Corporate Social and Environmental Responsibility

Chinese and Comparative Law Series

VOLUME 6

The titles published in this series are listed at *brill.com/ccls*

Corporate Social and Environmental Responsibility

Another Road to China's Sustainable Development

By

Menxing Lu

BRILL
NIJHOFF

LEIDEN | BOSTON

The Library of Congress Cataloging-in-Publication Data is available online at http://catalog.loc.gov
LC record available at http://lccn.loc.gov/

Typeface for the Latin, Greek, and Cyrillic scripts: "Brill". See and download: brill.com/brill-typeface.

ISSN 2213-4875
ISBN 978-90-04-36812-5 (hardback)
ISBN 978-90-04-36813-2 (e-book)

This book is printed on acid-free paper and produced in a sustainable manner.

Contents

Abbreviations

Asset Management Companies	AMCS
American Petroleum Institute	API
Badische Anilin & Soda-Fabrik	BASF
Bank of China	BOC
British Petroleum	BP
Business Case for Corporate Sustainability	BCS
Business in the Community	BITC
Chief Executive Officer	CEO
China Banking Regulatory Commission	CBRC
China Federation of Industrial Economics	CFIE
China National Petroleum Corporation	CNPC
China National Textile & Apparel Council	CNTAC
China Oversea Shipping Company	COSCO
China Securities Regulatory Commission	CSRC
Chinese Academy of Social Science	CASS
Chinese Communist Party	CPC
Committee for Economic Development	CED
Communication on Progress	COP
Corporate Assessment Methodology	CSA
Corporate Business Citizenship	CBC
Corporate Environmental Responsibility	CER
Corporate Financial Performance	CFP
Corporate Social Performance	CSP
Corporate Social Responsibility	CSR
Decade of Education for Sustainable Development	DESD
Department for Business, Innovation & Skills of the UK	BIS
Department of Energy of the US	DOE
Domestic Product	GDP
Dow Jones Sustainability Index	DJSI
Ecological Footprint	EF
Education for Sustainable Development	ESD
Emissions Trading System	ETS
Empowering Responsible Investment	EIRIS
Environmental Protection Agency	EPA
Environmental, Social and Governance	ESG
Environmental Supply Chain Management	ESCM
Essentially Contested Concept	ECC

European Entrepreneurship Fund	EuSFF
European Social Investment Forum	Eurosif
European Union	EU
Financial Times Stock Exchange	FTSE
Foreign Direct Investment	FDI
Forest Stewardship Council	FSC
Global Alliance of Banking Values	GABV
Global Corporate Citizenship	GCC
Global Environment Outlook	GEO
Global Industry Classification Standard	GICS
Global Oil and Gas Industry Association for Environmental and Social Issues	IPIECA
Global Reporting Initiative	GRI
Global Sustainable Investment Alliance	GSIA
Green Public Procurement	GPP
Greenhouse Gas	GHG
Green Supply Chain Management	GSCM
Human Development Index	HDI
Information Communication Technology	ICT
International Association of Oil & Gas Producers	IOCP
International Corporate Social Responsibility	ICSR
Initial Public Offering	IPO
International Monetary Fund	IMF
International Organization for Standardization	ISO
Lifelong Learning Programme	LLP
Media and Stakeholder Analysis	MSA
Millennium Development Goals	MDGS
Ministry of Civil Affairs of China	MOCA
Ministry of Commerce of China	MOFCOM
Ministry of Environmental Protection of China	MEP
Morgan Stanley Capital International	MSCI
Multinational Corporations	MNCS
Multinational Enterprises	MNES
National Contact Point	NCP
National Institute of Statistics and Economic Studies of France	INSEE
New Economic Regulations Act	NRE
Non-governmental Organizations	NGO
Oil and Gas Sector Supplement of GRI	OGSS
Organization for Economic Co-operation and Development	OECD
Outbound Foreign Direct Investment	OFDI

Organization of the Petroleum Exporting Countries	OPEC
People's Bank of China	PBOC
People Planet Profit	PPP
Principles for Responsible Investment	PRIS
Principles for Responsible Management Education	PRME
Product Label System	PLS
Public Procurement Contract Codes	PPCC
Purchasing Power Parity	PPP
Research and Development	R&D
Responsible Business Conduct	RBC
Shanghai Stock Exchange	SSE
Shenzhen Stock Exchange	SZSE
Small and Medium Enterprises	SMES
Social and Economic Council of the Netherlands	SER
Social Contribution Value Per Share	SCVPS
Socially Responsible Investment	SRI
State Environmental Protection Administration	SEPA
State Owned Enterprises	SOES
State-Owned Assets Supervision and Administration Commission	SASAC
Sustainable Consumption and Production	SCP
Sustainable Development	SD
Sustainable Development Goals	SDG
Sustainable Public Procurement	SPP
Tradable Pollution Permits	TPP
Triple Bottom Line	TBL
United Kingdom	UK
United Nations	UN
United Nations Conference on Environment and Development	UNCED
United Nations Education, Scientific, and Cultural Organization	UNESCO
United Nations Environmental Programme	UNEP
United Nations Global Compact	UNGC
United States of America	U.S.
World Business Council for Sustainable Development	WBCSD
World Commission on Environment and Development	WCED
World Health Organization	WHO
World Trade Organization	WTO
World Wildlife Fund	WWF
10-Year Framework of Programmes on Sustainable Development	10YFP

Illustrations

Figures

Table

CHAPTER 1

Introduction

1 Societal Developments and Environmental Challenges

1.1 *Societal Developments and the Global Environmental Crisis*

During the past centuries, society has experienced a profound revolution. While rapid economic growth and the related societal developments have achieved impressive progress in many aspects, these achievements also play a significant role in the creation of the current global environmental crises. As a result, we encounter the frequent occurrence of industrial environmental disasters around the world. The Bhopal disaster, the Exxon Valdez oil leak and the Mexican Gulf oil spill, became unprecedented in their nature, scale and speed at which they took place. In this context, there is a practical need to provide some basic insights into these societal developments.

Brundtland concluded in 1987 that "…. at the beginning of the 20th century, population numbers, the extent of human activities and the technologies available had little or no potential to change our planet earth radically and permanently. At the end of the 20th century, the size of the population, the technologies used and the increased level of prosperity did have that impact. At the close of the nineteen seventies global society was no longer within the limits of what the earth is able to provide and since then we have started to use up our available natural capital, while large sections of the world's population still have to live in poverty and under very poor social conditions….".[1] Since this statement, the environmental situation has become even worse due to the combined effect of world population growth, economic growth, globalization, the growth of corporate power, and last but not least, the technical innovations and the types of technologies used in production and consumption. To get a realistic perspective on the actual and possible roles of laws and regulations in addressing corporate behavior, it is necessary to take a closer look at some relevant developments.

First, population growth is an important indicator which has major effects on societal development. The growth in the number of living people on the earth—growth is an important underlying factor in creating many social and environmental problems. Over the last 100 years, the world population

1 See e.g. WCED 1987; De Hoo 2011.

 | DOI:10.1163/9789004368132_002

quadrupled to about 7 billion people in 2011,[2] and it is expected to reach 10 billion by 2100 (United Nations 2011).[3] This rapid population growth alone has caused far-reaching influence on the life quality of human beings. It has been observed that the earth's surface per head of world population[4] is shrinking substantially. According to the data from the Global Environment Outlook 4 (GEO-4)[5] and the Global Footprint Network (2012),[6] the average number of global hectares per head diminished from 7.9 in the year 1900, to ~ 5.2 in 1950, to ~ 3.3 in 1960, to ~ 2.8 in 1980, to ~ 1.9 in 2010. The projected number will further decline to ~ 1.6 hectares per head in 2050. Therefore, it is not surprising that the burgeoning world population is one of the major contributors to the current global environmental crisis.

The importance of population growth becomes even more evident in the context of China. According to the demographic data from the National Population Census of China,[7] the total population of China increased from 5626 million in 1953, to 6946 million in 1962, to 1 billion in 1982, to 1.13 billion in 1990, to 1.27 billion in 2000, and to 1.34 billion in 2010. The increasing population indeed poses significant challenges to China's societal, economic and environmental development and results in substantial frictions between those dimensions.

Second, *economic growth*. Over the last 100 years, the global economic output roughly increased 20-fold[8] and is expected to continue to grow throughout the 21st century. A fact that cannot be ignored is the dual effects of the rapid economic and societal development. The economic growth creates better living conditions for a substantial part of the world population, but in its

---

2 UNEP, GEO-5, 2012. In fact, there is a dispute on the accurate date of the world population reaching 7 billion. According to the United Nations (UN), the world population reached 7 billion on October 31, 2011. But the United States Census Bureau stated the 7 billion was reached on March 12, 2012. This book uses the data from the UN.

3 UN, Department of Economic and Social Affairs, '*Population Division, World Population Prospects: the 2012 Revision*'.

4 The earth surface per head of world population refers to what we have available for the production of raw materials for human consumption of products and services as well as for the compensation of their effects.

5 UNEP, GEO-4, 2007.

6 Global Footprint Network 2012.

7 The National Population Census is conducted by the National Bureau of Statistics of China. By the publication of this book, there are six censuses in total (1953, 1964, 1982, 1990, 2000 and 2010). The data is only applicable to Mainland China only, excluding Hong Kong, Macau and Taiwan. Available at: http://www.stats.gov.cn/english/Statisticaldata/CensusData/ (Accessed on February 1, 2017).

8 The data is based on the Maddison Project Database (2013). Available at: http://www.ggdc.net/maddison/maddison-project/data.htm (Accessed on February 1, 2017).

current pattern, this increased prosperity comes at the expense the depletion of natural resources and environmental degradation. Especially in the emerging economies, the rising per-person/per-capital resource consumption and the associated environmental impacts have been widely observed on their way for achieving economic prosperity.

The same type of development, on an even stronger scale, occurred in China. According to the latest data from the '*China Statistical Year Book*',[9] China's annual GDP (Gross Domestic Product) increased from ¥ 3678 billion RMB in 1978, to ¥ 18872 billion RMB in 1990, to ¥ 100280 billion RMB in 2000, to ¥ 413030 billion RMB in 2010, and to ¥ 689502 billion RMB in 2015.[10] Due to this impressive economic growth, China became the world's second largest economy surpassing Japan in 2010. Furthermore, the International Monetary Fund (IMF) claimed that China even overtook the United States as the world's largest economy in 2014.[11] Although China's economic growth has slowed down in recent years (particularly since 2012),[12] the outlook for China's economic growth in 2016 stays at 7.4%.[13] However, China's remarkable economic and social achievements come at the expense of environment deterioration and social problems. As a result, China is now confronting severe social and environmental crisis.[14]

Third, globalization. Since the late 1970s, the trend of globalization has taken command in the global (economic) development. This globalization process can be characterized by the intensification of cross-area and cross-border social relations between actors from very different locations, and by the growing transnational interdependence of economic and social activities.[15] Four constituting factors within globalization can be distinguished: trade, capital,

9 China Statistical Year Book is an annual publication, which covers the key data of China's economic and societal development.

10 China Statistical Yearbook 2016. Available at: http://www.stats.gov.cn/tjsj/ndsj/2016/indexeh.htm (Accessed on February 1, 2017).

11 IMF measures GDP in the terms of purchasing power parity. IMF estimated that by the end of 2014 China's GDP would reach 17.6 trillion US dollars against the US's 17.4 trillion US dollars.

See e.g. IMF, '*World Economic Outlook Database*', October 2014. Available at: https://www.imf.org/external/pubs/ft/weo/2014/02/weodata/index.aspx (Accessed on April 8, 2017).

12 According to the data of the World Bank, China's growth rate of GDP decreased from 10.6% in 2010 to 7.8% in 2012.

13 According to the databank of the World Bank, the growth rate of GDP (annual %) of China was 10.4 in 2010, 9.3 in 2011, 7.7 in 2012, and 7.7 in 2013.

14 For more information about China's environmental challenges, see Section 1.2.

15 See e.g. Beck 2000; Scherer and Palazzo 2009.

information, and people.[16] The development in these constituting factors of globalization has created an increasing magnitude of globalization over the last four decades.

This process of globalization has been theoretically and politically supported by the rise of the neoliberal economic paradigm and the related public policies of Western economies.[17] Worldwide—also in the case of China—the substantial changes in the role of the state have proven to be important for the speed in which the process of globalization could take place. States have been increasingly providing companies with the right of ownership, property rights and contract rights. States also created a facilitating environment by, for example, leaner enforcement systems, improved public goods (like infrastructure, education, and health care), more homogenous and stable societies and an endeavour to reduce unwanted consequences/externalities.[18] In the case of China, the process of globalization has been facilitated by China's economic reform since late 1978.[19]

The level of globalization can be measured by the globalization index. One of the widely used globalization indices is the KOF index of globalization. The KOF index measures the level of globalization in three dimensions: economic, social and political. The five graphics below respectively show the levels of globalization of the world in 1970, 1980, 1990, 2000 and 2011, implying the rapid development of globalization during the past four decades. Also, it is evident that the level of globalization differs widely in different regions and countries. The graphics (See Figure 1) are presented here to illustrate this development trend clearly: lighter blue shows the spreading out of globalization worldwide, and darker blue shows higher levels of globalization.

In its current form, globalization has shown that it can create both positive and negative impacts on society. It has been supportive of the rapid economic growth, but it also became a subject for a major debate as to whether

16 See e.g. Beck 2000; Scherer *et al.* 2009; IMF April 12, 2000.

17 The process of globalization did speed up since the administrations of Ronald Reagan (USA, President 1981–1989) and Margaret Thatcher (UK, Prime minister 1979–1990).

18 For more discussion on issues of privatization, see e.g. Megginson and Netter 2001; OECD, 2003.

19 China's reform and opening up policy, which is also known as the Chinese economic reform, started in December 1978. The former political leader Deng Xiaoping is often apprised as the chief architect of reform. The economic reform achieved the transformation from a 'centrally planned economy' to a 'socialist market economy' by introducing market mechanisms and reducing governmental control, and China increased its openness to foreign investments and the international community. Since 1978, China also issued relevant policies to welcome foreign investments and started to participate in IMF, World Bank and WTO.

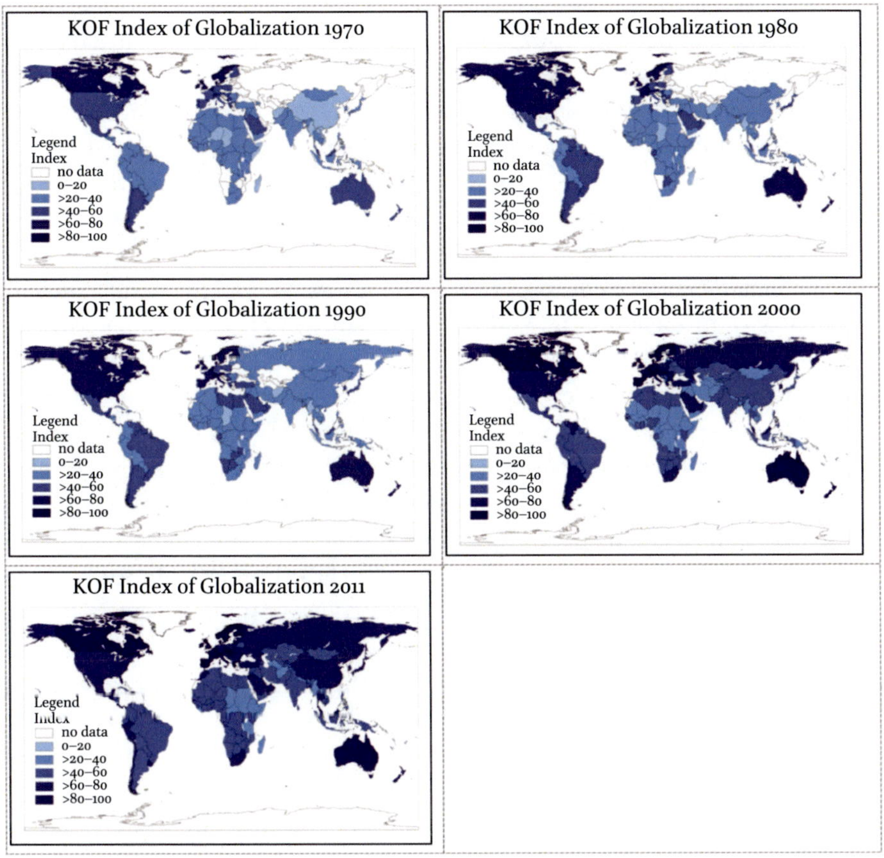

FIGURE 1 KOF Index of Globalization in 1970, 1980, 1990, 2000, and 2011. (Available at: https://www.kof.ethz.ch/en/forecasts-and-indicators/indicators/kof-globalisation-index.html (Accessed on February 1, 2017))
SOURCE: KOF INDEX OF GLOBALIZATION

globalization is a 'race to the bottom'[20] or a 'provider of individual freedom and democracy'.[21] In this discussion, the dual effects of globalization on the business–society relations are on the agenda,[22] and the major challenges are also under consideration like challenges as:

- The increasing volume of cross-border trade,—investments,—knowledge/innovation;

---

20 See e.g. Vogel 2001, pp. 163–172; Rudra 2008.

21 While some scholars hold that the process of globalization promotes democracy around the world, some scholars argue that globalization poses a threat to democracy. See e.g. Schwartzman 1998, pp. 159–181; Li and Reuveny 2003, pp. 29–54.

22 See e.g. Scherer, Palazzo and Matten 2009, pp. 327–347.

- The decreasing importance, power, and ability to control the national states;
- The growth in numbers, size, and power of corporations, in particular, the multinational corporations;
- The degree of inter-connectedness and pressures in global financial markets and the stability of the financial sector (takeovers and disinvestments);
- The ongoing worldwide economic growth and related innovation (like those in information and communication technology (ICT), biotechnology and renewable energy);
- The related resource consumption is already far beyond the earth's carrying capacity and increased (global) negative consequences in global environmental and social dimensions;
- The regulatory vacuum caused by a slow rise of proper global governance;
- The growing demand for Sustainable Development (SD), Corporate Social Responsibility (CSR) and Corporate Environmental Responsibility (CER).

Fourth, emerging economies. The process of globalization also substantially contributed to the share of the World's Total of Gross Domestic Product (GDP)[23] by the emerging economies. Over the last three decades (1984–2014) the share of emerging economies in World GDP went up from approximately 30% to 50% measured at Purchasing Power Parity (PPP) or from about 20% to 40% measured at Market Exchange Rates.[24] The rise in power of the emerging economies (for example BRICS)[25] is also visible in the case of China. Over the same period (1984–2014), the Chinese economy expanded at an average GDP annual growth rate of 10%.[26] However, the impressive number of GDP is only one facet that measures the progress of society. Another important indicator, namely GDP per capita, reflects the average living standard of people, and measured with this indicator China only ranked around 80th worldwide in 2016.[27]

Fifth, corporate numbers,—size and—power. The rise of corporations also plays an important role in the development of society. More particularly, within the same period (since the early 1980s) in which the process of globalization has taken command, the number, size and economic power of

23 GDP, according to OECD, is an aggregate measure of production equal to the sum of the gross values added of all resident institutional units engaged in production (plus any taxes, and minus any subsidies, on products not included in the values of their outputs).

24 IMF, '*World Economic Outlook Database*', October 2014. Available at: https://www.imf.org/external/pubs/ft/weo/2014/02/weodata/index.aspx (Accessed on April 8, 2017).

25 BRICS is a group acronym referring to the countries of Brazil, Russia, India, China and South Africa.

26 This data is based on the database of the World Bank Group. Available at: http://data.worldbank.org/(Accessed on April 8, 2017).

27 According to the World Economic Outlook Database 2016 from IMF, China ranks at 81st, and according to the World Development Indicators Database of the World Bank Group, China ranks 80th.

companies have also grown. The rapid process of industrialization and urbanization significantly changed people's lifestyle and influenced people's life quality and living standards for the better and for the worse. On the other hand, this process also brought about environmental degradation caused by climate change, air pollution, water pollution, acid rain, which all together severely threatens the existence and sustainability of human life. More particularly, some environmental pollution may pose direct risks and threats to public health. For example, air pollution is often known as the world's largest environmental health risk. According to recent data from the World Health Organization (WHO), about 7miilion people died as a result of air pollution exposure in 2012, which accounted for about 12.5 percent of the total global deaths.[28] As the natural environment is continuously deteriorating, people gradually suffer more and more from the economic development. In this context, corporations have frequently been blamed for the harm caused by their irresponsible business conduct. Today companies are expected to assume greater responsibility as their economic and political powers substantially increase.[29] In practice, more and more companies have started to assume social and environmental responsibilities by publishing environmental reports and trying to score higher on sustainability indices.

This case certainly counts for multinational corporations (MNCs) or multinational enterprises (MNEs). MNEs are large companies that own or control production facilities and service facilities and sell goods and/or service in one or more countries besides their country of origin.[30] MNEs play a role in the process of globalization: MNEs are co-creating economic growth, and they are at the same time a strong driving force.[31] Among the world's 100 largest economic entities, there are more than 40 MNEs, including companies like Royal Dutch Shell, Exxon Mobil, and Wal-Mart.[32] As MNEs continue to grow in numbers as well as in size, their economic and political powers also increase. Today it is widely observed that MNEs have played an active role in the international legal arena, despite the fact that private actors like MNEs are not qualified as subjects of the international law.[33] Today, the performance and power of MNEs provide hot topics in global economic and political debates.

---

28 WHO, '*7 million premature deaths annually linked to air pollution*', March 25, 2014. Available at: http://www.who.int/mediacentre/news/releases/2014/air-pollution/en/ (Accessed on April 8, 2017).

29 De Hoo 2011.

30 See e.g. Pitelis and Sugden 2000.

31 Buckley and Ghauri 2004, pp. 81–98.

32 Global Trends 2013.

33 Throughout the 19th century, only national states were deemed to be the subjects of international law. Available at: http://www.peacepalacelibrary.nl/research-guides/public

While the world is enjoying the substantial changes that MNEs have introduced, the social concerns over MNEs arise at the same time. In fact, it is an inconvenient fact that the transitional business activities have already caused many devastating environmental incidents. For example, the oil spills of Shell's Nigerian subsidiary have caused environmental devastation in the Niger Delta, which is now becoming one of the most polluted regions in the world.[34] Another oil spill caused by BP (also knowns as the Deepwater Horizon Oil Spill) triggered a severe ecological disaster in the Mexican Gulf, making it the worst oil spill accident in American history and also the biggest accident related to the release of oil into the ocean.[35] These two accidents caused by two oil giants show the potential magnitude of the adverse effects on the environment by MNE's operations worldwide as well as the difficulties to reach adequate compensation for those affected. The next example underlines this even more. The Bhopal Disaster is considered as the world's worst-ever industrial disaster due to its catastrophic devastation and the massive losses.[36] On December 3, 1984, a chemical factory located in India, exploded and released toxic gasses and substances, which caused the immediate deaths of 2259 person and about 8000 more deaths in the following two weeks.[37] Today, 30 years after the disaster, the total death toll has reached more than 25,000 and more than 100,000 are still suffering from the remaining toxic chemicals.[38] The chemical factory which was liable for this disaster belonged to an American MNE—the Union Carbide Corporation.[39] In the wake of this catastrophe, this company had been accused of adopting 'double standards' in environmental protection measures between its home factories and its overseas factories.[40] The Bhopal disaster put MNEs at the focus of public criticism. Consequently, the debates about the irresponsible business behavior of MNEs intensified, and the

-international-law/subjects-of-international-law/ (Accessed on February 1, 2017).

34 John Vidal, 'Shell faces payouts in Nigerian oil spill case', *The Guardian*, June 20, 2014. Available at: https://www.theguardian.com/environment/2014/jun/20/shell-faces-payouts-nigerian-oil-spill-case (Accessed on April 8, 2017).

35 Richard Black, 'Gulf oil leak: biggest ever, but how bad?', *BBC News*, August 3, 2010. Available at: http://www.bbc.co.uk/news/science-environment-10851837 (Accessed on April 8, 2017).

36 The official website of International Campaign for Justice in Bhopal is http://www.bhopal.net/ (Accessed on April 8, 2017).

37 *Id.*

38 The official website of the Bhopal Medical Appeal is http://www.bhopal.org/ (Accessed on April 8, 2017).

39 In 2001, the Union Carbide Corporation was 100% purchased by the Dow Chemical Company, as a subsidiary of Dow Chemical.

40 Union Carbide's own documents prove the company designed the plant with 'unproven' and 'untested' technology, and cut corners on safety and maintenance in order to save money.

public awareness and concerns about their environmental performance also increased.

Many of the current social and environmental challenges can be attributed to the reckless profit-seeking behaviour of corporations. As a response to the increasing public negativity, many companies started to participate in solving some social and environmental issues, through public welfare and environmental protection programs, which are traditionally important duties of public authorities.[41] The growing interest in sustainable development, corporate social responsibility, and corporate environmental responsibility is considered as an important step for the business community to internalize these social and environmental impacts of their business activities.

Sixth, technology choice and innovation. The level of global environmental impact is influenced by three factors: 1.) the total number of world population; 2.) the average level of prosperity per person; and 3.) the environmental impacts per unit of resources used per person. Factor 3 is to a large extent related to technology choices and innovation. As we have seen earlier, it is expected that factor 1 and 2 will continue to rise. So, if one wants to reduce environmental and social impacts at the same time, this means that technology choices and innovation need to contribute to that. Therefore, innovation and technology choices in the design of production processes, products, services and related consumption patterns have to incorporate minimization of their environmental and social effects. Over the last decades, it has become apparent that indeed this approach can play a role in reducing environmental and social impacts. But to what extent this can be the case is still under debate.[42] As described at the beginning of this paragraph, the relationship between the level of environmental impacts and the three constituting factors indicates a big dilemma of our global development. Specifically, the current economic growth patterns prove to be unsustainable because the increasing wealth and prosperity create higher environmental and social (sustainability) stress.

The combined result of these societal developments for achieving the goal of sustainable development can be visualized by two indices. The first one is the Human Development Index (HDI) and the second one is the Ecological

41 Scherer and Palazzo 2011, p. 899.

42 Optimists state that—only if supported by adequate government policies—within a decade, a factor 4 (which relates to a reduction by 75%) in reduction of used resources (incl. energy) and impacts on the environment is possible and a factor 10 (which relates to a reduction by 90%) could be achieved within five decades. However, pessimists argue these estimations are overstating the possible impact of innovation and technology choices as well as their possible introduction time, resulting in estimations holding lower reductions and longer lead-times.

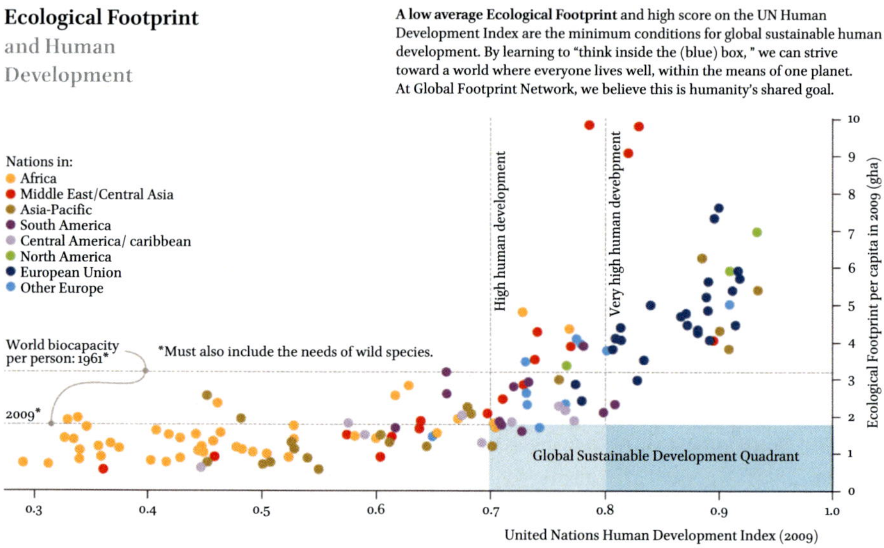

FIGURE 2 Ecological Footprint and Human Development Index
SOURCE: GLOBAL FOOTPRINT NETWORK, ANNUAL REPORT 2012

Footprint (EF). Both indices can be provided per head of population in a country or a region at a certain moment (the year 2009 in Figure 2).

The HDI index (the horizontal axis) provides a number between zero and one, which represents the level of the quality of living conditions. Three variables are used in a calculation of the HDI index: real living standard, life expectancy and access to primary education. The EF (the vertical axis) provides the number of hectares of biologically productive area needed to supply raw materials for consumption and to cope with the ensuing waste and emissions.

The relationship between these two indices results in a sustainability dilemma because nearly all countries perform outside the blue box (the 'Global Sustainable Development Quadrant'). In the current economic growth pattern, an increase in HDI seems directly connected to a substantial increase in EF. As presented in Figure 2, there are two scenarios concerning the interaction between HDI and EF: the one is that countries provide a too low HDI for their population and have an EF within the limits; the other one is that countries provide a high level of HDI for their population and have an EF (far) beyond its limits. Two questions arise from this situation: first, how to get a higher standard of living (HDI) while keeping the EF within its limits at the same time; second, how to reduce the EF to a level within its limits for those already having a high/very high standard of living.

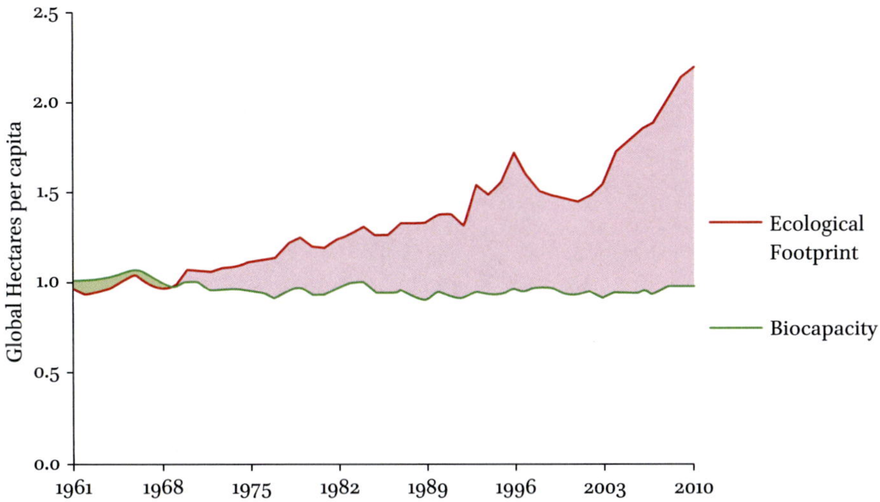

FIGURE 3 China's ecological footprint (Global Footprint Network for Nations. Available at: http://www.footprintnetwork.org/en/index.php/GFN/page/trends/china/ (Accessed on February 1, 2017))
SOURCE: GLOBAL FOOTPRINT NETWORK, FOOTPRINT FOR NATIONS

The seemingly causal link between HDI and EF is also relevant for China. The first graphic (Figure 3) shows the developments in China's ecological footprint and the second graphic (Figure 4) shows the developments in China's human development index and some of its constituting factors. Based on the information from the two graphics, from 1980 to 2015 there is a substantial increase in HDI and within the same period, the ecological footprint more than doubled.

It is against this background of social developments and their consequences for sustainable development (SD) that the role of the business community is regarded as important. Therefore, Corporate Social Responsibility (CSR) and as part of this Corporate Environmental Responsibility (CER)[43] are becoming urgent matters of concern and a high priority today. More particularly, John Elkington coined the so-called 'Triple Bottom Line' (TBL)—People, Planet and Profit, implying that companies should give equal attention to social, environmental and economic dimensions and should balance them into their business strategy. Because today the roots of many social and environmental problems can be ascribed to the profit-seeking activities of corporations, CSR and CER are considered as a response to solving these externalities caused by business.

43 In various publications, CER is also referred to as environmental dimension of CSR or environmental CSR.

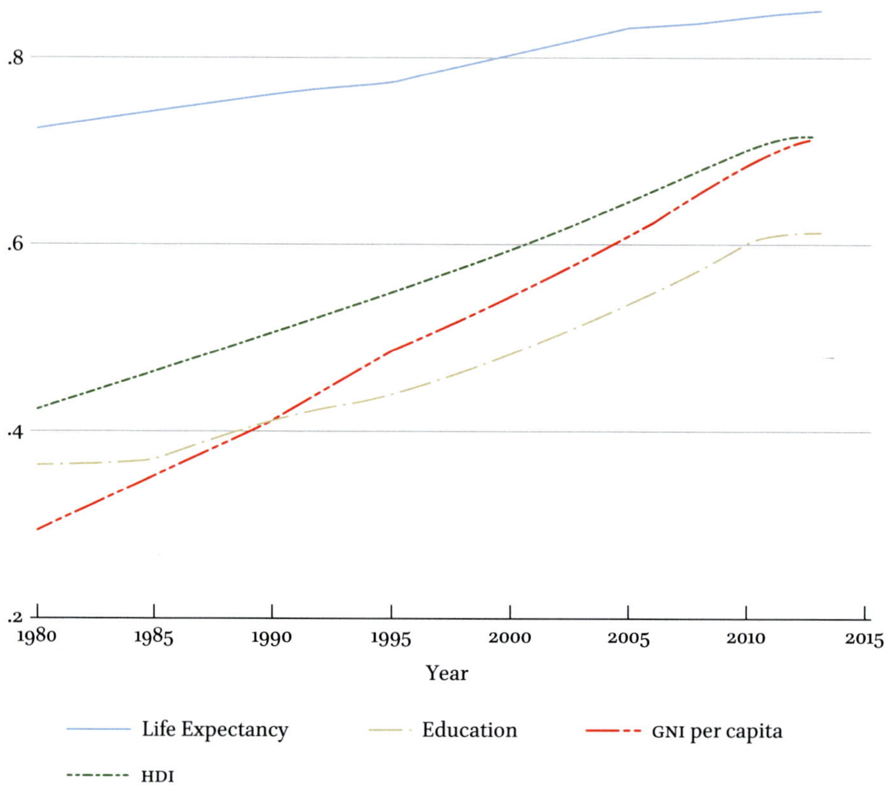

FIGURE 4 Trends in China's HDI component indices 1980–2013 (UNEP, Human Development Report 2014 (China). Available at: http://hdr.undp.org/sites/all/themes/hdr_theme/country-notes/CHN.pdf (Accessed on February 1, 2017))
SOURCE: UNDP HUMAN DEVELOPMENT REPORT 2014

As a result, the increasing demand for sustainable development, CSR, and CER is becoming more evident in academic circles and in practice. The evolution of CSR/CER shows that its emergence is not accidental, but the inevitable tendency of social and economic developments and its rise to prominence reflects the various societal and academic backgrounds.

1.2 *Environmental Challenges in China*

Since China's economic reform in 1978, China has experienced historical transformations in various aspects. From the economic perspective, China has achieved the historical shift from a centrally planned economy to a more market-based economy, also well known as the 'socialist market economy'. In this process, China's economic growth, industrialization, and urbanization have achieved remarkable progress. Today China has become one of the world's fast growing and the largest major economies.[44] Although the Chinese economy has taken a great leap forward during the past thirty years, there still exist many challenges before we can speak of a sustainable development in China. These challenges are related to a range of issues, such as deteriorating environmental pollution, rising income inequity, and administrative corruption. Particularly, China's rapid economic growth comes at the expense of excessive resource consumption and severe environmental deterioration.[45] The negative effects of China's extensive economic growth pattern have become more evident in recent years. According to a report from the Ministry of Environmental Protection of China (MEP), a total number of 471 pollution emergencies occurred in 2014, including three very severe incidents.[46] China's overall environmental situation therefore is and is expected to remain a cause for concern. The deteriorating environmental situation in China shows that the current development is far from sustainable from several aspects.

First, the increased economic costs to address the consequences of pollution. China's environmental pollution already harms its rapid economic growth. In particular, the contradiction between economic growth and environmental protection has gradually intensified in recent years and has become a bottleneck for China's further development. The adverse effects of environmental pollution on economic growth are becoming increasingly severe. The recent data indicated that the aggregated cost of pollution in China reached 13% of its GDP.[47]

Second, the adverse health effects of pollution. Today, environmental pollution has become one of the major threats to public health in China. It is reported that in China between 350,000 and 500,000 people die each year because of severe air pollution,[48] which makes air pollution one of the leading causes of death in China.

---

44 See supra footnote 12.

45 OECD 2008.

46 On January 23, 2015, the Ministry of Environmental Protection of China (MEP) released the '*Bulletin on Environmental Emergencies of 2014*'. Available at: http://www.zhb.gov.cn/gkml/hbb/qt/201501/t20150123_294725.htm (Accessed on February 1, 2017).

47 Olivia Boyd, 'Human toll of air pollution could be costing China 13% of GDP,' *Chinadialogue,* September 15, 2014. Available at: https://www.chinadialogue.net/blog/7316-Human-toll-of-air-pollution-could-be-costing-China-13-of-GDP/en (Accessed on April 8, 2017).

48 Malcom Moore, 'China's 'airpocalypse' kills 350,000 to 500,000 each year', *The Telegraph,* January 7, 2014. Available at: http://www.telegraph.co.uk/news/worldnews/asia/china/10555816/Chinas-airpocalypse-kills-350000-to-500000-each-year.html (Accessed on April 8, 2017).

Third, the social upheaval about environmental issues. The influence of environmental movement is growing, which is becoming an important factor in causing social upheaval in China in recent years. For example, the construction of a PX refinery[49] in Maoming, Guangdong Province in 2014 attracted considerable public attention, because of the high potential risk to the environment as well as on public health. Consequently, the large-scale protests against the construction of this and other PX refinery programs broke out in Xiamen (2007), Dalian (2011), and Kunming (2013). These protests did not only focus on the production process of a toxic substance but also on industrial safety standards of petrochemical installations in general.

Fourth, China's international environmental image is increasingly at stake. China's environmental pollution has also aroused big concerns in the international community and harmed China's international image. China is frequently mentioned as one of the largest contributors to global environmental problems, such as climate change and trans-boundary air pollution.[50] Taking climate change as an example, China has become one of the major contributors to global warming, accounting for about 8% of total greenhouse gas (GHG) emission.[51] In response to these international concerns, China, as a responsible country in the international community, commits to assuming its national responsibility for addressing climate change.

These adverse effects of environmental pollution in China have raised high concerns among Chinese policymakers and also the public.[52] As a result, the balance between environmental protection and economic growth is on the top of China's policy agenda. China has already paid more attention to the importance and urgency of addressing environmental pollution issues and started to make considerable efforts to improve the current environmental situation.

In 2003, the then Chinese leader Hu Jintao, put forward the concepts of the 'Scientific outlook on development'[53] (also known as 'scientific development')

49 The PX programme refers to the production of para-xyleen, which is used for example as a raw material for the production of plastic bottles, the so-called PET bottles.

50 Economy 2010, pp. 38–60.

51 Alex Morales, *"China Joins U.S. Among Biggest Global Warming 'Offenders'"*, *Bloomberg*, January 15, 2014. Available at: http://www.bloomberg.com/news/2014-01-15/u-s-joins-china-among-biggest-global-warming-offenders-.html (Accessed on April 8, 2017).

52 OECD 2008, Chapter 5.

53 The concept of 'Scientific outlook on development', also referred to as 'scientific development concept' is one of the guiding principles of Communist Party of China in terms of social, economic and cultural development, which was first initiated by the former Chinese leader Hu Jintao in 2003. This new ideology incorporates scientific socialism, sustainable development, social welfare, a humanistic society, increased democracy, and ultimately the creation of a socialist harmonious society.

and the 'Building a socialist harmonious society'[54] (also known as 'harmonious society'). These concepts are regarded as the guiding principles for China's economic, social and cultural development. The propagation of these two concepts reflects that the Chinese policymakers have realized that the environmental deterioration and degradation is one of the primary causes for an increase in social problems and a decrease in social welfare. It also shows their determination to strengthen environmental protection and to achieve the economic transformation towards a green economy. A green economy, as these policymakers see it, is characterized by lower resource consumption, high energy efficiency, sustainable energy resources, cleaner production and a more circular economy.

At the policy level, the central government has put environmental protection as a priority area in the '*Decision of the State Council on Implementing the Scientific Outlook on Development and Strengthening Environmental Protection*'.[55] This official document clearly states that environmental protection is one of China's fundamental national policies.[56] Since then, a series of laws, administrative decrees, and policies on environmental protection has been promulgated and implemented. By doing so, the Chinese legislators have developed a relatively comprehensive system of environmental laws and regulations.[57] However, the recent studies have been critical of the effectiveness of China's environmental regulation for many reasons.[58]

The first reason is that the weak enforcement by environmental authorities undermines the effectiveness of China's environmental regulation in reality.

---

54 The concept of 'Building a socialist harmonious society' stems from the philosophy of Confucius, and in modern times, it has been interpreted in a form of New Confucianism. The propagation of this concept is regarded as a response to the increasing social injustice and inequality, and also a solution to the increasing social conflicts.

55 State Council of China, '*Decision of the State Council on Implementing the Scientific Outlook of Development and Strengthening Environmental Protection*', December 2005. Available at: http://english.mep.gov.cn/ Resources/Policies/policies/Frameworkp1/200712/t20071227_115531.shtml (Accessed on April 8, 2017).

56 Environmental protection has become a basic national policy of China in the 1980s.

57 The Chinese government has formulated 9 laws on environmental protection, 15 laws on the protection of natural resources, 50 administrative regulations by the State Council on the environment.

58 Some organizations and scholars pointed out that today China has developed a relatively comprehensive framework of environmental laws and regulations, but there still remains deficiency in the enforcement of Chinese environmental laws and regulations, such as superficial enforcement, inadequate and weak punishments, lax investigations and delayed punishments, and so on. For more discussion on the various problems with environmental law enforcement in China, see e.g. Wang 2006, pp. 159–194; Ma and Ortolano 2000; OECD 2006.

In particular, the implementation conditions at the local level are even more worrisome, since economic growth is still a priority for local government and officials.

The second reason is that, due to the limits of the current environmental policy framework, the private actors, such as corporations, NGOs, and citizens, are expected to play an important role in environmental protection particularly in those cases where environmental regulations may fail. More particularly, the Chinese government also recognized the important role of corporations in addressing environmental pollution and the necessity of encouraging the environmentally responsible behaviour of companies. For example, the State-Owned Assets Supervision and Administration Commission of the State Council (SASAC) issued the '*Guidelines to the state-owned enterprise directly under the central government on fulfilling corporate social responsibilities*'.[59] But it is clear that during the recent decades—in the initial stage of the 'socialist market economy'—the priority for many corporations has been the pursuit of profits and still this is priority one. As a result of this fact, the environmental performance of companies varies but remains overall relatively limited. The environmental pollution accidents caused by corporations do still frequently occur.

The third reason is the influence of foreign direct investment (FDI) on China's fast growing economy and also on China's environmental conditions. This influence has the character of a 'two-edged sword'. According to data of the World Bank, China, as one of the most attractive destinations for foreign investment, saw its FDI increase from $ 338 billion US dollars in 2004 to $ 2535 billion US dollars in 2012. This phenomenal increase in FDI, on the one hand, induced many MNEs to transfer heavy pollution to China and to misuse China as a 'pollution haven'.[60] On the other hand, the rapid growth of FDI also made it possible for Chinese enterprises to learn from other foreign MNEs how to improve their sustainability performance and corporate governance.

Today more and more Chinese enterprises are going abroad as part of China government's 'go out' policy.[61] Especially after China joined the WTO in December 2001, China's outward (outbound) foreign direct investments (OFDI) have surged and became one of the leading sources of OFDI in the world. In 2012, China's OFDI amounted $ 1029 billion US dollars. In 2014, China ranked the world's third-largest foreign investor after the United States and

---

59 For more information about this Guidelines, see Chapter 9, Section 2.2.

60 See Chapter 6, Section 2.3.1.

61 China's 'Go Out' policy is China's current strategy to encourage more Chinese enterprises to invest overseas.

Japan.[62] However, Chinese MNCs are also facing a series of challenges in meeting the different environmental standards of the host countries and the international market.[63] In this context, it becomes imperative for Chinese enterprises to improve their environmental performance in order to meet the higher expectations and standards and to enhance their competitiveness in the international market.

The analysis above depicts a picture that corporations are on the one hand criticized as a leading cause of various social and environmental problems in the international society and in China. On the other hand, corporations are also regarded as part of the potential solution for addressing these challenges.[64] As a consequence, the concept of corporate social responsibility and corporate environmental responsibility gain an increasing popularity in the academic circles and in the business world.

2 Academic Background

2.1 *Sustainable Development, Corporate Social Responsibility, and Corporate Environmental Responsibility*

First of all, three closely related concepts are at the core of this book. These concepts are: sustainable development (SD), corporate social responsibility (CSR) and corporate environmental responsibility (CER).

2.1.1 Sustainable Development (SD)

As indicated at the beginning of this chapter, the term sustainable development (SD) was initially launched as a concept in the report '*Our Common Future*'[65] in 1987. In this report and in this book, the concept of sustainable development is defined as "a development that meets the needs of the present without compromising the ability of future generations to meet their own needs."[66] Today, sustainable development is mainly used in the policies pursued by national and supranational governments as well as by international organizations. The principal objective of sustainable development is to integrate three dimensions i.e. social, environmental and economic dimensions into an integral approach and to bring them into balance.[67]

---

62 The data of China's OFDI is based on the information available at: http://finance.chinanews.com/cj/2015/01-16/6977506.shtml (Accessed on April 8, 2017).

63 OECD 2008.

64 Scherer and Palazzo 2008, p. 414.

65 WCED 1987.

66 *Id.*

67 De Hoo 2011.

2.1.2 Corporate Social Responsibility (CSR)

The term of corporate social responsibility (CSR) does focus on the role of a corporation in an endeavour to achieve the goal of sustainable development.[68] CSR is used by or in relation to the business community, while sustainable development is applied by a range of actors in a broader context, including nations, international organizations, NGOs, and corporations. In literature and in practice, CSR is also referred to as corporate social performance and corporate sustainability performance. From a historical perspective, the modern theory of CSR originated in the United States where the American scholar Oliver Sheldon advocated the concept of CSR already in his book '*The Philosophy of Management*' in 1924,[69] and then another scholar Howard Bowen put forward the definition of CSR for the first time in 1954.[70] However, it was not until the middle of the 1960s and the beginning of the 1970s that CSR was widely known in the business community and in society as well.

In the 1990s, CSR became more prominent due to various reasons.[71] First, the concept of sustainable development did become a central perspective for societal development. As a prominent member of society, corporations are under pressure to integrate sustainable development into their corporate policy to retain acceptance and trust in society.[72] Second, because of the increasing strength of economic, political and social powers of the business community, corporations are expected to assume more responsibilities than ever. Third, many social problems, in particular, environmental pollution, are considered as the externalities of business activities, and thus corporations are expected to be responsible for internalizing these externalities of their business activities.

Despite the fact that CSR has been defined differently by numerous scholars, organizations, and nations, no consensus concerning the definition of CSR has been reached by now. In this book, the term of CSR can be defined as "a company is responsible for the social, environmental and economic consequences of its business decisions and activities, beyond what the law prescribes."[73] Based on this definition, the concept of CSR covers a broad range of social, environmental and economic issues, including human rights, labour, environment, anti-bribery.

---

68 COM (2002) 347 final.

69 Sheldon 2003. The first edition was published in 1924.

70 Bowen 2013. The first edition was published in 1954.

71 Crane *et al.* (eds.) 2008, p.3.

72 De Hoo 2011.

73 This definition of CSR is proposed on the basis of the understanding and analysis of other various definitions.

2.1.3 Corporate Environmental Responsibility (CER)

Corporate environmental responsibility (CER) can be defined as "a company going beyond compliance with mandatory environmental standards by adopting higher or stricter standards." CER is considered as the important environmental component of CSR. That is why in some publications the concept of CER is also referred to as 'Environmental CSR'. In more specific terms, CER is the environmental part of CSR theory and strongly relates to the field of environmental protection.[74]

The conceptual interrelationship between SD, CSR, and CER provides the possibility to approach and apply the theories and practices in the various fields of SD and CSR also in the perspective of CER. The more precise content of these concepts will be further discussed in Chapter 2.

2.2 *Major Disputes about CSR/CER*

As a consequence of the substantial increase of corporate power, the traditional corporate theory is facing new challenges. In contrast to the well-known position of Friedman, who insisted that the only responsibility of business was to increase profits, today modern corporations are expected to meet the expanding social expectations rather than the pursuit of profits alone. The development of CSR/CER in this context provides a tangible result of this statement, but the debates about where to draw the boundaries of CSR/CER still continue. Despite the various disputes, CSR/CER is increasingly popular in disciplines such as economics, law, and politics. Since the 1990s, the debate started to focus more on MNEs because their business expansions have caused serious harm around the world. The global environmental crisis has already become a primary concern for the international community and the national states. People become increasingly worried about their future, so they raised their voices to require MNEs to be more socially responsible and to enhance a common understanding and expectations of the international community about this issue. As a result, CSR/CER is becoming a prominent concept with its focus on various social and environmental issues caused by irresponsible corporate behaviour. Within the framework of CSR, human rights, labour conditions, environmental issues, anti-corruption, anti-bribery, production and product standards are the core issues.[75]

There is a range of highly controversial topics in the current debate of CSR/CER, but this book mainly focuses on the following three disputes:

74 Vogel 2006, p.110.

75 Gladwin and Walter 1976, pp. 57–74.

The first dispute is about the issue of to what extent does CSR/CER contradict the long proclaimed fundamental purpose of the corporation. Is making profit fundamentally incompatible with 'social responsibility' or not.[76] The opponents of CSR/CER have been mainly represented by Milton Friedman, who claimed that the only responsibility of corporations was to maximize their profits for their owners, i.e. shareholders. Arguing with this perspective, one is increasingly worried about the possibility that the engagement in CSR/CER will damage companies' competitive advantages in the market and thus decrease the profits of companies.

Over the past decades, Friedman's argument has been challenged and proven to be untenable even from an economic point of view. An inconvenient fact is that business activities do produce externalities on third parties. Environmental pollution is one of the typical examples of such an externality.[77] Corporations are responsible for the generation of these externalities. Furthermore, the recent literature equally argues that CSR/CER is not necessarily incompatible with the ultimate goal of profit maximization. Even in the case that in the short term, the investments in clean and environmentally friendly technologies will increase the production costs of corporations, but it does generate an increase in profits in the long term.[78] Today, in the business community, more and more companies desire to be regarded as socially and environmentally responsible. Those companies consider CSR/CER an effective way to solve a range of social and global problems caused by current corporate performance,[79] and to achieve long-term profits for corporations.[80] As companies are gradually recognizing the business value of being socially and environmentally friendly, it became a strategic trend to take good social and environmental performance as the key to business success. This trend occurs even more frequently when companies are confronted with increasingly intensive competition and strong public pressure. They start to integrate environmental strategies as an indispensable part of their management strategy. Recent literature also shows that CSR/CER has been successfully implemented in corporate business strategy on a voluntary basis by a relatively small but growing number of companies.[81]

The second dispute is about the relationship between shareholders, corporate managers and stakeholders within corporations. When the interests of

76 Drucker 1984, pp. 53–63.
77 Faure 2001, p. 9.
78 Falck and Heblich 2007, pp. 247–254.
79 Carroll 1979, p. 499.
80 Carroll 1999, p. 271.
81 Eccles, Ioannou and Serafeim 2014, p. 2836.

shareholders and corporate managers are not aligned, a principal-agent problem will arise between them. Traditional corporate theory views that corporations belong to their owners, i.e. shareholders, and managers should only be responsible to the owners of the corporations, i.e. the shareholders.[82] This idea is also known as 'shareholder primacy' and 'shareholder value',[83] which have been for several decades embraced as the dominant thinking on corporate purpose in the business world.

However, another theory claims that there are many other actors, which are affected by the decisions and activities of corporations. Those actors are known as the "stakeholders". In contrast to the traditional paradigm, the stakeholder theory[84] holds that there are other actors involved in business activities, such as employees, customers, investors, creditors, governments, NGOs and other public organizations. Therefore, the stakeholder theory perceives that a responsible company should balance the different interest of its shareholders and stakeholders. In reality, corporate managers cannot run the business "in vacuum conditions".[85] Their business decisions are frequently influenced by various external pressures. More particularly, the larger the corporations are, the more vulnerable the corporations are to external pressure.[86]

In this context, CSR/CER is considered as a potential instrument to fill this gap between the interests of shareholders and stakeholders, and between the profit-seeking purpose of corporations and the creation of social welfare. The development of CSR/CER provides a basis for a new approach in the field of business management which does focus on the close relationships between 'business, government, and civil society'.[87] Another motivation for corporations to engage in CSR/CER is to build or maintain a good reputation as a responsible social citizen and by doing so, to enhance their market competitiveness in the long run. However, there remains considerable uncertainty about the preferences of shareholders and managers concerning CSR/CER.

The third dispute is about the search for an optimal balance between the voluntary nature of CSR/CER and the compulsory nature of regulation. According to the various definitions, CSR/CER is a form of self-regulation, and a core characteristic of CSR/CER is its voluntary nature. The current literature generally agrees on this voluntary nature of CSR/CER. It can be characterized as

82 Dodd 1932, p. 1145.
83 The conventional shareholder value thinking has been challenged by many scholars. See e.g. Stout 2012.
84 Freeman 2010.
85 Levy and Kaplan 2008, pp. 432–451.
86 See Vogel 2006, p. 25.
87 Crane *et al.* (eds.) 2008, p. 304.

"a voluntary commitment of corporations to undertake responsibilities going beyond what law and public policies have prescribed."[88] In this view, CSR/CER is introduced as a form of self-regulation, complementary to mandatory regulation and law.

Some advocates of CSR/CER go even further and argue that the CSR/CER is primarily led by business and it should not be interfered by external regulation. In this view, CSR/CER could prohibit the development of new public policy or replace parts of existing ones. This view could even become a support of the so-called 'Pollution Haven Hypothesis', which states that the less stringent the environmental regulations, the more companies will choose for relocation, and therefore the more investments and job opportunities will be attracted.[89] Many empirical studies, particularly those about developing countries, support this hypothesis. The 'Pollution Haven Hypothesis' was also true for what happened in China during the last decades. Since China's economic reform in 1978, many foreign MNEs chose to invest in China mainly due to the cheap labour forces, abundant natural resources, and lenient regulations. China's lenient environmental regulation may be helpful for economic growth in the short run, but it proved to be very harmful to the sustainable development in the end.[90]

So far, the search for balance between voluntary CSR/CER and compulsory public policies has been represented by those proclaiming CSR/CER to be valuable in addition to the existing regulations and by those proclaiming that CSE/CER should more or less replace public policies and law. Another voice heard in this field is from Michael Porter. In contrary to the 'Pollution Haven Hypothesis' above, Porter argues that "properly and reasonably defined environmental standards will encourage innovations of corporations and will thus enhance their competitiveness in the market."[91] According to Porter, the well-designed regulation does not have a negative effect on corporate performance, but leads to various positive effects. This position in the debate is well known as the 'Porter Hypothesis' and has been substantiated with lots of evidence, even already in the decade before it was formulated. The 'Porter Hypothesis' also proclaims the possibility of a positive relationship between CSR/CER and regulation. Over the last two decades, the actual value of this relationship has been proven again and again.[92]

88 Dahlsrud 2008, pp. 1–13.

89 For more discussion on the 'Pollution Haven Hypothesis', see Chapter 3, Section 2.2.2.

90 Dean, Lovely, and Wang 2009, pp. 1–13.

91 Porter and Van der Linde 1995, pp. 120–134.

92 For more discussion on the 'Porter Hypothesis', see Chapter 6, Section 2.3.2.

Some scholars even argued that the voluntary-mandatory debate in CSR/CER seems to be a non-debate.[93] In this position, an argumentation is developed that there has been and still is a constant flow from pure self-regulation into soft law and into hard law regarding CSR/CER issues. In this view, the international community does respond adequately to CSR/CER issues at stake in practice. In reality, there is an increasing trend of introducing more regulation to accompany the good compliance and performance of CSR/CER. There are various endeavours in regulating CSR/CER at both the international and the national level. In the international arena, many international organizations are dedicated to developing the policy framework of CSR/CER in the form of guidelines, codes of conducts and principles.[94] Among those, the inter-governmental international organizations, like the United Nations and the European Union, make full advantage of their global influence by issuing international guidelines and pushing all members to comply and implement these guidelines to promote the development of CSR/CER. At the national level, the European countries, like the Netherlands, France and the United Kingdom, also strengthen and improve their domestic regulatory framework on CSR/CER.[95]

To conclude, with the rapid progress of globalization, today CSR/CER has become a global phenomenon. The worldwide popularity of CSR/CER is not accidental and has a profound societal and academic background. As a result of these social and academic developments, the role of corporations in society becomes more crucial. On the one hand, corporations are frequently condemned as the 'bad guys' because of the adverse effects of their wrongdoings; on the other hand, corporations particularly MNEs are also considered to have "an additional political responsibility to contribute to the development and proper working of global governance",[96] due to their strong economic and political powers. For advocates of CSR/CER, there is no doubt that corporations should be responsible for the internalization of the externalities they produce. Moreover, a vast amount of empirical evidence also shows that there is a business case for CSR/CER where "corporate responsibility can provide an enduring economic advantage for a company."[97] However, it is also argued that CSR/CER cannot provide satisfying results in a Chinese context without the support of

93 Eijsbouts 2011.
94 See Chapter 6, Section 4.
95 See Chapter 7.
96 Crane *et al.* (eds.) 2008, p. 414.
97 *Id*, p. 282.

proper regulation and enforcement in government policies. In my view, this provides enough ammunition to continue the research into the proper balance between voluntary and mandatory CSR/CER in general and more particularly in China.

3 Research Focus and Questions

When looking at the societal and academic developments described above, there are various angles from which to approach this research. In this context, it is important to make several choices to provide research focus for this book.

The first choice made is to focus on the environmental component (CER) within the broader framework of CSR. Since, CER has been taken as an important part of CSR, it is also necessary to provide a brief historical background about the evolution of CSR, including an overview of how CSR originates, flourishes and rises to the prominent position it has, as well as an overview of the specific contents of CSR in literature and also in practice.

The second choice is to focus on MNEs and to put MNEs, their performance and their significance at the core of this book. Because MNEs have caused enormous impacts on the economic, social and environmental developments worldwide and in China, as well as the magnitude of their expected impacts in the future. MNEs and their increasing engagement in CSR/CER could be of substantial importance in reducing the negative social and environmental effects of the economic growth in China.

The third choice is to adopt the broader definition of regulation as "an activity of attempting to control, order, or influence the behaviour of others"[98] in this book. In this approach, regulation can take various forms, including legislation, governmental regulations, self-regulation, third party regulation, co-regulation and market regulation. It also takes place at various levels, including the local level, the national level, and the global level. Therefore, this approach will provide a better starting point for a comprehensive understanding of the relationship between CSR/CER and regulation.

The goal of this book is to gain new insights on the increasingly popular phenomenon of CSR/CER, its relationship with regulation, and its relevance for China from a law and economics perspective. To reach this ultimate goal, the key research question of this book is: what is the role of CSR/CER in relation to government regulation in promoting sustainable development?

98 *Id*, p. 102.

To reach the conclusion, the following set of sub-questions will be answered in the coming chapters:

- *Research Question 1:* what are the different dimensions of CSR/CER in theory and in practice as laid down in various corporate codes or guidelines by the international community, national states and corporations?
- *Research Question 2:* why are a growing number of corporations apparently interested in CSR/CER even when this seemingly contradicts the traditional economic paradigm of profit maximization?
- *Research Question 3:* why do various actors, like shareholders, corporate managers, and (external) stakeholders engage in CSR/CER?
- *Research Question 4*: how to evaluate the efforts and the outcomes of companies in implementing CSR/CER in their business operations?
- *Research Question 5:* what new insights does the law and economics theory-based analysis bring to the current debates of CSR/CER?
- *Research Question 6:* should there be any role for regulation, more in particular for governmental regulation, to accompany CSR/CER? If so, what role could it play in the development of CSR/CER?
- *Research Question 7:* what can we learn from the European experience in promoting the development of CSR/CER?
- *Research Question 8:* what could the role of CSR/CER be in a Chinese context? More particularly, could CSR/CER play an important supplementary role in addressing China's environmental challenges?

As mentioned above, China's environmental challenges and environmental regulation serve as an important background for the book. However, the effectiveness and the constraints of China's environmental regulation are not the focus of this book due to two practical reasons. First, China's regulations have been a debated topic. A large number of studies has been conducted to discuss various issues in this domain, like the constraints of China's environmental policy framework, and how to improve its effectiveness. Therefore, this book is based on the academic achievements of the previous studies in this domain that the current state of China's environmental pollution remains a cause for concern and moreover, China's environmental regulation may fail to solve environmental issues in some cases. Second, this book is constructed on the idea that the ineffectiveness of the current environmental policy framework in China is an important reason for the private sector, more particularly the companies in this book, to play a role in addressing China's environmental challenges. In this context, the development of CSR/CER could possibly contribute to China's sustainable development.

4 Methodology

To answer the research questions mentioned above, this book mainly adopts three methodologies, including, law and economics analysis, comparative analysis, and case study.

4.1 *The Law and Economics of CSR/CER*

As one of the most important approaches in legal analysis, the law and economics analysis has been widely applied in a wide range of legal disciplines, including property law, contract law, tort law, corporate law, etc. Given the natural link between CSR/CER, corporate law and corporate governance, the law and economics analysis is adopted in this book to provide a better understanding of the increasingly popular phenomenon of CSR/CER, which is not desired by a group of traditional economists, as well the law and economics scholars, mainly represented by scholars like Milton Friedman. Comparing to the previous studies in this field, this book aims to contribute to the existing literature by providing some new insights into CSR/CER from a law and economics perspective. This is the research question 5 of this book.

More particularly, this methodology plays a crucial role in answering two key research questions of this book. The first question (Research question 2 and Research question 3) arises as to why there is a growing interest in participating in CSR/CER in the business world, which seemingly contradicts with the long-claimed logic of profit maximization. In this respect, the law and economics methodology will be applied to explore the motivations and the roles of various actors in CSR/CER.

The second important question concerns the relationship between CSR/CER and regulation (Research question 6). This book focuses on whether there should be any role for regulation (more generally, government intervention) to accompany the process of CSR/CER which in itself could be regarded as a self-regulatory mechanism.

4.2 *Comparative Studies of CSR/CER*

In this book, the methodology of comparative analysis will be adopted for answering Research question 7 and Research question 8. This book discusses the different approaches to CSR/CER in different institutional contexts. Three jurisdictions are chosen in this book and they are the international, EU and Chinese legal systems.

At the international level, today CSR/CER goes beyond the geographic boundary and becomes a global concern. Consequently, a set of international

CSR/CER standards, principles and guidelines have been developed by many influential international organizations, such as the United Nations, the World Bank, the OECD, etc. As a result, the international law on CSR/CER will also be included in this book.

Since the concept of CSR/CER originated in the Western countries, more particularly the United States and Europe, it is argued that the Western countries have been the frontrunners with more advanced knowledge and experience in this field. This book chooses the EU legal system rather than the American system primarily due to two reasons. First, in comparison with the US, the EU has adopted a more explicit approach to promoting CSR/CER at the policy level. A variety of CSR/CER related policies has been promulgated, which makes the topic of CSR/CER as the new field on the European policy agenda. Second, many Member States also actively develop their national policy frameworks on CSR/CER. In this sense, both the EU and the Member States set good examples in promoting the development of CSR/CER by means of various policy instruments.

Another important jurisdiction of this book is the Chinese legal systems. Although the appearance of CSR/CER is relatively late in China, the recent decades witnessed the rise of CSR/CER at the policy level and in practice. However, at its early stage, the development of CSR/CER is facing a variety of challenges. In this sense, it is important to find out what China can learn from the European experience for the further development of CSR/CER.

4.3 *Case Studies*

This book is to examine how and to what extent CSR/CER works in practice not only by studying literature and the legal systems but also by conducting some case studies. The main goal of the case studies is to have a closer look at the actual effects of CSR/CER-related regulations on corporate behavior. More particularly, the case studies aim to enquire to what extent the increasing number of CSR/CER policies could improve corporate sustainability performance, particularly in terms of sustainability reporting practices. This book chooses several MNEs from both the European and Chinese legal systems as the subject of the case studies.

In the European context, three European companies are selected from different countries and industries. They are: the Dutch chemical company—AkzoNobel, the French bank—BNP Paribas, and the British oil and gas giant—British Petroleum. In the Chinese context, two Chinese companies, more particularly state-owned enterprises (SOEs), are chosen in this book. They are the Bank of China (BOC) from the banking sector, and the China National Petroleum Corporation (CNPC) from the oil and gas industry.

By analyzing the formats and contents of the sustainability reports published by these selected companies, this book aims to gain more insights into the current state of sustainability reporting practices. More particularly, the case studies will focus on the changes that have occurred with regard to their sustainability reporting practice in different periods; and on the extent to which the sustainability reporting guidelines and standards have influenced the preparation of sustainability reports among these companies.

5 Structure of the Book

The structure of this book will be closely connected to the research questions defined above.[99] This book consists of ten chapters. It starts with the general introduction in Chapter 1 and provides conclusions and recommendations in Chapter 10. The Chapters in between can be divided into two main parts.

Part I focuses on the theoretical framework on CSR/CER. This part consists of three chapters.

Chapter 2 defines the subjects of this book: corporate social responsibility and corporate environmental responsibility from both theoretical and empirical perspective. From the theoretical perspective, this chapter encompasses various dimensions of CSR/CER, like its historical evolution, its definition and several closely related concepts (such as corporate governance, corporate citizenship, and corporate sustainability, and stakeholder orientation). This chapter also aims to gain more insights into how the business community converts the abstract idea of CSR/CER into their business strategies. Research Question 1 will be answered in this chapter.

Chapter 3 explains an interesting phenomenon being why do more and more corporations move towards CSR/CER. To answer this question, this chapter examines the roles and motivations of various actors towards CSR/CER, including companies, shareholders, managers, employees, consumers, and NGOs. Research questions 2 and 3 will be answered in this chapter.

Chapter 4 probes into another focus of CSR/CER: how to assess or evaluate the efforts and the outcomes of companies to address social and environmental issues. Therefore, this chapter has a look at the measurement of Corporate Social Performance (CSP) in theory and in practice. From the theoretical perspective, this chapter provides a brief literature review of CSP measurement.

99 See supra Section 3.

Next, this chapter turns to the practice of CSP measurement, by having a closer look at a newly emerging market—the rating industry. Research Question 4 will be answered in this chapter.

Part II turns to another key issue of this book regarding the relationship between CSR/CER and regulation from both theoretical and empirical perspectives. The main goal of this part is to gain more insights on whether regulation is needed in the case of CSR/CER, and if so what role it could play in promoting the development of CSR/CER in theory and in practice. Part II consists of five chapters.

Chapter 5 focuses on the law and economics analysis of CSR/CER. First, this chapter will discuss the relationship between CSR/CER and market failure. Second, this chapter will focus on the relationship between CSR/CER and government deficit. Then this chapter will discuss several possible solutions to cure market failure and governmental deficit respectively, including the Coase theorem, legal intervention, and private/self-regulation. Next, this chapter will discuss a principal-agent problem, i.e. the potential conflict of interest between shareholders and managers as far as the engagement of CSR/CER is concerned. Research Question 5 will be answered in this chapter.

Chapter 6 explores the possible roles of public authorities in promoting the development of CSR/CER. First, this chapter examines the role of governments in supporting and encouraging CSR/CER. Second, this chapter will have a closer look at the application of various policy instruments in several selected policy areas of CSR/CER, such as sustainability reporting, sustainable consumption, sustainable public procurement, socially responsible investment, and awareness raising. Third, the theoretical analysis of the role of government in CSR/CER will be substantiated by several important international CSR/CER standards developed by several important international organizations, such as the United Nations, the OECD, and the ISO. Research Question 6 will be answered in this chapter.

Chapter 7 focuses on the role of public authorities in promoting CSR/CER development in the European institutional context. First, this chapter begins with an overview of the development of CSR/CER at the EU level, by introducing several important CSR/CER directives and policies. Secondly, three Member States (the Netherlands, France, and the United Kingdom) are selected to exemplify the efforts of the states in developing their national policy frameworks on CSR/CER. Thirdly, this chapter also examines the effects of the CSR/CER policies on changing corporate behaviour by conducting the case studies of selected European companies. Research Question 7 will be answered in this chapter.

Chapter 8 and Chapter 9 explore the development of CSR/CER in China from both theoretical and practical perspectives. Research Question 8 will be answered in these two chapters.

Chapter 8 aims to depict China's CSR/CER landscape from a theoretical perspective. Particularly, given the significant difference between China and Western countries, Chapter 9 starts to provide some basic insights into China's institutional context, like China's political and economic systems, the cultural background, and the international situation. Next, this chapter provides an overview of the historical evolution of China's CSR/CER development, and the key actors and key issues of China's CSR/CER development will also be analysed in this chapter.

Chapter 9 discusses China's CSR/CER development at the policy level and in practice. First, this chapter describes China's policy framework on CSR/CER, by providing the literal analysis of several important CSR/CER regulations and policies. Moreover, this section will also examine how these CSR/CER-related policies motivate Chinese enterprises to improve their social and environmental performance by conducting case studies of selected companies, more particularly the state-owned enterprises in a Chinese context.

Chapter 10 seeks to systematically contextualize these findings and to answer the research questions of the book and provides recommendations on how to further promote the development of CSR/CER in China.

CHAPTER 2

What Does CSR/CER Mean?

1 Introduction

A proper starting point of this book is to define the research topic—the concept of CSR/CER. More particularly, CSR/CER has attracted a growing interest from both academic circles and the business community. Many efforts have been made to develop a widely accepted definition of CSR/CER. Therefore, the main goal of this chapter is gain more insights into the understanding of CSR/CER from both a theoretical and a practical perspective. More importantly, compared to the previous studies in this domain, this chapter addresses an important question, being what CSR/CER means for the business community.

Since the concept of CSR/CER is naturally related to the theory of corporation, this chapter starts with an introduction to the organizational and legal structure of companies (Section 2). More particularly, this chapter focuses on the changing forms of companies and their roles within society over time. Section 3 focuses on the historical evolution of CSR/CER during several crucial periods. Next, Section 4 discusses the definitions of CSR/CER developed by a number of scholars and international organizations. Section 5 introduces several competing concepts that are closely related to CSR/CER but with different focuses. These CSR related concepts are corporate governance, corporate citizenship, corporate sustainability and stakeholder orientation. After discussing the definition of CSR/CER from a theoretical perspective, Section 6 provides some idea as to how the business community converts the abstract concept of CSR/CER into their business strategies and operations. This chapter chooses four industries to demonstrate how companies from various industries integrate the ambiguous and abstract concept of CSR/CER based on their own background and expertise. These four industries are chemicals, oil and gas, banking and food and beverages. Finally, Section 7 concludes.

2 The Changing forms and Roles of Corporations

An important issue in corporate social responsibility and corporate environmental responsibility (CSR/CER) is the organizational and legal structure of corporations. Since the emergence of the corporate form, it has been subject to several fundamental changes. For a large part, these changes have been

 | DOI:10.1163/9789004368132_003

initiated by economic development, economic paradigm shifts, national policy shifts and last but not least corporate scandals. These factors, separately or in various combinations, contribute to the substantial transformations regarding corporate form and its role in society. Therefore, this chapter will start with a brief introduction of some significant developments in this regard.

As a dominant economic institution in the modern world,[100] the corporation played and plays a critical role in society. The rise of corporations from insignificance to their current dominance is a momentous event in modern history.[101] The first appearance of the corporate form dates back to the late 16th century[102] when corporations were created primarily for public or religious purposes. However, the corporate form was not widely accepted at that time, and their creation has even been restricted in some jurisdictions.[103]

The modern corporate form appeared in the middle of the 19th century when a set of fundamental principles of corporations had been settled in some major economic zones, like the US and Europe.[104] The five basic characteristics of the corporation include 'legal personality', 'limited liability', 'transferable shares', 'delegated management with a board structure', and 'investor ownership'.[105] These five core characteristics create a unique corporate form—the modern corporation. Several milestones in the history of modern corporations are worth mentioning.

The first Industrial Revolution (1760–1830) is a major turning point in history, which brought about wide-ranging changes in nearly every aspect of daily life. It has also been the beginning of the improvement of living standards for the general population.[106] During this period, the number and size of factories grew substantially (for example in textile, mining, iron making, chemical sectors), which marked the beginning of industrialization and urbanization. However, the emerging labour issues and the widening gap between the rich and the poor created an intense criticism of the newly emerging factory system and the modern corporate form.[107] As a result, the corporate form experienced substantial changes from the very beginning. A significant change in the corporate form occurred in the relationship between ownership and management,

100 Bakan 2005, p. 19.

101 *Id*, p. 1.

102 *Id*, p. 6.

103 In 1720, for example the English Parliament passed the Bubble Act to prohibit the creation of corporations.

104 Kraakman *et al.* 2009.

105 See e.g. Kraakman *et al.* 2009 , p. 5; Kraakman and Hansmann 2000–2001.

106 For more discussion about the first Industrial Revolution, see e.g. Berg and Hudson 1992, pp. 24–50; Inikori 2002.

107 Wren 2005.

which were closely united in partnerships or family business, but become separated and regulated in the corporate form.[108] This fundamental transformation, on the one hand, allowed corporations to grow at an unprecedented scale and speed by combining the capital of a vast number of investors,[109] but on the other hand did also provide managers with opportunities for notorious fraud and corruption by wielding the economic power of corporations.[110]

The 1920s and 1930s are characterized as the 'corporate period' by economist Nicholas Eberstadt[111] when the modern corporate form matured and began to take dominance in the economy. In particular, the market was controlled by several giant corporations, which were not only business organizations, but also institutions with strong economic powers, social powers as well as responsibilities.[112] This changing role of the modern corporation became increasingly visible in the Great Depression that took place in the 1930s. The Great Depression first started from a stock market crash in the U.S. in 1929, which rapidly became a worldwide economic depression. As for the causes of the Great Depression, the economic literature provides several competing theories, such as the well-known Keynesian economics[113] and the Monetarist economics.[114] In the eyes of the public, corporate greed and mismanagement played an important role in causing this devastating economic crisis.[115] The dramatic decrease in industrial production, wholesale prices, salaries and foreign trade occurred in combination with the massive growth of unemployment and created miserable societal conditions.[116] Consequently, modern corporations were seen as *'Frankenstein monsters',* who are capable of doing evil instead of assuming their new responsibility and serving the interests of society as a whole.[117]

108 Kraakman *et al.* 2009.
109 Bakan 2005, p. 8.
110 Bakan 2005, p. 15.
111 Eberstadt 1973, pp. 76–81.
112 Carroll 2008, p. 24.
113 Keynesian economics were developed by the British economist John Maynard Keynes during the 1930s in an attempt to understand the Great Depression. Keynes advocated increased government expenditure and lower taxes to stimulate demand and pull the global economy out of the Depression. For more information, available at: http://www.investopedia.com/terms/k/keynesianeconomics.asp (Accessed on April 9, 2017).
114 The Monetarist economics maintains that the money supply (the total amount of money in an economy) is the chief determinant of current dollar GDP in the short run and the price level over longer periods. Today, Monetarism is mainly associated with the work of Milton Friedman.
115 Bakan 2005, p. 19.
116 For more discussion about the Great Depression, see e.g. Temin 1991; Rothbard 1972.
117 Bakan 2005, p. 19.

Another severe economic recession took place in the 1970s, due to a surge in oil prices under the pressure of the formation of the Organization of the Petroleum Exporting Countries (OPEC).[118] This economic crisis again caused a series of negative consequences such as high unemployment and unstable inflation.[119] Governments faced intensive criticism for their incapability of dealing with this economic and societal crisis. In this context, economic policies started to embrace neoliberalism, which called for more freedom of individuals and corporations from regulations or other forms of government influence by limiting the role of government in the market.[120] Evidence of embracing neoliberalism can be traced back to the economic policies in the term of office of Margret Thatcher in the UK and of Ronald Regan in the US during the 1980s. The increasing popularity of neoliberalism contributed to the proliferation of CSR during this period.[121]

Since the 1980s, the rapid development of economic globalization has exerted a profound influence on the evolution of the modern corporation. The economic and political powers of corporations, particularly MNEs, increased substantially and even beyond the earlier known levels. One important factor is the advanced technical innovations in transportation and communications, which has dramatically enhanced the mobility and flexibility of business activities.[122] However, the strong powers of companies also made them more vulnerable to public pressure than ever.[123] In today's world, due to the worldwide exchange of goods, capital, labour, and information, the transboundary effects of business activities also intensify.[124] The adverse effects of corporate behaviour can be illustrated by an extensive list of global environmental accidents during the past decades, such as the Bhopal Disaster (1984), the Exxon Valdez oil spill (1986), and Deepwater Horizon oil spill (2010).

The adverse consequences of business activities have mainly been characterized in economic literature as 'externalities'.[125] Milton Friedman defines an externality as "the effect of a transaction...on a third party who has

118 *Id*, p. 21.
119 *Id.*
120 Bakan 2005, p. 21.
121 See Section 3.4.
122 Bakan 2005, p. 21.
123 Bakan 2005, p. 25.
124 See e.g. Mokhiber and Weissman 1999; Korten 2001.
125 An externality can refer to the positive effects of business activities, such as producing useful products and service and creating jobs, as well as the negative effects, such as environmental pollution. In this book, the term of externality mainly refers to the negative effects of business activities. For more discussion on the basic theories of externality, see e.g. Baumol 1988; Buchanan and Stubblebine 1962, pp. 371–384.

not consented to or played any role in carrying out of that transaction."[126] From a traditional economic perspective, the corporation is an 'externalizing machine',[127] and lacks the motivation to internalize externalities on a voluntary basis due to the extra costs which provide a burden on their profits. The public has gradually realized the fact that irresponsible corporate behaviour poses great threats to the quality of daily life since corporations consider these risks as externalities and impose the related costs on society. Consequently, irresponsible corporate behaviour is perceived as an important source of many social and environmental problems.

Another important trigger of corporate reforms is the intensifying criticism on corporate scandals. A landmark in corporate history has been the 'Enron Scandal' in the early 2000s, which led to the bankruptcy of the Enron Corporation, the implosion of their accountancy firm (Arthur Anderson), and the bankruptcy of many other closely related companies. The scandal shocked the world. As a world's leading Energy Corporation, Enron was prosecuted for fraud, insider trading, and money laundering. After the Enron Scandal and a series of corporate scandals and corruption in the early 2000s, corporations were faced with a severe crisis in public trust for being obsessively self-interested. In the post-Enron era, governments recognized the increasing need for regulation to prevent corporations from becoming dangerous institutions, which abuse their strong powers in a ruthless manner.[128] In the same period, the wide-spread public protests against corporate power led by various non-governmental organizations became frequent. Facing this increasing public pressure, business leaders did recognize the urgency to improve the corporate image to retain social trust, to maintain their licence to operate, and to secure their competitiveness in the international market. In this context, CSR/CER represents a corporate response to the increasing public pressure, which becomes an important driver for the rapid development of CSR/CER.

3 The Historical Evolution of CSR/CER

In the previous section, some significant developments of corporations were described in organizational forms and their changing roles within society. Irresponsible corporate behaviour has been targeted for its adverse effects on

126 Bakan 2005, p. 61.

127 Bakan 2005, p. 60.

128 For example, after the Enron scandal, the US Sarbanes-Oxley Act of 2002 was enacted—"An Act to protect investors by improving the accuracy and reliability of corporate disclosures made pursuant to the securities laws, and for other purposes".

employees, customers, the environment and local communities. At the same time, shareholders drew attention for their increasing vulnerability to management. Both civil society and shareholders believe that the corporation could provide a dangerous mix of power and unaccountability, which should be better addressed.[129] In this context, CSR/CER has been promoted as one of the answers to those concerns.[130] Therefore, this section provides an overview of the progressive agenda of CSR/CER, to better understand how the development of CSR/CER theory corresponds with the changing forms and roles of corporations over time.

3.1 *Early Forms of CSR: the Philanthropic Era*

In fact, the discussion about CSR is not a recent phenomenon. Although it has been regarded as the 'product of the 20th century',[131] the origins of CSR activities can be traced back to the era of the first Industrial Revolution. Considerable empirical evidence could be found to prove the existence of these earlier CSR activities, especially in Europe and the US.[132] During that period, the main concern for business leaders was the labour-related issues, like the welfare issues (related to health, safety, and living conditions) and the employment of female and children labour. So the dominant form of CSR of that time was the charitable contributions from the owners of various large corporations through establishing churches, hospitals, and schools. This period is categorized as the 'the philanthropic era'.[133]

However, corporate philanthropy was mainly regarded as the personal decisions of some generous entrepreneurs, like Cornelius Vanderbilt, Andrew Carnegie, John Rockefeller and Henry Ford, rather than as a result of corporate behaviour. Some scholars argued that it was hard to differentiate whether this philanthropy is corporate or personal behavior.[134] Their incentives behind the philanthropy were questioned for their genuine concerns for society or just for changing their image as 'Robber Barons'.[135] Despite these disputes, as one of the earliest forms of CSR, corporate philanthropy played a central role at the early stage of CSR development.[136]

129 Bakan 2005, p.27.

130 *Id.*

131 Carroll 2008, p.19.

132 *Id.*

133 Murphy 1978, pp. 19–25.

134 Carroll 2008, p.21.

135 'Robber Baron' was a term applied to a businessman in the 19th century who engaged in unethical and monopolistic practices, wielded widespread political influence, and amassed enormous wealth. See Bridges 1958.

136 Heald 1970, pp. 13–14.

3.2 *Some New Dimensions of CSR in the 1920s and 1930s*

Important decades in the development of CSR are the 1920s and the 1930s. In the middle of this period, the Great Depression started in the U.S. and then spread across the world. People perceived that the selfish and irresponsible conducts of corporations and their excessive use of corporate power were important causes of this devastating economic crisis.[137] They were convinced that the large companies dominated the economy and these companies combined their power to exert pressure on society.[138] Consequently, the word of 'corporation' started to represent an impersonal, immoral, selfish and evil image.[139] In this context, CSR was employed as a response to the increasing public negativity.

In this period a relevant and influential debate about the 'purpose of the corporation' took place between two law professors—Adolf Berle and Edwin Dodd. A critical issue of this debate was the question whose interest corporations should serve, which was still at the heart of the ongoing CSR discussion. In 1931, Adolf Berle, a corporate law professor at Columbia University, started the debate with the publication of *Corporate Powers as Powers in Trust*.[140] Berle argued that all powers of corporations were granted to corporate managers by the owners of the corporation, namely the shareholders, so managers had a fiduciary duty to their shareholders for achieving the maximization of profits. Berle, therefore, concluded that the corporate powers should be carefully exercised in line with the interest of the shareholders under any circumstance. Any business conduct that was not in support of this purpose was considered as a breach of obligations as the trustees of the corporation. Berle made his position clear that from a legal perspective, managers were trustees of the real owners of corporations, i.e. the shareholders, and they were therefore obliged to act in the shareholder's interests.

One year later, Berle's argumentation was challenged by a scholar from Harvard Law School, Edwin Dodd. As a response to Berle's position, Dodd published the article '*For Whom Are Corporate Managers Trustees?*' in 1932. At the beginning of this article, Dodd agreed with Berle's position that the fundamental purpose of corporations was to serve the interest of shareholders and managers should loyally serve for this purpose.[141] But he also pointed out that Berle's arguments were based on the assumption that a corporation was merely a private association of shareholders and managers were their

137 Bakan 2005, p.19.
138 Carroll 2008, p.23.
139 Bakan 2005, p.18.
140 Berle 1931, pp. 1049–1074.
141 Dodd 1932, pp. 1145–1146.

fiduciaries.[142] However, as discussed above,[143] the role of the corporation changed a lot during the past decades. There was a growing acceptance that a corporation had a broader societal responsibility for not only shareholders but also a large group of stakeholders who were directly or indirectly influenced by any decision or activity of corporations.[144] As a result, Dodd concluded that corporations should serve not only the interests of shareholders but also the interests of those affected by the business activities, such as employees, consumers, and the public.[145] Furthermore, he suggested that corporate managers should fulfil these responsibilities on a voluntary basis before they were compelled to do so.[146]

To summarize, it can be observed that in this debate Berle and Dodd share the same view on the accountability of corporate management but diverge in whom corporate management should finally serve.

3.3 *CSR Begins to Take Form in the 1950s and 1960s: the Awareness Era*

The third crucial period in the evolution of CSR is in the decades of the 1950s and 1960s. This period, particularly the period between 1953 and 1967, is characterized as the 'awareness era',[147] due to the growing acceptance of CSR and the substantial accumulation of writings regarding CSR issues.

Among a large amount of CSR literature, a landmark publication from the 1950s is the '*Social Responsibilities of the Businessman*' by Howard Bowen, which marked the beginning of a modern period of CSR writings.[148] In this book, Bowen suggested that as more and more business institutions appeared in the market, the whole world was entering 'the era of corporate capitalism'.[149] During this period, corporate capitalism showed a rapid growth in the size and power of corporations to a degree in which every business action would have a significant influence on people's life. Bowen, therefore, raised a fundamental question on "what responsibilities to society may businessmen reasonably be expected to assume."[150] As part of the answer to this question, Bowen put forward an initial definition of CSR as follows:

---

142 *Id*, pp. 1146–1147.

143 See Supra Section 2.1.

144 Dodd 1932, pp. 1145–1163.

145 *Id*, pp. 1153–1154.

146 *Id*.

147 The classification of CSR eras is developed by Murphy (1978). According to Murphy, the development of CSR can be classified into four periods: the 'philanthropic era' (the period before the 1950s), the 'awareness era' (the period 1953–1967), the 'issue era' (the period 1968–1973) and the 'responsiveness era' (from1974–1978 until now).

148 Carroll 1979, p.1.

149 Bakan 2005, p.14.

150 Bowen 1954, p.xi.

> the obligation of businessmen to pursue those policies, to make those decisions, or to follow those lines of action which are desirable in terms of the objectives and values of our society.[151]

Due to his notable contributions to the development of CSR, Bowen is awarded the honour of the 'Father of Corporate Social Responsibility.'[152]

However, despite the growing acceptance of CSR, the 'awareness era' was the decade of "more talk than action".[153] In this period, there was little action on CSR and the form of CSR was still limited to the earlier form of corporate philanthropy.[154]

3.4 *CSR Proliferates Rapidly in the 1970s and the 1980s: the Issue Era*

The decades of the 1970s and 1980s have far-reaching influence on the development of CSR. During this period, many influential scholars stepped into the discussion of CSR, as the number of CSR publications increased substantially. An influential writer in the 1970s is Keith Davis, who announced his return to the discussion of CSR[155] by publishing an article entitled *'The Case for and against Business Assumption of Social Responsibilities'* in 1973. At the beginning of this article, Davis introduced various cases for and against CSR by quoting from two distinguished economists' views on this topic.[156] Davis also presented the updated definition of CSR in this article as follows:

> a firm's consideration of, and response to, issues beyond the narrow economic, technical, and the legal requirements of the firm.[157]

Compared to his previous CSR definition in the 1960s,[158] Davis excluded firms' legal obligations from his new definition of CSR, based on his belief that mere

151 Bowen 1954, p.6.

152 Carroll 2006, p.5.

153 *Id.*

154 According to Carroll, there are few corporate actions in the 1950s. (See Carroll 2008, p.26)

155 Davis began to write on CSR topics and public several articles in the 1960s. See e.g. Davis 1960, pp. 70–76; Davis 1967, pp. 312–322.

156 In this paper, Davis firstly quoted Friedman's argument against CSR that "few trends could so thoroughly undermine the very foundations of our free society as the acceptance by corporate officials of a social responsibility other than to make as much as money for their stockholders as possible", and secondly, he quoted from Paul Samuelson's statement for CSR that "a large corporation these days not only may engage in social responsibility, it had damn well better try to do so." (See Davis 1973, pp. 312–322).

157 Davis 1973, p.312.

158 Davis (1960) first defined CSR as "businessmen's decisions and actions taken for reasons at least partially beyond the firm's direct economic or technical interest." (Davis 1960, pp. 70–76).

compliance with the mandatory legal requirements did not mean being socially responsible.

On the other hand, there were more critical views on the value of CSR as well. The position of Milton Friedman was well known in this respect; he treated CSR as a fundamental subversion of a free economy and even a free society.[159] Friedman strongly argued that in a free market the most important responsibility of the firm was to make as much money as possible,[160] and corporations had the freedom to use their resources for making maximum profits, as long as the firm conducts business activities within limits prescribed by the law.[161] Although being severely challenged in the following decades, Friedman's argument against CSR was still influential in today's discussion in this domain, but did lose much of its initial convincing power during the late 1990s and beyond.

A distinct feature of CSR in the 1980s was the proliferation of several alternatives and complementary definitions of CSR in academic writings as well as in practice. These concepts highlighted some new dimensions in the ongoing CSR debate. In general, most of these new insights strengthened the need to go from 'talk' to 'action', like providing a proper response, changing corporate performance and engaging more with stakeholders. As a result, several alternative concepts of CSR have gained considerable popularity in both academic and business circles, such as *corporate social responsiveness, business ethics,* and *corporate social performance*. The rapid growth of these new dimensions in the concept of CSR reflected that the focus of CSR became more practice oriented. Before the 1980s the efforts to better define the concept of CSR in a more detailed manner was obvious. After the 1980s, however, the primary concern shifted to establish a better understanding of CSR in its broader context. This change stemmed from some scholars' belief[162] that the term CSR was too narrowly defined to fully cover the various aspects of the related corporate social performance or actions.

An important concept from the 1970s became *'Corporate Social Performance'* (CSP). The term CSP was first introduced by Archie Carroll in the article *'A Three-Dimensional Conceptual Model of Corporate Performance'* (1979). To fully cover the wide-range of CSR issues, Carroll developed a three-dimensional *corporate social performance model* in which corporate social responsibility,

159 Friedman 1962, p.133.

160 Friedman 1970.

161 Friedman argued that "there is one and only one social responsibility of business—to use its resources and engage in activities designed to increase its profits so long as it stays within the rules of the game, which is to say, engages in open and free competition without deception or fraud." (Friedman 1962, p.133).

162 Carroll 1979, p.498.

corporate social responsiveness, and social issues were incorporated into a comprehensive system. In his three-dimensional CSP model, Carroll proposed a definition of CSR with four categories, which encompassed: economic responsibilities, legal responsibilities, ethical responsibilities and discretionary responsibilities.[163] He later incorporated these four categories to constitute a hierarchy of the "total social responsibilities".[164] In the 1980s, a group of scholars continued to advocate the concept of CSP. For example, Wartick and Cochran examined 'the evolution of the corporate social performance model' and further improved the CSP model, based on Carroll's work. They held that the first dimension of Carroll's CSP model 'social responsibility' should be taken as principles; the second dimension 'social responsiveness' as a process; and the third dimension 'social issues management' as policies.[165]

3.5 *CSR Rises to the Prominence in the 1990s and Starts to Flourish in the 21st Century*

The development of CSR entered a new stage in the 1990s, as fewer scholars focused on the conceptualization of a universally accepted definition of CSR.[166] The concept of CSR began to serve as starting point for other related research, such as corporate social performance, business ethics, the stakeholder theory, corporate sustainability, and corporate citizenship.[167] As a result, these new concepts matured and took a more central position in the CSR debates in the 1990s, which became apparent from the extensive literature on each subject mentioned above.[168]

A notable development from the 1990s was the establishment of a comprehensive conceptual framework of CSR by Carroll. By revisiting the previous four-part definition of CSR in 1979,[169] Carroll replaced the discretionary responsibilities with philanthropic responsibilities[170] and constructed the "the pyramid of corporate social responsibility" together with the three other types

163 Carroll further developed his four-part definition of CSR in the 1990s.
164 See Chapter 4, Section 2.1.
165 Wartick and Cochran 1985, pp. 758–769.
166 Carroll 2008, p.37.
167 *Id.*
168 *Id.*
169 Carroll proposed a four-part definition of CSR in 1979 as following: the social responsibility of business encompasses the economic, legal, ethical, and discretionary expectations that society has of organizations at a given point of time. (Carroll 1979, p.500).
170 According to Carroll, the philanthropic responsibilities entail that business should contribute to the local community where they operate and improve the quality of life and by doing so, respond to societal expectations as a good corporate citizen. (Carroll 1991, pp. 42–43).

of responsibilities, i.e. economic responsibilities,[171] legal responsibilities,[172] and ethical responsibilities.[173] In Carroll's CSR pyramid, he differentiated the philanthropic responsibilities from the ethical responsibilities, which could easily lead to confusion as has been the case. He claimed that the differences between these two responsibilities existed that the philanthropic responsibilities without ethical or moral restrictions, were more voluntary than the other three responsibilities and hence were not expected to be taken for economic, legal or ethical motivations.

As the figure (below) shows, the four types of responsibilities have a sequential order: the economic responsibilities served as the foundation of the CSR pyramid, and the philanthropic responsibilities were on top of the pyramid and less important than other three categories. Therefore Carroll has summarized that in his CSR pyramid a socially responsible firm *"should strive to make a profit, obey the law, be ethical, and be a good corporate citizen."*[174]

Next to Carroll's CSR pyramid, another important concept is 'People, Planet and Profit' (PPP) or the three P's as the major categories of CSR. This model is also well known as the 'triple bottom line' (TBL) and was developed and advocated by John Elkington in the late 1990s.[175] The notion of the 'bottom line' traditionally referred to profit making for corporations, and Elkington expanded the scope of the traditional bottom line by incorporating the social (people) and environmental (planet) dimensions. The triple bottom line approach requires corporations to balance the three dimensions in their business decisions and actions.

Another new feature of the 1990s is the proactive participation of the business community in advocating and implementing CSR. An increasing number of corporations developed their approaches to CSR, by translating the concept of CSR into their business strategies, depending on several variables, such as industrial sectors, production processes, products, and services as well as the major innovations (to be) provided. However, their corporate social

171 The economic responsibilities mean that companies should conduct business consistent with profit maximization, by providing jobs; generating investment; provide safe, desired, high-quality products and services; paying taxes; disseminating business standards; supporting technology transfer; supporting the creation of physical and institutional infrastructure.(Carroll 1991, pp. 40–41).

172 The legal responsibilities mean that business is expected to comply with the laws and regulations as the ground rules under which business must operate. (Carroll 1991, p.41).

173 The ethical responsibilities oblige a business to enter the field of what is right, just and fair. (Carroll 1991, p.41).

174 Carroll 1991, p.43.

175 Elkington 1999.

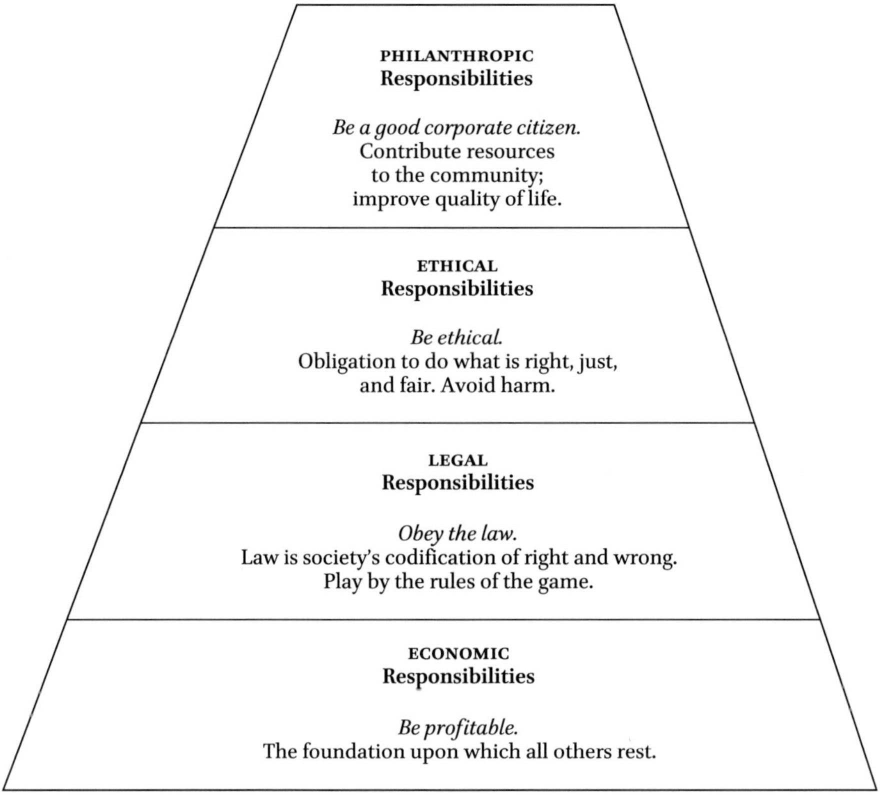

FIGURE 5 The pyramid of corporate social responsibility
SOURCE: CARROLL 1991, P. 43

performance did not always provide a typical learning curve or s-curve but showed a trial and error character. In some cases, we have even seen severe CSR-scandals in companies with high sustainability ratings, like Enron (in 2002) or Volkswagen (in 2015).[176]

After entering the 21st century, the emphasis of the CSR discussion changed from a theoretical perspective to an empirical one, and the interest of

176 Before the revelation of Enron and Volkswagen scandals, these two corporations have been regarded a paragons of CSR in their sectors. In particular, Volkswagen was ranked first on the Dow Jones Sustainability Index. After the outbreak of this scandal, Volkswagen has been removed from the DJSI. For more information about this scandal, available at: http://www.sustainability-indices.com/images/150929-statement-vw-exclusion_vdef.pdf (Accessed on April 9, 2017).

advocating the new concepts was continuously growing.[177] In 2003, Carroll reviewed his CSR pyramid again in the article '*Corporate Social Responsibility: A Three-Domain Approach*'. In this article, Carroll and Schwartz advocated a three-domain model of corporate social responsibilities, including the economic domain, the legal domain, and the ethical domain. The new model was, in essence, consistent with the earlier four-category pyramid of CSR, but it excluded the philanthropic domain. Carroll pointed out that corporate philanthropy could be prompted by different forces, like economic, legal or ethical motives and therefore could be subsumed under the other three domains.[178]

Today the importance of CSR has been widely accepted and became a global phenomenon in the era of economic globalization. Whether CSR will also be a success story in the future or not, is still in question. Different from the majority of CSR proponents, scepticism remained about the future of CSR. David Vogel, for example, recognized that the revival of CSR indeed brought many positive changes to business performance, but he also warned that "there are still significant limits to the market of virtue."[179]

4 What Is CSR/CER from a Theoretical Perspective?

4.1 *Definitions of CSR*

Irrespective of the increasing popularity and the wide acceptance of CSR in both academic circles and the business world, a major problem remains the lack of consensus about the definition of CSR.[180] The significant diversity regarding CSR-terminology, concepts, definitions, interpretations and practices is due to several important characteristics of the CSR domain, such as, the inherent diversity in content (the different dimensions of CSR: people, planet, profit); the diversity of applications (different companies in different sectors and with different management approaches); the diversity of stakeholders (international organizations, national states, NGOs, business institutions) as well as their respective power and interest; and the diversity in academic background (economists, scientists, sociologists). Therefore, CSR/CER is

177 Carroll 2008, p. 39.
178 Schwartz and Carroll2003, p. 508.
179 Vogel 2006, p. 3.
180 Crane *et al.* (eds.) 2008, p. 4.

identified as an 'essentially contested concept' (ECC),[181] because it has attracted a variety of arguments with respect to its proper meaning.[182]

Despite frequent disputes on the definition of CSR, there is still the need to share some well-established examples in this regard as a starting point of this book. As introduced in the previous section, many leading scholars contributed to establishing a precise definition of CSR in the academic circles, such as Bowen, Davis, and Carroll.[183] To grasp a broader picture of CSR definitions, this section provides some definitions developed by several international organizations and national governments. These definitions are selected on the basis of their influence and acceptance in society.

The first remarkable contribution comes from the *Committee for Economic Development* (CED).[184] The CED is a business-led public policy-oriented organization with the aim to "sustain and promote free enterprise, improve education and healthcare, reform campaign finance, enhance corporate governance, and improve the fiscal health of the United States."[185] In 1971, the CED published a report entitled '*Social Responsibilities of Business Corporations*'. In that report, CSR is perceived as a response to the changing expectations of business by stating that:

> business is being asked to assume broader responsibilities to society than ever before and to serve a wider range of human values.[186]

The CED further described the three concentric circles of responsibilities that business was expected to assume as follows:

> The inner circle includes the clear-cut basic responsibilities for the efficient execution of the economic function—products, jobs, and economic growth.
> The intermediate circle encompasses responsibility to exercise this economic function with a sensitive awareness of changing social values and priorities: for example, with respect to environmental conservation;

181 In 1956, Gallie established the essentially contested theory to address concepts, which by their very nature are inevitably contested.

182 Okoye 2009, pp. 613–627.

183 See supra Section 3.

184 The Committee for Economic Development, based in Washington D.C., was founded in 1942 by a group of business leaders.

185 For more information about the CED, available at: https://www.ced.org/about (Accessed on April 9, 2017).

186 CED 1971, p. 11.

> hiring and relations with employees; and more rigorous expectations of customers for information; fair treatment; and protection from injury. The outer circle outlines newly emerging and still amorphous responsibilities that business should assume to become more broadly involved in actively improving the social environment.[187]

The *World Business Council for Sustainable Development* (WBCSD) is an influential, CEO-led, global association of 200 company members, mainly MNES.[188] The WBCSD exclusively focuses on the role of the global business community in achieving the goal of sustainable development by playing a leading advocacy role for business. The WBSCD's understanding of CSR is based on its belief that business should play an important role in building a better future. The WBCSD defined CSR as:

> the continuing commitment by business to contribute to economic development while improving the quality of life of the workforce and their families as well as of the community and society at large.[189]

These two definitions are developed by international associations, which are led by the business community. The following CSR definitions are promoted by governmental organizations at both the international and the national level, such as the United Nations, OECD, GRI, the European Union and the UK government.

According to the Ten Principles of *the United Nations Global Compact*, corporate sustainability or corporate social responsibility means that:

> a company should operate in ways that, at a minimum, meets fundamental responsibilities in the areas of human rights, labor, environment, and anti-corruption.[190]

The *Organization for Economic Co-operation and Development* (OECD) uses the terminology of 'responsible business conduct' (RBC), and CSR is positioned as part of this much broader concept. The OCED Guidelines for Multinational Enterprises[191] define RBC as:

187 CED 1971, p. 15.
188 The WBCSD was founded on the eve of the 1992 Rio Earth Summit.
189 WBCSD, '*Corporate social responsibility: Meeting changing expectations*', 1999, p. 3.
190 For more information about the UN Global Compact, see Chapter 6, Section 5.1.1.
191 For more information about the OECD Guidelines, see Chapter 6, Section 5.2.

> all compliance with laws, such as those on respecting human rights, environmental protection, labor relations and financial accountability, even where these are poorly enforced. It also involves responding to societal expectations communicated by channels other than the law, e.g. intergovernmental organizations, within the workplace, by local communities and trade unions, or via the press. Private voluntary initiatives addressing this latter aspect of RBC are often referred to as corporate social responsibility (CSR).[192]

As a leading international organization, exclusively in the field of sustainability reporting, *the Global Reporting Initiative* (*GRI*) provides the detailed guidelines and information on what CSR means for corporations in different sectors. In this context, GRI defines CSR as:

> a firm's accountability to internal and external stakeholders for organizational performance towards the goal of sustainable development.[193]

The International Organization for Standardization (ISO) 26000 provides detailed guidance on the conceptualization and implementation of CSR. ISO defines social responsibility as:

> responsibility of an organization for the impacts of its decisions and activities on society and the environment that contributes to sustainable development, including health and welfare to society, takes into account the expectations of stakeholders, is in compliance with law and consistent with international norms of behavior, and is integrated throughout the organization and practiced in its relationships.[194]

The European Union also contributes to developing its CSR definitions. First, in 2001, the European Commission defined CSR as:

> a concept whereby companies integrate social and environmental concerns in their business operations and in their interaction with their stakeholders on a voluntary basis.[195]

192 OECD, '*Policy framework for investment user's toolkit: chapter 7*'. Available at: https://www.oecd.org/investment/toolkit/policyareas/responsiblebusinessconduct/42267935.pdf (Accessed on April 9, 2017).

193 GRI Sustainability Reporting Guidelines (the G3).

194 For more information about the ISO definition of CSR, available at: http://www.iso.org/iso/iso26000_sr.pdf (Accessed on April 9, 2017).

195 COM (2001) 366 final.

In 2011, the European Commission put forward a renewed, short and catchy definition of CSR as:

> the responsibility of enterprises for their impacts on society.[196]

This shift in definition makes clear that the EU started to move away from the voluntary character of CSR.

The *Government of the United Kingdom* is active in promoting the concept and the practice of CSR at the national level. In 2001, the UK defined CSR as follows:

> corporate social responsibility recognizes that the private sector's wider commercial interest requires it to manage its impact on society and the environment in the widest sense. This requires it to establish an appropriate dialogue or partnership with relevant stakeholders, be it their employees, customers, investors, suppliers or communities. CSR goes beyond legal obligations, involving voluntary, private sector-led engagement, which reflects the priorities and characteristics of each business, as well as sectoral and local factors.[197]

4.2 *Core Characteristics of CSR and Unsolved Disputes*

Notwithstanding the ambiguities and diversities among a variety of CSR definitions, the various definitions do provide the essential features, which could be considered as the core characteristics of CSR. For example, based on the extensive work on CSR definitions, De Hoo summarized six essential components that should be embedded in the definition of CSR. He perceived CSR as a form of entrepreneurship in which:

> a company:
> – subscribes to the social wishes of and the necessity for sustainable development,
> – accepts and assumes responsibility for making a contribution towards sustainable development,
> – implements the necessary changes in its governance,
> – is fully alive to the interests and wishes of its stakeholders,

196 COM (2011) 681 final.

197 Dahlsrud 2008, pp. 1–13.

- establishes those economic, social and environmental aspects of relevance to the company on the basis of widely accepted codes and integrates them in all its operational activities,
- and measures and evaluates the effects of its corporate performance and gives a transparent account thereof.[198]

By taking these six characteristics into account, a responsible company responds to expectations of society with respect to sustainable development, by running the company in a socially responsible manner and improving this in its overall performance regarding governance, strategic and operational processes, products, and services. This does align with the position that a range of scholars and international organizations have taken, as has been presented above.

Notwithstanding the enormous efforts in developing a universally accepted definition of CSR, many disputes remain unsolved in this field. The first dispute lies in *the voluntary or compulsory nature of* CSR. Since the modern era of CSR began in the 1950s, the notion of voluntarism or other synonyms, like the 'voluntary approach', 'on a voluntary basis', 'non-binding' and 'beyond legal compliance/obligations', does frequently appear as a crucial facet of the CSR definition.[199] However, the degree of voluntarism has brought about many debates as to whether CSR should be voluntary or mandatory, particularly given that the effectiveness of the voluntary approach is in doubt.[200] This debate will be mentioned again in various chapters of this book.

The second dispute is about the *multi-dimensional nature* of CSR, since the content of CSR and the priority CSR issues are dependent on many variables, such as place and time, corporate size and industrial sector. Important differences exist as to identify what CSR issues corporations are expected to address, because it is impossible to require corporations to fully cover all social and environmental impacts that they may bring about in practice. Also, the relevance and materiality of CSR issues vary widely between different industrial sectors and between different regions. This discussion will be referred to in the later chapter about measuring and benchmarking CSR.[201]

The third dispute has been about the degree to which a corporation should take a *multiple stakeholder orientation* in CSR. In a broad sense, stakeholders refer to any group or individual who is affected by corporate actions. According

198 De Hoo 2011, p.30.
199 Jones 1980, pp. 59–60.
200 See Chapter 5.
201 For more discussion about the measurement of CSR/CER, see Chapter 4.

to the stakeholder theory, corporations ought to be operated for the interest of all stakeholders, including its owners (shareholders), employees, customers, suppliers, investors, and local communities. Consequently, the term of stakeholder has frequently been used in defining what CSR means. For example, the European Commission (2001) defined CSR as "a concept whereby companies integrate social and environmental concerns in their business operations and in their interactions with their stakeholders on a voluntary basis."[202] In 2013, the European Commission made the position of stakeholders even more crucial by redefining CSR as hereinafter:"an enterprise is accountable for its impact on all relevant stakeholders."[203] This debate will be mentioned several times in the course of this book.

4.3 *Definitions of CER*

Compared to the extensive body of literature about the definition of CSR, there are relatively fewer efforts to define corporate environmental responsibility (CER) as a separate concept. This phenomenon can be partially explained by the fact that the environmental dimension is frequently regarded as an important component of CSR, and there seems no necessity to develop a separate CER definition. The Brundtland Commission even argued that a separate approach between the social and environmental dimension did harm the adequate policies to solve those issues.[204] Another possible reason for the relatively few numbers of CER definitions is due to the complicated nature of the environmental issues.[205]

In the current literature of CSR/CER, there are two basic approaches to defining CER. The first approach is to define CER within the much broader concept of CSR. In practice, many organizations prefer referring CER as the environmental dimension of CSR. For example, a report of the World Bank stated that:

> the environmental aspect of CSR is defined as the duty to cover the environmental implications of the company's operations, products, and facilities; eliminate waste and emissions; maximize the efficiency and productivity of its resources, and minimize practices that might adversely affect the enjoyment of the country's resources by future generations.[206]

202 COM (2001) 366 final.
203 COM (2011) 681 final.
204 WCED 1987.
205 Vogel 2006, p.110.
206 Mazurkiewicz 2004.

Several organizations do make a clear distinction between the social and environmental responsibilities of companies within the concept of CSR. An example is the World Business Council for Sustainable Development (WBCSD). In 1999, for example, the WBCSD released a report '*Corporate Social Responsibility: Meeting New Expectations*', in which corporate responsibility (also referred to as corporate sustainable development) is classified into three categories: corporate financial responsibility, corporate environmental responsibility, and corporate social responsibility.

Also in the academic circles, there are efforts to set forth a separate definition of CER. For example, Gunningham defines CER as:

> practices that benefit the environment (or mitigate the adverse impact of business on the environment) that go beyond those that companies are legally obliged to carry out.[207]

DesJardins defines CER as:

> corporate environmental responsibility should do two things: it should address the entire range of environmental and ecological issues affected by business decisions in a way that might actually turn the tide of environmental and ecological deterioration, and it should be capable of influencing business policy.[208]

Even if one does focus on CER as a separate field of policy and research for reasons of research or policy development, CER still is an indispensable part of the broader concept of CSR. In the efforts to conceptually differentiate between CSR and CER, the wording and meaning of the various definitions of CER show a close relation with the wording and meaning we have seen in the definitions of CSR.

5 CSR/CER-Related Concepts

As mentioned and argued above, the concept of CSR has been defined in various ways. A universally accepted definition of CSR is not to be expected in the academic circles and in the business world, despite the fact that the variety

207 Gunningham 2007, p.498.
208 DesJardins 1998, p.825.

of CSR definitions does share certain characteristics. This section introduces several strongly related concepts of CSR, which have exerted their influence on the conceptual understanding of CSR. These concepts are *corporate governance* as covered in business literature; *corporate citizenship* as covered in political science literature; *corporate sustainability* as covered in the social development/ecology related literature; and last but not least the *stakeholder orientation* as covered in the management literature.

5.1 *Corporate Governance*

Corporate governance deals with questions such as how to govern a corporation in an efficient and responsible way in view of the interest of stakeholders, how to organize proper governance in this respect as well as how to take account of the corporate policies implemented and the actual corporate performance? Not surprisingly, corporate governance is a concept that frequently appears in the discussion of CSR. The question of 'what is good corporate governance' has been for long at the centre of debates in the business community. From the traditional view, corporate governance deals with "investor protection devices vis a vis the company's management".[209] In this sense, corporate governance has "to protect a specific class of investors, the shareholders, for they are residual claimants on the corporate assets and thus they have the right incentives to maximize the firm's value."[210] This view represents a narrow understanding of corporate governance and has been challenged by the growth of CSR during the past decades. With the development of CSR, corporations try to absorb CSR as an integral part of corporate governance and management. In practice, the implementation of CSR could be achieved, for example, by developing specific policies and mechanisms for controlling, monitoring and reporting the social and environmental effects of business activities. Also, a number of scholars (Hopkins for example) also point out that for practical reasons it is necessary to advocate a broader conceptual approach to corporate governance, an approach that embraces CSR. However, for both proponents and opponents of this approach, an important question arises regarding the motivations for, as well as the outcomes of, corporations' engagement in CSR. More specifically, why corporations would like to engage in CSR did occur, and whether corporations' involvement in CSR indeed constitutes good corporate governance and performance or not. As a result, many studies have been conducted to examine relationships between CSR and corporate governance.

209 See e.g. Shleifer and Vishny 1997, pp. 737–783; Pacces 2011, p.297.

210 See e.g. Fama and Jensen 1983, pp. 301–325; Pacces 2011, p.297.

Harjoto and Jo[211] summarized four representative theories about the relationship between CSR engagement and corporate governance. The first theory, also known as the *'over-investment hypothesis'*, assumes that CSR engagement is a kind of principal-agent problem,[212] in which corporate managers (the agents) are inclined to invest in CSR activities with the aim of building a good personal reputation at the cost of shareholders (the principals)' interest.[213] If this hypothesis is confirmed, corporations with more effective governance mechanisms in place would invest less in CSR activities, because this more effective corporate governance will better control the behaviour of managers and thus, in this case, lead to a reduction of this particular principal-agent problem.

The second theory, also known as the *'strategic choice hypothesis'*, argues that the incumbent managers would strategically utilize CSR activities to reduce the potential risk of CEO turnover. If the hypothesis is confirmed, it could be expected that the incumbent managers would like to invest more in CSR activities.

The third theory, also known as the *'product-signalling hypothesis'*, supposes that firms can make use of CSR as a business strategy to differentiate their products or service from competitors in a competitive market. If this theory is valid, corporations are expected to invest more in CSR activities.

The fourth theory, also known as the *'conflict-resolution hypothesis'*, indicates that CSR is often employed to solve the conflict of interest between shareholders and stakeholders. If this theory is correct, there will be a positive relation between CSR engagement and corporate governance.

Based on those possible positive relationships between corporate management and CSR, Harjoto and Jo concluded[214] that there was a linkage between CSR, corporate governance, and corporate performance. They characterized this relationship as 'a governance-CSR nexus'. In a subsequent part of their research, they further tested whether CSR engagement and corporate governance could result in different corporate performance between corporations that engage in CSR and those corporations which do not. The results of their research indicated that the impact of CSR engagements on corporate performance was to a large extent determined by the way corporate governance was organized.

---

211 Harjoto and Jo 2011, pp. 45–67.

212 For more discussion on the principal-agent problem with respect to CSR engagement, see Chapter 5, Section5.

213 Barnea and Rubin 2010, pp. 71–86.

214 Harjoto and Jo 2011, pp. 45–67.

In this view, the concept of corporate governance indeed strongly influences the concept of CSR.

5.2 *Corporate Citizenship*

The second CSR-related concept is corporate citizenship. The term 'citizenship' takes its roots in political science and is traditionally characterized as a set of individual rights in civil, social and political aspects.[215] Later, with the rise of the corporate form, the notion of 'citizenship' began to be applied to corporations.[216] The starting point for a better understanding of this concept can be provided by answering two fundamental questions: the first one is 'what is corporate citizenship?' and the second one is 'which way of doing business can be considered to be good corporate citizenship?'

Today the term 'corporate citizenship' is frequently used to describe the relationship between society and business, and there are different approaches to defining what corporate citizenship means. In the first approach, a corporation is treated as a citizen, as an individual, and as a member of society. Therefore, corporations are expected to behave like a decent citizen. This approach has been widely adopted by many scholars. Davis, for example, argued that 'a socially responsible corporation should go beyond the minimum legal requirements as what a good citizen would do'.[217] Moreover, Marsden perceived corporations as "the legal entity with rights and duties, in effect, 'citizens' of states within which they operate".[218] In the second approach, one does not take the corporation as a citizen nor does it have citizenship rights, but one argues that corporations are expected to "assume some responsibilities to protect citizens' rights particularly where governments may fail."[219] For example, Matten and Crane described the corporate citizenship as "the role of corporations in administrating citizenship rights for individuals."[220]

In addition to these two approaches, some scholars pointed out that the process of globalization has played an important role in the proliferation of corporate citizenship, and thus advocated the development of a broader concept. The notion of 'Global Corporate Citizenship' (GCC) or 'Corporate Business Citizenship' (GBC) is the response to the changing role of business in the

215 Marshall 1964.
216 Moon *et al.* 2005, pp. 51–65.
217 Davis 1973, p.313.
218 Marsden 2000, p.11.
219 Matten and Crane 2005, pp. 166–179.
220 Matten and Crane 2005, p.173.

age of globalization.[221] For example, the joint statement on '*Global Corporate Citizenship—The Leadership Challenge for CEOs and Boards*' from the 2002 World Economic Forum suggested business leaders incorporate the idea of corporate citizenship into their business decisions and actions. Taking Exxon Mobil as an example, this world's largest oil and gas company made its commitments to being a good corporate citizen in all places they operated worldwide.

In answering the second question as to '*which way of doing business can be considered to be good corporate citizenship*', several organizations and scholars expressed their views. In 1973, the Confederation of British Industry published a report about the responsibilities of British companies (also known as the Watkinson Report). In this report, a new look at the responsibilities of companies was advocated, and corporations were recommended to behave like a good citizen by "taking account of the interests of others besides himself and trying to exercise an informed and imaginative ethical judgment in deciding what it should or should not do".[222] Carroll provided another definition of corporate citizenship, in line with his work on corporate social performance, which included four dimensions: economic, legal, ethical and philanthropic. Carroll argued that a good corporate citizen should "be profitable, obey the law, engage in ethical behavior and give back through philanthropy."[223]

In this respect, the discussions around the concept of corporate citizenship are closely related to the rise of CSR and do influence the conceptualization of CSR.

5.3 *Corporate Sustainability*

The concept of sustainable development is commonly defined as "development that meets the needs of the present without compromising the ability of future generations to meet their needs."[224] As mentioned earlier,[225] the concept of sustainable development and CSR are closely related, as CSR focuses on

221 Two professors of management Jeanne Logsdon and Donna Wood developed the theory of "Global Business Citizenship" (GBC), which is defined as a set of policies and practices that allow a business organization to abide by a limited number of universal ethical standards (called hyper norms), to respect local cultural variations that are consistent with hyper norms, to experiment with ways to re-conciliate local practice with hyper norms when they are not consistent, and to implement systematic learning process for the benefit of the organization, local stakeholders, and the larger global community.

222 Confederation of British Industry, and Company Affairs Committee. '*The Responsibilities of the British Public Company: Final Report of the Company Affairs Committee [of the Confederation of British Industry]*' Confederation of British Industry, 1973.

223 Carroll 1998, pp. 1–2.

224 WCED 1987.

225 See Chapter 1, Section 2.1.

the role of corporations in achieving the goal of sustainable development. This close relationship also becomes clear in some academic writings, which interchangeably use the term corporate sustainability as a synonym of CSR. When applied to corporations, corporate sustainability can be defined as "meeting the needs of a firm's direct and indirect stakeholders (such as shareholders, employees, clients, pressure groups, communities, etc.), without compromising its ability to meet the needs of future stakeholders as well."[226]

There are several periods in which the United Nations played an important role before sustainable development became a more generally accepted concept. Before the 1970s, the conflict did arise from five major trends of global concerns: accelerating industrialization and economic growth; rapid population growth; widespread malnutrition; depletion of non-renewable resources and a deteriorating environment.[227] The publication of '*The Limits to Growth*'[228] presented human's pursuit of economic growth within a finite world and the need to change course towards a more sustainable development. The report did have a direct influence on public policies worldwide and initiated various conferences organized by the UN.

In 1983, the World Commission on Environment and Development (WCED) was established on the call of the General Assembly of the UN. The goal of the WCED was to address the global environmental challenges. In 1987, the WCED, also known as the Brundtland Commission, issued the report '*Our Common Future*'. The report clearly defined the concept of sustainable development as a "development that meets the needs of the present without compromising the ability of future generations to meet their own needs."[229] Starting from this report, the significance of sustainable development has been acknowledged worldwide.

In June 1992, the United Nation Conference on the Environment and Development (UNCED) was held in Rio de Janeiro with more than 172 states (of which 108 states were represented by their head of state) participating. The remarkable outcomes of this conference are embodied in two official documents. The first one is the Rio Declaration on Environment and Development (the Rio Declaration), which sets forth 27 guiding principles for a sustainable

226 Dyllickand and Hockerts 2002, p.131.

227 Meadows *et al.* 1972.

228 Motivated by the concerns for the future of humanity, a group of industrialists, politicians, government officials and scientists became united in The Club of Rome (founded in 1968). The Club of Rome commissioned future-oriented research to a group of MIT-based scientists. As a result of this research, the book of '*The Limits of Growth*' was published in 1972.

229 WCED 1987.

development of the world. The second one is the adoption of '*Agenda 21*', which is, in essence, a comprehensive program for global action in all areas of sustainable development. The spirit of this conference is embodied by the expression '*Harmony with Nature*', which means that "human beings are at the centre of concerns for sustainable development. They are entitled to a healthy and productive life in harmony with nature".[230]

At the beginning of the new millennium, the UN set up the 'Millennium Development Goals' (MDGs), which consist of eight development goals ranging from eradicating extreme poverty and hunger, achieving universal primary education, to ensuring environmental sustainability. In 2012, the UNCED, also referred to as 'Rio+ 20', took place in Rio de Janeiro, Brazil. At this conference, the member states agreed to develop a new set of 'Sustainable Development Goals' (SDGs) to cover the development agenda for post-2015.[231] Also at this conference, the "Green economy in the context of sustainable development and poverty eradication" or in short the 'Green economy policies' were adopted. These green economy policies provide a possible tool to help member states achieve the goal of sustainable development based on their practical situations.

According to the Dow Jones Sustainability Index (DJSI), corporate sustainability is a business approach that creates long-term shareholder value by embracing opportunities and managing risks deriving from economic, environmental and social developments.[232] The 'business case for corporate sustainability' (BCS)[233] provides the rationale for a company to engage in sustainable development. Since the beginning of the 1990s, the BCS concept received more and more attention from the business community.[234]

In this context, the development of CSR and Sustainable Development have been naturally interlinked.

5.4 *Stakeholder Orientation*

As soon as a company holds the stakeholder orientation, the interest of a broader set of stakeholders is taken into account in its decision-making process rather than the interest of shareholders alone. The pros and cons of the stakeholder orientation versus the shareholder orientation are still a hot topic

230 For more information about the Rio Declaration available at: http://www.un.org/documents/ga/conf151/aconf15126–1annex1.htm (Accessed on April 9, 2017)

231 The target date of MDCs is the year of 2015.

232 Vogel 2006, p.11.

233 For more discussion on the business case of corporate sustainability/corporate social responsibility, see Chapter 3, Section2.

234 See e.g. Salzmann, Ionescu-Somers and Steger 2005, pp. 27–36.

of the ongoing debates in the business community as well as in academic circles. The key question of this discussion is the purpose of the corporation and particularly whose interests should be taken into consideration in business decision-making. In general, there are two approaches to answering this question: the shareholder primacy approach and the stakeholder approach.

The shareholder primacy approach. For quite a long time, the shareholder value thinking has been passionately embraced as a normative doctrine in business. This shareholder value thinking holds that shareholders are the true owners of the firm, so the firm should be operated primarily in the interest of shareholders.[235] Moreover, as the agents of the firm, corporate managers have "a fiduciary obligation to shareholders in the sense that the 'affairs of the corporation' must be conducted in the interest of shareholders."[236] In practice, some specific mechanisms are designed to constrain the behaviour of managers to avoid their abuse of corporate power. These mechanisms find their way into corporate law, corporate governance codes, regulation, and codes of conduct, to serve this goal. For example, company law already establishes the primacy of shareholders in the management structure of the firm, and it also contains specific articles to control manager behaviour, to ensure they will loyally fulfil their obligations to shareholders. However, it is argued that company law has "evolved to effectively constrain the pursuit of shareholder interests at the expense of other claimants on the firm."[237] In practice, legislators seem to turn to a multi-stakeholder orientation, which provides other parties as shareholders with a legal claim on the firm. As a result, more and more articles, with the aim of protecting the interests of customers, employees, suppliers and local communities, find their way in the legal system.

The stakeholder approach. This shareholder value primacy has been challenged by many scholars from different disciplines during past decades. Among all the competing theories, the stakeholder theory is one of the most influential and well-developed schools. The term 'stakeholder' was already used in an internal memorandum at the Stanford Research Institute in 1963.[238] But the stakeholder theory has not been widely accepted until the publication of Freeman's *Strategic Management: A Stakeholder Approach (1984)*. In this book, Freeman proposed a new way of thinking about corporate management in contrast to the shareholder value thinking. The stakeholder theory argues that besides the shareholders, there are other parties with a 'stake' in the company, in company decisions and actions. According to Freeman, the term 'stakeholder' refers

235 Freeman 1988, p.144.
236 *Id.*
237 *Id.*
238 Freeman and Reed 1983, p.89.

to "groups or individuals who benefit from or are harmed by, and whose rights are violated or respected by, corporation actions."[239] Freeman and Reed[240] further made a distinction between two levels of stakeholders: the 'narrow stakeholder' and the 'wide stakeholder', depending on whether they were vital to the survival and success of the firm or not. Freeman perceived that the major stakeholders of corporations included owners (the shareholders or stockholders), and next to those it included employees, suppliers, customers, and local communities in the narrow sense.[241] These stakeholders have a direct interest with any decision and action of the firm. Therefore, just as shareholders own the right to influence corporate decision-making based on their shares or stocks, stakeholders do also have a right to make claims and to get themselves involved in the strategic decision-making process of the firm.

In today's world, the stakeholder theory has frequently been used to support CSR, due to the obvious conceptual connection between the concept of CSR and the stakeholder theory.[242]

6 The Translation of CSR/CER into Business Contexts

Although today an increasing number of companies have placed sustainability at the core of their business principles and strategies, a key question is how to identify the CSR/CER issues that are financially material to their business. In fact, there is a broad range of issues within the environmental dimension that corporations are expected to address. The GRI Sustainability Reporting Guidelines (the G4) provide the specific indicators regarding the environmental dimension of sustainability. The environmental dimension should cover the potential environmental impacts related to materials, energy consumption, water, biodiversity, greenhouse gas (GHG) emissions, effluents and waste, products and services, compliance, transport, the overall environmental protection expenditures, supplier environmental assessment, and environmental grievance mechanisms.[243] These indicators apply to all types of organizations irrespective of size and industry, but the material sustainability issues vary significantly across sectors. Consequently, different industries may adopt different approaches to achieving the ultimate goal of sustainable development based on their respective background and expertise.

239 Freeman1988, p.144.
240 Freeman and Reed 1983, pp. 88–106.
241 *Id.*
242 Carroll 1991, p.43.
243 GRI Reporting Guidelines (the G4).

As mentioned above, a variety of CSR and CER definitions has been presented and the ambiguities embedded in these definitions raise another question about the interpretation of this concept under particular circumstances. Therefore, the main goal of this section is to describe how companies from different sectors translate the abstract concept of CSR/CER in practice, and further how they implement their own interpretations in their business strategies and daily operations. From this perspective, this section provides an overview of the various definitions of CSR/CER in different sectors, but the actual CSR/CER performance of these companies will not be measured and evaluated in this section.[244]

6.1 *Chemical Sector*

The first industry investigated in this section is the chemical industry. Chemical products are frequently associated with their significant impacts on the environment. This has been one of the various reasons for the global environmental movement to make a plea for the 'green or sustainable chemistry', which nowadays becomes a newly emerging field.[245] The term 'green chemistry' focuses on how to minimize the hazards of chemical products.[246] In fact, a large number of scientists and engineers make great efforts to find the creative and innovative methods of manufacturing green chemical products. Amongst these efforts, the achievements of Paul Anastas and John Warner are well known for the establishment of the '*12 Principles of Green Chemistry*'.[247] These principles are "prevention, atom economy, less hazardous chemical syntheses, designing safer chemicals, safer solvents auxiliaries, design for energy efficiency, use of renewable feedstocks, reduce derivatives, catalysis, design for degradation, real-time analysis for pollution prevention and inherently safer chemistry for accident prevention."[248] The green chemistry approach seems critical for the chemical industry and therefore, it is important to investigate how chemical companies implement these principles in their business activities.

---

244 For more discussion on the measurement of corporate sustainable performance, see Chapter 4.

245 For more information about the 'green chemistry', available at: http://www.acs.org/content/acs/en/greenchemistry/what-is-green-chemistry.html (Accessed on April 9, 2017).

246 For more information about the definition of 'green chemistry', available at: http://www.acs.org/content/ acs/en/greenchemistry/what-is-green-chemistry/definition.html (Accessed on April 9, 2017).

247 Anastas and Warner 2000.

248 *Id.*

In practice, an increasing number of chemical companies has seen sustainability as a core value of their business strategies. For example, the DJSI identifies the main challenges that the chemical industry is facing, like operational eco-efficiency, climate change, human capital management, and occupational health and safety.[249] To better demonstrate how the chemical industry integrates the sustainability into their business strategies, this section selects one of the world's largest chemical companies—'Badische Anilin- & Soda-Fabrik' (BASF)—to illustrate what the green chemistry means for this industry.

As one of the leading global chemical companies, BASF has acknowledged the metrics of sustainability for a long time. BASF has embedded sustainability into their corporate purpose: "we create chemistry for a sustainable future" as well as their strategic principle: "we drive sustainable solutions".[250] In particular, BASF aims to achieve this goal through three steps: 'sourcing and producing responsibly', 'acting as a fair and reliable partner' and 'connecting creative minds to find the best solutions for market needs'.[251] A critical step of BASF's sustainability management is to identify and prioritize the relevant sustainability issues through their materiality analysis.[252] Based on the results of their materiality analysis, the material sustainability aspects for BASF cover a range of issues in economic, environmental, and employees and social dimensions. The environmental dimension of sustainability encompasses five specific aspects. The first material environmental aspect for BASF is safety standards regarding emergency responses, process safety, and distribution safety. The second aspect is related to energy and climate protection by providing products with energy efficiency and climate change mitigation technologies. The third aspect is to enhance responsibility along with their value chain by promoting environmentally friendly technologies, recycling by-products, providing detailed information about their products, introducing the end-of-ripe technologies and reducing waste. The fourth aspect focuses on the sustainable use of water resources and the innovation of water protection products. The fifth aspect deals with the protection of diversity and ecosystems as well as the promotion of renewable raw materials.

---

249 For more information about the challenges of the chemical industry, available at: http://www.sustainability-indices.com/images/Industry_Group_Leader_Report_DJSI2015_Akzo-Nobel-NV.pdf (Accessed on April 9, 2017).

250 BASF Report 2014, p.22.

251 For more information about the sustainability issue of BASF, available at: https://www.basf.com/en/company/sustainability.html (Accessed on April 9, 2017).

252 For more information about the sustainability management of BASF, available at: https://www.basf.com/ en/company/sustainability/management-and-instruments/topics.html (Accessed on April 9, 2017).

6.2 *Oil & Gas Sector*

The sustainability of the oil and gas industry has become a hot topic in recent decades. That is, on the one hand, due to the crucial role of energy in "serving the needs of a growing population and helping people out of poverty."[253] On the other hand, in the wake of many devastating incidents caused by energy companies, such as Shell's oil spills in Nigeria and the Deepwater Horizon Oil Spill caused by British Petroleum, the significant environmental impacts of the oil and gas sector have raised considerable concerns. Consequently, it poses a significant challenge for the oil and gas industry: how to meet the increasing demands for energy while minimizing the potential impacts and risks to the environment?

Today the oil and gas industry is facing a variety of environmental challenges, such as the environmental damage due to oil spills, water, air emissions, flaring, biodiversity and ecosystem services, fresh water use and discharge, energy efficiency, climate change and potential impacts on local communities. Therefore, for energy companies, a crucial step is to identify and prioritize the material issues for their business operations and to develop their approaches to managing these challenges. In practice, many leading energy companies have already worked on integrating sustainability into their business strategies.

As the world's leading energy company, Royal Dutch Shell (Shell) has a solid history in addressing the sustainability challenges and subjects, by meeting the world's growing demands for energy in economical, environmentally and socially responsible ways. Shell positions its role in sustainability as "helping meet the world's growing demand for energy in ways that are economical, environmentally and socially responsible."[254] Therefore, Shell commits to assessing the potential environmental impacts on the environment before the projects, and to managing and minimizing these impacts during their operations. Beyond the compliance with environmental regulation and international standards, Shell also develops even stricter environmental standards than the mandatory environmental requirements, in the field of preventing operational spills, improving the energy intensity, reducing air emissions, minimizing the flaring and venting of natural gas, and managing the use of fresh water.[255] Also, a particular focus of Shell's sustainability strategy is the development of the decommissioning of an offshore facility, which is associated

253 Royal Dutch Shell plc Sustainability Report 2014, pp. 6–7.
254 *Id*, p.1.
255 *Id*, p.14.

with the disputes over the preparatory work for decommissioning the Brent oil and gas field.[256]

6.3 *Banking Sector*

In contrast with the sectors above featuring high pollution and energy consumption, the environmental impacts of the banking industry seem to be less significant. Banks play an important role in achieving the goal of sustainable development, not only by trying to become more sustainable themselves but also by influencing their clients to move towards sustainability through a range of financial products and services.[257] The environmental impacts of the banking sector can be categorized into two basic types: the direct environmental impact and the indirect environmental impact.[258] The direct environmental impact refers to the environmental footprints associated with their business operations, such as GHG emissions, paper, and electricity consumption. The indirect environmental impact relates to their financial products and services.[259] For the banking industry, there are three general approaches to managing their direct and indirect environmental impacts: by reducing their direct impacts on the environment, by financing and investing in sectors with significant environmental impacts, and by funding relevant research projects aimed at combating environmental pollution.

In this respect, as one of the world's most sustainable banks,[260] ING Group N.V. (ING) sets a good example of integrating sustainability into their business strategy. In the '*ING Environmental Approach*',[261] ING outlines their direct and indirect environmental impacts as well as how they manage these impacts through their financial activities. At ING, the direct environmental impact is associated with their operations and buildings, IT systems and business travels.[262] To reduce their direct impacts on the environment, ING works on measuring, monitoring and reporting their direct footprints regarding energy consumption, business travel, carbon off-setting, water use, paper use and waste. However, ING believes that the indirect environmental impact through their financial products and services is more far-reaching than their

256 *Id*, p.15.

257 For more information about the sustainability issue at ING, available at: http://www.ing.com/ING-in-Society/Sustainability/INGs-Sustainability-Direction.htm (Accessed on April 9, 2017).

258 ING Environmental Approach 2016.

259 *Id.*

260 In 2015, ING Group was named among the world leaders in banking industry by the DJSI.

261 ING Environmental Approach 2016.

262 *Id*, p.4.

direct environmental impact as mentioned above. Stemming from this belief, ING puts more emphasis on managing their indirect environmental impact through their financing activities and close cooperation with their suppliers. In particular, ING proactively works on "identifying and seizing opportunities to finance sustainable projects and companies with better environmental performance"[263] and "managing environmental risks"[264] via the ING Environmental and Social Risk (ESR) Framework. To ensure sustainability along their supply chain, ING also establishes the 'Sustainable Procurement Programme'[265] where ING's suppliers are asked to comply with the ING Procurement Sustainability Standards.

Unlike ING, some banks adopt a unique approach to achieving the goal of sustainable development. As a leading food and agriculture bank, Rabobank commits to making their contributions to sustainable development by accelerating sustainable agriculture and food supply worldwide and strengthening the vitality of communities under the corporate slogan of 'sustainably successful together'.[266] Rabobank's focus on the issues of a sustainable agriculture and the food supply chain is due to their long history and high-level expertise in the agriculture and food market. Rabobank aims to provide their clients with up-to-date knowledge and technologies on how to improve the efficiency of natural resources and how to reduce their impact on the environment.

6.4 *Food & Beverage Sector*

The importance of the food and beverage industry in today's world is due to the large environmental impacts related to food production and consumption through water and land use, the depletion of natural resources, greenhouse gas emissions, and the impact on ecosystems and biodiversity.[267] According to a recent report,[268] the world faces the urgent challenge to improve the way of food production and consumption. In this context, the food industry is expected to play an important role in contributing a more sustainable food system,

263 *Id*, p.6.

264 *Id*, p.7.

265 ING Annual Report 2014.

266 Rabobank Sustainably Successful Together: our contribution to sustainable development until 2020.

267 For more information about the importance of the food industry, available at: http://ec.europa.eu/environment/eussd/food.htm (Accessed on April 9, 2017).

268 World Resources Report 2013–2014, '*Creating a sustainable food future: a menu of solutions to sustainably feed more than 9 billion people by 2050*', available at: https://www.wri.org/sites/default/files/wri13_report_4c_wrr_online.pdf (Accessed on April 9, 2017).

and many governments have integrated the promotion of a sustainable food industry as part of their sustainability strategies. For example, the European Union defines a sustainable food industry as "encompassing a range of issues such as security of the supply of food, health, safety, affordability, quality, a strong food industry in terms of jobs and growth and, at the same time, environmental sustainability, in terms of issues such as climate change, biodiversity, and water and soil quality."[269]

As a world's leading nutrition, health, and wellness company, Nestlé firmly embed sustainability into their corporate value through 'creating shared value'. For Nestlé, environmental sustainability means delighting consumers by giving them another reason to trust Nestlé and enjoy their products and living up to employee's and external stakeholders' expectations about their environmental responsibility and practices.[270] Based on their own business operations, Nestle identifies four major material aspects and a number of specific issues under the banner of environmental sustainability: climate change; natural capital, including biodiversity, deforestation and soil fertility; resource efficiency and waste, including energy consumption, land use, littering and the environmental impacts associated with their manufacturing operations and packaging; and food waste.[271]

To manage these environmental risks, Nestlé sets up specific commitments and objectives:[272] (1) improving resource efficiency in their operations; (2) improving the environmental performance of package; (3) assessing and optimizing the environmental impact of their products; (4) providing climate change leadership; (5) preserving natural capital; and (6) providing meaningful and accurate environmental information and dialogue.

7 Summary and Some Concluding Remarks

This chapter focused on the meaning of CSR/CER and its related discussion, by presenting the historical evolution of CSR/CER, the conceptualization of CSR/CER, the competing concepts of CSR/CER, and the practical translation of CSR/CER. Based on the analysis of this chapter, one can notice that the

269 For more information about the European definition of sustainable food industry, available at: http://ec.europa.eu/environment/eussd/food.htm (Accessed on April 9, 2017).

270 Nestle in Society: Creating shared value and meeting our commitments in 2014.

271 *Id.*

272 *Id.*

concept of CSR/CER has been subject to many substantial changes from the very beginning.

From a historical perspective, it can be easily observed that the evolution of CSR/CER is closely related to the changing forms and roles of corporations in different periods. Therefore, we shortly showed that the organizational and legal structure of companies substantially changed over time. The corporate form did change over time in many aspects, like its purpose, type of legal personality, type of liability, type of ownership/shares, type of management and organizational structure, as well as its size, numbers, and powers. This created on the one hand opportunities for unprecedented corporate growth, but on the other hand also opportunities for notorious fraud and corruption by corporate management. It also created an increasing gap between a narrower defined corporate purpose (profit maximization) and the broader corporate purpose of serving the societal needs. The rise to dominance of neoliberal economics and related governmental policies of our times—in which the government itself became less powerful—provided the space to create corporate dominance. In this context, the corporation became a potential Frankenstein Monster—as was an expression during the Great Depression—and in some cases corporations proved this view to be real. One of those corporate scandals has been the Enron collapse (2002), a scandal that shocked the world and did lead to legal reform.

The changes about the relationship between business and civil society also gain enormous attention in academic circles, and a large number of scholars have made efforts to set forth a definition of CSR/CER. As a result, a variety of CSR/CER definitions is available in the literature, but a universally accepted CSR/CER definition is not expected. However, it proved that the search for a clear, widely-accepted and unbiased definition has been very helpful, but it is not necessary for the further development of CSR/CER for several reasons.

First, the establishment of a widely accepted definition of CSR/CER is confronted with many inevitable challenges, such as the multi-dimensional content, the multiple-stakeholder orientation, the variation in respective power and interest of actors, and differences in academic backgrounds. Notwithstanding these uncertainties, there are several essential elements inherent in the various definitions, which do provide companies and sectors of industry the ability to reach very relevant improvements in CSR/CER performance anyway. The business community incorporates the idea of CSR/CER in their business strategy and particular context.

Second, since the meaning of CSR/CER varies substantially depending on many variables, such as time, location, industry and culture, it is more important for the business community to incorporate the idea of CSR/CER into a business strategy based on their particular contexts. From this respect, a specific translation of CSR/CER is more useful than an abstract definition. In this chapter, we provided more insights into the sector-related difference in the translation of CSR/CER in four sectors: the chemical sector, the oil and gas sector, the banking sector and the food and beverage sector. Differences are clearly observed in their CSR/CER approach and relevant policies.

Third, even in the same scenario, the concept of CSR/CER could mean different things to different stakeholders based on their respective positions and interests, such as the corporation, corporate managers, shareholders, investors, consumers, employees and civil society. In the next chapter, we will look at the different view on CSR/CER of the corporate board, corporate managers, shareholders, investors, consumers, employees and civil society as well as what drives those stakeholders towards engagement in CSR/CER.

CHAPTER 3

Why CSR/CER? Theories and Empirics

1 Introduction

As examined in the previous chapter,[273] the concept of CSR/CER covers a broad range of issues in social, environmental and economic dimensions. In practice, this concept means different things to different stakeholders depending on their own positions and interest. Although the lack of a clear and widely accepted definition of CSR/CER remains an unsolved issue in this domain, the various definitions do provide the essential idea of CSR/CER, which can be interpreted as "going beyond mere compliance with mandatory environmental standards on a voluntary basis."[274] This implies that a corporation may adopt higher or stricter environmental standards required by mandatory environmental regulation on a voluntary basis. However, CSR/CER is not desired by a group of traditional economists, as well as the law and economics scholars. The traditional economists based their resentment against CSR/CER on the well-known position of Milton Friedman, who held that the only responsibility of business was to increase its profits.[275] Law and economics scholars like, Posner also equally argued that moving to charity, especially in a competitive environment, may not be a profit maximizing strategy; in the long run, it would lead to the bankruptcy of the corporation.[276] These arguments against CSR/CER are based on the assumption that the engagement of CSR/CER may impose higher costs on company interests. However, an interesting phenomenon is observed that today an increasing number of companies is moving towards CSR/CER in various ways, such as publishing annual reports concerning their social and environmental performance and competing to score highly on the sustainability rankings.[277] Furthermore, an extensive body of literature also indicates that CSR/CER is not always regarded as contrary to profit maximization.

---

273 See Chapter 2.

274 See Chapter 2, Section 4.

275 Friedman 1970.

276 Posner 2003, p. 435.

277 Some scholars observed that in recent decades, CSR rating agencies have experienced a pronounced growth. A CSR rating agency is any organization that assesses the social and environmental performance of corporations, and its mission is to make corporation's social and environmental effects transparent and available to stakeholders. A corporation will attempt to improve its image by publicizing positive ratings. The well-known rating agencies

 | DOI:10.1163/9789004368132_004

Therefore, a key question arises: why this would be the case? In particular, if as the traditional paradigm insists that CSR/CER would jeopardize profit maximization, why would more and more companie actively participate in CSR/CER on a voluntary basis? More particularly, considering a variety of market players whose interests are directly or indirectly affected by any business decision, what are their attitudes, motivations, and actions towards CSR/CER? Therefore, this chapter aims to gain more insight into the market demands for CSR/CER by exploring the roles and motivations of various market players towards CSR/CER.

To answer this question, this chapter begins with exploring why corporations would like to engage in CSR/CER on a voluntary basis, which seemingly goes against the traditional logic of the purpose of the company for profit maximization. More particularly, a large volume of literature indicates that CSR/CER does not always go against profit maximization in certain circumstances (Section 2). As one of the most important participants within companies, shareholders play an important role in business decision making. It is necessary to discuss what shareholder value is and in which context shareholders would like to accept CSR/CER as part of their interest (Section 3). The next section (Section 4) turns to another key actor in this domain, the corporate managers, whose personal preferences and values may influence business decision making. In addition to the actors within the corporate governance system, there is a group of other stakeholders who have direct or indirect stakes in the company, their roles and motivations also exert influence on the corporate decision making (Section 5). Finally, Section 6 concludes.

2 The Business Case for CSR/CER

2.1 *Towards a Broader Purpose of the Company*

Since its first emergence in academia, the theory of CSR/CER has raised longstanding disputes in the field of corporate law and corporate governance. Among a variety of controversies in this domain, a fundamental issue arises of why companies should accept social and environmental responsibility as an integral part of their business values? Therefore, a proper starting point of this discussion is to acquire a basic understanding of the purpose of the company. More particularly, what are the interests of a company and whose interests

include e.g. RobecoSAM, KLD, and Vigeo. However, despite the rapid development of CSR agencies, there are also growing concerns over the transparency and credibility of rating agencies. For more discussion on various issues of rating agencies, see Chapter 4, Section 4.

should the company and its managers serve? The heated debates over this issue have a long and rich tradition, started already in the 1930s.[278] Today it can be observed that there is a growing consensus in the current debate, especially in the law and economics literature.[279]

The conventional wisdom in this domain is known as the 'shareholder primacy' or 'shareholder-oriented model'. This theory is based on a fundamental assumption that shareholders are the owners of the company, so the primary purpose of the company is to maximize shareholder value. Furthermore, it is equally argued that the primacy of shareholder value does not necessarily contradict the pursuit of other corporate objectives, such as the environmental protection. It is supposed that the maximization of shareholder interests will result in the achievement of aggregate social welfare at large.[280] During the past decades, this conventional wisdom has been passionately embraced by many academic scholars, business practitioners, and policymakers as a dogma of corporate law and corporate governance.[281] The shareholder primary reached its peak in the 1990s[282] in both academic and business circles. More particularly, in 2001, Hansmann and Kraakman announced "the triumph of the shareholder-oriented model of the corporations over its principal competitors (the manager-oriented model, the labour-oriented model, the state-oriented model and stakeholder models)."[283]

However, in the wake of corporate scandals in recent years, particularly after the Enron Scandal, the shareholder value thinking has been continually blamed as a 'contributor' to many social and environmental problems. The work of Lynn Stout[284] stands out from other studies in this domain. Stout examined this classic doctrine from various perspectives, including company law, corporate economics, and the empirical evidence.[285] The primary results of her study indicate that despite the significant influence in the business

278 One of the most influential debates over the purpose of a company happened between Berle and Dodd in the 1930s. For more information about this debate, see Chapter 2, Section 2.2.

279 See e.g. Sjåfjell *et al.* 2015, p. 80; Hansmann and Kraakman 2000–2001.

280 Hansmann and Kraakman stated: "as a consequence of both logic and experience, there is convergence on a consensus that the best means to this end (that is, the pursuit of aggregate social welfare) is to make corporate managers strongly accountable to shareholder interests and, at least in direct terms, only to those interests." (Hansmann and Kraakman 2000–2001, p. 441).

281 Stout 2012, p. 6.

282 *Id*, p. 21.

283 Hansmann and Kraakman 2000–2001, p. 468.

284 Stout 2012.

285 *Id*, pp. 7–8.

community, there is a lack of any solid ground underpinning the shareholder value primacy in corporate law, corporate governance, and the empirical literature. On the contrary, Stout even argues that the shareholder value thinking could potentially damage shareholders' value in some circumstances.[286] Taking company law as an example, there is no jurisdiction that legally obliges the company and managers to prioritize the interests of shareholders over other interests.[287] In this context, many scholars from different disciplines began to rethink this traditional wisdom and have advanced several alternative theories to develop a broader view of the company purpose, such as the stakeholder theory and the theory of corporate social responsibility.[288]

2.2 *Towards Strategic CSR/CER*

2.2.1 The Strategic CSR/CER Hypothesis

As mentioned at the beginning of this chapter, there was little appreciation of CSR/CER in traditional economics. For example, Posner held that especially in a competitive market, CSR/CER would not have a bright future for the simple reason that for example, the additional investments in pollution reduction technology would only lead to higher prices, as a result of which customers would turn away from firms that engage in so-called corporate social responsibility.[289] The only way in which CSR/CER was viewed positively from an economic perspective was that charitable donations could in some cases be considered as effective advertising or public relations expenses and thus contributing to profit maximization.[290] In this context, the traditional paradigm views CSR/CER as "sacrificing profits in the social interests".[291] CSR/CER expenditure is perceived as a form of altruism,[292] which comes at the expense of corporate profits.

However, in the current debates, CSR/CER has gained increasing popularity in both academic and business circles. Many scholars equally argue that in addition to the philanthropic rationale, CSR/CER can also be derived from the aspect of profit maximization. Consequently, an increasing volume of academic

286 For example, Stout argued that the shareholder value thinking basically assumes that the interests of all shareholders are homogenous, but in fact different shareholders may have different values. The single focus on profit maximization simply ignores the preference of some pro-social shareholders.

287 Stout 2012, pp. 24–32.

288 For more discussion on the stakeholder theory and CSR, see *supra* Chapter 2, Section 4.4.

289 Posner 2003, pp. 435–436.

290 Engel 1979, p. 1.

291 Elhauge 2005, pp. 13–76.

292 In the case of altruistic CSR/CER, it basically assumes that the shareholder value would decrease while receiving noting in return. (Millon 2015, p. 44).

literature and empirical evidence presents that there is a business case for CSR/CER, also known as the 'strategic CSR/CER'. This hypothesis means that under various circumstances, CSR/CER could help companies to perform better financially and therefore enhance shareholder value. The strategic CSR/CER hypothesis can be simply interpreted as 'do well by doing good'.[293] A critical issue of the strategic CSR/CER hypothesis is to examine whether there is a market for virtue for companies to move towards CSR/CER. During the past decades, proponents of the strategic CSR/CER have worked on finding the convincing rationale to justify their position through various approaches.[294]

For example, Davis[295] proposed several possible reasons to incentivize companies to move towards CSR/CER, including "long-run self-interest, public image, viability of business,[296] avoidance of government regulation, socio-cultural norms, stockholder interest, let business try, business has resources, problems can become profits and prevention is better than curing."[297] Kurucz *et al.*[298] summarized four general types of strategic CSR/CER, and they were "cost and risk reduction by optimizing subject to constraints", "competitive advantage by adapting and leveraging opportunities", "reputation and legitimacy by building a responsible brand", and "synergistic value creation by seeking win-win-win outcomes". Orlitzky[299] also held that CSR/CER could improve corporate financial performance in four ways: first, CSR/CER engagement could enhance organizational reputation; second, CSR/CER engagement could improve the internal resources and skills (efficiency); third, CSR/CER could increase rivals' costs by attracting a more productive workforce; fourth, CSR/CER could boost the sales revenues and reduce business risk and reverse causation.[300]

Based on the prior studies, several important rationales for the strategic CSR/CER are identified in this book:

The first possibility, even recognized by Posner, is that corporate philanthropy (such as the charity donations to a local community) could provide rents from which the company ultimately would benefit as well. When a company

293 Kurucz, Colbert and Wheeler 2008, p. 84.

294 Carroll and Shabana 2010, p. 86.

295 Davis 1973, pp. 312–322.

296 According to Davis, the viability of business applies to the whole business system based on an assumption that the institution of business exists only because it performs valuable services for society. Therefore, if business wishes to retain its present social role and social power, it must respond to society's needs and give society what it wants. (Davis 1973, pp. 313–314).

297 Davis 1973, pp. 312–322.

298 Kurucz, Colbert and Wheeler 2008, pp. 83–112.

299 Orlitzky 2008, pp. 113–134.

300 *Id.*

embraces CSR/CER and reduces nuisance for the immediate environment where it operates, it would avoid the potential conflict with the local community. This could simply be an advertising strategy since the costs of enduring conflict with the local community could be higher than the costs of additional investments in nuisance control. But in addition to that, it is not unlikely that a large part of the workforce of firms is located closely to the company compound. Therefore, part of the workforce could be the primary victims of a nuisance. In this context, measures aiming at the reduction of nuisance would hence benefit the local community and the employees of the company. Thus, this would enhance the welfare of the workforce and in that sense contribute to profit maximization.

Second, investments in CSR/CER could be a marketing strategy to gain a better reputation whereby the company presents as a good corporate citizen. In this case, CSR/CER is used as a strategy of product differentiation, in which companies can differentiate their products from their competitors due to the good/better environmental quality of their products. By doing so, companies could ensure brand loyalty among their old consumers and attract more potential consumers with environmental preference. This will increase their sales and revenues in return. The product differentiation strategy has been widely used in the modern business world.[301] The environmental quality of the product can be differentiated and this differentiation can be signaled by a widely recognized label or logo. For example, companies could ask the permission from the World Wildlife Fund (WWF) to use its logo in order to demonstrate their contribution to the wildlife protection. By doing so, companies can benefit from reputational gains with potential customers.

Third, CSR/CER expenditure could reduce organizational costs and generate long-term revenues.[302] For example, the compliance beyond mandatory environmental standards leads to reduced nuisance for the local community and therefore results in lower (local) taxes for the firm. In this case, investments in CSR/CER fit in a strategy of profit maximization. From the societal perspective, CSR/CER also helps companies to boost trust by society and to retain the 'social license to operate',[303] because companies need to receive such permission from the government, local communities, and other related stakeholders.[304] Moreover, the investment in CSR/CER, for example, the R&D in eco-friendly technologies, will in the short run incur an increase in corporate

301 For more discussion on product differentiation, see Chapter 5, Section 4.1.1.

302 Millon 2015, pp. 67–69.

303 Moon and Vogel 2008, p. 303.

304 Porter and Kramer 2006, p. 80.

expenditure and a decrease in corporate profits. But these expenditures could pay off in the long-term prospect, by avoiding potential nuisance, saving more energy, or producing green products.[305]

Fourth, a pro-active CSR/CER strategy of the business community may prevent the potential risk of future regulation. This has been an important argument for corporations to engage in the so-called environmental (voluntary) agreements or environmental governance.[306] Those are in fact also voluntary agreements whereby firms engage in a contract with the government agreeing to comply with higher environmental standards, often on the condition that government will, during the duration of the environmental agreement, refrain from further regulating. Vogel also echoed this idea by arguing that self-regulation could reduce the likelihood of governmental regulation.[307] Companies may also use CSR/CER to improve their position within the current or future regulatory framework, which can be a potential source of market competitiveness compared to their peers who are not engaging in CSR/CER.[308] Therefore, many companies prefer to be one step ahead of the government legislation or intervention to anticipate social pressure and hence to be able to develop their policies in response to them.[309]

Finally, CSR/CER could fit in a so-called 'tit-for-tat' strategy in regulatory compliance and enforcement. This is a strategy that enforcement bodies often follow due to their limited budgets for monitoring and enforcement. As a result, enforcement agencies often engage in a strategy referred to as targeting, meaning that agencies will focus their efforts on specific categories of polluters or violators to achieve better results.[310] Enforcement agencies thereby implicitly or explicitly engage in regulatory dealings, using tolerance in some types of violation and increasing efforts in other types.[311] Hence, firms that present themselves as complying voluntarily with a high standard CSR/CER could thus, within a tit-for-tat strategy reduce pressures from environmental enforcement[312] and in that sense also gain from CSR/CER.

305 Millon 2015, pp. 65–67.

306 For more discussion on environmental agreements, see e.g. Orts and Deketelaere (eds.) 2001; Lyon and Maxwell 2008, pp. 246–248; Barrett 1994, pp. 878–894.

307 Vogel 2006, p. 16.

308 Reinhardt *et al.* observed that some firms may use over-compliance to spur further regulation, which would provide a competitive advantage over less adaptable firms. (Reinhardt *et al.* 2008, p. 225).

309 Crane *et al.* (eds.) 2008, p. 308.

310 See e.g. Arlen and Kraakman 1997, p. 687 and pp. 752–753.

311 Heyes and Rickman 1999, pp. 361–364.

312 See e.g. Oded 2013.

As has been presented, there are many reasons why one can argue that the engagement of CSR/CER does not necessarily run counter to the purpose of profit maximization. More particularly, the strategic CSR/CER does provide a variety of possibilities for companies to benefit from the engagement in CSR/CER without compromising profit maximization.[313]

2.2.2 The Porter Hypothesis

The argument that strategic CSR/CER could be profit maximizing has been hypothesized and developed in further detail by Michael Porter from a competitive strategy perspective. In contrast to the traditional economic paradigm that environmental regulation imposes additional costs on firms and thus may damage firms' competitiveness in the market,[314] Porter basically argues in many publications that firms that move beyond environmental compliance will automatically not only do more investment in environmental protection, but become more innovative in general. The innovations needed to reach higher environmental standards would, according to Michael Porter, also provide other benefits to the firm.[315] This argumentation is well known as the "Porter Hypothesis". In particular, Porter and Van der Linde believe that environmental regulation[316] can exert substantial influence on firms' environmental innovation in at least six aspects.[317] As a result, this further innovation would provide strategic gains to the firm as a result of which those firms that strive for higher standards of environmental protection, in the end, would also be more profitable.[318]

Porter has defended this Porter hypothesis not only with respect to corporations but also with respect to states. He holds that increased environmental

313 Kitzmueller and Shimshack 2012, pp. 74–75.

314 Jaffe *et al.* 1995, p. 133.

315 Porter and Van der Linde 1995, pp. 97–118.

316 According to Porter, environmental regulation could take in various forms not only limited to the command and control type, but also include market-based instruments, such as environmental taxes, trade emission trading system.

317 Porter and Van der Linde provide six seasons to explain the positive causal link between environmental regulation and innovation: "first, regulation can signals companies about likely resource inefficiencies and potential technological improvement; second, it focused on information gathering can achieve major benefits by raising corporate awareness; third, it reduces the uncertainty that investments to address the environment will be valuable; fourth, it creates pressure that motivates innovation and progress; fifth, it levels the transitional playing field; and sixth, it is needed in the case of incomplete offsets." (Porter and Van der Linde 1995, pp. 99–100).

318 See e.g. Porter and Van der Linde 1995, pp. 97–118; Faure and Johnston 2009, pp. 205–274; Lu and Faure 2015, pp. 239–266.

performance will lead to the increased competitiveness, of both nations and industries.[319] By examining the relationship between environmental regulation and the competitiveness of industries and nations in the context of America,[320] Porter observed that nations with strict environmental standards do not hinder the economic performance of nations but on the contrary can enhance the competitive advantages of nations in those affected industries.[321] For example, during the past decades, the Japanese vehicle industry has achieved an enormous growth and has become the worlds' largest automobile manufacturer, surpassing the U.S. and Germany. The success of the Japanese vehicle industry is to some extent related to its strict environmental standards in particular in gas emissions. In sum, Porter contends that the increased environmental performance will lead to increased competitiveness, of both nations and industries.[322]

A recent overview of literature shows that the empirical evidence of the Porter Hypothesis, although being mixed, to a large extent supports it. Ambec *et al.* distinguish between a weak and a strong version of the Porter hypothesis. The weak version only indicates that properly designed environmental regulation may spur innovation.[323] The strong version implies a relationship between environmental regulation and the business performance of a firm.[324] The authors conclude that the evidence for the weak version of the Porter hypothesis (that stricter environmental regulation leads to more innovation) is fairly clear and well-established. Empirical evidence concerning the strong version of the Porter hypothesis (that stricter regulation enhances business performance) is mixed: some studies find that environmental regulation has a direct negative effect on business performance,[325] but more recent studies also provide clearer support for that hypothesis.[326] Besides, Ambec *et al.* also points out that a critical premise for the Porter Hypothesis is the type of regulatory instruments which are employed. They further suggest that the most suitable instruments in favour of innovations are market-based and flexible instruments (like emission taxes, tradable allowances, or performance standards), industrial and patent policies and training, rather than command-and-control regulation.[327]

---

319 Porter 1991, pp. 168–170.

320 Porter 1991, pp. 168–170.

321 *Id*, p. 168.

322 Porter 1991, pp. 168–170.

323 Ambec *et al.* 2013, p. 9.

324 *Id.*

325 *Id.*

326 *Id*, p. 16.

327 *Id*, pp. 11–14.

Dan Esty and Michael Porter also examine the relationship between the stringency of environmental regulation and environmental quality in particular countries. They find out that not only the rigor and structure of environmental regulations have a particular impact on environmental performance, but also the enforcement.[328] The empirical evidence hence suggests that a country can benefit environmentally not only from economic growth but equally from developing the rule of law and strengthening its governance structures.[329] Interestingly, they also find evidence that countries that adopt a stringent environmental regime relative to their income are able to speed up economic growth rather than retarding it.[330] Therefore, the evidence at country level presented by Esty and Porter also confirms that countries adopting a stringent environmental regime do not have to be concerned that this endangers their competitive position. The evidence seems to show that it may speed up economic growth instead of retarding it.[331]

2.3 *Does a Company Do Well by Doing Good?*

Despite the various reasons to justify the strategic CSR/CER hypothesis, a fundamental premise underpinning this hypothesis is that the engagement of CSR/CER could pay off (at least in the long run). This argument raises a key question as to whether companies can do well by doing good. Many scholars have made great efforts to examine whether a positive relationship between CSR/CER investments and corporate financial performance exists in practice. The history of searching the empirical link between corporate social performance (CSP) and corporate financial performance (CFP) started from the 1970s,[332] when Bragdon and Marlin[333] conducted 'the very first empirical csp-CFP study' in 1972.[334] The major purpose for many of these empirical studies is to find the economic rationale for the business case for CSR/CER and more particularly, whether there exists a positive causal link between corporate responsibility and profitability. Since then, the empirical studies have rapidly

328 Esty and Porter 2005, p. 424.

329 *Id.*

330 *Id*, p. 425.

331 See e.g. Faure 2011, p. 393.

332 Margolis, Elfenbein and Walsh pointed out that "scholars have been searching for a link between corporate social performance (CSP) and corporate financial performance (CFP) for thirty-five years."

333 Bragdon and Marlin examine the relationship between corporate environmental performance and profitability from the perspectives of managers and investors. The results of their study indicated a positive link between CFP and CSP. (Bragdon and Marlin 1972, pp. 9–18).

334 Margolis, Elfenbein and Walsh 2008, p. 19.

accumulated in this domain. Scholars from different disciplines such as organizational behavior, business and society, and social and financial performance, examine the question whether the adoption of CSR/CER could enhance companies' performance, particularly in financial terms?

Among the large volume of the current empirical literature, the work of Margolis, Elfenbein and Walsh (MEW)[335] is one of the most representative and comprehensive empirical studies in this field. In general, the MEW is a meta-analysis and a comprehensive appraisal of 192 effects revealed in 167 studies from 1972 to 2007. It has been observed that due to the various indicators for measuring CSP, the current empirical studies vary widely in terms of content and methodology.[336] As a result, the MEW sorted these studies into nine categories: charitable contributions, corporate policies, environmental performance, revealed misdeeds, transparency, self-reported social performance, observers' perceptions, third-party audits, and screened mutual funds.[337] They further categorized CFP measures into two broad groups: accounting-based measures of financial returns and market-based measures of financial value.[338] Based on the categorization of various indicators to measure CSP and CFP, the MEW examined each category and found a modest positive average correlation between corporate social and environmental performance:[339] "58 percent indicated a non-significant relationship, 27 percent a positive relationship, and 2 percent a negative relationship between CSP and CFP."[340] Therefore, the authors concluded from their research that "the overall effect is positive but small, and moreover, that there is no evidence suggesting companies would suffer financially for CSP."[341]

Another important study in this domain is conducted by Eccles, Ioannou and Serafeim,[342] who empirically compare the effects of incorporating CSR/CER into business strategy on corporate organizational performance between two distinct types of companies: 'High Sustainability' companies and 'Low Sustainability' companies. In this study, the 'High Sustainability' companies refer to those having adopted a large number of CSR/CER policies for 'a significant period'.[343] In contrast, the 'Low Sustainability' companies are those who adopt

335 Margolis, Elfenbein and Walsh 2009, pp. 5–15.

336 *Id*, pp. 10–13.

337 *Id.*

338 *Id*, p. 13.

339 Kitzmueller and Shimshack 2012, p. 70.

340 According to their results, an additional 13% did not report sample size, so it was not possible to test for significance. (Margolis, Elfenbein and Walsh 2009, p. 21).

341 *Id.*

342 Eccles, Ioannou and Serafeim 2014, pp. 2835–2857.

343 'A significant period of time' refers to the time "prior to CSR becoming widespread, to reduce the possibility of potential measurement error due to the inclusion of firms that

none of these policies in their business strategy.[344] Empirically, they selected 90 samples from each group and matched the pairs of companies based on several indicators, including industry sector, corporate size, capital structure, operating performance and growth opportunities.[345] By carefully comparing the performance of the two groups, it is observed that the High Sustainability corporations outperform their counterparts from the Low Sustainability group regarding both stock markets and accounting performance from a long-term perspective.[346]

Both the theoretical rationale and the empirical evidence of the strategic CSR/CER hypothesis show that the social or environmental performance of firms does have a positive effect on firms' financial performance in some cases. Although the overall effect may not be significant, at the very least good environmental performance does not lead to poor financial performance.[347]

3 Why Shareholders Care about CSR/CER?

From the traditional economic perspective, shareholders are viewed as the natural opponents of CSR/CER. This argument is based on the assumption that shareholders have no other preference other than profit maximization. In other words, shareholders usually have little interest in CSR/CER, because it would impose potential costs and thus may reduce their aggregate wealth. Also, the traditional paradigm presumes that the interests of shareholders do conflict with those of stakeholders, like employees, consumers, investors and local communities. So, when companies act in the interests of stakeholders, it generally will lead to a decrease in shareholder value.

However, it has been equally argued that the interests of shareholders and stakeholders do not necessarily go against each other. The traditional shareholder value thinking simply premises that all shareholders are homogenous and they all share the same idea about their value, but in reality, shareholders' preference is highly diversified.[348] While the shareholder value model hypothesizes shareholders as purely selfish individuals who only care about the rise of stock price and their material returns, there are also many 'prosocial' shareholders who count on the long-term prospect of companies they invest in.

are either greenwashing or adopting these policies purely for public relations and communication reasons." (Eccles, Ioannou and Serafeim 2014, p. 2838).

344 Eccles, Ioannou and Serafeim 2014, p. 2837.

345 *Id.*

346 *Id.*

347 Vogel 2006, p. 33.

348 Stout 2012.

Moreover, evidence indeed indicates that there are several cases where shareholders would accept CSR/CER as part of their value, and even in some contexts they are willing to sacrifice at least part of their wealth for doing good.[349] Therefore, a key question arises here why shareholders desire CSR/CER, especially when it may damage their economic interest.

In practice, different shareholders have different preferences and interests in companies based on their diverse backgrounds and positions.[350] While some shareholders indeed only care about their share returns, other shareholders may be prosocial and would like to sacrifice some of their profits to contribute to the virtue of environmentally responsible business. In general, shareholders' motivations can be broadly categorized into two types: strategic and altruistic CSR/CER.

Today, the strategic CSR/CER has been passionately accepted as an important argument to motivate more and more companies to engage in CSR/CER. The strategic CSR/CER argues that it can be in line with the profitability of corporation and hence shareholders can benefit from CSR/CER expenditures. In this case, the strategic CSR/CER fits into the rationale of profit maximization and thus becomes desirable for shareholders. It is much easier to understand why shareholders accept strategic CSR/CER as their value rather than the problematic argument of the altruistic CSR/CER.

The more interesting hypothesis is hence the one where CSR/CER would not be a strategy of profit maximization, but where shareholders would want CSR/CER not for economic reasons, such as marketing or profit maximization, but for truly altruistic reasons. This is referred to as 'altruistic CSR/CER'. Some have described the desire for altruism as the preference for a 'warm glow'.[351] In practice, there are quite a few examples of shareholders striving for this 'warm glow'. For example, some financial institutions[352] focus on CSR/CER and explicitly call on the feeling good preference of depositors (and presumably shareholders). Also, the preference for ecological banking and green finance

349 Kitzmueller and Shimshack 2012, pp. 58–59.

350 Stout 2012, p. 9.

351 The warm glow preference refers to "utility derived from the mere fact of doing good yourself." (Kitzmueller and Shimshack 2012, p. 60).

352 An example is the bank Tridos in Belgium, which is one of the world's leading sustainable banks. Its mission is to make money work for positive social, environmental and cultural change. The environmental report of Tridos bank, available at: http://annual-report.triodos.com/en/2013/engagement/environmental-report.html?cat=b.

Besides, Deutsche Bank and BNP Paribas also constitute good examples that are devoted to becoming responsible banks, and more information about Deutsche Bank and BNP Paribas is available at: https://www.db.com/cr/en/responsible-business/index.htm and http://www.bnpparibas.com/en/responsible-bank (Accessed on April 10, 2017).

of shareholders, stakeholders, and customers does fit into this strategy.[353] This type of green finance corresponds to demands of customers and depositors, and it is a rational response of shareholders to insist on providing this green finance product. From that perspective, it could be considered as a form of strategic CSR/CER or product differentiation that fits into a profit maximizing strategy rather than altruistic CSR/CER that aims for a 'warm glow' preference.

Furthermore, some shareholders explicitly seek CSR/CER and for that reason become shareholders of companies by purchasing shares. Even if the number of shares they own may not give them control of the company, it grants them the rights as shareholders, e.g., to express their voice at the general shareholders meeting. Being a shareholder could, therefore, be regarded as a strategy attempting to change corporation policy. Finally, it should be mentioned that some shareholders, more particularly those striving for the warm glow, may demand other returns on their stock than simply dividends. In sum, there may be a variety of reasons to justify shareholders' option for 'doing good'.

4 Corporate Managers as CSR/CER Drivers

The role of managers in CSR/CER has become a subject of considerable debate in this domain, given their critical role in business decision making. In the case of CSR/CER, proponents believe that corporate managers, with their personal preference and ethical belief, can exert considerable influence on developing a business strategy towards a more responsible way and helping their companies shape ideas about the social role of business.[354]

4.1 *The Duty of Managers in Relation to CSR/CER*

To provide a proper view on the possible roles of manager, we have to recite some of the earlier remarks about the purpose of a company from the traditional economics and the law and economics literature.[355] Manager's involvement in CSR/CER was opposed by some classical economists as well as by some law and economics scholars. As discussed earlier, the shareholder-oriented model[356] insists that corporate managers have the fiduciary duties to act in the interests of shareholders and prioritize the maximization of shareholder value over other purposes.[357] This argument is based on the principal-agent theory,

353 For more discussion on green finance, see Bai, Faure and Liu 2014.
354 Swanson 2008, pp. 227–248.
355 See Chapter 2, Section 2.
356 For more discussion about the shareholder-oriented model, see *supra* Section 2.1.
357 Stout 2012, pp. 34–35.

which presumes that managers, as the agents of the owners of the firm, shall loyally serve the interests of the shareholders, namely the principals, by making as much money as possible.[358] For example, Davis argued that managers should focus on profit maximization, because they were trained for this purpose and they generally lacked the expertise in solving social and environmental issues.[359] Friedman also explicitly expressed his position against managers' involvement in CSR/CER, by stating that "in a free-enterprise, private-property system, a corporate executive is an employee of the owners of the business. He has direct responsibility to his employers. That responsibility is to conduct business in accordance with their desires, which generally will be to make as much money as possible while conforming to the basic rules of the society, both those embodied in law and those embodied in the ethical forum."[360]

As a result, many scholars insist that managers should concentrate on maximizing shareholder wealth other than those of stakeholders.[361] In this respect, the claim that corporate managers are important CSR/CER drivers goes against this conventional doctrine. However, this idea that managers could play an important role in advancing CSR/CER first stemmed from business leaders themselves.[362] Frank Abrams, the former chairman of Standard Oil of New Jersey, called corporate managers already in 1951 to recognize their responsibilities to society.[363] Ever since, CSR/CER became slowly but steadily an important issue for both corporate boards and executive managers, who were expected not only to improve corporate financial performance but also to balance a variety of interests between shareholders and stakeholders.[364] Particularly inspired by the stakeholder theory, many scholars began to focus on the managers' duty in order to address the conflict of interest between shareholders and stakeholders. Moreover, an extensive body of literature also indicates the possibility that managers could play "the pivotal role of moral leadership", because their personal values could exert a strong influence on business decision making."[365] Swanson[366] further examined the possible roles of managers in

358 See e.g. Berle 1931, pp. 1049–1074; Friedman 1970.

359 Davis 1973, pp. 312–322.

360 Friedman 1970.

361 *Id.*

362 Swanson 2008, p. 227.

363 Abrams said that "businessmen as professionals have responsibilities to many groups besides themselves and shareholders. Management's duty is to 'conduct the affairs of the enterprises to maintain an equitable and workable balance among the claims of various directly interested groups, a harmonious balance among stockholders, employees, customers, and the public at large.'" (Abrams 1951, pp. 29–34).

364 Frederick 2006.

365 *Id.*

366 Swanson 2008, pp. 227–248.

advancing CSR/CER in both the formal and the informal organizations. The results of her study showed that when leading the formal organizations, the social values of managers could be dictated in the form of the command to the lower-level managers; while in the informal organizations, the company culture was crucial and managers had considerable influence in shaping this culture.[367]

The role of managers in CSR/CER also gains legislative support in many jurisdictions. For example, the Section 172 (1) of the UK Companies Act 2006 prescribes that "a director of a company must act in the way he considers, in good faith, would be most likely to promote the success of the company for the benefit of its members as a whole, and in doing so have regards to a variety of interests, including: 1.) the likely consequences of any decision in the long term; 2.) the interests of the company's employees; 3.) the need to foster the company's business relationship with suppliers, customers, and others; 4.) the impact of the company's operations on the community and the environment; 5.) the desirability of the company to maintain a reputation for high standards of business conduct; 6.) and the need to act fairly as between members of the company."[368] It is clear that this article gives corporate managers more discretion to adopt CSR/CER policies and practices when conducting business.

4.2 *The Motivations of Managers towards CSR/CER*

Dozens of publications, as well as many legislative requirements, prove that corporate managers do play a role in promoting CSR/CER. Another important question is what are the actual attitudes and motivations of managers towards CSR/CER in practice? More particularly, if managers' performance is primarily benchmarked by the stock price, why should managers pay attention to social and environmental issues? Swanson[369] divided manager's motivations towards CSR/CER into two types: the positive and the negative motivations.

The positive motivation refers to the voluntary adoption of CSR/CER policies in business strategy. This occurs because more and more corporate managers have realized that corporate sustainability performance could contribute to corporate financial performance. This can be substantiated, for example, by a survey showed that "70 percent of global chief executives believe CSR is vital to their companies' profitability."[370] The results indicated that an increasing

367 *Id.*
368 Companies Act 2006, s. 172(1).
369 Swanson 2008, pp. 227–248.
370 Pricewaterhouse Coopers (PwC), '*Delivering the results: Growth and value in a volatile world*', the 15th Annual Global CEO Survey, 2012. Available at: https://www.pwc.com/gx/en/ceo-survey/pdf/15th-global-pwc-ceo-survey.pdf (Accessed on April 10, 2017).

number of corporate managers show genuine interest in finding the answer to the question: how to conduct their business in a more responsible or sustainable manner? Another indicator that substantiates the changing attitudes of managers toward CSR/CER is the reform of the measurement systems concerning managers' performance. It has been observed that many companies adopt a wider range of criteria to comprehensively assess managers' performance. One of the most popular measurement systems is the 'balanced scorecard' introduced by Kaplan and Norton in 1992,[371] which integrates both financial and non-financial indicators to evaluate managers' performance. The basic idea of this system stems from their belief that "pure financial measures of performance were not sufficient to yield efficient management decisions."[372] Therefore, a comprehensive measurement system does provide incentives to managers to play a more active role in advancing CSR/CER.

The negative motivation for CSR/CER involvement relates to the fact that some managers may strategically utilize CSR/CER for their personal benefits, such as to avoid the potential risk of CEO turnover, to increase job security, and to enhance their personal reputation. For example, Barnea and Rubin[373] perceived CSR/CER as a tool for managers to improve their personal reputation in sustainability leadership. Vespa and Cestone also observed that the incumbent CEOs strategically choose CSR/CER engagement in the present period to reduce the likelihood of CEO replacement in a future period,[374] because they could gain support from environmental activists and the general public.[375] This case may result in moral hazard where corporate managers may over-invest in CSR/CER activities to achieve their personal interests.[376] In this case, a risk of moral hazard may arise when managers' actions are not taken in pursuit of principals' interests, but for their personal interests.[377]

So far, our analysis is based on an assumption that managers' interests are aligned with those of shareholders. However, this is not always reflected in reality, a conflict of interest between shareholders and managers frequently occurs. This situation is well known as a principal-agent problem. This principal-agent problem could also occur concerning the issue of whether or not companies should engage in CSR/CER activities?[378]

371 Kaplan and Norton 1992, pp. 71–79.
372 Jensen 2002, p. 247.
373 Barnea and Rubin 2010, pp. 71–86.
374 Cespa and Cestone 2007, pp. 741–771.
375 Surroca and Tribó 2008, pp. 748–789.
376 See e.g. Baron 2008, pp. 328–340; Kitzmueller and Shimashack 2010, pp. 51–84.
377 See e.g. Philipsen 2003, p. 16.
378 For more discussion on the principal-agent problem, see Chapter 5, Section 5.

5 Other Key Stakeholders to Promote CSR/CER

Until now, this chapter has addressed a variety of motivations for corporations (as a whole entity), shareholders and their managers to adopt CSR/CER policies and practices. The following section further examines the role of other stakeholders, like investors, consumers, employees and civil society in promoting CSR/CER. They are regarded as major drivers for CSR/CER,[379] because their personal decisions about what to invest, what to buy and where to work do make a difference in business decision making. The internal and external pressure from investors, consumers, employees, and civil society provides incentives for companies and their managers to change their policies in order to satisfy their preferences.

5.1 *The Role and Motivations of Investors to Promote CSR/CER*

Investors usually have a large stake in the company and they could have more or less strong motives to participate in corporate governance and to promote CSR/CER engagement. More particularly, today it is observed that many corporations to a large extent rely on the funding from individual or institutional investors, so the personal values of investors could affect business decisions as to whether or not to adopt CSR/CER.[380] In this respect, investors could be important drivers for CSR/CER, because they could use their investment decisions to influence companies to move towards sustainable development and to embrace CSR/CER.

The socially responsible behaviour of investors is referred to as 'socially responsible investments' (SRI), also known as ethical mutual funds, social investment, etc.[381] Currently, there is no commonly accepted definition of SRI. Renneboog *et al.* defined SRI as "an investment process that integrates social, environmental, and ethical considerations into investment decision making."[382] The European Social Investment Forum (Eurosif) defined SRI as "any investment that integrates investor's economic objectives with their concerns with environmental, social and governance issues (ESG) when making investment decisions."[383] The recent literature of SRI shows the close relationship between

379 See e.g. Vogel 2006; Smith 2008, pp. 281–302.

380 Richardson 2015, p. 234.

381 In this book, the terms of socially responsible investment, social investment, sustainable investment, and sustainable and social impact investing can be used interchangeably. But today scholars generally differentiate ethical funds from SRI funds, considering that the traditional ethical funds are mainly driven by religious considerations.

382 Renneboog *et al.* 2008, p. 1723.

383 Eurosif, '*European SRI Study*', 2012. Available at: http://www.eurosif.org/publication/view/european-sri-study-2012/ (Accessed on February 23, 2017).

SRI, sustainable development, and CSR/CER. Specifically, the development of SRI is considered as an important contribution to building a sustainable financial market and a sustainable economy, and hence it is regarded as an implementation of CSR/CER by financial institutions.[384] This can be illustrated by the rise of the SRI market in the recent years.

SRI is not a recent phenomenon,[385] but it is only during the last years that SRI has gained considerable significance and prevalence in the global financial market. As an increasing number of ethical investors gradually recognize the potential effects of ESG issues on their long-term financial returns, the SRI market has experienced a substantial growth around the world. The recent data shows that the global SRI assets reached a total of $ 21.4 trillion US dollars at the beginning of 2014.[386] The world's fast-growing country in the SRI market is the U.S. where SRI has increased tenfold from 1995 to 2004. This showed a clear upward trend in SRI investment during the past decade. At the outset of 2014, the overall total value of the SRI market in the U.S. was $ 6.57 trillion US dollars, accounting for nearly 18% of $ 36.8 trillion US dollars in total assets.[387] In general, more than one out of every six dollars under professional management in the U.S. was invested in a portfolio with SRI strategies.[388]

Despite the worldwide popularity, SRI has been subject to an on-going discussion in the economic and the financial field. SRI has not been appreciated by the traditional investors due to their concerns about the potential reduction of their economic returns. Therefore, a crucial question arises here whether SRI performs as well as or even outperforms the traditional funds in the market? More particularly, the question arises as to how SRI motivates companies to improve their social and environmental performance in order to attract more environmentally conscious investors? In this respect, many studies have examined the influence of SRI or corporate environmental performance.

Vogel[389] examined the role of SRI in encouraging corporate sustainability performance from three perspectives: first, by enhancing their market

384 See e.g. OECD 2007; Steurer *et al.* 2008, p. 16.

385 According to the report of Eurosif (2014), the earliest origins of SRI can be traced back to the 17th century.

386 GSIA, '*Global Sustainable Investment Review*', 2014. Available at: http://www.gsi-alliance.org/wp-content/uploads/2015/02/GSIA_Review_download.pdf (Accessed on February 23, 2017).

387 US SIF, '*Report on US Sustainable, Responsible and Impact Investing Trends*', 2014. Available at: http://www.ussif.org/trends (Accessed on February 23, 2017).

388 *Id.*

389 Vogel pointed out that SRI can be an influential driver for CSR/CER in three ways: "first, if the demand of social investors for shares in responsible firms raised their share prices, thus lowering their costs of capital, those firms would have an advantage over their less

advantages over other less responsible competitors; second, by exerting a positive influence on corporate behaviour towards sustainability; third, by creating pressure for corporate governance reforms.

Richardson[390] pointed out that there were five ways in which SRI sought to exert influence: "a.) promoting SRI as a profitable alternative to conventional investment; b.) altering the cost of capital of targeted companies, such as by divestment, and thereby creating pressure for improved corporate behaviour. Positive investment, such as impact investing, can also reward and stimulate good behaviour; c.) advocating changes in companies as shareholders or lenders, such as by filing shareholder resolutions and informal engagement without corporate management; d.) designing codes of conduct for investors to engender more systemic changes across the market; e.) encouraging reforms to public policy and official regulations pertaining to the financial economy."[391]

Some empirical studies examined whether SRI funds outperformed the conventional funds or not. For example, Reeneboog *et al.*[392] conducted a relatively comprehensive research into the performance of socially responsible mutual funds. This research investigated the returns and risk of almost all SRI mutual funds around the world. The empirical evidence was mixed. In various cases, SRI funds underperformed compared to the traditional funds. Ronneboog *et al.* found out that "SRI funds in many European, North-American, and Asia-Pacific countries strongly underperform domestic benchmark portfolios. In particular, the average risk-adjusted returns of the SRI funds in Belgium, Canada, France, Ireland, Japan, Malaysia, the Netherlands, Singapore, Sweden, the UK and the US range from -2.2% to -6.5% per annum."[393]

Overall, the various findings above indicate several major trends of the SRI market. First, ethical investors do exert considerable influence on corporate social and environmental behaviour. Second, to what extent investors motivate companies to improve their social and environmental performance is still unclear. Third, the market for virtue for the SRI is still not strong enough, particularly since some of the SRI based funds do underperform the traditional investment funds.

---

responsible competitors. Second, the existence of a large pool of capital managed according to social criteria might encourage companies to change their policies in order to make their shares eligible for purchase by this pool of capital. Third, socially oriented investment funds can use informal mechanisms to press for changes in management policies, such as communicating with managers or submitting and supporting public interest proxy resolutions." (Vogel 2006, p. 61).

390 Richardson 2015, p. 236.

391 *Id.*

392 Renneboog *et al.* 2008, pp. 302–322.

393 *Id*, p. 321.

5.2 *The Role and Motivations of Consumers to Promote* CSR/CER

Another important force for CSR/CER comes from the consumer market. Over the past decades, consumers play an increasingly important role in society, as some scholars even claim that the current society in an era of globalization is a 'consumer society'.[394] Also, consumers are gradually aware of their powers to influence corporate behaviour by using their purchasing decisions. In this context, many new concepts have emerged, such as consumerism, 'consumer activism', 'consumer movement', 'conscience consumerism', 'ethical consumerism', and 'green consumer'. Smith[395] argued that the various terms shared the same idea that consumers cared about the issues of corporate responsibility and this would influence their purchase and consumption behavior. This provides incentives for companies to be more socially and environmentally responsible in order to satisfy consumers' preference for green products.

The term of ethical consumerism refers to "personal consumption where choice has been informed by some particular ethical issues—be it human rights, social justice, the environment or animal welfare."[396] In other words, it means that consumers' pro-social performance will have a potential influence on their purchasing decisions. A recent survey indicated that the market for green products or services is growing and about 90% of consumers show their concerns about the social and environmental attributes of products or service.[397] It reflects that a good social and environmental reputation of a company could become a factor which influences consumers' purchasing decisions. A crucial issue regarding consumers' role in the promotion of CSR/CER is whether or not consumers reward the companies for their environmental expenditure by paying a premium for environmentally friendly products. Consumers can be regarded as a key driver for CSR/CER by exercising their purchasing votes.[398] Consequently, an increasing number of companies start to use CSR/CER as a strategy to satisfy consumers' environmental preference.

The most prevailing strategy is known as the product differentiation or branding. In this case, to satisfy consumers' specific preference for green products, companies, particularly those who are closely related to end consumers, will use CSR/CER as a business strategy to differentiate their products from those of their competitors. In this case, consumers indeed play a role in influencing companies to improve their environmental performance.

---

394 Hilton 2009.
395 Smith 2008, p. 285.
396 *Id*, p. 287.
397 Smith 2008, p. 285.
398 Smith 1990, p. 7.

The substantial increase in the size of the green market over past years could also support this argument, as is substantiated by the survey data from the Co-operative's 'Ethical Consumer Markets Report 2015',[399] the total value of ethical market reached £ 80 billion GBP.

An increasing number of marketing surveys also show that CSR/CER has exerted influence on consumers' purchasing choice and thereby indicates that "consumers, on average, express an incremental willingness to pay for environmentally friendly and socially responsible products."[400] However, a significant gap has been observed between consumers' intentions and action in practice. It is argued that although many consumers claim to make their purchasing decisions based on the environmental performance of products, relatively fewer consumers indeed change their purchasing decisions primarily due to whether the products are produced in an environmentally friendly way.[401] A possible reason explaining the gap between consumers' intention and action was the lack of public awareness of CSR/CER.[402]

Another tactic of ethical consumerism is the use of consumer boycotts. The consumer boycott is considered as "the most manifest example of a broader phenomenon of consumer behaviour influenced by perceived CSR/CER lapses."[403] From a historical perspective, consumer boycotts achieved remarkable successes in influencing companies towards more socially and environmentally responsible way. A successful case in this respect is Greenpeace's boycott in response to Shell's disposal of the Brent Spar oil platform in the Atlantic Ocean. In 1995, when Greenpeace learned about Shell's plan to dump the Brent Spar in the North Sea, Greenpeace organized protest campaigns against Shell's dumping plan, given that "the ocean is not a dumping ground" and this dumping would potentially cause severe environmental pollution in the Atlantic Ocean. Shell was confronted with a consumer boycott in Germany and parts of the Northern Europe, which significantly damaged Shell's profitability and reputation. It was reported that this boycott led to a 50% decline in sales at some German Shell stations during the height of the protests.[404] Facing this tremendous public pressure, Shell finally decided to abandon the dumping plan due to falling sales and a drop in its stock price. The lessons from a large number of consumer studies prove that consumer boycotts do exert an

399 The Ethical Consumer Report 2015. Available at: http://www.ethicalconsumer.org/home/ethicalconsumer marketsreport2015downloadpage.aspx (Accessed on February 23, 2017).

400 Kitzmueller and Shimshack 2012, p. 73.

401 Vogel 2006, p. 48.

402 *Id*, p. 52.

403 Smith 2003.

404 Paine and Moldoveanu 1999.

effect on influencing corporate behaviour through the harm to the reputation of companies.

5.3 *The Role and Motivations of NGOs in Promoting CSR/CER*

Another important actor in driving CSR/CER is non-governmental organizations, NGOs (especially environmental NGOs). In an era of globalization, NGOs have gained considerable power on the international stage. Consequently, the relationship between the business world and NGOs has experienced remarkable changes. This changing relationship is evident in the field of environmental protection.

In the early times, the relationship between NGOs and the business community remained indifferent and they were even hostile to each other. This confrontational relationship could be partially explained by the divergence regarding their different goals, missions, and values. In this early period, many NGOs positioned themselves as spokesman and defender of public interests vis-à-vis corporate interests. The mission of NGO campaigns is to urge companies to adopt more socially and environmentally responsible policies. The popular strategy of NGOs is the so-called 'naming and shaming'. In practice, NGOs criticize and organize protest campaigns against irresponsible business behaviour and by doing so to impose public pressure on companies. As a result, the sales and prices of products from the target companies are usually affected. Today, more and more companies have changed their policies in response to the criticism and pressure from NGOs, given that the protest campaigns, even the threat of such campaigns, may cause significant damage to their reputation and profitability. There is a consensus about the powers of NGOs that although NGOs do not have 'hard powers' to change firms' behaviour, they do have considerable 'soft powers' by exerting pressures on them.

In practice, NGOs choose their targets based on the following considerations: first, they usually choose the well known and successful companies in order to attract more attention;[405] secondly, they chose "firms that are more likely to respond to their demands."[406] Facing the increasing magnitude of public campaigns, many companies started to respond to NGOs' criticism due to their concerns about the potential threat and risk of damaging their brand reputation and incurring substantial costs. In sum, the actual or potential threats from NGOs motivate firms to integrate CSR/CER as an important part of corporate strategy and even of profit maximization.

405 Porter and Kramer 2006, p. 79.

406 Kitzmueller and Shimshack 2012, p. 67.

However, NGO campaigns are not always credible and sensible as expected. In the Brent Spar case, for example, Greenpeace made a serious mistake in its estimation of the amount of oil left in the Brent Spar, and Greenpeace's campaign against Shell's dumping plan was criticized as 'completely misleading'. As a result, the reputation and the creditability of both Shell and Greenpeace were damaged. More and more companies and NGOs are recognizing the importance and necessity to develop more collaboration with each other to address a broad range of economic, social and environmental issues. In this context, the relationship between business and NGOs has experienced significant changes over time.

In recent years, it has been observed that many companies have integrated the partnerships with NGOs as a critical component of their CSR/CER strategies.[407] This so-called strategic corporate-NGO partnership has vast consequences for both companies and NGOs. On the corporate side, a good relationship could help companies to enhance their understanding of social and environment issues and hence to improve their reputation. On the NGO side, corporate support is also important to achieve their stated objectives (such as 'improving business practices for the better'[408]) in various ways, such as financial support, easier access to people and contacts, and innovation.[409]

Although many corporate managers, NGOs, and experts are quite optimistic about the future of the partnerships between companies and NGOs,[410] many disputes and challenges remain. According to the '*Corporate-NGO Partnerships Barometer 2013*',[411] there are three major challenges that limit the current and future development of the corporate-NGO partnership: first, a gap in terms of assessing the values of partnerships; second, a yawning gap between intention and performance; third, a wide gap between NGOs' and corporate perception of the value (or perceived value) of non-financial support. To be successful,

407 Rondinelli and London 2003, p. 61.

408 Guardian Sustainable Business blog, available at: http://www.theguardian.com/sustainable-business/future-bright-corporate-ngo-partnerships-challenges (Accessed on February 23, 2017).

409 C&E Corporate-NGO Partnership Barometer 2015. Available at: http://www.candeadvisory.com/sites/default/files/barometer_2015_final_3.pdf (Accessed on February 23, 2017).

410 According to the results of C&E Corporate-NGO Partnership Barometer 2015, sentiment about the mid-term prospects for corporate-NGO partnering remains very positive. 87% of respondents state that partnerships will become more or much more important over the next three years. (p. 6).

411 C&E Corporate-NGO Partnerships Barometer 2013. Available at: http://www.candeadvisory.com/sites/default/files/C%26E_Corporate_NGO_Partnerships_Barometer_2013_FINAL_0.pdf (Accessed on February 23, 2017).

"the future of this cross-sector collaboration will require businesses and NGOs to work harder."[412]

5.4 *The Role and Motivations of Employees in Promoting CSR/CER*

As an indispensable component of the company, the rights of the employee have been a priority on the CSR agenda.[413] Heald prioritized employee's issues over other topics by stating that "the first duty of an employer is to its employee by paying them a reasonable wage, providing decent and healthy working conditions, and treating them with utmost consideration".[414] In the current CSR framework, the issues of employee rights usually encompass fair wages, working time and conditions, health care, redundancy, and protection against unfair dismissal.[415] In this sense, employees seemingly show little interest as to whether a company has a good environmental reputation or not when choosing where to work. However, some scholars[416] worked on the link between employees and the promotion of CSR/CER. Their study results imply that employees could influence corporate environmental behaviour in various ways. For example, a good corporate sustainability performance can help companies attract and retain high quality employees. This can become a source of their competitive advantages.[417] Employees can also play a crucial role in encouraging companies towards sustainability by utilizing their choice about where to work. Some recent surveys show that a large portion of potential employees expressed their willingness to choose "an organization with a good reputation for corporate social responsibility and ethics."[418]

As a response to employees' increasing demand for sustainable development and CSR/CER, many companies start to take action by reforming corporate policies and by making commitments to promoting CSR/CER. For example, Shell sets a good example in this respect by voluntarily publishing sustainability reports since 1997. As mentioned in its reports, Shell made its commitments to sustainable development, particularly by enhancing its ability to attract and to retain the high-quality workforce. However, Vogel remained sceptical of the actual influence of the labour market on changing corporate sustainability performance for several reasons. First, there are no unified benchmarks for employees to measure what is a socially responsible or ethical

412 *Id.*
413 Matten and Moon 2008, pp. 404–424.
414 Heald 1970, p. 36.
415 Matten and Moon 2008, p. 412.
416 See e.g. Turban and Greening 1997, pp. 658–672; Albinger and Freeman2000, pp. 243–253.
417 See e.g. Turban and Greening 1997, pp. 658–672; Vogel 2006, p. 56.
418 Kitzmueller and Shimshack 2012, p. 73.

employer. Second, there does exist a gap between what employees thought to do and their actual action, because the financial rewards are still the most important factor when choosing jobs.[419]

6 Summary and Some Concluding Remarks

The traditional paradigm, primarily represented by Milton Friedman, insists that the only interest of business is to increase its profits, so CSR/CER is not appreciated by classical economics and the law and economic literature. Particularly during the past decades, the domain of company law and corporate governance was dominated by law and economic scholars who passionately embraced the maximization of shareholder value as the purpose of the company. The increasing popularity of CSR/CER in recent years challenges this conventional wisdom by arguing that CSR/CER does not necessarily go against the maximization of shareholder value and on the contrary, it can even create add-on value for the long term prospect of shareholder value. Important questions arise here as to why would be this case and which driving forces or market demands could be identified. This chapter contributes to a better understanding of CSR/CER by exploring the roles and motivations of various actors for engaging in CSR/CER, including the company (as a whole entity), shareholders, managers, investors, consumers, NGOs, and employees.

In Section 2, we went into various relevant dimensions of the business case for CSR/CER. First, the purpose of the company has been discussed. We argued that the conventional wisdom of 'shareholder value primacy' has been more or less routinely accepted as the leading doctrine of corporate purpose in economics, corporate law, law and economics and in the business community. We also found that the 'shareholder value primacy' has been embraced uncritically by academic scholars, business practitioners, and policymakers. Various corporate scandals (from ENRON-scandal in 2002 up to Volkswagen-scandal in 2015/2016) over the last two decades—which had vast negative economic, social and environmental consequences—did bring the narrow 'shareholder primacy' purpose of the company back to the 'corporate design table'. The 'shareholder primacy' seems to be replaced by a much broader corporate purpose, such as the stakeholder theory and the theory of CSR. Second, the rise of a strategic approach to CSR/CER has been discussed and substantiated. This approach holds that under various circumstances a better CSR/CER performance does help companies to perform better financially and therefore

419 Vogel 2006, pp. 56–60.

enhance shareholder value. One of the most prominent scholars and proponents of this approach is Michael Porter, who claims that strategic use of CSR/CER provokes substantial innovation, provides competitive advantages and creates better financial results. Some rationales for this approach are: improving relations with local communities/workforce; ensuring brand loyalty; improving the production process and product qualities; retaining the social licence to operate; better anticipating and reducing risks of future regulation and legislation. Third, the question is asked: are companies doing well by doing good? This concerns the relation between corporate financial performance or CFP (doing well) and corporate social performance or CSP (doing good). This relation can be non-significant, positive or negative and studies up to 2010 show a small positive effect and no evidence is found that companies suffer financially from investments in CSR/CER.

In Section 3, we provided some insights into the roles and motivations of shareholders to take CSR/CER on board. Often shareholders are presented as a single-minded group, all going after profit maximization; however, it appears to be a heterogeneous group with diversified preferences. Many of them accept strategic CSR/CER and some even go for the 'feel good experience' or the 'warm glow' and even accept lower financial returns for higher corporate social performance.

In Section 4, we focused on corporate managers as potential drivers of CSR/CER and analysed their duties and motivations to promote CSR/CER in their companies. First, we focused on managers' duties. It is not surprising that we find a strong link between their duties and our earlier remarks about the purpose of the company in economic theory as well as in law and economics. With the changes over the last years, the outcomes of studies prove that CSR/CER could provide a more positive influence on corporate financial performance. Consequently, more and more managers and business leaders did start to promote CSR/CER activities in and outside their companies in order to increase their corporate social performance. We also saw that this view is supported by new legislation where the duties of directors of a company are prescribed in more detail. This provides space for managers to fulfil their duties and while doing so strongly support better CSR/CER performance. Second, we focused on managers' motivation towards CSR/CER. We did find positive and negative types of motivation in the literature and in practice. The positive motivations for managers to engage CSR/CER appear to be strongly related to its contribution to corporate financial performance. The negative motives also became apparent and these mostly relate to the use of CSR/CER for personal benefits, such as: reduce CEO turnover; increase job security and enhance personal reputation.

In Section 5, we did focus on the roles and motivations in improving CSR/CER performance by key corporate stakeholders, such as: investors, consumers, NGOs, and employees. First, we did focus on the roles and motivations of individual and institutional investors to support CSR/CER. Also in this field of research, we have seen a moving away from the shareholder primacy doctrine. The spectacular rise in the last decade of Socially Responsible Investment (SRI) Funds is an example of this trend towards a balanced view on environmental, social and governance (ESG) dimensions of corporate social performance. However, in this relatively young investment discipline research is still not clear about the out-performance or under-performance of funds. Current literature still points to the under-performance of SRI versus conventional investment funds. Second, we did focus on the roles and motivations of consumers in CSR/CER. We saw that consumers care about CSR/CER levels in corporate performance and have the power to influence corporate decision making by their purchasing powers and behaviour. But also, consumers show a discrepancy between their positive CSR/CER attitude and their actual purchasing behaviour. Another important power of consumers (and as we will see later of NGOs in general) is to organize a consumer boycott to exert influence on the sales, brand, and reputation of the targeted companies. Depending on the organizational qualities of these consumer boycotts these can be very effective and also can have a deterrent effect on any rise of problematic corporate social performance. Third, we did look at the roles and motivations of non-governmental organizations (NGOs) in CSR/CER. With respect to the "NGO-business relationship", we encountered substantial changes from a mainly confrontational approach in the 1970th towards a partnership between business and NGOs in the late 1990s and beyond. Both types of relations have been substantiated by cases in which the goal "improving business practices for the better" has been reached. Fourth, we did look at the roles and motivations of employees in CSR/CER. As important stakeholders in the company, employees can also influence corporate CSR/CER behaviour in various ways, like their increased willingness to work for a high CSR/CER performing company; the use of their influence to guide corporate decisions in the direction of CSR/CER; etc. There are many examples of companies that explicitly state that their efforts in CSR/CER are partly taken with the preferences of their employees in mind. A good ranking in CSR/CER performance is frequently used by companies' human resources management to support the corporate brand and to help attract the best (high potential) employees.

The primary results of this chapter indicate that a variety of stakeholders has shown the increasing willingness as well as keen interest in promoting CSR/CER, while each actor may have specific motivations based on his own position and interest. The majority of stakeholders, however, perceive the most important reason for their involvement in CSR/CER as the business case of CSR/CER, also known as the strategic CSR/CER, which means that in certain circumstances, good social or environmental performance could to some extent improve corporate financial performance. Many empirical studies also indicate that the positive relationship between CSP and CFP does exist in business, although the mixed empirical evidence has been frequently questioned for the lack of solid groundings.

A substantial part of our analysis is based on the assumption that the interests of various stakeholders are aligned concerning whether companies should engage in CSR/CER or not. However, the situation could be much more complicated where a conflict of interest between different stakeholders may occur, such as the 'principal-agent problem'. Also, it is observed that the current CSR/CER world is facing a variety of challenges, which are the outcomes of its several characteristics, such as its voluntary nature. Therefore, these potential risks, as well as possible solutions, will be discussed in Chapter 5. Moreover, as mentioned at the beginning, this chapter primarily focuses on the motivations of various market players towards CSR/CER. Another important participant in CSR/CER, the government, is not yet included in our analysis. The interest and roles of government will be further discussed in Chapter 5 and Chapter 6. Before we enter into those Chapters, the following Chapter 4 will focus on the question: how to measure CSR/CER performance?

CHAPTER 4

Measuring Corporate Sustainability Performance

1 Introduction

Since its first emergence, the concept of CSR/CER has evolved significantly over time. As we have seen in the earlier chapters,[420] the contested nature of CSR/CER remains an unsolved obstacle for its further development. In academic circles, many efforts have been made to overcome these challenges. One of these efforts is the proliferation of alternative concepts of CSR/CER, such as corporate social performance, corporate social responsiveness, corporate citizenship, and corporate sustainability.[421] Among these alternative concepts, corporate social/sustainability performance (CSP) has gained considerable importance in this domain. In contrast to the ambiguous definition of CSR/CER, the notion of CSP focuses on the process and the outcomes of corporate actions for addressing social and environmental issues rather than on whether corporations should be accountable for the external effects of their behaviour. In recent years, the theory and practice of CSP measurement have become increasingly popular in both academic circles and the business world. We have witnessed an accumulating number of CSP studies as well as a rapid growth of the sustainability rating industry.

The main goal of this chapter is to better understand CSP measurement from both a theoretical and a practical perspective. This chapter begins with a brief introduction of the conceptual history of CSP and measurement (Section 2). By reviewing an extensive body of literature, three questions will be answered in this section: (1) what is CSP measurement? (2)what factors should be included in CSP? (3) why CSP should be measured?

On the basis of a brief overview of the theory of CSP, Section 3 turns to explore the practice of CSP measurement by having a look at a newly emerging market—the sustainability rating industry. Today a wide range of instruments has been designed to meet the increasing demand for CSP measurement, such as sustainability ratings, indices, rankings, and awards. Several well-established examples in this industry will be presented in this section to provide a brief description of how these instruments work in practice. The young and dynamic market of sustainability ratings gains increasing popularity but still has several

420 See Chapter 2, Section 3 and Section 4.

421 See Chapter 2, Section 5.

 | DOI:10.1163/9789004368132_005

notable challenges, such as the significant diversity of the rating systems, the lack of transparency, and the lack of accessibility. Therefore, Section 4 examines how these challenges affect the quality of a sustainability rating or ranking in terms of credibility, accessibility, and effectiveness, and what reasons cause these challenges. Finally, Section 5 provides some conclusive remarks.

2 The Theory of CSP and Its Measurement

2.1 *The Conceptual History of the CSP Model*

The theory of CSP has been a popular topic in exploring the interaction between business and society for a long time. Starting from the 1970s, a group of scholars has played an important role in constructing the theory of CSP. In this field, Carroll (1979), Wartick and Cochran (1985), and Wood (1991) have made considerable efforts to establish a comprehensive conceptual model of CSP. The concept of CSP was introduced for three reasons. First, it could describe what social expectations companies are expected to meet. Second, it could identify the social and environmental issues that are financially material to the long-term value of companies. Third, it could assist companies and their managers to recognize and manage the effects of their behaviour. Consequently, the concept of CSP differentiates itself from CSR/CER by integrating three factors, that is, social responsibilities, social issues, and social responsiveness, into one comprehensive model.

The conceptual model of CSP was first introduced by Carroll in 1979, who built a three-dimensional conceptual model of corporate performance by summarizing the various views on the meaning of social responsibility. In general, Carroll's CSP model consists of three dimensions: the definition of social responsibility, the social issues involved and the philosophy of responsiveness (See Figure 6). In the first dimension, Carroll categorized the entire range of responsibilities that a company is expected to assume into four basic groups: economic responsibilities, legal responsibilities, ethical responsibilities and discretionary responsibilities. Each group is given a different weight that reflects its relative magnitudes in the total responsibilities.[422] As shown in the figure below (See Figure 1), the economic responsibilities, as the principal responsibility of business, are given the largest weight. The second dimension of Carroll's CSP model (the social issues involved) identifies what type of social issues companies must address. However, Carroll also argued that the evolving social context posed considerable challenges for companies to fulfil this task.

422 Carroll 1979, pp. 499–501.

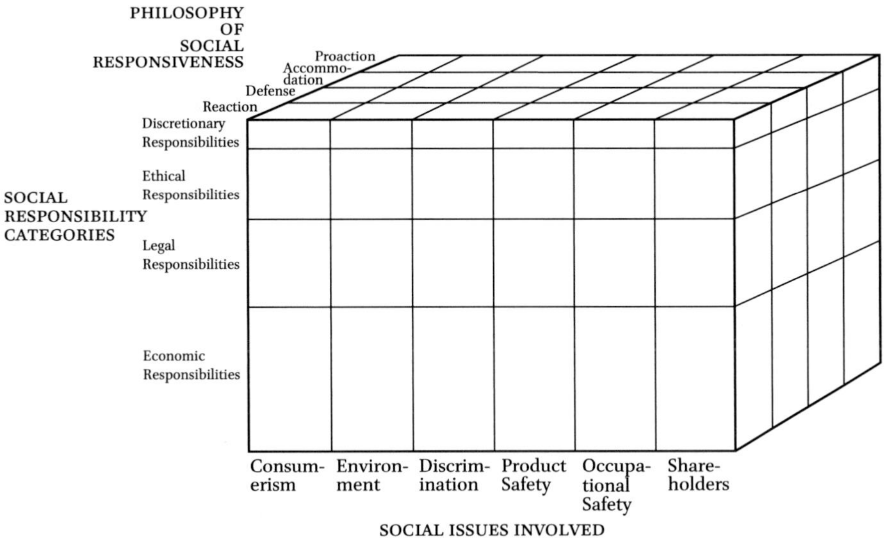

FIGURE 6 Carroll's CSP model
SOURCE: CARROLL 1979, P. 503

On the one hand, companies' focus on social issues could change over time, and on the other hand, companies' interest in specific social issues also could vary widely depending on different industries. The third important dimension of Carroll's CSP model is social responsiveness, which refers to how companies respond to the social responsibilities and the social issues.[423]

Carroll's CSP model was extended by Wartick and Cochran in 1985,[424] who further developed their three-dimensional CSP model (see Figure 7). The three dimensions are social responsibility, social responsiveness, and social issues management. Each dimension has its distinctive directions and orientations.[425] In the first dimension of their CSP model, Wartick and Cochran basically followed Carroll's hierarchical taxonomy of corporate social responsibility category as the principles of social responsibility.[426] But they further explored two fundamental premises on which the concept of CSR was constructed: the

423 Carroll pointed out that the social responsiveness "addresses the philosophy, mode, or strategy behind business (managerial) response to social responsibility and social issues."(Carroll 1979, p. 501)

424 Wartick and Cochran 1985, pp. 758–769.

425 *Id.*

426 The total social responsibilities of the company consist of economic responsibility, legal responsibility, ethical responsibility and discretionary responsibility.

social contract theory and moral agency theory.[427] In terms of social responsiveness, although Carroll pointed out that the corporate responsiveness could range from 'no response' to 'a pro-active response',[428] Wartick and Cochran further summarized four types of corporate social responsiveness as 'reactive', 'defensive', 'accommodative', and 'pro-active'. In the last dimension, Wartick and Cochran outlined three steps for companies to manage social issues through issues identification, issues analysis, and response management.

As mentioned above, the CSP model has been thoroughly studied by a large number of scholars and practitioners during the past decades, but none of these studies systematized the previous achievements in this field.[429] In this context, Wood recognized the necessity to fill this gap by contributing a comprehensive and coherent conceptual framework of CSP. Based on the academic achievements of the previous studies, Wood reformulated the CSP model into three new dimensions, that is, 'the principles of corporate social responsibility', 'the processes of corporate social responsiveness', and 'the outcomes of corporate behaviour' (See Figure 8). Compared to the previous studies in this field, Wood's CSP model provided an innovative understanding of the business-society relationship from the following aspects.

First, Wood clearly defined the concept of CSP as "a business organization's configuration of principles of social responsibility, processes of social

Principles	**Processes**	**Policies**
Corporate Social Responsibilities	Corporate Social Responsiveness	Social Issues Management
(1) Economic (2) Legal (3) Ethical (4) Discretionary	(1) Reactive (2) Defensive (3) Accommodative (4) Proactive	(1) Issues Identification (2) Issues Analysis (3) Response Development
Directed at:	Directed at:	Directed at:
(1) The Social Contract of Business (2) Business as a Moral Agent	(1) The Capacity of Respond to Changing Societal Conditions (2) Managerial Approaches to Developing Responses	(1) Minimizing "Surprises" (2) Determining Effective Corporate Social Policies
Philosophical Orientation	Institutional Orientation	Organizational Orientation

FIGURE 7 Wartick and Cochran's CSP model
SOURCE: WARTICK AND COCHRAN 1985, P. 767

427 Wartick and Cochran 1985, pp. 758–769.
428 Carroll 1979, pp. 501–502.
429 Wood 1991, pp. 691–718.

responsiveness, and policies, programs, and observable outcomes as they relate to the firm's societal relationships."[430]

Second, Wood distinguished between categories and principles.[431] Wood hence articulated the CSR principles at three levels of application: the principle of legitimacy at the institutional level,[432] the principle of public responsibility at the organizational level,[433] and the principle of managerial discretion at the individual level.[434]

The Corporate Social Performance Model
Principles of corporate social responsibility
Institutional principle: legitimacy Organizational principle: public responsibility Individual principle: managerial discretion
Processes of corporate social responsiveness Environmental assessment Stakeholder management Issues management
Outcomes of corporate behavior Social impacts Social programs Social policies

FIGURE 8 Wood's CSP model
SOURCE: WOOD 1991, P. 694

430 *Id*, p.693.

431 According to Wartick and Cochran, Carroll's four-category model of social responsibility can represent the principles of social responsibility as the first dimension of their CSP model. But Wood argued that the categories of social responsibilities were not the same as the principles, because "a principle expresses something fundamental that people believe is true, or it is a basic value that motivates people to act; categories, in contrast, show how to distinguish among different types of phenomena, but they do not represent motivation or fundamental truths". (Wood 1991, p.695).

432 The principle of legitimacy originates from Davis's *'Iron Law of Responsibility'* (1973)—"society grants legitimacy and power to business. In the long run, those who do not use power in a manner which society considers responsible will tend to lose it."

433 The principle of public responsibility at institutional level is based on Preston and Post's view (1975) that "business is responsible for outcomes related to their primary and secondary areas of involvement with society."

434 The principle of managerial discretion at individual level derives from Carroll (1979) and Wood's (1991) views that "managers are moral actors. Within every domain of corporate social responsibility, they are obliged to exercise such discretion as it is available to them, toward socially responsible outcomes".

Third, Wood also empirically tested several specific examples about how companies responded to social and environmental issues in terms of environmental management, stakeholder management, and issue management.[435]

Fourth, Wood further divided the collective outcomes of corporate behaviour into three basic types: the social impacts of corporate behaviour, the programs to implement social responsibility, and the policies to manage social issues.[436]

The three conceptual models of CSP elaborated above only constitute a small part of the long-lasting efforts made by many scholars to further develop and extend the solid and comprehensive theoretical foundations of the CSP model. However, Wood still perceived this domain as "controversial, fluid, ambiguous and difficult to research."[437]

2.2 *The Literature Review of CSP Measurement*

In addition to the construction of a conceptual model of CSP, CSP measurement also attracts considerable interest from academic circles. The extensive literature about CSP measurement shows the development of a wide range of assessment approaches. These approaches vary widely in terms of measuring scales, variables, and methodologies. In a literature review of CSP measurement, Wood categorized the current CSP measurement studies into four types.[438]

- The first type of CSP measurement literature describes the 'multi-category CSP measures', where CSP is measured in a broader sense and does not fit into one specific CSP category.[439] Examples are the company social or environmental reporting or the multi-faceted measures developed by the rating institutions.[440]
- The second type of CSP measurement literature refers to the measurement of Wood's structural (macro) principles of CSR:[441] the principle of legitimacy, the principle of public responsibility, and the principle of managerial discretion.[442]

---

435 Wood 1991, pp. 703–708.
436 *Id*, p.708.
437 Wood 2010, p.50.
438 Wood 2010, pp. 50–84.
439 Here one specific CSP category mainly refers to the principles of CSR, the processes of corporate social responsiveness, or the outcomes of corporate behavior, which is derived from Wood's CSP model. See *supra* Section 2.1.
440 Wood 2010, pp. 64–65.
441 *Id*, pp. 65–67.
442 See *supra* footnotes 435, 436 and 437.

- The third type of CSP measurement literature focuses on the measurement of the quality of the responsible process: how do companies address social and environmental issues, for example, the mode of corporate responsiveness, environmental scanning, stakeholder management practices, public affairs and issues management, and company practices?[443]
- The fourth type of CSP measurement literature relates to the outcomes and impacts of CSP measurement, such as information disclosure, environmental impacts, stakeholder-specific measures, consumer impacts, employee impacts, supplier impacts, and criminal conduct.[444]

Dommerholt also made a contribution to CSP measurement by categorizing the various approaches into two basic groups: the uni-dimensional measures and the multi-dimensional measures, based on the number of measuring criteria.[445] The uni-dimensional measures basically indicate that the corporate sustainability performance can be evaluated by only one specific issue or standard, such as pollution control, hazardous waste disposal, and greenhouse gas emission.[446] On the contrary, the multi-dimensional measures encompass the multiple indicators for measuring and assessing corporate sustainability performance. To date, the multi-dimensional measures are often used, because they could better present the multi-dimensional and complicated nature of the CSP model as presented above.[447] Dommerholt further illustrated several specific examples of multi-dimensional CSP measures, such as the construction of scales (like reputational scales) or content analysis. More particularly, the content analysis has become a widely acknowledged methodology in the practice of CSP measurement.

2.3 *Why Should CSP be Measured?*

Academic researchers and business practitioners have shown increasing interest in the conceptualization and practice of CSP measurement. Two important questions arise here: first, why CSP should be measured; second, what are the impacts of CSP measurement on corporate behaviour? More particularly, does CSP measurement truly change corporate behaviour and to what extent could the results of CSP measurement incentivise companies to improve their sustainability performance?

---

443 Wood 2010, pp. 67–69.
444 *Id*, pp. 69–75.
445 Dommerholt 2012, pp. 45–59.
446 *Id*, p.47.
447 *Id*, pp. 47–48.

The answer to the first question is related to the need to measure CSP in order to better manage it. The slogan often used in this context is "what is not measured is not managed."[448] At the same time, we can see that the specific motivations of CSP measurement vary widely depending on the values and positions of different stakeholders. To better understand the impacts of CSP measurement on business and society, this section will explore the motivations of various stakeholders, such as academic scholars, companies, investors, and consumers.

CSP measurement has been widely desired by academic scholars. This can be clearly proved by the accumulating number of studies in this respect. From an academic perspective, it is widely acknowledged that the CSP literature provides supportive evidence for the strategic CSR/CER hypothesis. As noted in the previous chapters,[449] a fundamental argument for the strategic CSR/CER is that companies can do well by doing good. In other words, it presumes that a good sustainable performance will enhance companies' financial performance. In this context, an increasing number of studies concerning the positive relationship between corporate social performance (CSP) and corporate financial performance (CFP) have been conducted. These studies try to find persuasive grounds underpinning this argument.[450] The CSP literature composes an important part of these efforts, because the empirical evidence of corporate performance and its effects is more convincing than pure theoretical analysis.

On the corporate side, companies play a key role in the development of CSP measurement. On the one hand, the operation of a CSP measurement system primarily relies on the extent of company responsiveness. The primary source of CSP information is company self-reporting, surveys or interviews with relevant corporate managers. Consequently, whether or not companies do proactively participate in the assessment process is an important determinant of a successful rating or ranking. On the other hand, nearly all CSP measurement systems set up a mission of improving corporate governance and sustainability performance. In this context, the impacts of CSP measurement on corporate behaviour are clear and substantial.

First, it helps companies and their managers to identify the key issues that are financially material for their long-term shareholder value as well as the impacts of their business activities on those variables.

448 Dillenburg, Greene and Erekson 2003, pp. 167–177.

449 See *supra* Chapter 3, Section 2.

450 *Id.*

Second, an in-depth and scientific analysis of CSP measurement is beneficial for companies, because it provides a possibility to monitor and manage their performance in addressing sustainability issues.

Third, it also creates a healthy and competitive environment in which companies rank against their competitors through improving their CSR/CER performance. More particularly, as a large number of investors and consumers tend to make their investment and purchasing decisions based on the environmental reputation or records of companies or products, a top ranking can be a potential source of competitive advantages in the market.

Finally, CSP measurement also constructs a platform to communicate best CSR/CER practices and to foster relevant debates among business practitioners and other stakeholders. In sum, CSP measurement indeed creates added values for business in various ways.

Therefore, it is clear that the participation in CSP measurement does create added value for business in various ways and it does exert a considerable influence on the quality of their corporate governance and performance.

Moreover, a wide range of stakeholders also shows growing interest in the field of CSP measurement. The burgeoning market for socially responsible investment (SRI) is a good example. As an increasing number of investors are aware of the potential risks and the opportunities associated with corporate sustainability management and performance, the information of CSP measurement has become an integral component of their investment decision making. According to a recent survey[451] conducted among 1000 investment professionals at both the international and the national levels, there was a clear upward trend among investors to take environmental, social and governance (ESG) issues into consideration. The interviewees pointed out that a CSP ranking or rating could help investors better acquire the relevant information of a company's strategy and performance on sustainability and thus could help them make more informed investment decisions.[452] Similar to the financial market, this story also happens in the consumer market, where an increasing number of environmentally conscious consumers may base their purchasing decision on the information they acquire from a well-established provider of sustainability rankings.

Based on the analysis above, an increasing demand for CSP measurement is observed from both academic circles and the business community. Although the motivations behind this demand vary significantly among scholars, companies, investors, and consumers, there is a growing consensus among the

451 Sadowski *et al.* November 2012.

452 *Id.*

various stakeholders that CSP should be measured. As a result, a new market has emerged in recent years.

3 Rating CSP: an Emerging Market

A growing number of players participate in measuring, comparing and analyzing corporate sustainability performance, such as rating organizations, companies, sustainability professionals, financial institutions, NGOs, and mass media. Consequently, a wide range of instruments has been developed, including sustainability ratings, indices, ranking, awards, and polls. According to a recent research program '*Rate the Rates*' launched by SustainAbility,[453] the most widely employed instruments in the current CSP domain are ratings, indices, and rankings.[454] Given the incredibly large number of measuring instruments available today, this section could not provide a complete inventory of the vast universe of CSP measurement. For the purpose of this book, this section selects three prominent instruments to provide some basic insights of this new market: sustainability rating, indices, and awards.

3.1 *A Newly Emerging Market*

Today people are overwhelmed by enormous ranking information from newspapers, magazines or mass media. In the modern business world, rating has been widely used as a tool for measuring and communicating a company's financial and non-financial performance.[455] The proliferation of sustainability ratings has exerted a significant influence given the wide use of these data. The rated companies and rating users like consumers, investors, and employees, are inclined to take rating information into account when making decisions. In this context, a new market has emerged, as a large number of actors have stepped into this fast-growing market by establishing their own measurement systems. These institutions are well known as the sustainability rating agencies, which refer to "the organizations that rate or assess corporations according to a

453 SustainAbility, founded in 1987 by John Elkington and Julia Hailes, is a think tank and strategy consultancy. It is working to inspire transformative business leadership on the sustainability agenda. From 2010 to 2012, SustainAbility launched a five-phrase research program '*Rate the Raters*' which provides a comprehensive understanding of the key trends of the current development of sustainability rating market as well as the shortcomings they are facing.

454 Sadowski *et al.* October 2010, p.8.

455 Sadowski *et al.* May 2010.

standard of social and environmental performance that is at least in part based on non-financial data."[456]

Several remarkable trends have been observed in this dynamic market. First, although the CSP measurement is not a new topic,[457] it is the last decade[458] that has witnessed the surge of the rating market. According to a recent survey of the '*Rate the Raters*', there are more than 100 rating agencies.[459] An increasing number of new players continually appear in this market every day.

Secondly, in addition to the expanding number of rating agencies, the significant diversity between rating agencies is obvious in terms of target audiences, rating methodologies, key issues, and geographic scales. In practice, some rating agencies target specific groups as their audiences, such as consumer-orientated or investor-orientated rating agencies, while others cover the multiple stakeholders. Some rating agencies focus on specific issues, sectors or geographic regions, while others attempt to establish a set of comprehensive rating standards across sectors and regions. Consequently, the current state of the rating industry presents a remarkable diversity. This phenomenon can be explained by several reasons, like the lack of a widely accepted definition of CSR/CER, the multi-dimensional nature of sustainability issues and the fierce competition between rating agencies in this new market.

Thirdly, to follow the changing societal and environmental context, many rating agencies keep updating their data and methodologies on a regular basis.[460] The dynamic nature of the sustainability rating industry, on the one hand, allows it to catch up with the latest trends in sustainability agenda. On the other hand, it also poses significant challenges to people to have a comprehensive and consistent understanding of this industry. As a result, this young, diverse and dynamic market has attracted considerable attention from academic scholars, business practitioners and policy makers.

The fierce competition in the sustainability rating market forces many rating agencies make great efforts to differentiate from their competitors, by creating their own unique screening instruments and measuring methodologies.[461] Sustainability rating agencies usually measure, analyse, and compare corporate sustainability performance based on a set of pre-determined benchmarks.

456 Scalet and Kelly 2010, p.70.

457 The conceptual debate on CSP measurement can be traced back to the 1970s. See *supra* Section 2.1.

458 A recent survey shows that more than a third of rating institutions have been established since 2005.

459 Sadowski *et al.* May and October 2010.

460 Sadowski *et al.* May and October 2010.

461 Dommerholt 2012, p.49.

This, so called, sustainability assessment methodology consists of a screening instrument and an assessment procedure. Specifically, the screening instrument does measure or evaluate corporate sustainability performance, which can be divided into two types. A negative screening instrument works with the exclusion of specific issues or industry sectors, like tobacco and alcohol companies. A positive screening instrument does rank the actual corporate sustainability performance, such as a sustainability ranking. The assessment procedure describes how the outcomes are processed through the screening instrument.[462] A complete rating procedure is conducted through three phases: information collection, data analysis, and outcomes.[463]

3.2 *Sustainability Ratings and Indices*

Today a variety of sustainability ratings and indices are provided by different organizations, like rating agencies, asset management companies, financial institutions, academic institutions, NGOs and mass media. Given the formidable challenges to fully cover the vast universe of sustainability ratings and indices, four examples are selected: the Dow Jones Sustainability Index (DJSI), RobecoSAM, FTSE, and MSCI. They are chosen based on several standards. First, they are all well-established and influential organizations with a rich sustainability rating expertise and experience. Second, the rating products provided by these agencies are frequently mentioned as one of the largest, most trusted or most comprehensive sustainability ratings and indices. Third, these indices and rating agencies provide sufficient information to the public. By exploring these four examples, this section aims to gain more insights into this dynamic and complicated market. Three questions will be answered in this section:

- How these rating agencies measure and evaluate corporate sustainability performance in practice?
- How do they make their rating products different from their peers?
- What are the effects of their rating results on the rated companies and other relevant stakeholders, like the rating users?

3.2.1 Dow Jones Sustainability Index (DJSI)

As the first global sustainability index, the Dow Jones Sustainability Index (DJSI) was launched in 1999. The DJSI is based on the cooperation of two distinguished organizations in the rating industry: the Standard & Poor Dow Jones Indices and Sustainable Asset Management (SAM) Research, later

462 *Id*, p.45.
463 *Id*, p.49.

RobecoSAM.[464] Since its establishment, a wide range of sustainability indices has been integrated into the DJSI index family. Today the DJSI has become one of the most prominent providers of the integrated assessment of corporate economic, environmental and social performance.[465] The DJSI index family consists of the DJSI family and the DJSI Diversified family. In order to meet the specific requirements of different stakeholders, these two families differ in terms of rating approaches and scopes.

The DJSI family encompasses a series of global, regional and national indices.[466] Within the DJSI family, rated companies are selected in accordance with a set of pre-designed economic, social and environmental criteria. But the percentages of selected companies vary depending on different types of sustainability indices. For example, the top 10% sustainable companies from each industry can be included in the DJSI World index. The top 20% companies can be included in the World enlarged index and regional indices (such as the DJSI Asia Pacific, the DJSI Europe, and the DJSI North America). The top 30% companies can be included in the country indices (such as the DJSI Australia and the DJSI Korea).[467] The exclusive trademark of the DJSI family is well-known as the 'best-in-class' rating approach, which means that only the sustainability leaders of each industry group can be included in this index family. This unique approach is adopted due to the significant diversity of sustainability issues across sectors. Therefore, the DJSI believes that the industry-specific indices play an important role in helping companies from different industries to identify the material sustainability challenges and opportunities for their long-term shareholder value. Moreover, this approach can motivate companies to compete with their peers to achieve a better ranking within the same industry. The DJSI family also keeps monitoring rated companies by conducting the annual assessment. Based on the results of the annual assessment, all companies face the potential risks of downgrading or even being excluded from the ranking lists. This mechanism also provides an important driver for companies to continuingly improve their sustainability performance.

The DJSI Diversified family, as a new member of the DJSI index family, was first launched in 2013. It also consists of various global and regional rating

464 For more information about the DJSI Family, available at: http://www.sustainability-indices.com/index-family-overview/djsi-family-overview/index.jsp (Accessed on February 23, 2017).

465 *Id.*

466 The DJSI family consists of the DJSI World, DJSI Asia Pacific, DJSI Europe, DJSI North America, DJSI Australia, DJSI Korea, DJSI World Enlarged and DJSI Emerging Market.

467 The data is based on the DJSI Annual Review 2015. Available at: http://www.sustainability-indices.com/review/annual-review-2015.jsp (Accessed on February 23, 2017).

indices.[468] In contrast with the DJSI family as mentioned above, the DJSI Diversified family is customized for a specific group of investors, who are interested in SRI. These investors traditionally evaluate companies through a set of standard market benchmarks (like the stock price), but they also show keen interest in integrating sustainability standards.[469] However, they are facing obstacles to integrating sustainability benchmarks into their investment portfolios without making any substantial change regarding the asset allocation. To meet their special requirements, the DJSI Diversified indices, on the one hand, track the financial performance of the rated companies in terms of the risk-return profile, and on the other hand, they also reflect the sustainability performance of the rated companies.

Today, the DJSI has been widely recognized as one of the most prominent ratings. According to a survey among 1000 sustainability experts and professionals, the DJSI stands out from the 16 well-established ratings for its highest credibility.[470] As a result, an increasing number of companies lists a high ranking on the DJSI as an important achievement in the field of sustainability.

3.2.2 RobecoSAM

Among the various rating agencies, one of the most influential rating agencies is SAM Research founded in 1995, and later it has been acquired by Robeco in 2007.[471] As a specialist in sustainability investing, RobecoSAM provides a wide range of products and services for asset owners and managers, such as asset management, indices, engagement, voting, impact analysis, sustainability assessment and benchmarking. Today, RobecoSAM has gained a global reputation in the field of sustainability rating. Every year more than 3000 publicly traded companies around the world are invited to participate in its annual assessment,[472] which makes it one of the most comprehensive databases on corporate sustainability performance. In the domain of CSP measurement, RobecoSAM differentiates itself from other competitors by developing its unique

468 The DJSI Diversified family consists of the DJSI Diversified World, the DJSI Diversified Select, the DJSI Diversified World Developed, the DJSI Diversified North America, the DJSI Diversified Europe, the DJSJ Diversified Asia and the DJSI Diversified Emerging.

469 For more information about the DJSI Diversified family, available at http://www.sustainability-indices.com/index-family-overview/djsi-diversified-family-overview/index.jsp (Accessed on February 23, 2017).

470 Sadowski *et al.* October 2010, p.15.

471 For more information about RobecoSAM, available at: http://www.robecosam.com/en/about-us/about-robecosam.jsp (Accessed on February 23, 2017).

472 The total number of invited companies is 3,470, among which 2500 companies are invited for the DJSI World Universe and the rest companies are invited for the regional DJSI indices.

measuring system—the RobecoSAM's Corporate Assessment Methodology (CSA) in 1999. Since then, the CSA has been regularly updated to catch up with the latest developments on sustainability agenda.

Generally speaking, the CSA aims to provide a comprehensive analysis of the progress and performance of companies in addressing sustainability issues, and of the quality of the related information disclosure by those companies.[473] Compared to other rating schemes, the rating results of the CSA are derived from the information directly provided by the rated companies through the pre-designed online questionnaire rather than solely publicly available information.[474] Given the significant diversity across sectors, the questionnaire is designed based on general criteria and industry specific criteria, both covering the various issues in economic, environmental and social dimensions. Each dimension consists of 6–10 criteria, and 2–10 questions need to be answered under each criterion.[475] But the numbers and weight of each criterion and sub-question vary depending on different sectors. The general criteria refer to a set of benchmarks related to the standard management practice and performance measures in economic,[476] environmental[477] and social dimensions.[478] On average these account for 40%-50% of the total assessment.[479] The other 50% of assessment criteria is industry-specific,[480] which details the specific risks and opportunities for an industry about how to address the economic, environmental and social issues that are financially material for its long-term success. Based on the Global Industry Classification Standard (GICS),[481] RobecoSAM designs 59 different online questionnaires covering 59 RobecoSAM industries derived from 24 GICS industry groups.

---

473 CSA Guide—RobecoSAM's Corporate Sustainability Assessment Methodology. Available at: http://www.sustainability-indices.com/images/corporate-sustainability-assessment-methodology-guidebook.pdf (Accessed on February 23, 2017).

474 *Id*, p.3.

475 *Id*, pp. 5–9.

476 The general criteria of the economic dimension contain: corporate governance, customer relationship management, risk &crisis management.

477 The general criteria of the environmental dimension contain: environmental policy/management system, environmental reporting.

478 The general criteria of the social dimension contain: corporate citizenship and philanthropy, human capital management, labor practice indicators, and talent attraction & retention.

479 The accurate percentage depends on the industry.

480 The general criteria accounts for 40%-50% of the assessment, and the industry specific criteria take up at least 50% of the assessment.

481 The Global Industry Classification Standard (GICS) was launched by MSCI and Standard & Pool's in 1999, which consists of 10 sectors, 24 industry groups, 67 industries and 156 sub-industries.

In general, a RobecoSAM questionnaire consists of approximately 80–120 questions covering those economic, environmental and social issues. These issues are uncovered under the traditional financial performance analysis. Moreover, to guarantee the objectivity of answers, the majority of the questionnaire is designed in the form of multiple-choice questions, and each answer is assigned some points ranging from 0 to 100. The sum of all question scores is a company's 'Total Sustainability Score', which determines whether a company can be included in the prestigious DJSI family and it also determines its rating positions.

In addition to the online questionnaire analysis, another important component of the CSA is the Media and Stakeholder Analysis (MSA). This assessment scheme is based on news coverage from mass media, and the complementary information from a large group of stakeholders, such as consumers, NGOs, international organizations, and national states.

3.2.3 FTSE

As one of the new leaders in the global rating industry, the FTSE (Financial Times Stock Exchange) Russell[482] provides a variety of global and regional indexes focusing on SRI.[483] Among the variety of products and services, the FTSE ESG Ratings provide a set of comprehensive and daily-updated benchmarks on companies' risks and performance concerning ESG issues. The FTSE ESG Ratings aim to offer objective information and scientific analysis for users (more particularly asset owners, asset managers, and consultants) and thus to help them integrate ESG factors into investment decision-making. Today, the FTSE ESG Ratings have been widely used by a wide range of market players, including 90 of the world's top 100 asset managers, the top 10 investment banks, the top 5 global custodians, and more than 100 of the world's largest asset owners.[484]

A remarkable feature of the FTSE ESG Ratings lies in the unique method of data collection. Within the FTSE ESG Ratings, all data used for assessing a company's ESG risk and performance should be publicly available information and any privately provided information is not accepted. The reason for adopting this approach is to guarantee information transparency and thus to enhance

482 FTSE Russell is a trading mark of FTSE International Limited ('FTSE') and Frank Russell Company ('Russell') and their respective subsidiary undertakings, which are members of the London Stock Exchange Group plc group.

483 For more information about FTSE index families, available at: http://www.ftse.com/products/indexmenu (Accessed on February 23, 2017).

484 For more information of FTSE, available at: http://www.ftserussell.com/about-us (Accessed on February 23, 2017).

the credibility of rating results.[485] Based on the comprehensive database of the FTSE ESG Ratings, the assessment results are calculated through two procedures: first, the score assessments for measuring practice and performance; second, the exposure assessments for measuring relevance and materiality.

In the first process of score assessment, a company's overall ESG practices will be evaluated through a range of indicators under a given theme. For example, the qualitative indicators are used to assess the quality of management. The quantitative indicators are used to measure corporate data disclosure. The sector-specific indicators are tailored for different industrial sectors. The performance indicators use the quantitative data to make performance judgments.[486] In the second assessment procedure, a company's exposure is mainly evaluated through a detailed analysis under the Industrial Classification Benchmark (ICB)[487] Subsectors where a company is located[488] and its presence in specific countries.

In today's business world, the FTSE ESG Ratings are used in various ways, such as building a basis for active portfolio management, company engagement, customized indices, ESG risk analysis or ESG research and analysis. As one prestigious product of the FTSE ESG Ratings, the FTSE4Good Index Series (the FTSE4Good indices)[489] are designed to measure the corporate performance on ESG issues. In practice, the FTSE4Good indices play an important role in four scenarios. First, they can be used as tools in the creation of index-tracking investments, financial instruments or fund products focused on responsible investment. Secondly, they can help investors to distinguish between companies with better ESG performance and those with poor ESG performance. Thirdly, they can be used as the transparent and evolving global and regional standards for companies to assess their progress and achievements on ESG issues. Fourthly, they can be used as a benchmark to track the performance of responsible investment portfolios.[490]

485 For more information about FTSE ESG Ratings, available at: http://www.ftse.com/products/downloads/FTSE-ESG-Methodology-and-Usage-Summary-Short.pdf?32 (Accessed on February 23, 2017).

486 *Id.*

487 The Industry Classification Benchmark (ICB) is a definitive system categorizing over 70,000 companies and 75,000 securities worldwide, enabling the comparison of companies across four levels of classification and national boundaries.

488 The ICB consists of 114 Subsectors.

489 The FTSE4Good index series consist of the FTSE4Good Global Minimum Variance Index, the FTSE4Good Environmental Leaders Europe 40 Index, the FTSE4Good IBEX Index, and the FTSE4Good Bursa Malaysia Index.

490 For more information about the FTSE4Good indices, available at: http://www.ftse.com/products/indices/ftse4good?_ga=1.134764273.1417608972.1449521509 (Accessed on February 23, 2017).

3.2.4 MSCI

As a leading provider of data and analysis on risk and portfolio measurement, the Morgan Stanley Capital International (MSCI) has more than 40-years experience in helping clients to make more informed decisions based on their research and analysis. MSCI attempts to contribute to a more sustainable future by providing their clients with professional products and services on risk and performance. Throughout its history, MSCI has expanded its business scale through a series of takeovers and mergers with other influential players in the rating industry, such as Barra, Measurerisk, IPD, Investor Force and Governance Holdings Co.[491] As a result, MSCI has accumulated a comprehensive database by continually integrating a variety of expertise in various fields of expertise: portfolio risk analysis, risk management and governance, risk transparency, real estate performance management, performance reporting and corporate governance. This consequently enhanced MSCI's competitive advantages in the rating market.

MSCI ESG Research Inc. was launched in 2010 as an important subsidiary of MSCI.[492] Today it has become one of the world's largest providers of in-depth analysis, ratings and data exclusively on economic, social and governance factors (ESG) to a variety of clients, including 45 of the top 50 asset managers, asset owners, consultants, advisors, and academics.[493] The key mission of MSCI ESG Research is to help investors to understand how ESG factors could influence the long-term returns of their investment portfolios and thus help them to integrate ESG issues into their investment decisions. During the evolution of MSCI ESG Research, new rating activities were designed—the MSCI ESG ratings. These were designed to help investors to identify the potential risks and opportunities of ESG integration through in-depth ESG research, analysis, and rating. The MSCI ESG Index family is designed to "to represent the most prevalent environmental, social and governance (ESG) investment strategies, utilizing our award-winning ESG data and ratings of thousands of companies

491 An important merger is the 2010 acquisition of a leading provider of risk management products—RiskMetrics, which also owns three prominent rating agencies: Center for Financial Research and Analysis, Innovest Strategic Value Advisor, and KLD Analytics Inc. For More information about the history of MSCI, available at: https://www.msci.com/our-story (Accessed on February 23, 2017).

492 MSCI ESG Research Inc. is an indirect wholly-owned subsidiary of MSCI, a Registered Investment under the Investment Adviser Act of 1940.

493 MSCI ESG Research: Overview and Product. Available at: https://www.msci.com/documents/1296102/1636401/MSCI_ESG_Research_Factsheet.pdf/411954d3-68af-44d6-b222-d89708c5120d (Accessed on February 23, 2017).

worldwide."[494] The broad MSCI ESG Index family[495] provides customized products and services to meet the specific requirements of different investors. For example,

- The MSCI Global Sustainability Indexes are reconstituted annually and designed for investors "seeking exposure to companies with strong sustainability profiles and with relatively low tracking error to the underlying equity market."[496]
- The MSCI Global ex Controversial Weapons Indexes are "designed for investors who wish to avoid investments in cluster bombs, land mines, chemical and biological weapons, and depleted uranium weapons."[497]
- The MSCI Global Environmental Indexes focus on investors who demand low-carbon investment strategies, fossil fuel exclusion strategies, and other thematic issues.[498]

3.3 *Sustainability/CSR Awards*

CSR/Sustainability awards evaluate and compare against each other on sustainability. The winners are named in the title of sustainability awards for their better performance on sustainability. Today sustainability awards become a popular instrument in promoting responsible business through public recognition. As a result, a wide range of organizations has launched their own CSR or sustainability awards, including governments, international organizations, industrial associations, financial institutions, academic institutions, NGOs, and mass media. The mass media have been significantly active in this field. Many influential newspapers and magazines have launched a variety of awards for sustainability or CSR, for example, Fortune's '*Most Admired Company Award*', Financial Times' '*Most Respected Companies List*', and the '*Guardian Sustainable Business Awards*'. The governments are also important players in this domain. For example, the US Department of Energy (DOE) praises the contribution of individuals and groups in sustainability through DOE Sustainability Awards.

494 For more information about MSCI ESG Indices, available at: https://www.msci.com/esg-indexes (Accessed on February 23, 2017).

495 The MSCI Index families consists a variety of products covering different ESG issues, including MSCI Global Sustainability Indexes, MSCI Global SRI Indexes, MSCI Global ex Controversial Weapons Indexes, MSCI Global Environmental Indexes, Barclays MSCI ESG Fixed Income Indices, and Custom MSCI ESG Indexes.

496 MSCI ESG Indexes. Available at: https://www.msci.com/documents/10199/242721/MSCI_ESG_Indices.pdf/42ef2d23-c4ef-4672-8476-52bbb8c98cca (Accessed on February 23, 2017).

497 *Id.*

498 *Id.*

The Australian government also launched the '*Australian Business Awards*' to encourage the well-managed, high-performing leading industry initiatives.[499] In 2012, the European Commission launched the '*European CSR Award Scheme*', with the aim of demonstrating the excellent CSR practice and to exchange the best experience across Europe.[500]

As the major provider of sustainability ratings and indices, the rating agencies also pro-actively participate in rewarding companies for their good performance on sustainability. For example, RobecoSAM launched the '*RobecoSAM Sustainability Award*' in several hierarchical categories, which consists of the 'industry leader', the 'gold class', the 'silver class', the 'bronze class' and the 'industry mover'. Companies will be evaluated and granted with correspondent awards based on their CSA scores. To be exact, only one company with the highest CSA scores from each industry can receive the honor of '*RobecoSAM Industry Leader*', while those companies that score within 1% less than the Industry Leader can be named the '*RobecoSAM Gold Class*'. For example, in 2015, AkzoNobel, ING, and Unilever were named the '*RobecoSAM Industry Leader*' in their respective industries.[501]

4 Challenges and Opportunities for the Future of Sustainability Rating

Despite the increasing popularity and significance of CSP measurement within the agenda of CSR/CER and sustainable development, serious challenges remain about the quality and robustness of sustainability ratings. Particularly in the wake of the Volkswagen emission scandal,[502] sustainability ratings are also facing increasing public negativity about their credibility. Before the outbreak of this scandal, Volkswagen was awarded the honour of the leader of the Automobiles & Components Industry group of 2015 by one of the most prominent

---

499 For more information about the Australian Business Awards, available at: http://www.businessawards.com.au/ (Accessed on February 23, 2017).

500 For more information about the European CSR Award Scheme, available at: http://www.csreurope.org/ european-csr-awards (Accessed on April 30, 2017).

501 For more information about the DJSI Industry Group Leaders 2015, available at: http://www.sustainability-indices.com/review/industry-group-leaders-2015.jsp (Accessed on February 23, 2017).

502 The Volkswagen emission scandal was first revealed by the United States Environmental Protection Agency (EPA) on 18 September 2015 when the German automaker was found to be in violation of the Clean Air Act by intentionally manipulating the results of emission controls. More information about the Volkswagen emission scandal is available at: http://www.epa.gov/vw (Accessed on February 23, 2017).

sustainability indices— the DJSI—which is frequently cited as one of the most well-established and most credible ratings.[503] The journalist John Gapper had already set the tone about the recent rating failures and scandals as "rating agencies have extended their grip and lulled investors and institutions into a false sense of security."[504] In the Volkswagen Emission scandal, Volkswagen apparently found a fraudulent way to pass all security guarantees in the DJSI rating schemes, which should have alarmed the analysts. The exposure of this scandal made various stakeholders doubt the robustness levels of sustainability ratings. Therefore, it is necessary to evaluate the current state of the sustainability rating in a broader sense.

4.1 *Rate the Rater*

Many scholars have made great efforts to assess the quality of the current rating schemes. Chatterji and Levine provided three benchmarks of the ideal non-financial performance measurement: reliability, comparability, and validity. They, therefore, argued that if a measurement failed to meet these three benchmarks, the rating results could damage corporate sustainability performance and decrease the overall social welfare.[505] Moreover, by comparing three widely used sustainability indices(the DJSI, KLD 400 and FTSE4Good Indices), they also found that the significant diversity between these ratings was evident in terms of weighting systems, bars of performance, data collection, transparency, and other concerns.[506] Scalet and Kelly described the current state of the sustainability ratings as "the early stage of development with a variety of challenges."[507] These challenges were related to various issues, such as the lack of uniform standards, the diversity of weighting systems, the lack of comparability across rating agencies, the overwhelming requests of information disclosure, the low response rate of rated companies, and the lack of transparency. Windolph, based on a review of previous studies in this domain, systematized the challenges the sustainability ratings were facing as follows: "the lack of standardization, lack of credibility of information, bias, trade-offs, lack of transparency, and lack of independence."[508] Dommerholt compared the contents of screening instruments of SAM and KLD, and the results of his

503 Sadowski *et al.* October 2010.

504 Jon Gapper, 'Time to rein in the ratings agencies', *Financial Times*, April 28, 2010. Available at: http://www.ft.com/cms/s/0/28df0210-52f8-11df-813e-00144feab49a.html#axzz3t66C26SM (Accessed on February 23, 2017).

505 Chatterji and Levine 2006, pp. 25–51.

506 *Id.*

507 Scalet and Kelly 2010, pp. 69–88.

508 Windolph 2011, pp. 61–80.

study indicated that the current instruments were imperfect in measuring corporate sustainability performance and the validity of the rating results remained questionable.[509]

The literature review above generally shows that today sustainability ratings are facing a variety of challenges that potentially impede their further development. Three values that are frequently cited as the important benchmarks of a rating or ranking will be explored in more detail, i.e. credibility, accessibility, and effectiveness.[510] Any factor that may damage these values is considered as a challenge or a risk that may influence the quality of sustainability ratings. In this section, we also identify possible reasons behind these problems and recommendations to overcome them.

4.2 *Credibility*

The first value of sustainability rating is credibility, which can be simply described as "whether a rating or ranking is trustworthy or not." The answer should be provided to the following two questions: do these ratings or indices convey the real information of corporate sustainability performance and do they help stakeholders make more informed decisions? Despite the significant lack of consensus in the CSR/CER and CSP domain, the majority of current studies deems credibility as the most fundamental virtue to benchmark the quality of a rating or ranking.[511] The degree of credibility of a rating or ranking can be influenced by a variety of factors. In the five-phase research project '*Rate the Raters*', SustainAbility[512] together with GlobeScan[513] interviewed more than 1000 sustainability experts, from the business communities, governments, NGOs, and academia,[514] about their views about the important factors contributing to a credible rating or ranking. The influencing factors mentioned include: (1) the objectivity/ credibility of data sources, (2) the disclosure of rating methodology, (3) the consistency of methodology over time, (4) the focus on material issues, (5) the direct engagement of companies under evaluation,

509 Dommerholt 2012.

510 See e.g. Windolph 2011, pp. 37–57; Chatterji and Levine 2006, pp. 29–51; Scalet and Kelly 2010, pp. 69–88.

511 *Id.*

512 See *supra* footnote 435.

513 GlobeScan is an evidence-led strategy consultancy focused on stakeholder intelligence and engagement.

514 The GlobeScan/SustainAbility, '*Rate the Raters 2012: Polling the experts*'. Available at: http://www.sustainability.com/library/rate-the-raters-phase-five-polling-the-experts-2012#.VmaoknarS70 (Accessed on February 23, 2017).

(6) the experience and size of the research team, and (7) the stakeholder involvement in the development of the methodology.

Among these various factors, the objectivity of data sources and the disclosure of rating methodology received the highest values of the "very high importance" among the interviewees.[515] Three out of the seven important factors are examined in more detail in this section, that is, the objective of data sources, the disclosure of rating methodology, and the independence of rating organizations. This section aims to provide an answer to the question: how these factors potentially damage the credibility of a rating or ranking?

4.2.1 Objectivity of Data Sources

Data collection is a fundamental step in the assessment procedure of a rating. Rating agencies collect data related to corporate sustainability performance in various ways, such as publicly available information (like corporate sustainability/CSR report or corporate website), information privately provided by companies, surveys or interviews with the companies to be rated, and the relevant media coverage. Different rating agencies may adopt different approaches to collecting and selecting the useful information they need for assessing corporate sustainability performance. For example, RobecoSAM and the DJSI use their pre-designed online questionnaires as the primary source of data collection. On the contrary, the FTSE ESG ratings solely rely on the publicly available information. Due to the lack of standardization in this field, it is difficult to judge which approach is superior over the other. In fact, these two approaches have their respective strengths and shortcomings. For example, the usage of surveys and questionnaires could collect more direct information privately provided by companies than purely publicly available information. But the exclusion of any private information could "improve the credibility of data and ensure transparency across the market."[516]

As many rating agencies have claimed, one of the supposed objectives of their work is to solve information asymmetry between companies and stakeholders.[517] Nevertheless, it is difficult for investors and consumers to verify the sustainability claims made by companies due to their limited access to information. As a result, it occurs that some of the less sustainable companies may strategically make use of this situation by disclosing incomplete or even

515 *Id.*

516 For more information about the FTSE Index Inclusion Rules, available at: http://www.ftse.com/products/ downloads/F4G-Index-Inclusion-Rules.pdf (Accessed on February 23, 2017).

517 Chatterji and Levine 2006, pp. 25–51.

incorrect information to mislead their investment or purchasing decisions. It could lead to 'a market for lemons'[518] where companies with truly sustainable performance are crowded out of the market, but the less responsible companies remain in the market. Such opportunistic behaviour is well known as 'greenwashing'.[519] In this context, sustainability rating systems provide a solution to deter the risk of greenwashing, by providing a third-party and independent information assessment of corporate sustainability performance. By doing so, they aim to assist the rating users to make more informed decisions.

Ironically, the lack of transparency of the sustainability raters themselves just goes against their stated objective of overcoming information asymmetry. Generally speaking, there are two scenarios where the risks of greenwashing may occur in the rating process. The first scenario happens between rating agencies and rated companies. Since for nearly all rating systems, the most important data source is from companies,[520] the quality of corporate self-reporting is a key factor in determining the credibility of a rating. However, in practice companies usually have incentives to greenwash their sustainability/CSR reports, by opportunistically withholding some negative information or even disclosing some misleading information to obtain a better ranking or rating score. In this case, the external verification of company information (by a third party like an accountancy firm) is critical for raters to ensure their own credibility. But the practice in this respect is still lacking.[521] The second scenario of greenwashing could come into play between raters and rating users, given the significant lack of the transparency about data collection process, data quality, data analysis and data evaluation. Not surprisingly, Porter and Kramer perceived some of the rating results as "a jumble of largely meaningless rankings, allowing almost any company to boast that it meets some measure of social responsibility, and most do."[522]

4.2.2 Disclosure of Rating Methodology

The disclosure of rating methodology is also regarded as one of the most important determinants of the credibility of a rater.[523] According to the results of the '*Rate the Rater*', 90% of sustainability professionals think that the disclosure of

518 Akerlof 1970, pp. 488–500.
519 Green washing refers to the fact that the environmental claims made by the label cannot be sustained. (Martinez Gandara 2013, p.134)
520 Windolph 2011, p.43.
521 Sadowski *et al.* February 2011.
522 Porter and Kramer 2006, p.3.
523 Sadowski *et al.* October 2010.

rating methodology is one of the most important factors of a credible rating.[524] However, the reality is exactly the opposite. For many rating agencies, the disclosure of rating methodology is quite sensitive and more or less regarded as a company secret, because it is closely related to their commercial interests, competitive advantage and their market positions in the rating industry. Not surprisingly, to date, the majority of raters only make partial disclosure of their rating methodologies. Only a few raters provide a relatively sufficient disclosure about how the rating results are processed and calculated.[525]

Many ratings place emphasis on improving the information disclosure and transparency of rated companies. However, the inconsistency between raters' stated objectives and their own lack of transparency has raised ongoing controversies. As explained earlier, raters' reluctance to disclose their rating methodologies is understandable given the proprietary nature of the rating methodology. The rating methodology is their "trademark" or "secret source".[526] However, at the same time, the significant lack of transparency (particularly regarding the disclosure of rating methodologies) seriously damages the credibility of a rating. Windolph argued that "as long as rating processes are not transparent, their reliability may be questioned just like the reliability of the companies to be examined."[527] One can also argue that the disclosure of the methodology could become a potential source of competitive advantage for raters,[528] because the credibility of their ratings will be substantially enhanced if raters disclose more information about how the data is collected and how the scores are calculated. In fact, a majority of rating users have expressed their willingness to accept and adopt a rating when they better understand how the rating results are processed.[529] In this case, the disclosure of the rating methodology could become a potential source of competitive advantages for a rater.

Consequently, rating agencies have frequently been advised to improve the transparency of their rating methodologies to boost trust among rating users, watchers, and other stakeholders. Chatterji and Levine, for example, proposed a possible solution that raters could provide several detailed case studies to demonstrate how data is collected and scored, and why companies are included, downgraded, or even excluded from the rating or ranking lists.[530] Other scholars, given the commercial sensitiveness of the disclosure of rating

524 *Id.*
525 *Id.*
526 Sadowski *et al.* October 2010, p.14.
527 Windolph 2011, pp. 45–46.
528 Sadowski *et al.* February 2011.
529 *Id.*
530 Chatterji and Levin 2006, pp. 29–51.

methodologies, suggested a reasonable compromise that rating agencies could be at least "fully transparent with rated companies and primary users".[531]

In practice, some rating agencies began to respond to the increasing demand for the disclosure of rating methodologies. For example, the FTSE4Good publishes its Index Inclusion Rules for the FTSE4Good Index series,[532] which provides a set of criteria for inclusion and exclusion from its rating system. By doing so, it helps companies to better understand why they are included or excluded from the FTSE4Good Index and more importantly how they should improve their performance to meet the criteria of the Index.

4.2.3 Independence of Rating Agencies

The level of independence of rating agencies also affects the credibility of the rating results. In the rating market, the close cooperation with rated companies has been cited as a competitive advantage by raters, because it means that they can collect more data privately provided by rated companies than their peers. However, it has also been strongly criticized for the potential risks of the biased rating results. In fact, the conflict of interest between raters and rated companies is quite common, particularly in the financial markets,[533] where some raters are funded or compensated by rated companies in various ways. For example, as the major providers of ratings, indices, and rankings, many financial service institutions also provide other paid products and services for rated companies, such as financial analysis, risk management, and consultancy services. This may result in a conflict of interest between raters and rated companies, considering the rated company could influence the rating results.[534]

To avoid the potential conflict of interest, an increasing number of rating agencies have developed a formal policy on conflict of interest. This policy generally explains the approach of rating agencies to managing the possible conflicts in the rating process, such as the principle of independence or the specific provisions of providing services to the evaluated companies.[535] The Ethical Investment Research and Information Services (EIRIS)[536] present a good example about how to publicly disclose the relevant policies on independence,

531 Sadowski *et al.* February 2011.

532 For more information about the FTSE4Good Index Series, available at: http://www.ftse.com/products/downloads/F4G-Index-Inclusion-Rules.pdf (Accessed on February 23, 2017).

533 Windolph 2011, pp. 48–49.

534 See e.g. Windolph 2011, pp. 37–57; Sadowaki *et al.* February 2011.

535 Sadowski *et al.* February 2011.

536 EIRIS is a long-established sustainability rating organization and a leading global provider of environmental, social and governance (ESG) research. After a merger in 2015–2016

confidentiality, stakeholders and code of conduct.[537] For example, EIRIS explicitly declares its independence by stating that "the grading, rankings, and other outputs of EIRIS research may not be influenced by an existing or potential business relationship between EIRIS and a researched company or a third party representing a company."[538]

Based on the analysis above, it appears that the deeper reason behind the various disputes about the credibility of sustainability ratings is the significant lack of transparency of raters. Therefore, to boost the trust among their clients, it is an urgent task for raters to improve their transparency particular regarding the data collection, the disclosure of rating methodologies, and the relationship with rated companies and other stakeholders.

4.3 *Accessibility*

The second challenge of the rating industry is to increase its level of accessibility, which in this context can be simply described as "the extent to which a rating user or rated company can understand, value and use sustainability ratings". Currently, the significant diversity of assessment approaches creates the situation of "the wall of codes" or "chaos of codes".[539] A broad range of measurement tools or codes of conducts competes against each other for attracting more attention and more adoption. In this race, a magnitude of benchmarks, questions, weighting and scoring system have been incorporated into the rating systems, which make the current rating industry much more complicated.[540]

The diversity of the rating market is, on the one hand, widely welcomed by rating users, because the different metrics of each assessment approach can meet their specific requirements across regions, countries, and industries. For example, some ratings provide the global benchmarks, while some focus on the regional or national standards; some ratings provide an overall evaluation or assessment on corporate performance on sustainability, while some ratings only focus on some specific issues (like environmental pollution and employee issues); and some ratings put more emphasis on the environmental dimension,

between the French based organization Viego and the UK based organization Eiris, it is now operating as ViegoEiris.

537 For more information about EIRIS policies, available at: http://www.eiris.org/about-us/policies/ (Accessed on February 23, 2017).

538 EIRIS Independence Policy, available at: http://www.eiris.org/wp-content/uploads/2013/04/Independence-Policy.pdf (Accessed on February 23, 2017).

539 Chatterji and Levine 2006, pp. 29–30.

540 Lucy Kellaway, 'A good employer offers more than Botox', *Financial Times*, January 30, 2015. Available at: http://www.ft.com/cms/s/0/8691574c-2b0f-11e0-a65f-00144feab49a.html#axzz1CdnIbd1E (Accessed on February 23, 2017).

while some ratings specialise in the area of human rights or anti-corruption. In this context, the diversification of sustainability ratings does provide a broad portfolio with a wealth of sustainability rating products and services.

However, there is a substantial disadvantage to this significant diversification in the sustainability rating market, because it creates a low level of accessibility for both rated companies and rating users. For rating users, the diversification of the current rating industry creates considerable complexity and confusion. It even poses significant challenges to decide which ratings to trust.

The rated companies and their managers are confronted with various challenges, including: first, the potential costs of the various rating systems; second, the great pressure to understand the differences between these rating agencies and their rating systems; third, to fill in various long, slightly different or sometimes profoundly different questionnaires. Even for sustainability experts, it is a 'mission impossible' to understand all rating systems and to decide which system is better than others and which one they need to comply with. This situation results in two different responses from the rated companies. Some companies simply ignore this challenging task and do not bother about the sustainability ratings.[541] Other companies decide to participate in the rating process due to different motivations. The latter companies usually have to spend considerable time and resources to fill in the detailed questionnaire or to prepare the materials that are required by rating agencies. For example, RobecoSAM and the DJSI require the rated companies to fill in a detailed online questionnaire with more than 100 pages.

There are also other downsides of the lower accessibility of the sustainability rating industry. First, the high compliance costs potentially crowd out small and medium companies from the rating market. More particularly, it is argued that SMEs could not afford to participate in the endless rating process even though they out-perform on sustainability. Consequently, it creates a danger of the biased rating results that companies with higher responsiveness (such as completing the questionnaire and submitting more materials) are awarded higher rating scores. Second, the significant overlaps between different rating systems also contribute to the significant diversification of the rating industry. In practice, some ratings are simply constructed on the basis of other ratings or a combination of several ratings. This phenomenon is well known as "build a rating from ratings".[542] For example, Newsweek's Green Rankings are based on a combination of ratings from RickMetrics, TruCost, and CorporateRegister.com.

---

541 Chatterji and Levine 2006, pp. 29–30.

542 Sadowski *et al.* October 2010, p.13.

To summarize, the increasing diversity of sustainability ratings is expected to meet the different demands of various stakeholders. But instead, the larger the number of sustainability ratings, the greater the challenges posed for rating users and rated companies to have a proper understanding and trust in these ratings. In this context, a strong demand for fewer and higher quality ratings is socially desired today.[543] As a result, raters are urged to put more focus on the quality of ratings rather than on the quantity. This is needed because the quality of a rating or ranking plays an increasingly important role in determining which rater will survive in this competitive market in the end.[544]

4.4 *Effectiveness*

The third challenge that the rating industry is currently facing is to improve the effectiveness of sustainability ratings on corporate behaviour. The actual impact of sustainability rating is even more important, because nearly all rating agencies share the same objective to "improve corporate social or environmental performance" or to "enhance corporate transparency."[545] Several studies have been conducted to examine the impacts of sustainability ratings, and more particularly to what extent companies would adjust their behaviour towards sustainability in response to being rated. Scalet and Kelly[546] investigated the impacts of the rating agencies on corporate behavior. Their primary findings indicated that "a CSR ranking appears to do little to encourage firms to acknowledge and address problems related to their social and environmental performance."[547] Chatterji and Toffel[548] empirically examined the responses of hundreds of companies towards sustainability ratings. They found out that companies with poor rating results have a more active response than companies with good rating results or never being rated.

The mixed impact of sustainability ratings is the outcomes of several characteristics of the sustainability rating industry. First, it is difficult to evaluate the actual impacts of a rating or ranking. According to the results from '*Rate the raters*', only a few raters could provide the specific examples to demonstrate the impacts of their rating products on corporate behavior. The majority of raters generally cite some broad and abstract indicators to reflect their influence, such as the number of rating users, the adoption of influential institutions

543 Sadowski *et al.* July 2011.
544 *Id*, p.5.
545 Sadowski *et al.* February 2011, p.7.
546 Scalet and Kelly 2010, pp. 69–88.
547 *Id*, p.69.
548 Chatterji and Toffel 2010, pp. 917–945.

and media coverage.[549] The second possible reason is the potential bias of the rating results, which could occur in various forms. For example, one common form of the biased ratings is related to the specific types of rated companies. It is observed that most ratings including the most prestigious ones tend to only focus on the large or well-known companies, while SMEs are usually not included.[550] Taking the DJSI as an example, the 'best-in-class' approach basically limits the scope of the rated companies to MNEs that own more resources to improve their sustainability performance. The second danger of the biased ratings is derived from the so-called 'rewarding strategy' used by raters. Since the effectiveness of a rating or ranking to a large extent depends on how companies respond to ratings, many rating agencies make use of this strategy to spur company responsiveness, which implies that companies with pro-active responsiveness probably will be rewarded by higher rating scores. This strategy, on the one hand, could motivate companies to improve the quality of their self-reporting, but on the other hand, it may result in biased results which exclude lower responsive companies, because the lack of responsiveness does not necessarily indicate a bad sustainability performance. In this case, the rating results are strongly questioned as to whether they truly identify the more sustainable companies.

5 Summary and Some Concluding Remarks

Just as a saying goes, "what gets measured gets managed".[551] This slogan is also true in the discussion of CSR/CER and CSP. The shift of focus means that we move from CSR, which puts more emphasis on whether a company should be responsible for its behaviour, to CSP, which focuses on the progress and outcomes of corporate actions in addressing social and environmental issues. Consequently, the theory and the measurement of CSP have gained increasing popularity and considerable significance from both the academic circles and the business world in recent years. To better understand this increasingly popular phenomenon, three questions were answered in this chapter:

1) What is CSP measurement? More particularly, what dimensions, aspects and issues should be included in CSP measurement?
2) Why should CSP be measured?

549 Sadowski *et al.* Feburary 2011, p.8.
550 Windolph 2011, p.44.
551 Chatterji and Levin 2006, p.31.

3) How CSP measurement works in practice, and what are the challenges and opportunities it is currently facing?

To answer these questions, a short overview of the history of CSP, its achievements and challenges were provided. The core of this chapter was created by the academic CSP theories, the practical CSP measurement, and their translation into a wide range of CSP rating products and services.

To answer the first question, this chapter addressed some important stages in the development of CSP theory and measurement. The CSP studies have a long and rich tradition and especially during the 1980s, CSP-theory made large progress in its development. Many scholars have made great efforts to establish a comprehensive CSP model during the past decades. Considerable first input in this domain comes from Carroll (1979). Carroll's work has been further expanded in a more corporate practice-oriented theoretical framework by Wartcik and Cohran (1985). Wood (1991) reformulated the earlier CSP models into a comprehensive and coherent conceptual framework of CSP. Their systematic analysis and improvements of CSP models certainly provided very useful input into the design of measurement practices and methodologies in the rating industry.

This chapter also provided an answer to the second question: why CSP should be measured? The answer to this question could be simply formulated as "without measuring CSP, it cannot be managed". It has been observed that the values of CSP measurement have been widely desired by both academic scholars and the business practitioners. More particularly, CSP measurement has exerted substantial impacts on corporate behaviour in various ways: first, it helps corporate managers to identify material issues and it evaluates the influence of their reactions on those issues; second, it helps corporate managers to monitor and manage their impacts on society and on environment; third, it creates action towards rising CSP-levels which could become a competitive advantage for companies; fourth, it creates corporate best CSR/CER practices.

In addition to the considerable attention from academia, the business world also shows a growing interest in the practice of CSP measurement, which creates a newly emerging market—the sustainability rating industry. To answer the third question: how CSP measurement works in practice, this section explored this fast growing sustainability rating market. Due to the strong market demand for assessing and comparing corporate sustainability performance, a wide range of organizations has stepped into this young and dynamic market by providing a wide range of products or services, such as ratings, indices, rankings, and awards. Consequently, the recent decades have witnessed substantial growth of the sustainability rating market. To provide some depth in the sustainability rating market, four well-established rating agencies and their products or services were discussed in more detail: the Dow Jones Sustainability Indices (DJSI), RobecoSAM, Financial Times Stock Exchange (FTSE) and Morgan Stanley Capital International (MSCI). This clearly reflects the proliferation of the various rating systems today, as well as the announced differences between these approaches in terms of target audiences, rating scales, and methodologies.

Despite the increasing popularity, the current rating market is facing many challenges that may undermine the positive effects of sustainability ratings. These challenges are related to various issues, such as the lack of transparency, the objectivity of data sources, the lack of independence and the significant diversity. Considering the increasing importance of the rating system for companies, stakeholders, and society at large, a profound reform is needed not only for rating agencies but also for rating users and regulatory bodies. On the one hand, to survive the fast-growing and competitive market, it is important for rating agencies to manage the risks above and thus to boost trust among users. On the other hand, rating users should pay more attention to the assessment of a rating or ranking before using them. A more interesting hypothesis here is whether governmental regulation should intervene in this self-regulatory market to accompany its success and hence guarantee its contribution to a more sustainable world.

CHAPTER 5

The Law and Economics of CSR/CER

1 Introduction

As an essentially contested concept,[552] the definition of CSR/CER remains an unsolved issue in this domain.[553] Since its first appearance in academic writings in the 1950s, many scholars, business practitioners, and organizations have made great efforts to develop a universally accepted definition of CSR/CER. Although their attempts fail for many reasons, the various definitions do share the essential idea of this concept, which can be simply interpreted as "going beyond mere compliance with mandatory environmental standards on a voluntary basis." It implies that companies would like to adopt higher or stricter environmental standards. In this sense, CSR/CER has been widely recognized as a form of self-regulation and more particularly a form of private environmental governance. Also, as mentioned in the previous chapters,[554] there may be a variety of reasons for companies and stakeholders to participate in CSR/CER. All these arguments are based on a fundamental assumption that the development of CSR/CER should be primarily led by corporations. In this view, there is little room for government intervention. However, the necessity of government intervention in CSR/CER has attracted considerable interest from both academic and policy circles. Therefore, this chapter provides a law and economic analysis of CSR/CER, by putting it in the broader discussion of addressing market failure and governance deficit.

This chapter first discusses the context of which CSR/CER is gradually becoming socially desirable to a large extent, due to the existence of market failure and governance deficit (Section 2 and Section 3). This chapter positions CSR/CER within a broader framework, pointing at the need to internalize the environmental externalities and will then discuss the feasibility of various approaches to fulfilling this task (Section 4). The question will hence be addressed to what extent self-regulation could, under the circumstances, be an alternative for public regulation in internalizing environmental externalities. The reason to focus on self-regulation is related to the fact that CSR/CER is, as a voluntary mechanism, also considered as a self-regulatory tool. A complication

552 Moon *et al.* 2005, pp. 426–453.
553 See supra Chapter 2.
554 See supra Chapter 3.

 | DOI:10.1163/9789004368132_006

which arises within the corporate context, is that the conflict of interest between shareholders and managers may occur concerning the engagement of CSR/CER. In this case, the traditional principal-agent problems could equally be relevant for our discussion of CSR/CER (Section 5). In that respect, the question obviously arises of whether in the emergence of CSR/CER, there may be a risk of market failure (such as information asymmetry) which regulation could potentially remedy. Based on the analysis above, Section 6 discusses in which contexts and to what extent CSR/CER as a voluntary mechanism may still need accompanying regulation to increase its effectiveness. Section 7 concludes.

2 CSR/CER and Market Failure

According to welfare economics, if all markets with perfect competition reach a general equilibrium,[555] the state of resource allocation is referred to as a situation of Pareto efficiency,[556] in which individual's value could be maximized without making anyone worse off. However, in reality, the situation of a general equilibrium and Pareto efficiency cannot always be achieved for many reasons, such as incomplete information, the existence of externalities, and imperfect competition. Therefore, often a market failure remains.[557] The law and economics literature[558] indicates market failure has four different sources: monopoly/market power, externality, information problems, and public goods. More particularly, three sources of market failure find their relevance for the discussion of CSR/CER, and they are externality, information asymmetry, and public goods.

2.1 *Externality*[559]

An externality is considered as a typical form of market failure.[560] From a traditional economic perspective, an externality can be defined as the external

555 Philipsen 2003, pp. 10–11.

556 Pareto efficiency generally refers to a situation of allocation of resources in which at least one person is made better off and no one is made worse off.

557 Philipsen argued that a Pareto-efficient situation requires a number of conditions: (1) on every market there should be many small and identical producers, who cannot significantly influence the price level and who sell homogenous products in their respective markets; (2) there should be perfect information in that economy, meaning that all market participants are informed about all (equilibrium) prices and characteristics of goods; (3) there are no externalities; and (4) the products are private goods. (Philipsen 2003, pp. 10–11).

558 See e.g. Cooter and Ulen 2011, pp. 38–42; Philipsen 2003, pp. 10–19.

559 In this book, externality generally refers to the negative externality.

560 Cooter and Ulen 2011, pp. 39–40.

benefit or cost that spills over onto third parties who are not involved.[561] Based on this definition, the externality can be categorized into two basic types: the positive externality (the external benefit) and the negative externality (the external cost). Taking business activity as an example, while companies are producing goods or service for consumption, they may also generate some adverse effects (such as waste disposal, water and air pollution) onto third parties (like local communities and the environment). An externality is quite relevant for the case of CSR/CER, because environmental pollution is considered as a typical example of a (negative) externality.

From the perspective of companies, the negative effects of their business operations on third parties are externalities, and they usually lack incentives to internalize these externalities at the expense of corporate profits. Since these externalities are not internalized, there is a divergence between private cost and social cost.[562] The private cost only refers to the cost of production, and the social cost refers to the sum of private cost and other additional costs. In this case, the additional costs mainly refer to the costs to internalize externalities. Welfare economics, therefore, perceive the overall market under this circumstance as not Pareto-efficient. In other words, it means that the existence of an externality results in a market failure. Therefore, an important question arises as to how to motivate firms to take the internalization of externalities into account.

2.2 *Information Asymmetry*

The second source of market failure is information asymmetry, which refers to an imbalance of information between parties in transactions. The asymmetric information causes market distortions in the form of adverse selection and moral hazard. The risk of adverse selection was first discussed in the insurance market,[563] but this discussion also finds its importance in other markets, such as the labour market and the product market. The well-known phenomenon of adverse selection is developed by George Akerlof,[564] who established a model by using cars as an example to elaborate the problem of adverse selection and its effects on the market. Akerlof held that due to the asymmetric information concerning the quality of cars between sellers and buyers, the products with 'bad' quality (which is referred to as a lemon in his paper) would drive out those with good quality in the market. Akerlof described this situation as the 'market for lemons'.

---

561 The concept of externality has been defined by many scholars. For more discussion on the basic theories of externality, see e.g. Baumol 1988; Buchanan and Stubblebine 1962, pp. 371–384.

562 Dahlman 1979, p. 141.

563 Cooter and Ulen 2011, pp. 48–49.

564 Akerlof 1970, pp. 488–500.

The problem of adverse selection is quite relevant for CSR/CER, considering that it may also result in the 'market for lemons' in the green market.[565] Supposing that environmentally conscious consumers have a demand for green products, it will, of course, lead to an increase in the supply of green products.[566] A danger that may cause severe negative effects on the green market is that sellers have the possibility to opportunistically utilize consumers' demands for green products, because in general, they have more information about the quality of their products or service than consumers (i.e. buyers). In this case, the information mainly refers to whether their products or services contain environmental attributes. More importantly, it seems more advantageous for sellers to provide 'brown' products under the banner of green products. As a result, the green products will be driven out by the 'brown' products.[567]

In practice, several strategies are designed to cure the problem of 'market for lemons', such as the eco-labelling system and CSR/CER information disclosure. However, the effectiveness of these regimes to a large content depends on whether they are credible. Taking CSR/sustainability reporting as an example, today the general public is overwhelmed with a flood of information regarding corporate sustainability performance, but the quality of information disclosure has become a long-standing concern. A fundamental premise is that this self-reporting mechanism is derived from the public trust in what the companies have claimed in their reports. In this case, the risk of information asymmetry is that a company may selectively disclose the positive information concerning its social or environmental performance and hide the negative information, to build a good image. This risk is also well-known as greenwashing, which may damage public trust in companies and in this system.[568]

2.3 *Public Goods*

Another instance of market failure is the public goods, which refer to "commodities the benefit from which is shared by the public as a whole",[569] such as national security, fresh air, and lighthouse. This definition suggests

565 Green market refers to a distinguished market where environmentally friendly products and services are more desirable.

566 Green product can be generally described as a type of product with good environmental attributes or that has fewer negative environmental effects. Available at: http://www.isustainableearth.com/green-products/what-is-a-green-product (Accessed on February 26, 2017).

567 In this book, brown product is described as the opposite type of green product.

568 Green washing refers to the fact that the environmental claims made by the label cannot be sustained. (Martinez 2013, p. 134).

569 Ogus 1994, p. 33.

two fundamental characteristics of public goods: non-rivalry[570] and non-excludability.[571] In this respect, public goods could be an appropriate starting point for the discussion of CSR/CER, because the environmental goods and externalities are often characterized as non-rivalry and/or non-excludability.[572] The traditional paradigm views the internalization of environmental externalities as one of the most fundamental tasks for the government. In this view, the private provision of public goods seemingly goes against this classic dichotomy of duties between the government and business.[573] However, the recent literature[574] has shed light on the feasibility and desirability of private provision of public goods, due to the limitations of governments in providing public goods in some cases. A typical example of the private provision of public goods is that individuals make donations for public preference. In this sense, CSR/CER can be regarded as "the corporate provision of public goods or curtailment of public problems independent of legal benchmarks."[575] Thereby, a key question arises here why companies would like to act in line with public preference rather than simply the preference of their shareholders. More importantly, does the corporate provision of public goods have a positive or adverse effect on the total social welfare?

Advocates of CSR/CER basically argue that in some cases public goods may be naturally bundled with the production of private goods.[576] In practice, it is quite common for the business community to engage in the provision of public goods. Although the primary mission of companies is to produce private goods or service for consumption, it is observed that companies often produce public goods or a joint product bundled with both private and public goods in this process.[577] This joint provision of private and public good is described as an 'impure public good'.[578] Eco-product or green product is an example of this 'impure public good', which is constituted by a private product and a public good associated with good environmental attributes. For example, when a vehicle

570 Non-rivalry means that the consumption of public goods by one person does not leave less for any other consumer. (Cooter and Ulen 2011, p. 40).

571 Non-excludability means that the costs of excluding nonpaying beneficiaries who consume the goods are so high that no private profit-maximizing firm is willing to supply the goods. (Cooter and Ulen 2011, p. 40).

572 Kitzmueller and Shimaschack 2010, pp. 54–55.

573 See Section 3.1.

574 For more discussion on the private provision of public goods, see e.g. Andreoni 1988, pp. 57–73; Bergstrom *et al.* 1986, pp. 25–49; Warr 1983, pp. 207–211; Kotchen 2006, pp. 816–834.

575 Kitzmueller and Shimshack 2012, pp. 55–56.

576 Besley and Ghatak 2007, p. 1647.

577 Kitzmuller and Shimschack 2010, p. 55.

578 Buchanan 1968.

company decides to produce hybrid cars or less polluting cars, they also make a contribution to the improvement of air quality. In this case, consumers also make their contributions to the provision of public goods by purchasing this type of environmentally friendly cars. Moreover, companies are also rewarded by consumers' willingness to pay a premium. In this case, the corporate provision of public goods results in an increase of total welfare. Besley and Ghatak described this situation as "sustaining a level of public provision".[579]

To summarize, the existence of CSR/CER can be considered as a contribution to curing market inefficiency by the business community. Some scholars hold that companies' endeavour to cure a market failure may lead to a Pareto-efficient result where the maximization of social welfare may be achieved.[580] However, in some cases, CSR/CER activities do not solve market failure, but create new problems, such as the risk of greenwashing.[581] Therefore, a key question is to what extent CSR/CER could cure the market failure and whether legal intervention is still needed for accompanying the success of CSR/CER.

3 CSR/CER and Governance Deficit

The governance deficit or regulatory failure is another important justification for CSR/CER. The classical dichotomy insists on the strict division of duty between the government and the corporation. The position of Milton Friedman in this respect is quite well-known. He insisted that the only responsibility of business was profit maximization, and the government assured the responsibility of the provision of public goods and the reduction of externalities.[582] Therefore, the emergence of CSR/CER is regarded as an invasion of the government's duty to tackle market failure, such as the internalization of externalities, and the provision of public goods.[583] With the rise of corporate power, the strict division of duty has gradually become blurred.[584] In fact, today more and more companies start to assume some responsibilities that have traditionally been regarded as duties of governments, such as environmental protection, labour rights, public health, and education.[585] This phenomenon implies that private actors like corporations could play a political role and act in line

579 Besley and Ghatak 2007, p. 1660.
580 Reinhardt *et al.* 2008, pp. 232–233.
581 For more discussion on greenwashing, see Section 4.1.2.
582 See e.g. Friedman 1970.
583 Kitzmuller and Shimschack 2012, p. 54.
584 See Chapter 2, Section 2.
585 Scherer and Palazzo 2011, p. 899.

with the benefits of society. This argument can be supported by the corporate provision of public goods as discussed above.[586] Many studies describe the political role of corporations in CSR/CER as 'political CSR/CER'.[587]

More particularly, it has been observed that private actors, such as corporations, do play a role in governance not only at the national level but also at the international level,[588] particularly in cases where the government fails.[589] This can be better illustrated by the historical fact that the development of CSR/CER was closely associated with addressing governance deficits.[590] Matten and Moon observed that CSR/CER encouraged companies to assume more responsibilities beyond the law particularly in the field where the government was facing limits to solve.[591] The development of CSR/CER in the UK is just a good example.[592] In the late 1970s and the early 1980s, the UK government was confronted with a serious governance crisis characterized by higher unemployment rates and urban riots. At that time, the Thatcher government decided to employ CSR/CER to address the serious governance deficit.[593] In fact, companies probably would like to voluntarily engage in addressing governance deficit to avoid the threats of potential legal intervention.[594]

In the age of globalization, the scope of CSR/CER has expanded from the national level to the international level, and the global CSR/CER also finds its importance for global business regulation. Due to the strong power and influence of MNEs, the negative impacts of international business on society and environment also substantially intensified during the past decades. However, the effectiveness of international business regulation is relatively weak or a failure in solving the problems caused by MNEs, which can be described as 'global governance deficit'.[595] What makes this situation even worse is that the national states are reluctant to impose regulations on international business, to a large extent due to the restriction of territory and the potential threats of hindering the domestic economic developments and weakening their national

586 See supra Section 2.3.

587 Political CSR refers to an extended model of governance with business firms contributing to global regulation and providing public goods. (Scherer and Palazzo 2011, p. 901).

588 Moon and Vogel 2008, pp. 314–317.

589 Matten and Crane 2005, pp. 166–179.

590 Moon and Vogel 2008, pp. 307–308 and p. 319.

591 Matten and Moon 2008, pp. 404–424.

592 For more discussion about the governance crisis in the UK, see Moon 2005, p. 54.

593 Moon and Richardson 1985.

594 See Chapter 3, Section 2.2.

595 See e.g. Moon and Vogel 2008, pp. 303–326; Scherer and Palazzo 2008, pp. 413–431; Levy and Kaplan 2008, pp. 432–451.

competitiveness.[596] As a result, Moon and Vogel argued that a regulatory vacuum of international business was created by the deficit of both national governments and international organizations.[597]

In this context, the appeal for MNEs to assume more responsibility for addressing global issues, such as the global environmental crisis, is becoming much stronger than ever.[598] Global CSR/CER is regarded as "a possible response to the failure of national and international business regulation."[599] Vogel described global CSR/CER as a new dimension of 'global civil regulation'.[600] In other words, CSR/CER may be quite important where the national and international business regulations fail.

Global CSR/CER may play an especially important role in the emerging market, like China, where the government may be more vulnerable to serious governance deficit, such as corruption, low standards, weak enforcement, and the unwillingness to impose regulation on foreign investments. Therefore, the role of CSR/CER in China and its relationship with environmental regulation of course merit further and detailed research in this book.[601]

4 Possible Approaches to Addressing Environmental Pollution

The traditional law and economics approach to environmental problems is that a variety of legal and policy instruments can be needed to internalize (environmental) externalities.[602] Only in the case where transaction costs would be low, could this internalization automatically take place via the Coase theorem, which equally has some relevance for the discussion of CSR/CER (4.1). Otherwise, a market failure will remain, as a result of which some form of legal intervention will be necessary (4.2). In this regard, the question arises of to what extent one could rely on self-regulation (4.3).

596 Moon and Vogel 2008, p. 310.

597 Moon and Vogel 2008, pp. 303–326.

598 Levy and Kaplan 2008, pp. 432–451.

599 Moon and Vogel 2008, p. 309.

600 Vogel perceived global civil regulation as a type of voluntary regulation for addressing the social and environmental impacts of global firms and markets without governmental intervention. (Vogel 2008, pp. 261–282)

601 For more discussion on the relationship between CSR/CER and China's environmental regulation, see Chapter 8 and Chapter 9.

602 The traditional instrument for environmental protection is environmental regulation, and governmental officials at various levels are responsible for developing, implementing and enforcing the public environmental regulation. (Van den Bergh 2013, pp. 130–133).

4.1 *The Coase Theorem*

The traditional starting point for any economic analysis of environmental pollution is well known as the Coase theorem.[603] Coase stated that if transaction costs are zero (or low),[604] an optimal allocation of resources (hence, also an internalization of an externality) will automatically follow without any necessity for the legal system to intervene. When applied within the context of the corporation, the Coasean transaction happens between a company (as a whole entity) as one party and the stakeholders of the company as the other party, such as its employees, consumers, investors, suppliers. Pointing at the importance of (implicit) negotiations (via the price mechanism) and hence of the importance of the market, the Coase theorem also finds its relevance for CSR/CER in some cases.

4.1.1 The Relevance of the Coase Theorem for CSR/CER

A lesson from the Coase theorem is if it were possible to differentiate various consumer groups, corporations could engage in product differentiation, whereby, for example, fair trade or organic products would be provided to those consumer groups who would have a specific demand. This business strategy can be described as 'product differentiation' or branding, and CSR/CER is frequently regarded as "a means of product differentiation" in today's business world.[605] The assumption of this strategy is that consumer groups would be willing to reward corporations that meet their critical demands for 'green' products, by paying a correspondingly higher price.[606] This assumption is substantiated by the incremental willingness of consumers to pay for environmentally friendly and socially responsible products.[607] If environmentally conscious consumers prefer higher environmental standards and have a willingness to pay a corresponding price, the resulting product differentiation perfectly fits into the Coase theorem. Thus, this would as such, as the Coase theorem assumes, not entail a need for additional regulation. Moreover, in this hypothesis, CSR/CER also perfectly fits into the profit maximization rationality, since corporations would be rewarded for investments in higher environmental standards by consumers. Going beyond environmental compliance and thus investing more in environmental protection may lead to additional costs which correspond to

603 Coase 1960, pp. 1–44.

604 Coase held that transaction costs included search costs, bargaining costs, and monitoring costs.

605 Kitzmueller and Shimshack 2012, p. 65.

606 *Id*, p. 64.

607 *Id*, p. 72.

higher prices. However, since consumers demand the application of higher environmental standards, the higher prices do not result in a loss, but may rather serve as a market argument.

Today, product differentiation or branding has become a prevailing business strategy for firms. Examples include the Body Shop, organic food, etc. The Body Shop achieves its success in the competitive cosmetic industry, by creating its ethical brand images, such as using natural-derived ingredients, being against animal testing, treating people well, supporting community fair trade and protecting the planet.[608] It turns out that the ethical business strategies do work. According to a consumer survey of The Body Shop, their natural and fair trade products are becoming a purchasing trend among consumers. Also, it is assumed that 83% of their regular customers tend to choose products or services from retailers that take social and environmental issues seriously, and meanwhile 64% of them are willing to pay a premium for an ethical product.[609]

Another example is the global boom in the production and consumption of organic food. Today more and more people are becoming passionate or even obsessed with organic food, because it is typically advertised as safer, healthier and more nutritious than conventional food. Largely due to consumers' concerns about well-being, health, and environmental protection, a sharp increase has been observed in organic food sales. For example, the estimated sales of organic products in the U.S in 2012 amounted to $28.4 billion US dollar, which accounted for over 4 percent[610] of total food sales. In Germany—the largest market for organic food in Europe, the organic food sales reached € 6.6 billion EUR and the total food sales reached € 170 million EUR, accounting for about 4 percent of the total food sales in 2011, and in 2013 the organic food sales reached more than € 7.6 billion EUR.[611] Also, the increasing demand for organic food shows consumers' willingness to pay a premium for purchasing organic food.

---

608 For more information about the story of the Body Shop, available at: https://www.thebodyshop.com/nl-nl/ (Accessed on April 13, 2017).

609 The data is from The Body Shop International Values Report 2011. Available at: http://www.thebodyshop.com/content/pdf/global-values_report.pdf (Accessed on February 26, 2017)

610 The percentage varies depending on different food categories. For example, organic products account for larger shares in some categories, such as dairy, fresh fruits and vegetables.

611 The data is from a report The Food & Beverage Industry in Germany (Issue 2012/2013) of Germany Trade & Invest (GATI). Available at: http://www.gtai.de/GTAI/Content/EN/Invest/_SharedDocs/Downloads/GTAI/Industry-overviews/industry-overview-food-beverage-industry-en.pdf (Accessed on February 26,2017).

4.1.2 The Limits of the Coase Theorem

To what extent the Coase theorem is successfully applied may depend on several factors, such as the bargaining power of two parties, the existence of strategic behaviour, and the zero-transaction cost condition.[612] In practice, the application of the Coase theorem for CSR/CER also meets some constraints, of which one significant limit is known as the risk of greenwashing.

As indicated above, one important condition for this product differentiation case is that companies can signal their environmental attributes to the market and particularly to the consumers who have this special preference. Eco-labels are one of the most widely employed tools by companies to convey relevant environmental information about their product to the appropriate consumers. As a result, it is not a surprise to witness the substantial increase of eco-labels during the last few years. According to the latest data from the Ecolabel Index, there are 465 eco-labels in 199 countries and 25 industry sectors.[613] However, the danger is that this market may only work if consumers can trust the environmental claims that are made. In practice, the risk of greenwashing means that companies will selectively disclose the positive information on their environmental or social performance, and withhold the negative information on these dimensions, so as to create an overly positive corporate image. Also, more importantly, because eco-labelling is a voluntary mechanism for rather limited regulation and weak enforcement, firms can easily get away from punishments. Therefore, greenwashing is quite common in the green market. The results of some studies showed that more than 90 percent of consumer products claiming to be green are greenwashed, which means that environmental claims made by the eco-labels are not substantiated.[614]

As discussed above, from a law and economics perspective, greenwashing is a market failure and in particular an adverse selection problem. According to the economic model of greenwashing established by Lyon and Maxwell,[615] greenwashing can be utilized as an opportunistic business strategy. Companies can choose whether they will disclose environmental information or withhold it, or what information they would like to disclose, positive or negative type, or to what extent they would like to publicize it all or partially, based on the cost-benefit analysis of this strategy. As a result, it will lead to a 'market for lemons'[616] in which 'brown' products marked by misleading or even

612 Faure and Weishaar 2012, pp. 400–401.
613 The relevant data is available at: http://www.ecolabelindex.com/ (Accessed on April 13, 2017).
614 Martinez 2013, p. 134.
615 Lyon and Maxwell 2011, pp. 3–41.
616 Akerlof 1970, pp. 488–500.

false eco-labels will remain in the market while the 'green' products with genuinely good environmental performance may be driven out of the market. In other words, greenwashing is a significant problem that has adverse effects on the eco-labelling mechanism. Since the effectiveness of the eco-labelling mechanism largely depends on consumers' trust, the risk of greenwashing can damage consumers' confidence on green products marked by eco-labels and thereby erodes their willingness to pay a premium for green products.

The evidence of greenwashing indicates the need for accompanying regulation. In other words, regulation is not only necessary but also needed to deter greenwashing, which could take place via a certification, e.g. eco-labelling schemes. Again, also certification is a form of a self-regulatory scheme. There are criticisms on certification schemes as well (such as weak standards, ineffective enforcement), and the empirical evidence also proves that a certification system alone is not enough to deter greenwashing. Hence, there may be some role for government intervention in supporting the certification of eco-labelling schemes and it is assumed that the role of government in regulating eco-labelling is critical because governmental intervention provides some coercion for consolidating the eco-labelling mechanism.[617]

This section only discussed the application of the Coase theorem in the case of product differentiation. Of course, the Coase theorem can also be applied in various cases. For example, some employees may prefer to work in a company with a good reputation on social or environmental responsibility, so some companies may adjust their business strategy or policy on CSR/CER to attract or retain high-quality employees. Based on the analysis above, we suppose that regulation may equally be needed in all other cases where environmental externalities cannot be internalized via the low transaction costs setting as presented in the Coase theorem.

4.2 *Legal Intervention*[618]

One important condition for the Coase theorem is the low or zero transaction cost, but in reality, critics could argue that the Coase theorem will not be applied in practice due to information problems (and hence high transaction costs). In other cases, environmental harm may have a wide-spread nature, latency problems may occur, or the number of potential injurers and victims

---

617 For more discussion on the regulation of eco-labeling, see Chapter 6, Section 4.2.2.

618 The legal intervention to internalize market failure will be briefly introduced in this section. For more discussion about the relationship between CSR and legal intervention, see Chapter 6.

is simply too large, making Coasean bargaining impossible. In that case, the market failure constituted by the negative externality will remain, and some legal intervention will be indicated. Moreover, some scholars argue that internalizing externalities is the main goal of the environmental law, and the legal intervention, in this case, is unavoidable.[619] The legal invention can also be presented in different forms.

4.2.1 Environmental Liability

First, one possibility is to use the deterrent effect of liability rules, hence of environmental liability.[620] By imposing accident costs[621] on potential parties, liability rules provide them with incentives to pay attention to the consequences of their behaviour and thus to minimize the accident costs. However, it has been argued that private law solutions (like liability rules) may not be effective under some circumstances. Shavell[622] examined the choice between liability rules and safety regulation, by establishing some criteria to decide which one is more socially desirable. According to Shavell, liability rule may be ineffective and safety regulation will be more desirable, when the government holds better information on optimal abatement techniques, when insolvency problems arise, and when for some reasons a liability suit for environmental damage can never be brought.[623]

4.2.2 Command and Control Regulation

As indicated above, Shavell posited several conditions under which environmental regulation may be more effective than liability rules, and therefore public law approach for addressing environmental pollution is still needed. Empirical evidence also confirms that the quality of the environment has improved substantially as a result of regulatory efforts and not so much in response to the legal action in tort.[624] Government intervention should, however, not always necessarily take the form of safety standards set by the government. The latter is also referred to as so-called command and control

619 Faure and Niessen 2006, p. 26.

620 Shavell 1980, pp. 1–25.

621 Calabresi 1970.

622 Shavell 1984, pp. 357–370.

623 For example, because the damage can be wide-spread, victims can believe damage has natural causes, victims cannot be identified, and long latency periods and problems of causation may exist. (Shavell 1984, pp. 357–370).

624 Dewees and Trebilcock 1996, p. 315.

regulation.[625] An alternative would consist of so-called economic or market-based instruments.[626] The empirical evidence indicates that the relative effectiveness of either command and control or market-based instruments is very much dependent upon the specific context, type of pollutant regulators, institutional design, and other elements.[627]

4.2.3 Economic/Market-Based Instruments[628]

The traditionalists view environmental pollution as one of the most important tasks for the government, and the government has a variety of instruments to fulfil this task, such as regulation, policies, and economic instruments. Among the various tools, preference for the economic or market-based instruments has been advocated by the traditional economic paradigm.

One possibility is to impose an environmental tax on polluting activities, which is also well-known as the 'Pigouvian tax'.[629] Economists argue that by imposing a tax on the firm which equals the marginal benefits and marginal costs of pollution activities, firms would have enough incentives to engage in internalizing externalities. Compared to the traditional command and control environmental regulation, environmental taxation has some advantages, such as environmental effectiveness, economic efficiency, the ability to raise public revenue, and transparency.[630] Empirical evidence also shows the effectiveness of environmental taxation in abating environmental pollution, such as water pollution, air emission, and waste disposal.[631]

Another possibility is the emission trading system, also known as the tradable or marketable pollution permits.[632] The emission trading system aims to influence polluters' activity by issuing pollution permits with a specific amount of emissions pre-determined by policy makers.[633] Today, the tradable permits have become a prevailing tool for the government to control pollution, and the European Emissions Trading System (ETS) is a good example.

---

625 The command and control regulation may refer to a direct regulation of activities prescribed by legislation that clearly states what is permitted and what is illegal.

626 See supra Section 4.1.

627 Faure 2012, pp. 309–310.

628 For more discussion on market-based instruments, see e.g. Faure and Weishaar 2012, pp. 399–421.

629 Pigou 1951.

630 OECD 2011.

631 *Id.*

632 Johnston 2007, pp. 353–385.

633 *Id.*

4.3 *Private/Self-Regulation*

4.3.1 The Economic Analysis of Self-Regulation

As discussed in the previous chapter,[634] CSR/CER can be simply defined as "going beyond mere compliance on a voluntary basis".[635] In that sense, CSR/CER could be considered as a form of self-regulation,[636] whereby corporations would voluntarily go beyond compliance with environmental standards prescribed by governmental regulation. In some cases, other parties may stimulate corporations to engage in CSR/CER. Of course, many environmental NGOs, in a consultation with corporations, will try to convince corporations to move towards CSR/CER. In other cases, it is more particularly buyers in the supply chain that impose high(er) environmental standards upon their suppliers. The latter is referred to as supply chain control or private environmental governance.[637] The latter can equally be important in the context of China: often large retail chains downstream in the supply chain (often situated in Europe and in the US) may impose private environmental (for example food safety) standards on providers upstream in the supply chain, sometimes located in China. Via this supply chain control, private parties (buyers) will impose high standards upon suppliers in order to be able to correspond to demands of consumer markets in Europe.[638]

Again, the contracting via the supply chain control to a large extent fits into the notion of private contracting and can thus be considered as an application of the Coase theorem. Self-regulation more generally has in some cases been advanced in law and economics literature as an effective tool to regulate externalities at lower costs than via government regulation. Arguments presented in the law and economics literature in favour of self-regulation[639] relate *inter alia*

634 See Chapter 2.

635 Kitzmueller and Shimshack 2012, p. 53.

636 Ogus defined self-regulation in four types: (1) formally binding, non-compliance leading to public law or private law sanctions; (2) codes of practice which presumptively apply unless an alleged offender can show that some alternative conduct was capable of satisfactorily meeting the regulatory goals; (3) norms the breach of which leads to non-legal sanctions, such as ostracism; or (4) standards compliance with which is purely voluntarily. (Ogus 2000, pp. 587–602).

637 Van den Bergh 2013, pp. 129–199.

638 For example, the flower industry of Colombia, as one of the major exporters of cut flowers to Europe, had created the Florverde program to encourage members to adopt a set of environmental friendly standards, in order to satisfy the high standards of the European Union. (Lyon and Maxwell 2008, p. 244).

639 Miller has posed three arguments in favor of self-regulation inter alia the specific knowledge of professionals, the flexibility of self-regulating agencies and the lower costs of self-regulation. (Miller III 1984, p. 897).

to higher expertise of the stakeholders involved (thus leading to lower information costs), lower organizational and administrative costs, and to the fact that business actors may have a larger willingness to apply norms and standards that they would have created themselves.[640] Self-regulation could in that sense lead to a 'crowding in' of norms.[641] The main advantage of self-regulation from that perspective would be that it could lead to a higher intrinsic motivation of stakeholders to comply, given that they were involved in the creation of the norms and standards. All aforementioned factors may be seen as valuable arguments in favour of CSR/CER, even as a cost-efficient alternative to governmental (command and control) regulation.

However, the law and economics literature on self-regulation has equally argued that there are many problems with self-regulation as well.[642] One problem is that there may be free-riding of particular members. Therefore, some may join the body that would be responsible for self-regulation, thus benefiting from reputational gains with no incentive to comply with the agreed standards. Second, compliance with self-regulation is also based on a voluntary system. Enforcement may hence be weak, which can be particularly risky since some emissions can cause substantial environmental harm. Indeed, there are a few typical features of environmental pollution which might make it an unsuitable candidate for self-regulation (only), such as the latency problems,[643] and the widespread scope of the environmental damage, the causal uncertainty and the transboundary nature of environmental pollution. All those typical features of environmental pollution may make it substantially more difficult to solve via self-regulation. Consequently, government intervention, either via command and control or market-based instruments, may still be the primary tool needed to control environmental externalities.

4.3.2 The Application of Self-Regulation

Nevertheless, there are some successful stories with respect to private environmental governance. For example, private supply chain standards are becoming a popular business strategy for more and more companies (buyers) who would like to impose private environmental standards on their suppliers. Wal-Mart shares some experience in this respect. In order to achieve the target of a safe and responsible supply chain, Wal-Mart imposes high standards on

640 See e.g. Cheffins 1997.

641 See e.g. Frey 1997, pp. 56–57 and p. 64; Frey 1999, pp. 395–408.

642 For more discussion on the problems with self-regulation, see e.g. Philipsen 2003.

643 Indicating a potential long time lapse between the moment of the emission and the moment that the damage may occur.

their suppliers regarding their social and environmental conditions.[644] With regard to the environment, besides the mandatory compliance with domestic environmental law, local laws and regulations, and international treaties and protocol, Wal-Mart requires its global suppliers to comply also with its specific standards on waste management, air emissions management, water management, energy consumption and greenhouse gas management, land use and biodiversity, environmental management system, hazardous substances management and pollution prevention, noise pollution and nuisance.[645] A similar strategy is implemented by the Body Shop. In order to manage the sourcing process of natural ingredients, it requires new suppliers to comply with its ethical, social and quality criteria, besides the compliance with legal and financial checks.[646] However, as mentioned before, many of those cases relate to examples where traders already comply with basic mandatory environmental standards, and CSR/CER (in all of its different forms and shapes) mainly presents an instrument to go beyond compliance with mandatory standards without being a substitute for those standards.

Although there are a variety of instruments for policymakers at their disposal for addressing environmental pollution, recent literature has also indicated that each of these instruments has its strengths and weaknesses. In practice, policymakers cannot solely count on one specific type of these instruments. Therefore, the optimal mixes of these instruments have become an important task for policymakers.[647] This section only provides an overview of these instruments from a law and economics perspective, and the issues about the optimal regulatory mix will be further presented in Chapter 6.

5 Complication: Principal-Agent Problem

So far, our analysis is based on an assumption that the interests of the managers and the shareholders were aligned. However, the situation may be more

644 Wal-Mart publishes and regularly updates Standards for Suppliers, which are utilized to evaluate employment practices and environmental compliance in facilities producing merchandises for sale by Wal-Mart. The latest version was adopted in April, available at: http://corporate.walmart.com/global-responsibility/ethical-sourcing/standards-for-suppliers (Accessed on February 26, 2017).

645 Wal-Mart' Standards for Suppliers. Available at: http://corporate.walmart.com/global-responsibility/ ethical-sourcing/standards-for-suppliers (Accessed on February 26, 2017).

646 The Body Shop International Values Report 2011. Available at: http://www.thebodyshop.com/content/ pdf/global-values_report.pdf (Accessed on February 26, 2017).

647 Faure and Weishaar 2012, pp. 399–421.

complicated in reality, as a principal-agent problem may arise between shareholders and corporate managers. It is the well-known problem that there may be a conflict of interest between the shareholder (principal) and the manager (agent), which is to be solved in what is now commonly referred to as corporate governance. As long as the interest of shareholders and managers align, there is obviously no problem. However, it is possible that there is a divergence of interest between shareholders and corporate managers concerning the corporate engagement in CSR/CER, which raises the question how to deal with those divergences.

A principal-agent problem can be generally defined as the conflict of interest between the principal and the agent, which is mainly due to the separation of ownership and control.[648] Within companies, this conflict could occur between the owners of companies (i.e. shareholders) and their managers, or between the majority shareholders and the minority shareholders, or between the firm and its other contractual parties, such as employees, suppliers, and customers.[649] But this section focuses on the discussion of the first type of agency problem, i.e. the conflict of interest between shareholders and the hired managers. In this agency problem model, managers are delegated authorities to act on behalf of the shareholders. However, a risk that endangers this model is that in practice managers have the possibility of abusing their discretion for their private interest. As a result, how to motivate managers to act in line with shareholders' interest has always been an important issue for the corporate governance literature.

5.1 *Shareholders Want CSR/CER; Managers Do Not*

The first scenario of the principal-agent problem refers to the hypothesis where shareholders would desire that the companies could engage in CSR/CER (or simply charity), but managers refuse. Especially in the case of altruistic CSR/CER, shareholders who desire a feeling of warm glow and would like to sacrifice some of their wealth for social welfare. But managers may refuse to enforce shareholders' altruistic desire, if "they are given a contract in which incentives are tied to the financial performance of the firm."[650]

In corporate governance literature, a variety of strategies has been designed for addressing this principal-agent problem. Kraakman *et al.* distinguish these strategies into two categories: regulatory strategies and governance

648 Posner 2003, pp. 440–442.

649 For more discussion on agency problems, see Kraakman *et al.* 2009.

650 Salazar and Husted 2008, p. 148.

strategies.[651] The regulatory strategies regulate managers' behaviour directly by imposing a fiduciary duty of care and loyalty. The duty of loyalty requires managers to conduct business "in good faith and in the best interests of the corporation", and the duty of care requires managers to "exercise that degree of skill, diligence, and care that a reasonably prudent person would exercise in similar circumstances."[652] Since the corporate fiduciary duty has been prescribed by law, the breach of fiduciary duty will lead to personal liability for managers.[653] From the perspective of corporate governance, there are six governance strategies to motivate and constrain director's behaviour, including selection and removal,[654] initiation and ratification,[655] and trusteeship and reward. Today, the reward strategy is widely employed by many firms to provide incentives for their directors. For example, in the United States, many chief executive officers (CEOs) are rewarded by stock ownership, in order to align their interests with shareholders' interests. In this case, CEOs' compensation is closely linked to stock price and therefore the financial performance of the firm. As a result, managers will have stronger incentives to act in line with profit maximization

Of course, the possibilities that are at the disposition of a shareholder will largely depend upon the corporation concerned and the applicable legal rules in the specific legal system.[656] However, it is well-known that the traditional remedies provided in corporate governance do not always serve to align interests of shareholders and managers.[657] Moreover, empirical evidence also indicates that the corporate fiduciary duty is largely unenforceable.[658] Hence, shareholders may fail in the sense that they are not able to enforce their preferences upon the management. Of course, the extent to which this problem will arise depends on the size of the corporation, but also upon the question of whether the particular shareholder has a majority or minority position, or more generally, whether the shareholder is able to control corporate policy or not. As the corporate governance literature has indicated, many problems can arise where the management is, more specifically in publicly held companies, not always acting in line with the preferences of the majority of the

651 Kraakman *et al.* 2009, pp. 37–45.
652 Reinhardt *et al.* 2008, p. 222.
653 Scalise 2005, p. 282.
654 Removal and selection refer to shareholders' appointment rights.
655 Initiation and ratification refer to shareholders' decision rights.
656 For a more detailed analysis from a corporate law perspective, see e.g. Olaerts and Schwarz (eds.) 2012.
657 See e.g. Ryan and Wiggins 2004, pp. 497–524.
658 Scalise 2005, p. 284.

shareholders.[659] Those principal-agent problems that generally affect corporate policy can therefore also lead to managers not always acting in correspondence with the preferences of the shareholders as far as CSR/CER is concerned.

5.2 *Managers Want CSR/CER; Shareholders Do Not*

The second hypothesis concerns the opposite one, being that shareholders do not want CSR/CER, but managers would nevertheless do so. Again, a classic principal-agent problem arises. This is the situation harshly criticized by the traditional economic paradigm mainly represented by Milton Friedman. He argued that a corporate executive, as an employee of shareholders, has a direct responsibility to conduct the business in accordance with shareholders' desires of "making as much money as possible while conforming to the core rules of the society, both those embodied in law and those embodied in ethical custom."[660] In this context, Friedman criticized managers, who deviated from profit maximization to practice CSR/CER, for cheating their employers, misallocating the society's resources, and destroying wealth.[661] Therefore, it would seem strange to posit a hypothesis where managers rather than shareholders would desire CSR/CER. Still, one could imagine a situation where e.g. institutional investors are completely indifferent as far as CSR/CER is concerned and where managers for a variety of reasons want to engage in CSR/CER, such as the ethical beliefs of managers and the potential risk of CEO turnover.[662]

Of course, managers always had discretionary funds at their disposition that they could use for the benefit of the corporation. To the extent that the discretionary use of those funds by the managers would substantially reduce shareholder wealth, the company would become a potential target for a corporate take-over for the simple reason that share prices would drop. In that case, the market for corporate control would lead to the replacement of the management that is not maximizing shareholder value.[663] But, more generally, shareholders obviously have other remedies at their disposition to align the performance of the managers with their interests.[664] Hence, this does not seem to be a problem that necessarily merits a specific remedy.

659 This can especially be the case where the ownership of shares is widely spread and dispersed as a result of which a group owning e.g. less than 50% of share can de facto control corporate policy.

660 Friedman 1970.

661 Friedman 1962.

662 See Chapter 3, Section 4.

663 *Id*, pp. 428–432.

664 See supra Section 5.3.

An important point with respect to regulation is obviously how one would have to cure principal-agent problems if they risk preventing the development of CSR/CER. As we have argued above, principal-agent problems may indeed arise concerning the desirability of CSR/CER. However, they do not seem specific or different from other principal-agent problems between shareholders and managers. Thus, this does not merit specific regulatory solutions since the traditional remedies for the principal-agent problem prescribed in the corporate governance literature can be applied.

6 Summary and Some Concluding Remarks

The starting point of this chapter is derived from the definition of CSR/CER as discussed in the previous chapters. Despite the conceptual uncertainty in this domain, the various definitions of CSR/CER do share the essential idea of this concept as "going beyond mere compliance with mandatory environmental standards on a voluntary basis". In this sense, CSR/CER could be regarded as a form of self-regulation and more particularly a type of private environmental governance. Therefore, this chapter provided a law and economic analysis of CSR/CER, by positioning it in the broader framework of addressing environmental issues.

From a traditional law and economic perspective, an internalization of environmental externalities should not be voluntary and hence should not take place via CSR/CER. As argued above, the market failure, particularly the environmental externality, should be cured either where possible through bargaining (if transaction costs are low) or through liability rules, command and control or market-based instruments.[665] However, CSR/CER, as a form of self-regulation did show various advantages over other approaches (particularly legal intervention), such as higher expertise of the stakeholders involved, lower organizational and administrative costs, and the fact that the business actors may have a larger willingness to apply norms and standards which they have created themselves. On the other hand, the governance deficit of the business regulation at both national and international levels also necessitates engagement in CSR/CER in addressing environmental pollution.

Based on the analysis above, we can see that CSR/CER does find its relevance and importance in curing a market failure and governance deficit. In this context, CSR/CER is viewed as complementary to environmental regulation for addressing some complicated social and environmental issues. However,

665 See supra Section 3.

this chapter also equally indicated that many problems remain with this self-regulatory approach. There may be various ways in which government could play a role in accompanying the success of CSR/CER. It is already indicated above that the product differentiation applied to a green market, may be problematic to a certain extent because eco-labelling often leads to greenwashing. Greenwashing could lead to an adverse selection, which equals the 'market for lemons' as a result of which no real green products (which are presumably more costly) would be put on the market. Regulation may be needed to cure this information asymmetry, for example via certification. However, certification of eco-labels should not necessarily take the form of government regulation since it can equally be based on self-regulation. Many of the current certification schemes for eco-labelling are already de facto based on self-regulation. However, some of these certification schemes do not go without criticism and have raised questions whether government regulation should intervene to accompany the certification process.[666]

Market failure resulting from information asymmetry could also occur related to environmental reporting by corporations. Consumers may be overloaded with sustainability reports or reports on CSR/CER performances by a variety of companies. However, for consumers, it may be very difficult to verify the environmental claims that are made in sustainability reports. This raises the question of the need for regulation, but once more to a large extent this can and has been cured through self-regulation. One can now increasingly notice the emergence of rating indexes whereby a variety of sustainability reports is indexed, compared and rated.[667] However, as mentioned in the previous chapter,[668] the emerging rating market is also faced with a range of challenges that may damage its effects on improving corporate environmental performance. In this case, there is also a need for government intervention to accompany the success of this self-regulatory market.

One aspect where CSR/CER may require regulation is in the international business domain, particularly in the so-called North-South relationship. Some argue that corporations, especially MNEs, from the North doing business in the South, have to comply with global CSR/CER guidelines, more particularly as far as respecting environmental norms and human rights are concerned. A problem is that often relocation to developing countries takes place because of lower standards and norms in developing countries which precisely reduces production costs for the industry from developing countries. This has led to

666 Martinez 2013.

667 See e.g. Dommerholt 2012, pp. 45–64.

668 See Chapter 4, Section 4.

quite a few conflicts; for example, with indigenous communities for violation of human rights in developing countries by multinational corporations.[669] As a result, scholars[670] have held that MNEs can be held liable on the basis of international law or even on the basis of national tort law for violations of human rights or environmental pollution. It is sometimes even held that CER/CSR would require MNEs from developed countries to apply the same standards in developing countries as they apply at home. That, however, raises the question whether one generally should impose the standards from the North to developing countries as well. Schäfer has rightly indicated that given the different level of development in the South such a requirement may lead to paternalism, forcing developing countries to come to e.g. safety and environmental standards for which they have no need and no preference.[671] However, this is a domain where undoubtedly regulation and more particularly international CSR/CER norms can play an important role.

Based on the analysis of this chapter, we can conclude that CSR/CER as a form of self-regulation has advantages over governmental regulation, such as the flexibility of self-regulating agencies low information cost and lower organizational costs.[672] Therefore, in this book, CSR/CER is viewed as a complementary, not an exclusive to environmental regulation in addressing some complicated environmental issues.[673] However, many problems remain with this self-regulatory approach. To the extent that government oversees this self-regulatory process (e.g. of sustainability reporting, eco-labelling, and certification), government regulation would merely play a supplementary role. It then fits into what is referred to as conditional self-regulation. The interdependencies between government regulation and CSR/CER and more particularly the specific roles of public authorities in promoting the development of CSR/CER definitely merit further research in the following chapters.

669 For an overview of this problem and various examples, see Choukroune 2013, pp. 50–80.
670 See e.g. Van Dam 2011, pp. 221–254.
671 Angara *et al.* 2010.
672 Philipsen 2003, pp. 37–38.
673 Moon and Vogel 2008, p. 312.

CHAPTER 6

Possible Roles of Public Authorities for Promoting CSR/CER

1 Introduction

The law and economic analysis from the previous chapter[674] shed light on the necessity of government intervention in supporting and promoting the development of CSR/CER in various ways. From the theoretical perspective, CSR/CER, as a kind of self-regulation, can be used as a supplement instrument to cure market failure on a voluntary basis. However, the law and economic literature also argues that it is not always effective to leave all the problems to the market. Many problems remain with this self-regulatory approach, such as the 'market for lemons' problem and principal-agent problem.[675] Therefore, the success of CSR/CER needs government intervention to be successful. Public authorities gradually recognize the importance of promoting CSR/CER where a governance deficit occurs in addressing social and environmental issues. Empirical research supports the idea that public authorities can play an important role in shaping and promoting the development of CSR/CER. To better understand the relationship between regulation and CSR/CER, two relevant questions will be answered in this chapter:

- Is there a role for regulation or, more generally government intervention, to accompany the process of CSR/CER?
- If so, what specific roles could governments play in promoting CSR/CER?

Section 2 starts with a literature review of the role of government in promoting CSR/CER. Moreover, this section also provides an inventory of policy instruments that could be used by public authorities to achieve their commitments to sustainable development and CSR/CER. Section 3 examines how those instruments can be employed in some selected areas, including sustainability reporting, sustainable consumption, sustainable public procurement, socially responsible investment, and awareness raising. Several examples will be presented in this section to illustrate the application of these instruments in practice. Section 4 introduces several important international CSR/CER

674 See Chapter 5.

675 *Id.*

 | DOI:10.1163/9789004368132_007

guidelines and principles, such as the United Nations Global Compact, the OECD Guidelines for Multinational Enterprises, and the ISO 26000 Guidance on CSR. Section 5 provides a summary and some concluding remarks.

2 Government as a Driver for Promoting CSR/CER

2.1 *The Role of Government in Promoting CSR/CER*

An extensive body of academic studies does shed light on possible roles of the government in promoting CSR/CER.[676] Despite the different research focuses, these studies convey the same idea that the government could play and actually does play an important role in the development of CSR/CER in various ways. The literature often takes different starting points in the categorization process but does converge as soon as one describes the tools and instruments which can be used. For example, Fox *et al.*[677] categorized four types of roles that government could play in this process, as mandating, facilitating, parenting and endorsing. McBarnet examined three types of relationship between CSR and the law as: (1) 'CSR beyond law', (2) 'CSR through law', and (3) 'CSR for law'.[678]

The study of Gond *et al.* stands out in this domain for a relatively comprehensive analysis of the relationship between CSR and government. According to Gond *et al.*, the relationship between CSR and government can be generally categorized into five ideal types. These five types of CSR-government relationships are not exclusive to each other. In practice, some CSR/CER public policies may reflect several types of relationships at the same time.

- The first type is CSR as self-government. This echoes our previously mentioned discussion of CSR/CER as a type of self-regulation, complementary to government intervention.[679]
- The second type is CSR as facilitated by government. Government could facilitate the development of CSR "through endorsement in the forms of speeches and other means of giving their imprimatur to business."[680]
- The third type is CSR as a partnership with government. Government could foster CSR by building a partnership with the business community and other stakeholders, like NGOs.

676 See e.g. Fox *et al.* 2002; Moon 2002, pp. 385–408; Moon 2004, pp. 1–27; McBarnet 2009, pp. 9–56; Moon and Vogel 2008, pp. 303–326; Steurer 2010, pp. 49–72.

677 Fox *et al.* 2002.

678 McBarnet 2009, pp. 9–56.

679 See Chapter 4.

680 Gond *et al.* 2011, p. 649.

- The fourth type is CSR as mandated by government. Government could employ a variety of regulatory approaches in mandating CSR.
- The fifth type is CSR as a form of government.[681] In the fifth type, CSR is regarded as a functional substitute in fulfilling government obligation, especially in situations where there is a regulatory vacuum.

On the basis of various studies, five important roles of public authorities for promoting CSR/CER are identified in this book, as mandating, facilitating, partnering, endorsing and demonstrating.

First, *the mandating role* means that public authorities can enforce CSR/CER by establishing specific minimum standards or prohibiting certain activities. In this mandating role, public authorities could employ a wide range of policy instruments, including laws, regulations, legal and fiscal awards and penalties. A good example is the French government's legislative measures to establish the compulsory non-financial information reporting mechanism.

Second, *the facilitating role* means that public authorities could create favourable conditions for encouraging environmentally responsible conduct. More particularly, it is observed that many companies expect governments to set a clear and consistent governmental expectation of CSR/CER. Moreover, companies also expect to receive some recognition if they can meet governmental expectations. In this context, public authorities have developed a wide range of public policies, which can be characterized as facilitating instruments. Examples include the national action plan on CSR/CER, awareness raising campaigns, economic incentives, taxes and subsidies, CSR/CER education, training and research program, and CSR/CER awards.

Third, *the partnering role* means that public authorities could build a collaborative network with private sectors as partners, by establishing a multistakeholder forum, organizing dialogues among a range of stakeholders, and developing cross-sector agreements and guidelines.

Fourth, the *endorsing role* means that public authorities could support and foster the development of CSR/CER by providing public political support in various forms, such as public procurement policies, business representatives in the policymaking process, CSR/CER label mechanism, and the demonstration of best CSR/CER practices.

Fifth, the *demonstrating role* means that public authorities could "demonstrate their leadership to business in the exemplary way that they engage with stakeholders or promote and uphold respect for fundamental rights."[682]

681 Gond *et al.* 2011, pp. 640–671.
682 *Id.*

This role is also called 'leading by example' or 'walking the talk'. Governments could make themselves a good example of CSR/CER through "making public procurement more sustainable; applying SRI principles to governmental funds (such as pension funds); adopting CSR management system and audits in governmental institutions; reporting on the sustainable performance of governmental bodies."[683]

This categorization above provides a possibility to distinguish between relevant options in the vast universe of public sector roles for promoting CSR/CER. It should be noted that there is no strict distinction between the various roles that public authorities can adopt for addressing specific CSR/CER issues, which means that in some cases government could act as a legislator, facilitator, or partner at the same time.

2.2 *Typology of Policy Instruments in Promoting CSR/CER*

A wide range of policy instruments is designed and applied by governments for promoting CSR/CER. It is observed that the CSR/CER policies present a significant diversity, not only with respect to the forms and methods used in the design of policy instruments, but also concerning the key issues they address.[684] This section provides the different types of policy instruments in CSR/CER and the main themes laid down in the international CSR/CER guidelines.

2.2.1 Typology by Type of Instrument

Policy instruments refer to "the set of techniques by which government authorities wield their power in attempting to ensure support and effect or prevent social change."[685] In this definition, government designs and employs a range of policy instruments to achieve their public goals. There are several different types of classifications in the current literature, such as the Anderson typology of basic policy choice (non-intervention and intervention), the simple twofold classification (normative and affirmative), and the threefold classification (coercive, remunerative and normative).[686] Vedung proposed a new typology by distinguishing the various policy instruments into three categories: (1) regulations, (2) economic means, and (3) information, which respectively can be metaphorically characterized as 'sticks', 'carrots' and 'sermons'.[687] However, in

683 Steurer 2010, pp. 49–72.
684 Steurer 2010, p. 57.
685 Vedung *et al.* 1998, p. 21.
686 Vedung *et al.* 1998, p. 21.
687 Vedung *et al.* 1998, pp. 29–30.

a real world, there are no 'one-size-fits-all' answers, and one single instrument may fail to address the complicated problems in many cases. A mix of different policy instruments has become a popular strategy for policymakers. For this purpose, one additional category was added to the Vedung's classification– the instrument mix.

The legal instruments (*'sticks'*)[688] refer to "a set of techniques undertaken by governmental bodies to influence people's behaviour, by means of publishing laws, directives, regulations, and decrees."[689]

The economic/ market-based instruments (*'carrots'*) refer to a set of tools that make use of economic incentives to influence others' behaviour. Some economic instruments are becoming more desirable to resolve environmental issues, such as environmental taxation and emission trading.[690]

The informational instruments (*'sermons'*) aim to influence people's behaviour or attitude by disseminating and exchanging relevant information. Examples are guidelines, manuals, websites, and brochures.

The instrumental mix refers to an optimal collaboration or combination of instruments mentioned above. Since each instrument has its own strengths and weakness, the combination of different instruments has become a popular strategy for policymakers. Therefore, there are two types of instrumental mix. One is partnering instruments,[691] in which different stakeholders collaborate to solve specific issues. This is a kind of co-regulation, such as a multi-stakeholder forum. Another type of instrumental mix is the hybrid instruments,[692] which combines various policy instruments to be more effective.

2.2.2 Typology by Themes and Issues

Given the multi-dimensional nature of the CSR/CER domain,[693] it is difficult to fully cover the wide range of social and environmental issues that corporations are expected to deal with. Therefore, the key themes and issues of CSR/CER also reflect the various areas of government policy. This section introduces a few examples of the theme-based classification in international CSR/CER policies.

The United Nations Global Compact focuses on four key areas in the domain of CSR/CER: human rights, labour rights, environmental protection, and

688 See supra Chapter 5, Section 2.3.
689 See Bemelmans-Videc, Rist and Vedung 2011.
690 See supra Chapter 5, Section 2.2.
691 Steurer 2010, p. 57.
692 *Id.*
693 See supra Chapter 2, Section 2.

anti-corruption.[694] *The OECD Guidelines for Multinational Enterprises* focus on the development of CSR in eight different policy areas of (1) human rights, (2) employment and industrial relations, (3) environment, (4) combating bribery, bribe solicitation and extortion, (5) consumer interests, (6) science and technology, (7) competition and (8) taxation.[695]

The European Commission's renewed strategy CSR puts emphasis on policy areas like sustainable consumption, public procurement, socially responsible investment, CSR education, training, and research.[696] A systematic analysis of CSR public policies at both the EU and the Member States level identified the five key CSR policy themes:[697]

1) raising awareness and building capacities for CSR among companies and stakeholders;
2) fostering philanthropy and charity;
3) fostering disclosure and transparency on economic, social and environmental issues of business activities;
4) fostering socially responsible investment (SRI); and
5) leading by example in particular by making public procurement more sustainable, applying SRI policies to governmental funds, adopting CSR management systems and audits in government institutions, and reporting on the sustainable development performance of government agencies.

3 Public Policies to Advance CSR/CER

This section explores in more detail how governments promote the development of CSR/CER by means of various policy instruments in five selected areas: (1) sustainability/CSR reporting, (2) sustainable consumption, (3) sustainable/green public procurement, (4) socially responsible investment, and (5) awareness raising for CSR/CER. By doing so, this section provides a more detailed insight into the vast universe of CSR/CER policies in specific areas.

---

694 For more discussion on the UN Global Compact, see Section 5.1.1.

695 For more discussion on the OECD Guidelines for Multinational Enterprises, see Section 5.2.

696 For more discussion on the European Commission' renewed strategy on CSR, see Chapter 7, Section 2.

697 Steurer *et al.* 2008.

3.1 *Sustainability or CSR/CER Reporting*

3.1.1 The Theory and Practice of Sustainability Reporting

A sustainability report refers to "a report published by a company or organization about the economic, environmental and social impacts caused by its everyday activities."[698] A sustainability report is presented periodically or annually and it can be presented in print or online. Moreover, a sustainability report has various formats, such as a stand-alone sustainable report (non-financial information), an integrated report (financial and non-financial). In this book, similar terms such as sustainability report, CSR report, corporate responsibility (CR) report, and environmental report are used interchangeably.

Sustainability reporting has become one of the priority areas in the field of CSR/CER, as the necessity and the value of sustainability reporting are widely recognized by the business community. To date, the disclosure of corporate social and environmental information has been widely accepted as a practical instrument to help companies measure, monitor, and manage the social and environmental impacts of their business activities. It is also recognized as a useful tool for companies to communicate their sustainable performance to shareholders and other stakeholders. In practice, it has been observed[699] that sustainability reporting has become a standard practice in the business world. According to a recent survey, 72% of companies included in the S&P 500 Index[700] claimed their involvement in sustainability reporting practice in 2013.[701] The data from GRI also showed that about 7205 organizations produced sustainability reports in 2015.[702] Despite this increasing popularity of sustainability reporting, several obstacles may hinder its further development.

The first obstacle is the variety of sustainability report formats. Despite many efforts made by the Global Reporting Initiative, there are no commonly accepted standards about how a sustainability report should be prepared and what content should be included in this report. As a result, the forms and the contents of the current sustainability reporting practice vary widely.

---

698 This definition is based on the information from the official website of GRI. Available at: https://www.globalreporting.org/information/sustainability-reporting/Pages/default.aspx (Accessed on March 2, 2017).

699 KPMG *et al.* 2013.

700 S&P 500 Index is an American stock market index based on the market capitalizations of 500 large companies having common stock listed on the NYSE or NASDAQ.

701 The data is based on the study of Governance and Accountability Institute, Inc. Available at: http://www.ga-institute.com/nc/issue-master-system/news-details/article/seventy-two-percent-72-of-the-sp-index-published-corporate-sustainability-reports-in-2013-dram.html (Accessed on March 2, 2017).

702 The data is based on the sustainability disclosure database of GRI. Available at: http://database.global reporting.org/ (Accessed on March 2, 2017).

The second obstacle is the insufficient number of the reporting companies. Although there is a remarkable increase in the number of companies that publish sustainability reports, the number is still very small compared to the existing number of all types of originations in total. It is observed that the majority of companies are still not engaging in sustainability reporting.[703] The question of how to motivate more companies to engage in sustainability reporting remains a big concern for policymakers.

The third obstacle is the questionable credibility levels of sustainability reports, which has become subject to enormous controversies. More particularly, corporate greenwashing scandals continue to create doubt on the credibility and the transparency of corporate information disclosure.

These three potential risks also explain why public authorities are expected to play a role in accompanying the success of the sustainability reporting mechanisms. The various sustainability reporting policies can be characterized into two basic types: the voluntary approach and the mandatory approach. There is an on-going debate on which approach prevails, and advocates of each approach have many arguments for and also against each other.[704] These two approaches do not contradict each other, and they are in fact highly complementary.[705] In this complementary relationship, the mandatory approach sets up the appropriate minimum standards or requirements for sustainability reporting. The reporting entities have the discretion to decide to what extent they would like to go beyond the mandatory reporting standards. The overlap between voluntary and mandatory approaches is widely observed in the existing sustainability reporting frameworks.[706] In recent years, both voluntary and mandatory sustainability reporting standards, guidelines and principles increased substantially.

3.1.2 Sustainability Reporting Policies and Guidance at the International and the National Level

3.1.2.1 *Global Reporting Initiative* (GRI)

At the international level, the reporting framework developed by Global Reporting Initiative (GRI) is regarded as the leading and most comprehensive sustainability reporting framework. GRI is an international NGO based on a global multi-stakeholder network, but the governmental organizations

703 Maguire 2011.

704 KPMG *et al.* 2010.

705 *Id.*

706 KPMG *et al.* 2013, p. 14.

play an important role in its history. GRI is formally inaugurated as a UNEP collaboration program, and it has a close partnership with the UN Global Compact and the OECD. There is a governmental advisory group within the GRI's network. This advisory group aims to help GRI to "better understand governments' perspectives on their role in corporate social responsibility and sustainability reporting."[707]

As a leading organization in the field of sustainability reporting, GRI continuously has worked on advancing the sustainability reporting agenda since the 1990s. GRI focuses on designing a comprehensive policy framework on sustainability reporting, which could be universally applicable to organizations of all types and sectors and also to be compatible with different reporting formats.[708] The GRI policy framework consists of three main blocks: the Sustainability Reporting Guidelines, Sector Guidelines, and other resources. The Sustainability Reporting Guidelines mainly provide the general guidance on the preparation of a sustainability report. The Sector Guidelines focus on the reporting issues in specific sectors, such as financial service, oil and gas, construction and food industry.

As the cornerstone of this framework, the Sustainability Reporting Guidelines were first launched in 2000 and have been updated four times.[709] The latest version is its fourth generation launched in May 2013 (the G4 Guidelines). The main aim of the G4 Guidelines is to provide a comprehensive and up to date guidance as to how to prepare effective sustainability reports, and how to promote the standard practice of sustainability reporting across the world. In order to avoid the potential risk of standards chaos,[710] the G4 Guidelines are designed as "a consolidated framework against different codes and norms".[711] The G4 Guidelines make references to other widely used frameworks, such as the UN Global Compact, the UN Guiding Principles on Business and Human rights, and the OECD Guidelines for Multinational Enterprises. Moreover, what makes the G4 Guidelines different from other frameworks in this domain is the emphasis on the principle of materiality. The materiality of sustainability reporting means that reporters only need to disclose information that is critical

---

707 For further information about the governmental advisory group, available at: https://www.globalreporting.org/network/network-structure/governmental-advisory-group/Pages/default.aspx (Accessed on April 16, 2017).

708 The sustainability report can be presented in the following formats: standalone sustainability reports, integrated reports, annual reports, reports that address particular international norms, or online reports.

709 The first Guidelines were launched in 2000, followed by the second generation (the G2 Guidelines) in 2002, and the third generation (the G3 Guidelines) in 2006.

710 De Hoo 2011, pp. 31–32.

711 GRI Sustainability Reporting Guidelines (the G4 Guidelines) 2013.

to their endeavours to achieve the goal of sustainability development and to manage their economic, environment and social impacts.[712]

The G4 Guidelines consist of two separate documents. The first document is the 'Reporting Principles and Standard Disclosures', which sets up a set of principles for reporting entities to prepare their reports 'in accordance with the G4 Guidelines'. The 'Reporting Principles' are categorized into two groups: the 'principles for defining report content'[713] and the 'principles for defining report quality'.[714] The 'Standard Disclosures' explains what information should be included in a sustainability report. The second document is an 'Implementation Manual', which provides guidance on how to understand, interpret and implement the 'Reporting Principles and Standard Disclosures' in preparing a sustainability report.

3.1.2.2 *EU Directive on Non-Financial Information Disclosure*

The European Union sets an example in promoting sustainability reporting practices by developing a series of policies. At the beginning of the 21st century, the European Commission had already recognized the importance and the necessity of encouraging corporate non-financial disclosure. In 2002, the European Commission published its first communication concerning CSR,[715] which explicitly stated that promoting convergence and transparency would be desirable in the fields of accounting, auditing, and reporting. In 2011, another communication entitled '*A renewed EU strategy 2011–2014*'[716] listed "improving company disclosure of social and environmental information" high on the agenda of the European Commission for its further actions in promoting CSR across Europe.

In December 2014, the European Commission adopted a directive specifically addressing CSR reporting issues—'*Directives on disclosure of non-financial and diversity information by certain large companies*' (Directive 2014/95).[717] By

712 GRI & ISO 26000, GRI G4 Guidelines and ISO 26000: 2010 How to use the GRI G4 Guidelines and ISO 26000 in conjunction, 2014. The report can be accessed at: http://www.iso.org/iso/iso-gri-26000_2014-01-28.pdf (Accessed on April 16, 2017).

713 Principles for defining report content include stakeholder inclusiveness, sustainability context, materiality, completeness.

714 Principles for defining report quality include: balance, comparability, accuracy, timeliness, clarity and reliability.

715 COM (2002) 347 final.

716 COM (2011) 681 final.

717 *OJ* L 330/1, 15.11.2014. This directive is an amendment of Directive on the annual financial statements, consolidated financial statements and related reports of certain types of undertakings (Directive 2013/34).

setting up the minimum legal requirements, this Directive aims to "enhance the relevance, consistency, and comparability of non-financial information disclosed by certain large undertakings throughout the Union."[718] This Directive prescribes that public-interest undertakings with more than 500 employees are subject to this directive and have an obligation to prepare a non-financial statement to report environmental matters, social and employee-related matters, human rights matters, and anti-corruption matters. The Directive does exclude small and medium-sized enterprises (SMEs) from the target group of these new disclosure requirements.

3.1.2.3 *Sustainability Reporting Policies at the National Level*

At the national level, today many governments have started to make non-financial information disclosure mandatory. According to a recent report from KPMG, about two-thirds of national reporting policies are mandatory.[719] Two examples will be highlighted here to show this development in different contexts: the French and the Chinese policy initiatives.

The French government sets an example in promoting sustainability reporting practice through the mandatory approach.[720] As early as in 2001, the French Parliament passed the New Economic Regulations Act (Nouvelles Régulations Economiques, NRE), which required companies listed on the stock exchange to disclose information about the environmental and social impacts of their activities. The NRE Act is regarded as the first legal framework for the French Parliament's efforts to make sustainable reporting a mandatory requirement for business.[721] Later, the Grenelle I Act (2009), and the Grenelle II Act (2010) were adopted, which indicated that the French government had taken a very strong stance in promoting sustainability reporting and non-financial information disclosure. In particular, the Grenelle II Act is regarded as a milestone for France towards mandatory sustainability reporting. The Article 225 of the Grenelle II Act required companies with over 500 employees to incorporate "information on the way in which society takes account of the social and environmental consequences of its activity as well as its societal commitments for sustainable development" in their annual report.

Sustainability reporting is a relatively new area in China. But the recent decade witnessed the rapid development of sustainability reporting in China.

---

718 *OJ* L 330/1, 15.11.2014.

719 KPMG *et al.* 2013, p. 13.

720 For more discussion on French mandatory information disclosure mechanism, see Chapter 7, Section 2.1.

721 Doucin 2013.

Particularly, the Chinese government has made significant efforts in regulating sustainability reporting practices. A variety of regulatory agencies has issued various policies on sustainability reporting. In 2008, the State-owned Asset Supervision and Administration Commission of China (SASAC) released *Guidelines to the State-owned Enterprise Directly under the Central Government on Fulfilling Corporate Social responsibilities,*[722] which encourage state-owned enterprises to actively engage in CSR practices. Article 18 prescribes that one of the main measures to fulfil their social responsibilities is to establish a CSR reporting system. In the same year, the then-State Environmental Protection Administration (SEPA) in partnership with the China Securities Regulatory Commission (CSRC) launched a new environmental economic policy—the 'Green Securities Policy',[723] which required the listed companies to disclose detailed information about their environmental records. As a response to government endorsement of sustainability reporting, the private sectors, such as the stock exchange, industrial associations, academic institutions, and NGOs also actively engage in developing their own reporting guidelines.[724]

The overview of sustainability /CSR reporting policies at the international and the national level showed that governments indeed take the lead in promoting and regulating sustainability reporting practices. A variety of sustainability reporting policies is regarded as an important driver for the development of sustainability reporting. However, the current policy framework on sustainability reporting has significant limits. Fox example, the target groups of mandatory reporting entities are still limited to the particular types of companies that meet a certain threshold, such as listed companies and companies with more than 500 employees. SMEs are exempted from the mandatory reporting obligations. Given that SMEs account for a substantial part of the economy in many countries, how to motivate SMEs to engage in sustainability reporting remains a big challenge for the further development of sustainability reporting practices.

3.2 *Sustainable Consumption*

3.2.1 The Importance of Sustainable Consumption

Sustainable consumption refers to "the use of services and related products which respond to basic needs and bring a better quality of life while minimizing the use of natural resources and toxic materials as well as emissions of waste and pollutants over the life cycle of the service or product so as not to

722 See Chapter 9, Section 2.

723 See Chapter 9, Section 2.4.1.

724 See Chapter 8, Section 2.6.

jeopardize the needs of future generations."[725] The concept of sustainable consumption is naturally related to sustainable development. Specifically, it has been widely acknowledged as the cornerstone of achieving the goal of sustainable development.[726] At the United Nations Conference on Sustainable Development (Rio+20), the concept of sustainable consumption and production (SCP) has been reaffirmed as "one of the three overarching objectives of, and essential requirements for sustainable development."[727]

Sustainable consumption also has substantial relevance in the discussion about CSR/CER. As mentioned in the previous chapter,[728] today consumers are aware of their roles and power in influencing companies' behaviour. In fact, consumers' increasing demands for goods or service with environmental attributes have become an important force to motivate more companies to engage in CSR/CER. If consumers express their preference for green products and also have a willingness to pay a premium for green products, companies could use product differentiation as a business strategy. This could, on the one hand, satisfy consumers' special demands, and on the other hand, enhance the competitiveness of companies in the market. In order to shed some light on the relation between CSE/CER and sustainable consumption, the book places an emphasis on the eco-labelling scheme in the consumer market.

3.2.2 Eco-Labelling—a Signalling Strategy to Identify Green Products

As mentioned before,[729] as an important instrument to identify green products, eco-labelling is very relevant to the discussion about CSR/CER. Today an increasingly popular tool for companies to differentiate their products from their competitors is known as eco-labels or environmental labels and declarations. According to ISO, eco-labels convey "the relevant information about a product or service in terms of its overall environmental character, a specific

725 The definition of sustainable consumption was proposed in the Oslo Roundtable on Sustainable Production and Consumption in 1994.

726 For further information on Rio+20, available at: https://sustainabledevelopment.un.org/rio20 (Accessed on March 5, 2017).

727 The Report of the United Nations Conference on Sustainable Development Rio+ states that "[w]e recognize that poverty eradication, changing unsustainable and promoting sustainable patterns of consumption and production and protecting and managing the natural resource base of economic and social development are the overarching objectives of and essential requirements for sustainable development." Available at: http://www.uncsd2012.org/content/documents/814UNCSD%20REPORT%20final%20revs.pdf (Accessed on March 5, 2017).

728 See supra Chapter 5, Section 1.1.

729 See supra Chapter 5, Section 1.1.

environmental aspect, or any number of aspects."[730] The eco-labels are now widely accepted as an important management and communication instrument for both companies and consumers. For companies, eco-labels can help them to measure their environmental performance and more importantly to communicate their environmental attributes to consumers and the market. For consumers, particularly for those who have specific environmental demands or preferences, eco-labels can help them to make the right purchasing decisions.

As a result, it is not surprising to witness the rapid growth of the eco-labelling market in recent years. However, several drawbacks of the current eco-labelling mechanism may endanger the quality and the positive effects of this dynamic market. The competition in the market of eco-labels (in particular those belonging to the same category) leads to a labyrinth of eco-labels, which may create confusion to consumers as to which labels are better and which labels to trust. In some cases, the label designs are too vague or ambiguous to understand. As mentioned above,[731] an important pre-requisite for eco-labelling as an adequate mechanism is that consumers could trust what companies have claimed through eco-labels and would reward companies by paying a premium. All these drawbacks will damage consumers' confidence about this mechanism in the end. Another significant risk of eco-labelling is known as greenwashing.[732] Greenwashing occurs due to the information asymmetry between producers and consumers in combination with the voluntary character of the eco-labelling mechanism. In this context, regulation (both public and private regulation) may be needed to deter greenwashing and to guarantee the transparency and credibility of eco-labels.

One way to overcome these problems is via certification (also well known as eco-labelling schemes). Certification refers to "voluntary, multiple-criteria-based third party program that awards a licence which authorizes the use of environmental labels on products indicating overall environmental preferability of a product within a particular product category based on life cycle considerations" (ISO 14024:1999).[733] Today a wide range of certification programs on eco-labelling are established and operated by both public and private

730 ISO 14020: 2000 'Environmental labels and declarations'.

731 See Chapter 5, Section 1.2.

732 Green washing refers to the fact that the environmental claims made by the label cannot be sustained. (See Martinez 2013, p. 134)

733 ISO categories eco-labels into three types: Type I Environmental Labelling (ISO 14024), Type II Self-declared Environmental claims made by manufactures (ISO 14021), and Type III Environmental Declarations (ISO 14025). The eco-labels mentioned in this paper refer to the type 1 labels.

organizations at the national and the international level. For example, some countries have initiated an eco-labelling scheme, such as the 'Blue Angel' initiated by Germany government, the 'Energy Star' run by the Environmental Protection Agency (EPA) of the U.S., and the 'Nordic Ecolabel' established by the Nordic countries. Some international organizations also developed various certification schemes in the different industrial sectors, such as 'Forest Stewardship Council' (FSC) in forest management, 'Rainforest Alliance', and 'Green Business Opportunities for the Global Plastic Card Industry'.

These certification schemes are voluntary guarantee mechanisms. This self-regulation approach has been frequently questioned for their weak standards and ineffective enforcement. This has become an important argument in favour of a more mandatory approach to regulating the eco-labelling schemes. In practice, the adoption of mandatory standards on eco-labels is increasing. The U.S. EPA, for example, imposed mandatory labelling requirements on pesticide products, by introducing the Pesticide Product Label System (PPLS) under section 3 of the Federal Insecticide, Fungicide, and Rodenticide Act (FIFRA).[734]

The EU eco-label regulatory framework is another good example as to how public policies are applied to encourage and guarantee higher environmental performance by means of eco-labelling. The EU has developed a series of directives and regulations on eco-labelling. In 2010, the EU eco-label schemes were established under the Regulation (EC) No 66/2010 on the EU Ecolabel,[735] in which the EU made its commitment to establish an EU eco-label scheme within its internal market. Further, the EU also introduces specific requirements and standards for eco-labels in different sectors, such as the food industry, the energy industry, the vehicle industry, and the chemical industry. Taking the food industry as an example, the EU issued two regulations to set up environmental criteria for the labelling of organic food: the regulation of organic production and labelling of organic products,[736] and the regulation laying down detailed rules on organic production and labelling of organic products with regard to organic production, labelling, and control.[737]

Based on the analysis above, we have seen that sustainable consumption, as an integral part of sustainable development, also plays an important role in promoting CSR/CER. In this context, a wide range of public policies has been developed to encourage sustainable consumption.

---

734 US EPA Pesticide Product Labels. Available at: http://www.epa.gov/pesticides/regulating/labels/product-labels.htm (Accessed on March 4, 2017).

735 *OJ* L 27/1, 30.1.2010.

736 *OJ* L 189/1, 20.7.2007.

737 *OJ* L 250/1, 18.9.2008.

3.3 *Sustainable Public Procurement (SPP) and Green Public Procurement (GPP)*

3.3.1 What Are SPP and GPP?

While the previous section focuses on the sustainable consumption in the private sector, this section has a look at sustainable consumption in the public sector. Public procurement refers to the behaviour of the public sector to purchase products, works, and services from the private sector, which are needed to better execute their functions for public purposes.[738] In this process, public authorities are not only the regulators but also one of the most influential consumers in the market. According to the recent data from the World Trade Organization (WTO), the spending of public procurement accounts for 10–15% of gross domestic product (GDP) of a national state.[739] With a demand in this volume, public procurement exerts a considerable influence on shaping the trends of production and consumption. Therefore, the management of public procurement is an important issue on the policy agenda of public authorities.

During a long period of time, the predominant benchmarks for measuring public procurement have been cost and efficiency.[740] Due to the rising need of sustainable development and CSR/CER in recent years, public authorities tend to integrate social and environmental criteria into their purchasing decision making. In this context, two new concepts are developed to align public procurement with sustainable development and CSR/CER, and they are sustainable public procurement (SPP) and green public procurement (GPP). Theoretically, the two concepts are not totally equivalent.

SPP refers to "a process whereby organizations meet their needs for goods, services, works and utilities in a way that achieves value for money on a whole life basis in terms of generating benefits not only to the organization, but also to society and the economy, whilst minimizing damage to the environment."[741]

GPP refers to "a process whereby public authorities seek to procure goods, services and works with a reduced environmental impact throughout their life cycle when compared to goods, services and works with the same primary function that would otherwise be procured."[742]

---

738 McCrudden 2007, p. 93.

739 This data is based on WTO's work on public procurement. Available at: https://www.wto.org/english/ tratop_e/gproc_e/gproc_e.htm (Accessed on March 3, 2017).

740 Steurer *et al.* 2007, p. 8.

741 Procuring the future—Stainable Procurement National Action Plan: Recommendations from the Sustainable Procurement Task Force. Available at: https://www.gov.uk/government/uploads/system/uploads/ attachment_data/file/69417/pb11710-procuring-the-future-060607.pdf (Accessed on April 16, 2017)

742 COM (2008) 400 final, p. 4.

The two definitions indicate that the difference between SPP and GPP lies in which criteria are taken into account for purchasing decision making. If multiple criteria are taken into account, such as social criteria, environmental criteria, innovation criteria, and human rights criteria, one can speak of SPP. On the contrary, GPP only focuses on the environmental criteria. Therefore, GPP is regarded as an important component of the broader SPP framework.[743]

In practice, public procurement policies constitute an important part of governmental policy agenda. An important question arises why governments should integrate social and environmental criteria into the public procurement process. The answer to this question can be simply articulated that the benefits of an open, sustainable and green public procurement market are clear and immense to the public authorities in various aspects.[744] First, public authorities could make use of the public procurement policies to achieve their policy targets and commitments to sustainable development and environmental protection. Second, by using their purchasing power, public authorities also set a good example to influence other market participants, such as suppliers, investors, and private consumers. Third, public authorities provide economic incentives for corporations to improve their environmental performance, such as managing their supply chain and developing green technologies.

3.3.2 Public Polices on Public Procurement

Many public sectors at both international and national levels have endorsed SPP and GPP as an important policy instrument to achieve their commitments to sustainable development. The European Union is a good example to illustrate the role of public authorities in implementing SPP and GPP at the policy level. In the Europe context, the public authorities at both EU and Member States levels are major consumers in the European market. The recent data

743 Steurer *et al.* 2007, p. 3.

744 The European Commission illustrates the multiple benefits of GPP in environmental, social, economic, and political aspects. For example, in the environmental field, GPP allows public authorities to achieve environmental targets, to set a good example for private consumers, raise awareness for environmental issues. GPP can also improve the quality of life, and help to establish higher environmental performance standards for products and services. The economic benefits of GPP include saving money and resources, providing incentives for industry innovation, and price reduction for environmental technologies. From the political aspect, GPP is an effective way to demonstrate the public sector's commitment to environmental protection and to sustainable consumption and production. For more discussion on the benefits of GPP, see '*Buying Green-a handbook on green public procurement*'. Available at: http://ec.europa.eu/environment/gpp/pdf/Buying-Green-Handbook-3rd-Edition.pdf (Accessed on March 4, 2017).

shows the expenditure of public procurements amounted to 14% of GDP.[745] The importance of GPP was explicitly recognized in the EU Communication on public procurement,[746] which provided guidance "on how to reduce the environmental impact caused by public sector consumption and to use GPP to stimulate innovation in environmental technologies, products, and services."[747] As a result, the European Commission has taken various actions to promote GPP within the EU market. The EU policy framework on public procurement mainly consists of three currently applicable directives: Directive 2014/24/EU on public procurement (the 'Public Sector Directive'),[748] Directive 2014/25/EU on procurement by entities operating in the water, energy, transport and postal services sectors (the 'Utilities Directive')[749] and Directive 2014/23/EU on the awards of concession contracts (the 'Concession Directive').[750] Compared to the old directives,[751] the 2014 procurement directives ensure the inclusion of the social and environmental targets into the process of public procurement,[752] such as "environmental protection, social responsibility, innovation, combating climate change, employment, public health and other social and environmental considerations."[753] To help public authorities to identify the green products or services when making purchasing decisions, the EU has also developed a set of common GPP criteria covering 21 product and service groups.[754]

745 This data is based on the information from the European Commission. Available at: https://ec.europa.eu/ growth/single-market/public-procurement/strategy_en (Accessed on March 3, 2017).

746 COM (2008) 400 final.

747 *Id*, p. 4.

748 *OJ* L 94/1, 28.3.2014, p. 65.

749 *OJ* L 94/1, 28.3.2014, p. 243.

750 *OJ* L 94/1, 28.3.2014, p. 1.

751 On April 16, 2014, the new EU public procurement initiatives came into force and meanwhile the older directives on public procurement are being replaced: Directive 2004/17 on procurement in the water, energy, transport and post service sectors ('Sector Directive') and Directive 2004/18 on procurement-contracts for public works, public supply and public services ('Classical Directive').

752 McCrudden (2007) argued that the old public procurement directives opened up opportunities to introduce the social and environmental criteria in the procurement process, but they did not explicitly prescribe them.

753 For further information on EU's GPP framework, available at: http://ec.europa.eu/environment/gpp/eu_ public_directives_en.htm (Accessed on March 3, 2017).

754 The 21 product and service groups include: cleaning products and service, combined heat and power, computer and monitors, copying and graphic paper, electrical and electronic equipment used in the health care sector, electricity, food and catering services, furniture, gardening products and services, imaging equipment, indoor lighting, and office building design, construction and management.

3.4 *Socially Responsible Investment* (*SRI*)

3.4.1 The Rise of the SRI Market

As noted in the previous chapter,[755] investors are regarded as an important driver of CSR/CER development, who can use their investment decision to influence corporate decision making. If investor's decisions are based not only on economic but also on social and environmental considerations, they are called socially responsible investment (SRI). In recent years, SRI has gained considerable significance and prevalence in the global financial market. According to a recent report of Global Alliance of Banking Values (GABV),[756] despite the devastating global financial crisis, the SRI market continues to grow significantly. There is an increasing significance of the SRI market not only for the financial market but also for the sustainable economy. Therefore, how to foster the further growth of SRI has become a new emphasis of public policy. Some scholars[757] thus suggested that SRI public policies would have positive effects on the SRI market and even on the overall financial market. With respect to the role of public policies in fostering the growth of SRI, it is argued that "national regulation might be one of the main drivers of SRI."[758] In practice, a variety of policy instruments are designed by public sectors to create a conducive environment for the development of SRI, and pension funds have become the focus of public policies.

3.4.2 Public Policies on SRI

3.4.2.1 *SRI Policies at the International Level*

At the international level, two international principles are frequently mentioned in the domain of SRI. The first principle—United Nation's Principles for Responsible Investment is supported by the United Nations (UN). In 2005, the United Nations Environmental Program (UNEP) Finance Initiative and the United Nations Global Compact launched the Principles for Responsible Investment (PRIS). The PRIS consist of six core principles,[759] which make

755 See supra Chapter 3, Section 5.1.

756 Global Alliance of Banking Values, '*Strong, Straightforward and Sustainable Banking: Financial Capital and Impact Metrics of Values Based Banking*', 2012. Available at: http://www.gabv.org/wp-content/uploads/Full-Report-GABV-v9d.pdf (Accessed on March 4, 2017).

757 Friedman and Miles 2001, pp. 523–548.

758 Eurosif, '*European SRI Study 2014*'. Available at: http://www.eurosif.org/publication/european-sri-study-2014/ (Accessed on April 16, 2017).

759 The six principles are:
Principle 1: We will incorporate ESG issues into investment analysis and decision-making processes.

commitments to incorporate ESG issues into investment decision-making and to encourage the investment industry to implement these principles. In essence, the PRIs is a voluntary framework with the aim to provide guidance to enable investors to better align their investments with the broad expectations of society. By now, the PRIs have 1359 signatories from more than 50 countries.[760] The PRIs have been accepted by asset owners, investment managers and professional service partners across the world. However, it is argued that the non-binding character and weak enforcement prevent this voluntary framework from providing an efficient guidance on SRI and the actual implementation of PRIs is questionable.

Comparing to the broad scope of PRIs, the Global Alliance of Banking Values (GABV) devotes itself to building a sustainable banking sector by establishing a set of sustainable banking principles.[761] The GABV's principles of sustainable banking, consist of six principles,[762] provide the practical guidance on how to define and identify sustainable banks and moreover how sustainable banks distinguish their roles in the SRI market.

3.4.2.2 *SRI Policies at EU Level*

The European Commission has fallen short of regulation SRI compared to its regulation of other CSR/CER issues, like sustainability reporting and public procurement discussed above. It is observed that the EU directives on SRI are

---

Principle 2: We will be active owners and incorporate ESG issues into our ownership policies and practices.

Principle 3: We will seek appropriate disclosure on ESG issues by the entities in which we invest.

Principle 4: We will promote acceptance and implementation of the Principles within the investment industry.

Principle 5: We will work together to enhance our effectiveness in implementing the Principles.

Principle 6: We will each report on our activities and progress towards implementing the Principles.

760 The latest data is from the official website of PRIs. Available at: http://www.unpri.org/signatories/signatories/ (Accessed on March 4, 2017) .

761 Global Alliance of Banking Values. Available at: http://www.gabv.org/about-us/our-principles (Accessed on March 4, 2017).

762 The six principles are: (1) triple bottom line approach at the heart of the business model; (2) grounded in communities, serving the real economy and enabling new business models to meet the needs of both; (3) long-term relationships with clients and a direct understanding of their economic activities and the risks involved; (4) long-term, self-sustaining, and resilient to outside disruptions; (5) transparent and inclusive governance; (6) all of these principles embedded in the culture of the bank.

still pending.[763] One important step for the European Commission in promoting SRI is the establishment of European Social Entrepreneurship Funds (EuSEF) in December 2011. The EuSEF aims to "provide support to the market for social businesses by improving the effectiveness of fundraising by investment funds that target these businesses."[764]

Another focus of the European SRI policies is the information disclosure requirements of pension funds. In the 'Communication concerning corporate social responsibility: a business contribution to sustainable development',[765] the Commission clearly required "occupational pension schemes and retail investment funds to disclose whether and how they take account of social, environmental and ethical factors in their investment decisions."[766] Moreover, the Commission also "encouraged initiatives aiming at monitoring and benchmarking practices of pension funds and investment funds with regard to and in support of CSR, and invites the EU Multiple-stakeholder Forum on CSR to consider whether a common EU approach can be established."[767]

France regulates the SRI information disclosure in the Grenelle II Act (in French: Loi Grenelle II), which was passed in 2010 and is considered as a milestone for France towards integrated sustainable and financial reporting system.[768] Article 224 of this Act (in French: L' article 224) specifically addresses the information disclosure of investment funds, by requiring all asset management companies and alternative investments funds to disclose information as to how they integrate ESG issues into their investment policies in their annual reports.[769] However, the regulatory frameworks vary widely in different nations. According to an OECD report,[770] in some countries, such as Japan and Canada, there are no governmental initiatives to encourage investors to take ESG issues into account or to require them to disclose relevant information.

Based on the analysis above, the governmental SRI initiatives are comparatively limited in comparison with public policies on SPP and GPP, and SRI is considered as one of the "least developed themes of CSR policies."[771]

763 Steurer *et al.* 2008.

764 ESDN, '*Sustainable Investment: options for a contribution to a more sustainable financial sector*', 2012.

765 COM (2002) 347 final.

766 *Id.*

767 *Id.*

768 See Chapter 7, Section 2.1.

769 The Original version of this article is: "obligation pour les sociétés de gestion de présenter 'l'information relative à la prise en compte des critères sociaux, environnementaux et de qualité de gouvernance [ESG] dans leur politique d'investissement."

770 OECD 2007, p. 19.

771 Steurer *et al.* 2008.

3.5 *Awareness Raising for CSR/CER*

The awareness for CSR/CER refers to the recognition and acceptance of CSR/CER not only among companies, but also among other stakeholders, such as employees, consumers, investors, and NGOs. The importance of raising awareness for sustainable development and CSR/CER has been widely accepted. Particularly as a relatively new concept, the further development of CSR/CER to a large extent depends on how CSR/CER is perceived by companies and stakeholders.[772] In a recent report, the European Commission also expressed its concerns that if corporations were unaware of how CSR/CER could make a contribution to their long-term interest and a more sustainable world, CSR/CER will just remain as a concept in the book.[773] As a result, how to raise public awareness for CSR/CER has been regarded as a key task for governments to strengthen the further development of CSR/CER.

The first already widespread approach to raising public awareness is to encourage CSR/CER education, training program, and academic research. A broad consensus in this respect is that education and training play an important role in the development of CSR/CER. For citizens, CSR/CER education provides them with a broader awareness of sustainable development and CSR/CER. For managers, employees and future business leaders, CSR/CER training could help them to improve management skills in this field. As a result, the integration of CSR/CER into education curriculum and training programs is becoming popular worldwide. For policymakers, high-quality CSR/CER academic research could provide valuable recommendations for their decision making.

At the international level, the UN Education for Sustainable Development (ESD) launched the '*Decade of Education for Sustainable Development* (DESD) *2005–2014*' initiative, delivered by the United Nations Educational, Scientific, and Cultural Organization (UNESCO). The DESD initiative seeks to make use of educational resources of the world to further develop a sustainable world by integrating several important issues on sustainable development into general education, such as biodiversity, climate change, sustainable consumption into teaching and learning.[774] In 2007, the '*Principles for Responsible Management Education*' (PRME) were established under the coordination of UN Global Compact and several leading academic institutions. The PRME consists of six

---

772 *Id.*

773 COM (2002) 347 final.

774 UNESCO, '*Education for Sustainable Development*'. Available at: http://www.unesco.org/new/en/education/themes/leading-the-international-agenda/education-for-sustainable-development/ (Accessed on March 5, 2017).

principles,[775] with the aim to lay a foundation for the promotion of responsible management education.

The EU has also acknowledged the necessity to promote CSR/CER education, training and research. At the policy level, the European Commission has listed "further integrating CSR into education, training, and research" on the agenda of its new CSR communication.[776] In this communication, the Commission made commitments to further financing academic research and innovation on CSR. Moreover, the Commission also required Member States to play an important role in fostering CSR education establishment. Under the guidance of the Commission, some Member States have started to introduce sustainable development and CSR issues into the curriculum. For example, the French Education Ministry launched the Generalized Provision for Sustainable Development Education[777] which integrates sustainable development into the national education system. Whereas, some Member States choose to focus on increasing the awareness of SMEs by funding specific training programs for SMEs. For example, Germany funded the Employee development through Engagement (*Personalentwicklung durch Engagement*), which aims to improve employee's skills related to CSR/CER in SMEs.

775 Principle 1 Purpose: We will develop the capabilities of students to be future generators of sustainable value for business and society at large and to work for an inclusive and sustainable global economy.
Principle 2 Values: We will incorporate into our academic activities and curricula the values of global social responsibility as portrayed in international initiatives such as the United Nations Global Compact.
Principle 3 Method: We will create educational frameworks, materials, processes and environments that enable effective learning experiences for responsible leadership.
Principle 4 Research: We will engage in conceptual and empirical research that advances our understanding about the role, dynamics, and impact of corporations in the creation of sustainable social, environmental and economic value.
Principle 5 Partnership: We will interact with managers of business corporations to extend our knowledge of their challenges in meeting social and environmental responsibilities and to explore jointly effective approaches to meeting these challenges.
Principle 6 Dialogue: We will facilitate and support dialog and debate among educators, students, business, government, consumers, media, civil society organizations and other interested groups and stakeholders on critical issues related to global social responsibility and sustainability.
For further information on the 'Principles for Responsible Management Education', available at: http://www.unprme.org/about-prme/the-six-principles.php (Accessed on March 5, 2017).

776 COM (2011) 681 final.

777 UNESCO, '*Good Practices in the UNECE region*', 2007. Available at: http://unesdoc.unesco.org/images/0015/ 001533/153319e.pdf (Accessed on March 5, 2017).

The second approach is to facilitate the exchange of CSR /CER information and experience by establishing CSR/CER centres or platforms. For example, in 2001, CSR Netherlands (*MVO Nederland*) established a network of companies and an independent platform with the aim of exchanging CSR information and knowledge among companies, in particular, SMEs.[778] Today some networks, websites, and platforms on CSR are continuing to appear across the globe.

4 CSR/CER-Related Policies at the International Level

After discussing the roles and the policy areas that government could play in promoting CSR/CER, this section focuses on the international CSR/CER guidelines and standards developed by several influential international governmental and non-governmental organizations. The global CSR/CER guidelines present a great variety in terms of forms and contents, which can generally be divided into two categories: comprehensive and issue-oriented guidelines. For the purpose of the discussion on corporate environmental responsibility, the selection of international CSR/CER standards in this section is based on two criteria: first, they are widely accepted or adopted by companies and public sectors; second, they include environmental issues or they are oriented to environmental issues.

4.1 *The United Nations (UN) Global Compact*

As one of the world's most influential international organizations, the United Nations set up the missions to "promote sustainable development, to end poverty, promote prosperity and well-being for all, protect the environment and address climate change."[779] On its sustainable development agenda,[780] the UN is committed to "protecting the planet from degradation, including through sustainable consumption and production, sustainably managing its natural resources and taking urgent action on climate change."[781] As an important part

778 For further information on CSR network of the Netherlands (*PARTNERS EN NETWERKEN*), available at: http://www.mvonederland.nl/taxonomy/term/316/27893 (Accessed on March 5, 2017).

779 United Nations, '*Time for Global Action for People and Planet 2015*'. Available at: http://www.un.org/ sustainabledevelopment/ (Accessed on March 5, 2017).

780 On January 1, 2016, the 17 Sustainable Development Goals (SDGs) of the 2030 Agenda for Sustainable Development—officially came into force.

781 UN General Assembly, '*Transforming our world: the 2030 agenda for sustainable development*'. Available at: http://www.un.org/ga/search/view_doc.asp?symbol=A/RES/70/1&Lang=E (Accessed on March 4, 2017).

of the UN's actions to achieve the goal of sustainable development, the UN has made remarkable efforts in developing several influential CSR principles and guidelines, such as the ten principles of the UN Global Compact, the UN Guiding Principles on Business and Human Rights, and the UN Principles for Responsible Investment.[782]

The United Nations Global Compact is a strategic policy initiative to encourage corporations to align their business strategies and operations with sustainable development. First proposed by then UN Secretary General Kofi Annan in 1999, the Global Compact was officially launched in July 2000 with two goals: the one is to "mainstream the Ten Principles in business strategy and operations around the world"; and the other is to "catalyze business action in support of UN goals and issues, with emphasis on collaboration and collective action."[783]

The Global Compact is, in essence, a principle-based framework, which consists of ten universally accepted principles. The Global Compact provides guidance on responsible business in four policy areas: human rights, labour, environment, and anti-corruption.

Specifically, the first two principles are concerned with *human rights*:

- Principle 1: Businesses should support and respect the protection of internationally proclaimed human rights;
- Principle 2: make sure that they are not complicit in human rights abuses.

The next four principles focus on *labour aspects*:

- Principle 3: Businesses should uphold the freedom of association and the effective recognition of the right to collective bargaining;
- Principle 4: the elimination of all forms of forced and compulsory labour;
- Principle 5: the effective abolition of child labour;
- Principle 6: the elimination of discrimination in respect of employment and occupation.

The seventh, eighth and ninth principles deal with *environmental matters*:

- Principle 7: Businesses should support a precautionary approach to environmental challenges;
- Principle 8: undertake initiatives to promote greater environmental responsibility;

782 For further information on the UN Principles on Responsible Investment, see supra Section 4.4.

783 This is based on the information from the website of the United Nations Global Compact. Available at: https://www.unglobalcompact.org/AboutTheGC/index.html (Accessed on March 5, 2017).

- Principle 9: encourage the development and diffusion of environmentally friendly technologies.

Then the last principle is about *anti-corruption*:

- Principle 10: Businesses should work against corruption in all its forms, including extortion and bribery.

Due to the global influence of the UN in the international society, the Global Compact has become one of the world's largest as well as one of the most influential CSR initiatives. Today more than 13,000 participants in both business and non-business communities are signatories to the Global Compact.[784] A recent survey of European Commission explicitly stated that "the UN Global Compact is the most frequently referenced CSR instrument."[785]

The Global Compact is not a regulatory framework by nature, but a voluntary and non-binding global framework. The Global Compact provides platforms for participants and other stakeholders to share and exchange ideas and best practices regarding the development and implementation of critical issues on sustainability agenda. The participation of this voluntary mechanism can bring about a wide array of benefits to business and the civil society as well, such as "instilling a culture of corporate leadership and innovation", "moving corporate responsibility from a concept to a fact", and "giving voice to people's concerns".[786] By participating in the Global Compact, corporations commit to incorporating the 'ten principles' into their business strategies and daily operations. Moreover, they are also required to issue the 'Communication on Progress' (COP)[787] annually to disclose the progress of the implementation of the 'ten principles' on the website of the Global Compact.

4.2 *The OECD Guidelines for Multinational Enterprises*[788]

In the age of economic globalization, the importance of international investment and multinational enterprises is widely acknowledged.[789] The OECD Guidelines for Multinational Enterprises (the OECD Guidelines) are initiated

784 For further information on the participation of the Global Compact, available at: https://www.unglobalcompact.org/HowToParticipate/index.html (Accessed on March 5, 2017).

785 European Commission 2013.

786 Latham & Watkins LLP 2009.

787 A COP should include a statement by the chief executive, a description of practical actions and a measurement of outcomes, and failure to produce this report will degrade the status of participants to non-communicating and even lead to expulsion from the Global Compact.

788 The OECD Guidelines for Multinational Enterprises were first adopted in 1976 and have been reviewed and updated five times. The latest edition was updated in 2011, and all references concerning to the Guidelines are based on this edition.

789 See Chapter 1, Section 1.

in this context as a comprehensive set of recommendations addressed by governments to MNEs for encouraging responsible business conduct. The OECD Guidelines have already been established for the first time in 1976. During the past year, the OECD Guidelines have been revised frequently as a result of developments in the business-society relationships. In 2011, the fifth revision of the OECD Guidelines was completed, mainly to confirm The Guidelines with the UN Guiding Principles on Business and Human Rights.

As a part of the '*OECD Declaration on International Investment and Multinational Enterprises*',[790] the ultimate goal of the OECD Guidelines is to encourage MNEs to "contribute to economic, environmental and social progress with a view to achieving sustainable development."[791] To achieve this goal, the OECD Guidelines provide a set of voluntary and non-binding principles and standards for responsible business conducts of MNEs, in areas of human rights, employment and industrial relations, environment, combating bribery, bribe solicitation and extortion, consumer interests, science and technology, competition and taxation. The OECD Guidelines also include a series of initiatives focusing on specific sectors, such as agricultural supply chains, financial sector due diligence, textile and garment supply chains, extractive sector stakeholder engagement and mineral supply chains.

An important characteristic of the OECD Guidelines is that they are addressed by adhering governments to MNEs. The pro-active role of governments in promoting responsible business conducts is clearly identified by the OECD Guidelines. More particularly, governments play an irreplaceable role in the implementation of the OECD Guidelines.

First, in contrast to other global CSR policies, the OECD Guidelines are knowns as "the only government-backed international instruments on responsible business conduct with a built-in grievance mechanism."[792] This unique feature can be substantiated by the common aim of the adhering governments to "encourage the positive contributions that multinational enterprises can make to economic, environmental and social progress and to minimize the difficulties to which their various operations may give rise."[793]

Second, the commitments to adhering to the OECD Guidelines create binding obligations for governments. For example, the governments adhering

790 The OECD Declaration on International Investment and Multinational Enterprises was adopted in 1976 as a policy commitment by adhering governments to provide an open and transparent environment for international investment and to encourage the positive contribution MNEs can make to economic and social progress.

791 OECD Guidelines 2011 Edition, p. 19.

792 OECD Guidelines for Multinational Enterprises: Responsible Business Conduct Matters.

793 OECD Guidelines 2011 Edition, p. 15.

to the OECD Guidelines are obligated to establish National Contact Points (NCPs), which are the unique implementation mechanism. NCPs aim to "further the effectiveness of the OECD Guidelines by undertaking promotional activities, handling inquiries and contributing to the resolution of issues that arise related to the implementation of the OECD Guidelines in specific instances, taking account of the attached procedural guidance."[794] Moreover, the adhering governments also have the flexibility to develop domestic policy frameworks within their jurisdiction, to better fit their different institutional contexts.[795]

Today, many MNEs show genuine interest in improving corporate environmental performance, since it has been regarded not only as a corporate responsibility but also a business opportunity in many instances.[796] In this context, the OECD Guidelines have a specific chapter on environmental matters, which provides a set of recommendations for MNEs as to the improvement of corporate environmental performance. In particular, they encourage MNEs to establish and maintain a 'sound environment management' system as an important part of their business strategy.

4.3 *The ISO 26000 on Social Responsibility (ISO 26000)*

As the world's largest developer of international voluntary standards, ISO has published more than 19,500 international standards, covering a wide range of issues of business, society, and government, such as quality management, environment management, and food safety.[797] In November 2010, ISO launched an international standard on social responsibility—the ISO 26000 Guidance on Social Responsibility (ISO 26000), which is regarded as the most important development in the standardization of global CSR standards.[798]

ISO 26000 is a set of voluntary standards in promoting socially responsible conduct that is applicable for all types of organizations. The implementation of such standards could bring multiple benefits to organizations, such as "the competitive advantage; reputation; the ability to attract and retain workers or members, customers, clients or users; the maintenance of employee's morale,

794 Implementation Procedures of the OECD Guidelines for Multinational Enterprises, 2011 Edition, p. 68.

795 For more information about the implementation of OECD Guidelines by adhering governments, see Chapter 7, Section 3.

796 See Chapter 3, Section 2.

797 For further information on ISO, available at: http://www.iso.org/iso/home/about.htm (Accessed on April 14, 2017)

798 Moratis 2015, p. 39.

commitment and productivity; the view of investors, donors, sponsors and the financial community; and the relationship with companies, governments, the media, peers, customers, and the community in which it operates."[799]

Environmental management has been a critical component of the ISO standard system, and ISO has developed the ISO 14000 for environmental management and ISO 900I for quality management in this field. As opposed to other ISO management system standards, ISO 26000 is not a management system standard. In fact, the ISO 26000 only provides guidance rather than requirements and it cannot be used for certification whereas many other ISO standards can.[800] Instead, ISO 26000 only seeks to assist all types of organizations to put CSR into practice, by sharing a common understanding of what CSR is, what its basic principles are, what the core subjects and issues it includes are, and how to integrate it throughout an organization. Moreover, the target groups of ISO 26000 are all types of organizations, including but not limited to corporations.

Specifically, ISO 26000 identifies seven basic principles /aspects of social responsibility: (1) accountability, (2)transparency, (3) ethical behaviour, (4) respect for stakeholder interests, (5) respect for the rule of law, (6) respect for international norms of behaviour, and (7) respects for human rights. The ISO 26000 includes six core issues that are most likely to arise in business operations: (1) human rights, (2) labour practices, (3) environment, (4) fair operating issues, (5) consumer issues, and (6)community development and involvement. Under each core subject, a range of specific issues should be taken into account. ISO 26000 perceives that all core issues can find their relevance for any type of organizations, but it is not necessary to include all issues. Instead, corporations could identify the most relevant issues to their business operations.

ISO 26000 also clearly states that this standard does not intend to "provide guidance on what should be subject to legally binding obligations; nor to address questions that can only properly be resolved through political institutions."[801] But the governments may use this standard as part of their policy framework on sustainable development and CSR/CER. More particularly, by applying this standard, governments could help the organizations make their positive contributions to sustainable development. Today, ISO 26000 has

799 ISO 26000 Guidance on Social Responsibility 2009, p. vi.

800 Certification is a useful tool to check whether the system works and is a vital part of management systems, such as ISO 9000-quality management and ISO 14000-environment management. The certification is usually issued by independent third parties.

801 ISO 26000 Guidance on Social Responsibility 2009.

been adopted by 64 countries and been translated into 24 languages,[802] which makes it one of the most influential global CSR initiatives. For example, ISO 26000 has been referred to as one of the core internationally recognized CSR principles and guidelines in the European Commission's renewed strategy for corporate social responsibility,[803] in which the European Commission invites all large European companies to take account of this standard in developing their CSR strategies.

5 Summary and Some Concluding Remarks

As mentioned at the very beginning of this chapter, the traditional paradigm views CSR/CSR as a business-led activity by its nature and insists that the development of CSR/CER should be primarily driven by the market demands for responsible business behaviour. However, the law and economics analysis from the previous chapters equally indicate that many problems remain with this self-regulatory approach. Government intervention is needed in various ways to accompany the success of CSR/CER. In this context, this chapter discussed the relationship between public authorities and CSR/CER by answering two questions:

- Is there a role for regulation or, more generally government intervention, to accompany the process of CSR/CER?
- If so, what specific roles governments could play in promoting CSR/CER?

This chapter started with a literature review about the various roles that government could play in promoting CSR/CER. Despite the different focus, we found a broad consensus of the various studies that government could play and already have played an important role in promoting CSR/CER. More particularly, the work of Gond *et al.* merited a detailed discussion in this chapter. According to Gond *et al.*, there are five ideal types of relationship between CSR and government and these are: CSR as mandated by government, CSR as facilitated by government, CSR as a partnership with government, CSR as self-government, and CSR as a form of government. Based on the academic achievements of the previous studies in this domain, this chapter identified five roles that public authorities could play in CSR/CER as: mandating, facilitating, partnering, endorsing and demonstrating. In some cases, governments could act as a legislator, a partner or a facilitator at the same time.

802 Moratis 2015, p. 25.
803 COM (2011) 681 final.

We also had a look at the wide range of policy instruments that are designed and applied by the government to achieve their commitment to CSR/CER. This chapter provided two types of typologies of CSR/CER public policies. The first typology is an instrument-based classification. Benchmarked against this criterion, a wide range of policy instruments can be categorized into five types: legal instrument (sticks), economic or market-based instrument (carrots), informational instrument (sermons), and the instrumental mix. The second typology is based on the key CSR/CER issues that are expected to be addressed by making reference to international CSR/CER policies.

This chapter provided some insights into how governments promote CSR/CER, by describing relevant policies and practices in five selected policy areas: sustainability reporting, sustainable consumption, sustainable public procurement, socially responsible investment and awareness-raising for CSR/CER. As far as *sustainability reporting* is concerned, we concluded that there were some substantial obstacles in its further development, like the contra-productive amounts in varieties of sustainability report formats; the slow growth and insufficient amount of reporting companies compared to the number of companies worldwide; and the still questionable credibility of reporting quality. We consider the standardization in reporting materiality, content, and format coming from the Global Reporting Initiative - which is now in its 4th generation of guidelines - as a large advantage compared to earlier days of reporting. More and more national (examples of French initiatives and Chinese initiatives) and supra-national entities (an example of the EU) steadily increase their support to non-financial reporting as such and the use of GRI reporting formats.

Sustainable consumption proves to be an important part of CSR/CER. It directly reduces the consumption quantity as well as the negative effects of production processes, products, and services. One of the instruments used quite effectively in order to push sustainable consumption is eco-labelling, with the aim to better identify "the real" green products and services. But the initial effectiveness of eco-labelling seems more and more undermined by the rise in numbers and reduced comparability of eco-labels as well as by the behaviour of those companies trying to greenwash their products compared to others. Also in this area, the government is expected to take a regulating force in the market to increase the affected transparency and credibility of eco-labels and substantially decrease greenwashing possibilities. One of the possibilities for public and private parties is to increase the support provided to certification schemes. Examples are provided from Europe and the U.S.

Sustainable Public Procurement and Green Public Procurement differ in content from each other as do respectively CSR and CER. The latter does focus on the environment and the former takes the broader spectrum of non-financial aspect and issues in sustainability as its starting point. Public Procurement is the purchase by the state of production capacity, products and services needed to better fulfil its public obligations. If one takes the initiative to make public procurement *Green* or *Sustainable,* this leads to substantial support for those production processes, products, and services that match the new requirements based on CSR/CER practices. The EU is providing good examples of supporting policies implemented in the EU itself and the Member States while including its social and environmental targets in public procurement.

Socially Responsible Investment (*SRI*) has been presented as another important driver of CSR/CER exercised by individual and institutional investors. The SRI market attracted the substantial attention of public authorities to build part of their CSR/CER supporting policies upon the further growing strength of SRI. Guidance for those policies is provided by UN Financial Initiative and the UN Global Compact. In cooperation, these UN bodies launched the six Principles for Responsible Investment which gained strong support and many adherents. Also, private organizations set the tone in stimulating the growth of this SRI market. With respect to public policy in this domain, we provided some examples of actions taken within the EU (the European Social Entrepreneurship Funds and transparency rules for SRI investments by Pension Funds) as well as in France.

Awareness raising and capacity building are fundamental requirements for the introduction of innovations, as in this case the rise of CSR/CER knowledge and actions by companies, stakeholders, and public authorities. A wide range of actions are and still can be taken in existing and new education—and training programs as well as in academic research. Guidance is provided by mentioning UN programs and the EU. Another type of action taken by private and public authorities is the organizational approach in which CSR/CER centres are established to provide information, networks, websites and platforms to a variety of stakeholders, such as small and medium sized enterprises.

Moreover, several important general and comprehensive CSR/CER policies and guidelines are developed by international organizations. In this chapter, we presented the United Nations Global Compact, the OECD Guidelines for Multinational Enterprises, and the ISO 26000 on Social Responsibility.

To summarize, this chapter supported the idea that although the development of CSR/CER does not call for government intervention in the first instance, the significant constraints of a pure self-regulatory approach need the intervention of government in various ways. This argument has been explored and substantiated by a wide range of public policies at both the international level and the national level. Given the significant differences in CSR/CER across countries, there is no one-fits-all answer for all public sectors. In this context, there is a practical need to examine the roles of public sectors in promoting CSR/CER in specific institutional contexts.

CHAPTER 7

CSR/CER Policies and Practices in the European Institutional Context

1 Introduction

The analysis from the previous chapter showed that public authorities could play and have already played an important role in encouraging environmentally responsible business in various ways.[804] More particularly, it has been widely observed that the understanding and implementation of CSR/CER vary widely from continent to continent, from country to country and from industry to industry. In fact, the comparative studies of CSR/CER present remarkable differences between different approaches and there is no 'one fits all' approach for all governments.[805] The frontrunners in this field, Europe and America, have adopted two different approaches to promoting the development of CSR/CER. Matten and Moon observed that the American companies made more explicit commitments to their involvement in CSR/CER, but the European companies tended to be more implicit in this respect.[806] This phenomenon can be partially explained by the different 'historically grown institutional frameworks' between Europe and America.[807]

The main goal of this chapter is to better understand the role of public authorities in promoting the development of CSR/CER in the European institutional context. More particularly, this chapter is constructed at three levels: the EU level, the Member States level and the company level. Section 2 introduces the developments of CSR/CER policies at the EU level. The European Union has played an active role in supporting and shaping the development of CSR/CER across Europe. Consequently, the topic of CSR/CER has taken up a position on the EU policy agenda. A series of strategies and initiatives have been developed by the EU public authorities, which construct the European approach towards CSR/CER. Member States have taken a range of measures to implement the EU strategy on CSR/CER. Section 3 selects three Member States to exemplify their efforts in developing the national policy frameworks on

804 See Chapter 6.

805 Matten and Moon 2008, p. 404.

806 *Id*, p. 405.

807 *Id*, pp. 407–409.

 | DOI:10.1163/9789004368132_008

CSR/CER. After exploring the variety of public policies on CSR/CER, another key question of this chapter is how European companies respond to these policies. In other words, to what extent do CSR/CER policies change corporate sustainability performance. Section 4 examines this impact of CSR/CER policies on corporate sustainability performance by conducting case studies of three selected European companies in the field of corporate sustainability reporting. Finally, Section 5 concludes.

2 CSR/CER Policies at the EU Level

2.1 *The European Approach towards CSR*

The European Union has acted as a pioneer in promoting and institutionalizing the development of CSR across Europe by means of various policy instruments. Particularly, the European institutions[808] show increasing interest in enhancing a common understanding of CSR at the EU level. As a result, it is observed that the development of CSR has been integrated into the EU's political strategy and has become a new policy field at both the EU and the Member States level. Within the EU, the development of CSR was first explicitly identified in the year 2000 as a positive contribution to achieve the EU strategic goal (also known as the Lisbon goal).[809] It clearly stated that "by the year of 2010, EU becomes the most competitive and dynamic knowledge-based economy in the world, capable of sustainable economic growth with more and better jobs and great social cohesion."[810] As an important part of achieving the Lisbon goal, European companies were encouraged to make their contributions by conducting business from "a corporate sense of social responsibility regarding the best practices of lifelong learning, work organization, equal opportunities, social inclusion and sustainable development."[811]

---

808 In this book, the European institutions generally refer to the Parliament, the Council of Ministers, the Commission as well as the Economic and Social Committee and the Committee of Regions.

809 The European Council held a meeting on 23–24 March, 2000 in Lisbon, in which a strategic goal of European Union was reached regarding employment, economic reform, social cohesion, and the transformation of the new 'knowledge-based economy'. More particularly, the Lisbon European Council made a special appeal to companies' sense of social responsibility regarding best practices on lifelong learning, work organization, equal opportunities, social inclusion and sustainable development.

810 Lisbon European Council: Presidency Conclusions 29/13/2000.

811 *Id*, Article 39.

The Lisbon goal is subsequently endorsed by the new EU's 10-year growth strategy—the 'Europe 2020',[812] in which the significance of CSR development has been reaffirmed. In a nutshell, the 'Europe 2020' strategy seeks smart, sustainable and inclusive growth by setting common targets on employment, research, and development, climate change and energy, education as well as poverty and social exclusion. Particularly for the EU, sustainable growth means "building a competitive low-carbon economy, protecting the environment, exploiting Europe's leadership in the race to develop new green technologies, introducing efficient smart electricity grids, harnessing EU-scale networks, improving the business environment, and helping consumers."[813] In this context, the role of CSR in achieving sustainable growth is emphasized, and several flagship initiatives were launched to stimulate CSR practices across Europe, such as '*A resource-efficient Europe*'[814] and '*An integrated industry policy for the globalization era*'.[815]

In addition to the endorsement of the EU institutions, the European companies have a long tradition of embracing CSR, which can be traced back to the 19th century, for example, French companies did already engage in addressing social and environmental issues on a voluntary basis in this period of time.[816] This phenomenon can be explained on the one hand by the increasing pressure from a variety of stakeholders, including consumers, investors, public authorities and local communities, and on the other hand by the stakeholder-oriented tradition of European company law.[817]

2.2 *Key CSR Initiatives at the EU Level*

The significance of CSR has found recognition among the EU institutions and the business community. Nevertheless, the question "how to better promote the development of CSR across Europe" has become a priority on the EU policy agenda. As a result, from the beginning of the 2000s, European institutions (particularly the European Commission and the European Parliament) have taken various measures to establish the European policy framework on CSR.

812 'Europe 2020' is the EU's growth strategy for the current decade of 2010–2020. Available at: https://ec.europa.eu/info/strategy/european-semester/framework/europe-2020-strategy_en (Accessed on March 8, 2017)

813 COM (2010) 2020 final.

814 COM (2011) 21 final.

815 COM (2011) 614 final.

816 Beaujolin and Capron 2005, p. 97.

817 Millon 2015, pp. 47–53.

2.2.1 The Green Paper on Promoting a European Framework for CSR

In July 2001, the European Commission (the Commission) published its first CSR policy—the '*Green Paper on promoting a European framework for corporate social responsibility*' (the Green Paper),[818] with the aim to "stimulate a wide debate on new ways of promoting corporate social responsibility at both the European level and international level."[819] In the Green Paper, the Commission first defined CSR as "a concept whereby companies integrate social and environmental concerns in their business operations and in their interaction with their stakeholders on a voluntary basis."[820] The Commission further explained its understanding of CSR as "being socially responsible means not only fulfilling legal expectations but also going beyond compliance and investing 'more' in human capital, the environment and the relations with stakeholders."[821]

More particularly, the Commission explored the meaning of responsible business practices in two dimensions: the internal dimension and the external dimension.[822] The internal dimension focuses on business behaviour within the company, related to the employee issues and environmental issues, such as human resources management, health and safety, managing changes, and the management of environment impacts and natural resources.[823] The external dimension expands to the interests of stakeholders beyond the company and even beyond Europe, such as the interests of consumers, suppliers, public authorities, local communities and the global community.[824]

Another important goal of the Green Paper was to launch a wide consultation among stakeholders to communicate their ideas as to "how to build a partnership for the development of a European framework for the promotion of CSR."[825] The consultation aimed to collect ideas of the following questions:

- What role could the European Union play in this process?
- What role could CSR play in enhancing the competitiveness of companies?
- What are the respective roles of main stakeholders within this framework?
- How to ensure and evaluate the effectiveness of this framework.[826]

---

818 COM (2001) 366 final.
819 COM (2001) 366 final, p. 23.
820 COM (2001) 366 final, p. 6.
821 *Id*, pp. 6–7.
822 *Id*, p. 8.
823 *Id*, pp. 8–11.
824 *Id*, pp. 11–15.
825 *Id*, p. 22.
826 *Id*, pp. 22–23.

By collecting and summarizing the responses from various stakeholders during this consultation process,[827] the Commission published the '*Communication concerning corporate social responsibility: a business contribution to sustainable development*'[828] in 2002. This Communication presented a European action framework for CSR, including the definition of CSR and the proposed action plans in seven priority areas:[829]

1) increasing knowledge about the positive impact of CSR on business and societies in Europe and abroad, in particular in developing countries;
2) developing the exchange of experience and good practice on CSR between enterprises;
3) promoting the development of CSR management skills;
4) fostering CSR among SMES;
5) facilitating convergence and transparency of CSR practices and tools;
6) launching a Multi-Stakeholder Forum on CSR at EU level; and
7) integrating CSR into community policies.

In 2006, the Commission launched a business-led initiative called '*the European Alliance for CSR*',[830] with the aim of encouraging EU companies of all sizes to make positive contributions to the development of CSR.

2.2.2 EU Strategy 2011–2014

To catch up with the latest development of sustainability and the CSR agenda, the Commission updated its strategy on CSR by launching '*A renewed EU strategy 2011–14 for corporate social responsibility*' in October 2011.[831] Several essential elements of this 2011 CSR strategy should be emphasized here.

Frist, in this renewed CSR strategy, the Commission re-defines CSR as "the responsibility of enterprises for their impact on society",[832] which indicates an important shift from the previous definition shared by the Green Paper and the Communications from 2002[833] and 2006.[834] This updated definition, on

827 The Commission received more than 250 responses to the Green Paper, from employers' organizations, business associations, and individual enterprises, trade unions, civil society organizations, organizations at local, regional, national, European and international level as well as academics and other interested individuals.

828 COM (2002) 347 final.

829 *Id*, p. 8.

830 COM (2006) 136 final.

831 COM (2011) 681 final.

832 *Id*, p. 6.

833 COM (2002) 347 final.

834 COM (2006) 136 final.

the one hand, expands the scope of CSR from "the integration of social and economic concerns" to "any possible impacts of their business operations". On the other hand, it also shows that the modern understanding of CSR is no longer restricted to the traditional voluntary approach, but tends to adopt a combined voluntary and mandatory approach. In this context, the Commission identifies the respective roles of public authorities and companies in promoting the development of CSR: companies should take the lead in this process, and public authorities should play a supporting role through a smart mix of voluntary and mandatory policy instruments.[835]

Secondly, the Commission maps a new agenda for action, which identifies eight priority areas to fulfil the EU's commitments to actively promoting the development of CSR practices at the national, the European and the international level:

1) Enhancing the visibility of CSR and disseminating good practices;
2) Improving and tracking levels of trust in business;
3) Improving self- and co-regulation processes;
4) Enhancing market reward for CSR;
5) Improving company disclosure of social and environmental information;
6) Further integrating CSR into education, training, and research;
7) Emphasizing the importance of national and sub-national CSR policies; and
8) Better aligning European and global approaches to CSR.

For each area, the Commission also provides companies, Member States and other stakeholders with specific commitments and suggestions about how to implement this agenda in practice.

Thirdly, a priority of this agenda for action is to align European and global approaches to CSR. As a result, an important source of the European CSR framework is a set of internationally recognized CSR principles and guidelines. More particularly, the following sets of global CSR principles and guidelines are highlighted by the European Commission, including:

1) the United Nations Global Compact,[836]
2) the Universal Declaration of Human Rights,
3) the United Nations Guiding Principles on Business and Human Rights,[837]
4) the OECD Guidelines for Multinational Enterprises,[838]

835 COM (2011) 681 final, p. 7.
836 See Chapter 6, Section 5.1.1.
837 See Chapter 6, Section 5.1.2.
838 See Chapter 6, Section 5.2.

5) the ISO 26000 Guidance on social responsibility,[839]
6) the Global Reporting Initiative,[840]
7) the International Labor Organization Tripartite Declaration of Principles Concerning Multinational Enterprises and Social Policy, and
8) the International Labour Organization Core Conventions and the Declaration on Fundamental Principles and Rights at Work.

Finally, the Commission also invites "all large European enterprises to make a commitment by 2014 to take account of at least one of the following sets of principles and guidelines when developing their approach to CSR: the UN Global Compact, the OECD Guidelines for Multinational Enterprises, and the ISO 26000."[841]

To monitor and evaluate the implementation progress of this agenda for action, the Commission, in partnership with the Member States, enterprises, and other stakeholders, organized seven peer review meetings[842] in 2013. The primary results of these meetings showed that in general, the progress achieved in the implementation of the CSR strategy was significant.[843] The Commission also launched a public consultation to evaluate the outcomes, shortcomings and the key future issues in the area of CSR. The feedbacks from a wide range of respondents indicated "the overall impact of the Commission's (CSR) policy was regarded as generally useful or very useful."[844]

2.2.3 EU Multi-Stakeholder Forum on CSR

In addition to developing a series of initiatives and strategies on CSR, another important role of the Commission in advancing CSR is to facilitate dialogues between business and various stakeholders to exchange ideas and to share good practices on CSR. One achievement in this field is the establishment of the European Multi-Stakeholder Forum on CSR (also known as CSR EMS Forum), which is chaired by the Commission with the aim of "promoting transparency and convergence of CSR practices and instruments."[845] To date, the

839 See Chapter 6, Section 5.3.
840 See Chapter 6, Section 1.2.
841 COM (2011) 681 final.
842 The seven peer review meetings were held in the UK, Denmark, France, Sweden, Finland, Italy and the Netherlands in 2013.
843 For further information on the peer review meetings, available at: http://ec.europa.eu/social/keyDocuments.jsp?advSearchKey=CSRprreport&mode=advancedSubmit&langId=en&policyArea=&type=0&country=0&year=0 (Accessed on March 8, 2017).
844 European Commission Ref. Ares (2014)4124533—09/12/2014.
845 COM (2002) 347 final, p. 17.

CSR EMS Forum has become an important platform to disseminate ideas and best practices of responsible business conduct at the EU level.[846] The CSR EMS Forum 2015 attracted 450 participants from various sectors, and twelve CSR related issues[847] were discussed at this Forum.

3 CSR/CER Policies at Member States Level

Due to the continuous efforts, the EU institutions have developed a European framework on CSR at the EU level. As the key actors within this framework, Member States are expected to play a pro-active role to extend the benefits of CSR policies throughout the Europe. In the 2011 CSR strategy, the Commission invited the Member States to "develop or update by mid-2012 their own plans or national lists of priority actions to promote CSR in support of the Europe 2020 strategy, with reference to internationally recognized CSR principles and guidelines and in cooperation with enterprises and other stakeholders, taking account of the issues raised in this communication."[848] As a response, many Member States have taken actions to meet this requirement. A recent survey showed that by 2014, 24 of the 27 Member States claimed that they had developed or would develop a national action plan on CSR.[849]

This section aims to gain more insights on how Member States develop their own national CSR policy frameworks. Three Member States are selected to exemplify how they respond to the Commission's requirements to develop their national action plans on CSR: the Netherlands, France, and the United Kingdom.

From the outset, it is necessary to make a distinction between two basic types of policy instruments deployed by governmental organizations: the voluntary approach and the mandatory approach. As noted above,[850] the Commission points out that the development of CSR should be primarily led by

846 Executive Summary of 2015 CSR forum, available at: http://ec.europa.eu/growth/industry/corporate-social-responsibility/ (Accessed on March 13, 2017).

847 The twelve issues include international market access, education and human capital, Small and Medium Enterprises (SMEs), international development cooperation, business and human rights, public procurement, innovation, competitiveness and Growth, human Rights and access to remedies, responsible investment, responsible supply chains, national and regional policies on CSR and financial institutions.

848 COM (2011) 681 final, pp. 12–13.

849 Corporate Social Responsibility: National Public Policies in the European Union, Compendium 2014, pp. 9–10.

850 See *supra* Section 2.2.2.

business, and public authorities could play a supporting role through a mix of voluntary and mandatory instruments.[851] For example, in some areas, public authorities promote the development of CSR by recognizing and adopting the voluntary CSR principles and guidelines initiated by companies and other stakeholders into their domestic policy framework. There are some areas where public authorities take the lead in developing mandatory regulations to promote and shape the development of CSR, such as improving the transparency of corporate reporting and providing economic incentives. As a result, a mix of mandatory and voluntary approaches is widely observed in developing their national policy frameworks on CSR.

3.1 *CSR Policies in the Netherlands*

3.1.1 The Development of CSR in the Netherlands

From a historical view, CSR is not a recent topic in the Netherlands. The roots of CSR in this country can be traced back to the end of 19th century, when some 'socially-aware entrepreneurs', like Van Marken, provided social services to the local community on a voluntary basis, such as health care funds, pension, and relief funds.[852] However, it was not until the mid-1990s that the importance and values of CSR have been widely acknowledged by the Dutch society.

The rise of CSR in the 1990s was to a large extent attributed to the changing relationship between public authorities, business, and civil society. In particular, the 'deregulation movement' in the 1980s and the 1990s[853] led to the corresponding changes concerning the division of duties between public and private sectors.[854] In this context, corporations were given more flexibility to self-regulate their business operations. Moreover, a favourable political and social environment also contributed to the rapid development of CSR in the Netherlands. At the policy level, the Dutch government has played an active role in promoting and stimulating the development of CSR.[855] Particularly in the Dutch context, a socio-political decision is generally reached through a multi-stakeholder approach, which means that a variety of stakeholders can participate in the process of decision making. This mechanism can to some extent stimulate various stakeholders to share their views on CSR. From a societal perspective, the Dutch public also expresses a higher expectation for responsible business behaviour.

---

851 COM (2011) 681 final, p. 7.

852 SER, '*Corporate Social Responsibility: A Dutch Approach*', 2001, pp. 23–24.

853 For more information about the deregulation movement, see e.g. Keeler 1984; Cramer 2005.

854 Cramer 2005, pp. 87–96.

855 *Id.*

In response to the EU 2011 CSR strategy, the Dutch government has taken various measures to develop its national action plans on CSR. In particular, the Dutch government focused its efforts on four key areas:[856] first, aligning European CSR with global approaches to CSR; second, improving disclosure of relevant non-financial information by companies; third, providing market incentives for CSR; and fourth, enhancing the visibility of CSR and disseminating good practices. In the Netherlands, there is a division of the duty to develop CSR policies at the national and the international levels. To be more exact, the Ministry of Economic Affairs is responsible for the national CSR policy, while the Ministry of Trade and Development focuses on the international CSR policy. Another important governmental organization in this field of CSR development is the Social and Economic Council of the Netherlands (SER), which is an important advisory and consulting agency of the Dutch government and the Parliament. The SER plays a critical role in promoting the adoption of the international CSR guidelines and more importantly in drafting the first recommendation report on CSR.

3.1.2 Key CSR Policies

3.1.2.1 *Corporate Social Responsibility: The Dutch Approach*

The first important CSR policy is an advisory report on CSR- '*Corporate Social Responsibility—A Dutch Approach*'- in 2001.[857] This advisory report was prepared by the SER at the request of the Dutch government. In this report, the Dutch approach to CSR was defined as "values adding business activities in relation to people, profit, and the planet, and it concerns continuous transparent stakeholder engagement."[858] The SER viewed CSR as an important part of core business and also an integral element of corporate policy. The SER's CSR definition consisted of two key elements in determining "whether one can rightly refer to socially responsible business in this day and age."[859] The one was "consciously focusing business activities on creating values in three dimensions (people, planet, and profit), thus contributing to society's prosperity

856 Government of the Netherlands, '*Contribution by the government of the Netherlands to the renewed strategy of CSR*', 2012. Available at: https://business-humanrights.org/en/pdf-contribution-by-the-government-of-the-netherlands-to-the-renewed-eu-strategy-for-csr (Accessed on April 8, 2017).

857 SER was asked to prepare an advisory report on the issues of corporate social responsibility by the Dutch government in 1999. SER submitted its final report in December 2000, which was published in March 2001.

858 SER, '*Corporate Social Responsibility: A Dutch Approach*', 2001.

859 *Id, p.* 2.

in the long term."[860] The other one was "maintaining relations with the various stakeholders on the basis of transparency and dialogue, so as to provide answers to reasonable questions from society as a whole."[861]

This report also identified the various roles of the Dutch government in promoting CSR as legislator, supplier, stimulator, and facilitator.[862] In particular, as a legislator, public authorities could directly intervene in the market by prohibiting certain activities or by setting up specific minimum standards. Moreover, they were also expected to create favourable conditions for the further development of CSR.[863] As a supplier, public authorities could support the development of CSR by providing various public services relating to CSR issues, such as CSR education and training programs.[864] As a stimulator and facilitator, public authorities could develop a strategic partnership with companies and other stakeholder groups through various market incentives, such as taxes and subsidies.[865]

3.1.2.2 *The CSR Policy of the Netherlands*

The Dutch government updated its national CSR policy- '*Corporate Social Responsibility pays off*' (the Dutch CSR Policy)[866]- in 2013 as a response to implementing the EU 2011 CSR strategy. This document is also well known as the Dutch national action plan for CSR. First, the Dutch CSR Policy identified five key tasks for the Dutch government to promote the development of CSR, including:

1) ensuring that the frameworks of CSR are as clear as possible and that business is fully informed about them;
2) promoting a level playing field for Dutch business;
3) making other governments aware of their responsibilities, for example through economic diplomacy;
4) promoting transparency and stakeholders dialogue; and
5) setting a good example.[867]

---

860 *Id.*
861 *Id.*
862 *Id*, p. 10.
863 *Id*, p. 10.
864 *Id*, p. 11.
865 *Id*, pp. 11–12.
866 Government of the Netherlands, '*Corporate Social Responsibility pays off*', 2013. Available at: https://www.government.nl/documents/policy-notes/2013/06/28/csr-pays-off (Accessed on April 8, 2017).
867 *Id*, p. 6.

In addition to these five tasks, this policy letter also pointed out four priority areas where the Dutch government could take further actions in order to fulfil the tasks above, including sector risk analysis, information, transparency, and monitoring.[868]

Another key feature of the Dutch CSR policy is the strong emphasis on the 'International Corporate Social Responsibility' (ICSR).[869] The Dutch government expects Dutch companies to comply with these international guidelines when operating abroad, especially when the local legislation is inadequate or not effectively enforced.[870] At the international level, the OECD Guidelines for Multinational Enterprises are regarded as one of the most influential international CSR guidelines in the Netherlands,[871] which makes up the solid ICSR framework for the Dutch corporations. The OECD Guidelines express the Dutch government's expectations on how Dutch companies should operate internationally to prevent potential violations related to human rights, employment and industrial relations, environment and so on. The Dutch government has taken various measures to improve the compliance of the OECD Guidelines, for example, translating and disseminating information material, organizing workshops, and building a dedicated website that provides relevant information.[872] Another significant action is the revitalization of the National Contact Point (NCP). According to the OECD Guidelines, all adhering governments are required to establish a NCP, and the Dutch NCP[873] was created by a government decree in 2007.[874] Moreover, a detailed and user-friendly website of the Dutch NCP was built[875] to channel better access to the public. The Dutch NCP claims its two main missions on its website. The first mission is to promote and raise awareness of the OECD Guidelines among the business community, trade unions, and civil society organizations, and the Dutch NCP fulfils

868 *Id.*

869 *Id.*

870 *Id.*

871 For more information on the Dutch NCP, available at: http://www.oecdguidelines.nl/ (Accessed on March 13, 2017).

872 *Id.*

873 The Dutch NCP operates independently from the Dutch government and consists of four independent members and four advisory members from different ministries.

874 The Dutch NCP was formalized by government decree in 2007, and extended in 2011. In June 2014, a revised government decree on the establishment of the NCP has been published by the Dutch Ministry of Foreign Affairs. Available at: http://www.oesorichtlijnen.nl/actueel/nieuws/2014/7/23/instellingsbesluit-2014-zorgt-voor-verfijning-en-versterking-werkzaamheden-ncp (Accessed on March 13, 2017).

875 For more information on the Dutch NCP, available at: http://www.oecdguidelines.nl/ (Accessed on March 13, 2017).

this task through publishing promotional material and organizing workshops or events. The second important task is to mediate between parties in case of different opinions about the implementation of the OECD Guidelines or non-observance of the Guidelines. The parties involved can bring the disputes to the NCP for solution.[876]

The second important international CSR guideline within the Dutch CSR policy framework is the UN Guiding Principles on Business and Human Rights (the UN Guiding Principles). The implementation of the UN Guiding Principles is regarded as a priority for the Dutch government. The Ministry of Foreign Affairs of the Netherlands is responsible for developing the national action plan for implementing the Guiding Principles. In preparation for this action plan, a series of interviews and consultations were conducted among a broad range of stakeholders, including 50 representatives from implementation organizations, the business community, civil society, and academic experts. The consultations finally reached a broad consensus concerning the role of public authorities in the integration of the UN Guiding Principles into the Dutch current policy framework. Furthermore, through this consultation process, the Dutch government also mapped out its agenda of developing the national action plan, on which several important points were listed, including policy coherence, clarifying due diligence, transparency and reporting, and providing scope for remedy.[877]

In addition to the two international CSR guidelines mentioned above, the Dutch CSR policy framework also makes references to other internationally recognized guidelines, such as the UN Global Compact and the ISO 26000.

3.1.2.3 *Dutch Law on Non-Financial Information Disclosure*

A key policy area for the Dutch government in promoting the development of CSR is sustainability reporting. The mandatory requirements on non-financial information disclosure can be found in the Dutch Civil Code 1992 (the Code)[878]

876 *Id.*

877 National Action Plan on Business and Human Rights of the Netherlands, 20 December 2013. Available at: http://business-humanrights.org/sites/default/files/documents/netherlands-national-action-plan.pdf (Accessed on March 9, 2017).

878 The Dutch Civil Code (in Dutch: the Burgerlijk Wetboek) is the civil code of the Netherlands, which was reformed in 1992. The Code consists of 10 Books, dealing with natural persons and family law, legal persons, property law, law of succession, real property rights, obligations and contracts, particular contracts, transport law and means of transport, intellectual property and international private law. Available at: http://www.dutchcivillaw.com/civilcodegeneral.htm (Accessed on April 8, 2017).

and the Environmental Management Act 2004 (the Act).[879] To be exact, the Article 2: 391 of the Code[880] is the direct implementation of the EU '*Modernization Directive on the annual and consolidated accounts of certain types of companies, banks and other financial institutions and insurance undertaking*'[881] into the Dutch law. According to this Article, "an organization should, to the extent necessary for an understanding of their development, performance or position as far as relevant, give some information (financial and non-financial) about the environment, employees, and risks in their annual reports."[882] A specific chapter on environmental reporting[883] of the Act provides detailed requirements for the preparation of an environmental report. In addition to the national reporting standards, the Dutch government also adopts the international guidelines and principles on sustainability reporting to improve transparency, such as the GRI Sustainability Reporting Guidelines.

In addition to the legislative actions, a unique action to enhance information transparency taken by the Dutch government is the establishment of the 'Dutch Transparency Benchmark' by the Ministry of Economic Affairs in 2004. Through this Transparency Benchmark, the Dutch government aims to enhance the content and quality of CSR reports of the largest Dutch companies by providing non-binding guidance on how to report their policies and the outcomes in the area of CSR. The Transparency Benchmark[884] is performed every year to "assess the extent to which businesses account for their

879 In the Netherlands, almost all national environmental regulations have been incorporated into the integrated Environmental Management Act. Since about 80% of Dutch environmental regulations are derived from EU legislation in this respect, the Environmental Management Act is generally based on EU legislations and regulations Available at: https://www.government.nl/topics/environment/contents/roles-and-responsibilities-of-central-government/eu-legislation (Accessed on April 7, 2007).

880 Paragraph 1 of Article 2:391 prescribes that "if necessary for a good understanding of such development, of the results or of the situation of the legal person and group companies, the analysis comprises both, financial and non-financial performance indicators, including environmental and employee matters". Available at: http://www.dutchcivillaw.com/civilcodebook022.htm (Accessed on April 8, 2017).

881 *OJ* L 178/16, 17.7.2003.

882 KPMG *et al.* 2013, p. 69.

883 The title of Chapter 12 of the Act is 'Reporting, Record-Keeping and Monitoring Obligations'.

884 This Transparency Benchmark consists of 50 criteria, including a content-oriented framework of standards and a quality-orientated framework of standards. '*Criteria Transparency Benchmark 2016*.' Available at: https://www.transparantiebenchmark.nl/sites/transparantiebenchmark.nl/files/afbeeldingen/criteriatbeng.pdf (Accessed on March 13, 2017).

activities in the field of Corporate Social Responsibility (CSR) in their annual reports."[885]

3.1.2.4 *MVO Nederland* (*CSR Netherlands*)

To further raise awareness of CSR particularly among SMEs, the Dutch Ministry of Economic Affairs established a nationwide knowledge and information centre for corporate social responsibility—MVO Nederland (in English: CSR Netherlands) in 2004.[886] The most important mission of this national knowledge centre is to encourage more corporations, particularly SMEs, to integrate social and environmental issues into their business strategies and daily operations. By establishing a broad and dynamic business network with more than 2000 partners[887] from business and other organizations, MVO Nederland can bring companies, governmental organizations, trade unions, and NGOs together to facilitate collaborations, provide practical information and exchange best and worst experiences of CSR.

3.2 *CSR Policies in France*

3.2.1 The French Approach to Developing CSR

In the past decade, the recent development of CSR in France is remarkable.[888] According to a survey from the National Institute of Statistics and Economic Studies (INSEE)[889] in 2012, more than half of the French companies with more than 50 employees have acclaimed their involvements in CSR practices in their business. Particularly in the wake of corporate scandals and serious environmental pollution issues caused by French companies,[890] both the French government and the French public have paid more attention to the adverse effects of irresponsible business conduct. The then Premier Minister of France said that: "the deep crisis we are experiencing is not only a financial and economic one but also an environmental one."[891] In this context, the French government set up an ambitious goal to become a leading nation in supporting the development

885 For more information on the Dutch Transparency Benchmark, available at: http://www.transparantie benchmark.nl/ en/node/2 (Accessed on March 13, 2017).

886 For more information on MVO Nederland, available at: http://www.mvonederland.nl/ (Accessed on March 13, 2017).

887 *Id.*

888 Beaujolin and Capron 2005, pp. 97–108.

889 INSEE, '*Corporate social responsibility: an already widespread approach*', 2012. Available at: http://www.insee.fr/en/themes/document.asp?ref_id=ip1421 (Accessed on March 10, 2017).

890 For example, the AZF explosion accident happened in Toulouse, France in 2001.

891 Excerpt from the closing speech of Jean-Marc Ayrault, the then Prime Minister of France at the Environmental Conference on 14 and 15 September 2012 in Paris.

of CSR. As a result, a wide range of policies and strategies has been launched to achieve this goal. Several characteristics of the French national framework on CSR make it different from those of other Member States.

First, the role of the French government is traditionally strong,[892] and it also plays a leading role in promoting the development of CSR. In practice, the French government strengthens the development of CSR by means of mandatory approaches, such as the mandatory information reporting policy.[893]

Second, the French understanding of CSR is explicitly related to the concept of sustainable development. Therefore, the CSR-related policies constitute an important part of the French national strategy on sustainable development and of its national strategy on ecological transition.[894]

Third, the wide adoption of the global CSR guidelines and principles also take a position within the French CSR policy framework. In contrast with the Dutch CSR approach mentioned above, the French approach does not develop its own definition of CSR, but chooses to make reference to a set of globally recognized CSR standards, such as the UN Global Compact, the ISO 26000, the OECD Guidelines for Multinational Enterprises, the UN Guiding Principles on Business and Human Rights, and the EU 2011 CSR strategy. This phenomenon echoes the French government's ambition of being a leader on CSR and sustainability at both the EU level and the international level. As a result, the French government wants to keep its national CSR policy framework consistent and coherent with the international standards on CSR. There are several critical moments in the efforts of the French government to establish its national policy framework.

First, in 2001 the disclosure requirements were first introduced by the New Economic Regulations Act (Nouvelles Régulations Economiques Act, NRE Act). Since then, the French government has actively worked on enhancing information transparency.

Secondly, in 2007, the '*Grenelle for the environment*' multi-stakeholder forum was organized with the aim to take a step forward in the CSR development in France, which led to the promulgation of two new laws: the Grenelle I Act (2009) and the Grenelle II Act (2010). Several important conclusions of this forum have been embodied in these two laws, including "widening of compulsory non-financial reporting, promotion of socially responsible investment, the creation of labels for companies of all sizes attesting to the quality of their

892 Beaujolin and Capron 2005, p. 99.

893 For further discussion on French mandatory information disclosure, see Section 3.2.2.1.

894 Government of France, '*Preparatory document for the French national plan for the development of corporate social responsibility* (CSR),' 2013, p. 4.

management in environment and social fields and their contribution to environmental protection, training of employees on the environment, sustainable development and risk prevention".[895]

Thirdly, at the 2012 Environmental Conference to the National Council for Ecological Transition, the first 'Roadmap for Ecological Transition'[896] was adopted. In this roadmap, the French government put an emphasis on the importance of implementing CSR policies to the nation by stating that "it is essential that France continues to play a leading role at a time when, at European level, Member States are invited to take a new step forward."[897] Moreover, the deployment of policy instruments in promoting CSR was also strengthened in this official statement.[898]

Fourthly, a comprehensive action platform was also established under the supervision of the French Prime Minister,[899] in order to facilitate regular dialogues between a range of stakeholders for sharing ideas and best experiences of CSR.

3.2.2 Key CSR Policies

As mentioned above, an important feature of the French policy framework is the strong position of public authorities in promoting the development of CSR. This feature can be best exemplified in two policy areas: the mandatory reporting system and the socially responsible investment (SRI).

3.2.2.1 *Mandatory Non-Financial Information Disclosure in France*

A significant achievement of the French CSR policy framework is the establishment of the mandatory non-financial information disclosure. The French government started to improve the disclosure of non-financial information in 2001, and many regulations and policies have been subsequently developed in the following decade.

As early as in 2001, the French Parliament passed the 'New Economic Regulations Act' (Nouvelles Régulations Economiques), also well-known as the NRE Act. The NRE Act required all companies listed on the stock exchange to disclose information "on how the company takes into account the social

895 *Id*, p. 9.

896 The first 'Roadmap for Ecological Transition' was presented in 2012, and to date it has been updated twice: the second version in 2013 and the third version in 2015.

897 The French Ministry of Ecology, Sustainable Development and Energy, '*Roadmap for Ecological Transition*', 2012.

898 Government of France, '*Preparatory document for the French national plan for the development of corporate social responsibility* (CSR),' 2013.

899 *Id*, p. 10.

and environmental consequence of its activity and impact on its societal commitments in support of sustainable development, combating discrimination and promoting diversity."[900] A subsequent implementation decree of the NRE Act was enacted in 2002, which identified about 40 social and environmental topics on which a company should report.[901] The NRE Act is frequently regarded as the first legal framework on extra-financial reporting with far-reaching influence because it provides access for shareholders and stakeholders to understand the overall performance of companies.[902] However, the NRE Act also contains some obvious imperfections. One of the most significant challenges in this framework lies in the lack of sanctions in case of violations or non-compliance, which can be attributed to the long tradition of 'orientation laws'[903] in France.

So far, the compliance of the NRE Act has been regularly assessed by a variety of institutions, including governments, auditing institutions, and rating agencies. The assessment results indicate that the NRE Act has achieved positive results in incentivising more and more companies to disclose environmental, social and governance (ESG) issues in their reports. For example, according to an analysis conducted by the Ministry of Ecology, Sustainable Development and Energy in 2007, about 81% of companies had at least made some efforts on reporting.[904] The C3D organization (College of Sustainable Development Executives) also observed that the publication of a sustainability report became a prevailing trend among the top French companies.[905] Furthermore, according to a survey of KPMG in 2013, France has won the first place in terms of corporate responsibility reporting rates among large companies.[906] However, a clear disparity of reporting levels is also observed between different sectors. According to a French rating agency Vigeo,[907] the average reporting percentage in the

900 Article L 225-102-1(5) of the Commercial Code.

901 These topics are on the one hand inspired by the GRI performance indicators, and on the other hand are taken from the "French social report", a list of social data required from all companies to show compliance with labor regulation.

902 Government of France, '*Preparatory document for the French national plan for the development of corporate social responsibility* (CSR),' 2013, p. 11.

903 The 'orientation law' is a specific type of law adopted in France with the aim of setting important objectives for the nation reinforced with significance that preliminary decisions carry.

904 The French Ministry of Foreign Affairs, '*The French legislation on extra-financial reporting: built on consensus*', 2012.

905 *Id.*

906 KPMG 2013.

907 Vigeo is a French rating agency founded in 2002 as the leading European expert in the assessment of companies and organizations with regard to their practices and performance on environmental, social and governance (ESG) issues.

telecommunications sector reached 76%, while the proportion in the financial sector was only 53%.[908]

To further improve the non-financial information disclosure, the French government launched a nationwide multi-stakeholder forum on sustainable development in 2007, also known as the '*Grenelle for the environment*'. At this forum, representatives from central government, local authorities, business, trade unions, environmental and consumer NGOs, and academics gathered to discuss the environmental issues that France confronted. The forum concluded by committing to set up goals for sustainable development, which led to the adoption of two new laws: the Grenelle I Act (2009) and the Grenelle II Act (2010).[909] It also sends a clear signal that the French Government acts as an interventionist in promoting sustainability reporting and non-financial information disclosure.

The milestone for France moving towards the mandatory non-financial information disclosure is Section 225 of the Grenelle II Act,[910] which requires companies to disclose information "on how they take into account the social and environmental consequences of their activity and social commitments in favour of sustainable development."[911] After two-years of lengthy and tough negations, the implementation decree of Section 225 was published in 2012, amending Section 225-102-1 of the Commercial Code, with several significant changes compared to the NRE Act.

First, it widens the scope of reporting entities by setting up certain thresholds, such as the number of employees, total assets or annual net sales. In short, Section 225 encompasses all types of companies with more than 500 employees, including all listed companies and non-listed companies. Even for the subsidiaries of foreign companies operating in France, as long as they meet the specific thresholds in terms of employee numbers and net revenue, they are also required to disclose their social and environmental performance.[912] To help companies to better implement this new reporting requirement, it also provides different timetables for every type of company. Considering the varieties of different types of companies, the implementation schedule is a

---

908 Vigeo, '*CSR: what do companies do report on?*', February 2010. Available at: http://www.vigeo-eiris.com/en/2010/02/11/csr-what-do-companies-do-report-on/ (Accessed on April 8, 2017)

909 French Decree No. 2010–788

910 Institute RSE 2012.

911 The French Ministry of Foreign Affairs, '*The French legislation on extra-financial reporting: built on consensus*', 2012.

912 The thresholds vary depending on the specific types of companies.

progressive one.[913] Article L 225-102-1 of the Commercial Code clearly prescribes that all state-owned companies irrespective of size are also subject to the mandatory reporting requirements.

Secondly, it broadens the scope of information that is required to be reported. The decree lists 42 topics on which companies must report. The 42 reporting topics can be divided into three basic categories: environmental, social and governance (ESG) indicators. For each category, companies have the discretion to choose the most important indicators that are financially material for their business operations.

Thirdly, the 'report or explain' principle is applied in this decree. This principle generally means that companies could decide to omit certain information on several subjects in this report, but they need to explain the reason why they choose to exclude such information from their reports.

Fourthly, it also states that a parent company also should consolidate ESG issues of all their subsidiaries in the report.

Fifthly, it ensures the quality of company self-reporting by prescribing that a company's report must be signed by the Board of Directors, and must also be audited or verified by an independent third-party body. The independent auditors should provide opinions on the quality of the report as well as the possible reasons for the omission of certain information.

In September 2012, the French government organized the '*Environmental Conference for the Ecological Transition*', during which, the importance of mandatory non-financial information disclosure was confirmed.[914] It also concluded that after more than ten years' efforts, the French policy framework on sustainability reporting has been successfully built on consensus.[915]

3.2.2.2 *French Policies on Socially Responsible Investment*

Another key area of the French CSR policy framework is socially responsible investment (SRI). France is one of the most developed SRI markets in Europe,[916] because its SRI assets have experienced substantial growth in the recent decade. According to a recent survey of Novethic,[917] during the past ten years, the

---

913 The French Ministry of Foreign Affairs, '*The French legislation on extra-financial reporting: built on consensus*', 2012.

914 *Id.*

915 *Id.*

916 Eurosif 2014, p. 43.

917 Novethic is a research and media expert in sustainable finance based in Paris. The subsidiary of the Caisse des Dépôts group pursues three main goals: first, fostering quality of responsible investment, conducting high quality of research, and raising awareness of ESG topics.

SRI assets in France have increased from € 3.9 billion EUR in 2003 to € 169.7 billion EUR in 2013.[918] A series of regulatory instruments to promote SRI is regarded as an important driver for the dynamic growth of the SRI market in France.

The first regulation is the 'Act of 19 February 2001 on a generalisation of employee savings', which introduced "an incentive into the Monetary and Financial Code for managers of employee savings funds to take into account environmental and social criteria in their asset management policy."[919] The second legal provision is the amended Section 224 of the Grenelle II Act and its subsequent implementation decree (2012). Section 224 requires the Asset Management Companies (AMCs) to integrate ESG issues into their investment policies, and they must disclose information as to how they deal with ESG issues in their annual reports.[920]

In addition to the legislative actions above, the French government also encourages stakeholders to participate in developing the voluntary SRI initiatives. For example, the French public authorities lead by example in creating several public pension funds, such as the 'Pension Reserve Fund', the 'Additional Civil Service Pension Establishment', and the 'Civil service complementary retirement fund'.[921] All these public pension funds are required to comply with the SRI principles and policies endorsed by the French government. Furthermore, the French government also supports the development of NGOs in the field of SRI and CSR, taking Vigeo and Novethic as examples. Vigeo,[922] founded in 2002, has dedicated itself to become a leading organization in evaluating the practice and performance of companies and organizations on ESG issues. Vigeo regularly publishes thematic studies on CSR and SRI to provide investors and companies with a better understanding as to how to incorporate ESG issues into their business operations. Novethic was launched in 2001 as a leading research and analysis center on SRI. In 2009, Novethic launched the first European label for SRI funds. The introduction of SRI Label aims to "provide individual investors with a framework for Sustainable and Responsible Investment (SRI) products offered by investment managers".[923] Novethic also established

918 Novethic, '*The transformation of Responsible Investment in France*', April 2014.

919 Government of France, '*Preparatory document for the French national plan for the development of corporate social responsibility* (CSR),' 2013.

920 *Id.*

921 *Id.*

922 For more information about Vigeo, available at: http://www.vigeo.com/csr-rating-agency/en/1-2-qui-sommes-nous-2 (Accessed on March 10, 2017).

923 For more information about the SRI Label, available at: http://www.novethic.com/socially-reponsible-investment/french-european-sri/sri-market.html (Accessed on March 10, 2017).

the 'Green Fund Label',[924] which is awarded to the financial organizations that focus on solving environmental issues.

3.3 *CSR Policies in the United Kingdom*

3.3.1 The UK-Approach to CSR

The UK government has been a major driver for the contemporary development of CSR in the UK for a long time.[925] As a pioneer and practitioner, the efforts of the UK government in this respect could be traced back from the Thatcher and the Blair governments, who have actively advanced the development of CSR during their terms of administration despite their different political standings. The rapid growth of CSR in the UK was closely related to the profound governance crisis, particularly in the 1980s, when the UK government was confronted with a profound governance crisis of high unemployment, urban decay, and social unrest.[926] In this context, CSR was employed by the UK government as a solution to overcome governance deficits as well as a positive contribution to society for a variety of reasons. Moon[927] summarized three key rationales to justify the involvement of the UK government in promoting CSR, that is, "substitute for government effort", "complement of government effort", and "legitimation of government policies".

In practice, the UK government has taken many actions to promote CSR.

Appointment of a Minister of CSR. A landmark event happened in 20002 when the then Prime Minister Tony Blair appointed the world's first Minister for CSR[928] under the Department of Trade and Industry (DTI).[929] The main responsibility of CSR ministers was to promote CSR in the UK. The DTI further clarified its attitudes and duties of the UK government in directing the discourse of CSR as follows: "the government has an ambitious vision for corporate social responsibility: to see private, voluntary and public sector organizations in the UK take account of their economic, social and environmental impacts,

924 For more information about Green Fund Label, available at: http://www.novethic.com/socially-reponsible-investment/environmental-funds/sri-market.html (Accessed on March 10, 2017).

925 Moon 2004, pp. 1–24.

926 Moon and Richardson 1985.

927 Moon 2002, pp. 385–408.

928 Since 2000, the UK government has appointed 7 CSR ministers, but then it stopped appointing a new minister. Available at: http://3blmedia.com/CSR-Blogs/UK-sees-no-need-CSR-Minister-anymore (Accessed on March 10, 2017).

929 The UK Department of Trade and Industry was replaced with the creation of the Department for Business, Enterprise and Regulatory Reform and the Department for Innovation, Universities and Skills (BIS) on June 28, 2007.

and take complementary action to address key challenges based on their core competencies—locally, regionally, nationally and internationally."[930]

Establishment of CSR institutions. The UK government also actively develops a strategic partnership or collaboration with other stakeholders by supporting the establishment of many CSR institutions. Examples include the 'Business in the Community', the 'Ethical Trading Initiative', and the 'LEAD International'. For example, the Business in the Community (BITC) is one of the largest and also oldest CSR organizations in the UK[931] and also a Prince's responsible business network,[932] with the aim to encourage the governmental organizations to work together for addressing CSR issues and thus making contributions to society.

Implementation of international CSR guidelines. In addition to a range of domestic policies, the UK government also takes the implementation of international CSR guidelines as a priority of its policy agenda. A breakthrough action in this field is the implementation of the UN Guiding Principles on Business and Human Rights. At the time when the UN Guiding Principles were published in 2011, the then Prime Minster Cameron made the implementation commitment in the UK. In 2013, the UK launched the national action plan '*Good Business: Implementing the UN Guiding Principles on Business and Human Rights*'.[933] The UK became the first nation to fulfil this commitment, and it sent a clear message of the UK government's expectation for the responsible business operations of companies operated both within the UK and abroad.

3.3.2 Key CSR Policies

3.3.2.1 *National Action Plan on Corporate Responsibility (CR)*

As a response to the EU 2011 CSR strategy,[934] the UK government made the commitment to developing its national action plan on CSR. According to the peer review report from the European Commission,[935] the UK government promised to develop a comprehensive CSR framework covering a wide range of

930 Smith 2003, p. 4.

931 The BITC was founded in 1980 in the UK. Available at: http://www.bitc.org.uk/about-us/what-we-do/our-history (Accessed on March 10, 2017).

932 The BITC is one of The Prince's Charities, a group of not-for-profit organizations of which The Prince of Wales is President.

933 The UK Foreign & Commonwealth Office, '*Good Business: Implementing the UN Guiding Principles on Business and Human Rights*', first published on September 4, 2013 and last updated on May 12, 2016.

934 See *supra* Section 2.2.2.

935 For more information about the peer review reports on CSR, available at: http://ec.europa.eu/social/keyDocuments.jsp?advSearchKey=CSRprreport&mode=advancedSubmit&langId=en (Accessed on March 10, 2017).

relevant themes, including the alignment with global CSR approaches, improving business reporting and disclosure, improving understanding of responsible supply-chain management, encouraging more SMEs to adopt responsible business activities, enabling profession and career development for practitioners of CSR, strengthening the relationship between business and society, improving understanding of the relationship between business and human rights, and improving consumer awareness and trust.[936]

For the preparation of this framework, a public consultation '*Corporate responsibility: a call for views*' was launched from 27th June to 27th September 2013.[937] The consultation finally received 152 replies in total from a wide variety of stakeholders. The summary of these responses was published in '*Good for Business & Society: government response to call for views on corporate responsibility*' in March 2014.[938] This report first declared its position by defining corporate responsibility (CR) as "voluntary action business taken over and above legal requirements to manage and enhance economic, environmental and societal impacts."[939] According to this definition, the UK approach primarily viewed CSR as a business-led activity that could create shared values for business and for society.

The main body of this report is the synthesis of the 152 responses, which covers several related themes, that is, 'CR revolution', 'horses of courses',[940] 'collaboration', 'community and role of government'.[941] Concerning the role of government, there was a divergence between respondents who called for more legislation through updating the existing laws or enacting new laws and those who were against it. People against legislation argued that CSR should be mainly business-led activities and hence should not be driven by external pressure. Moreover, they expressed their worries that the regulatory defects, such as bureaucratic inefficiency and weak enforcement, would impede the

936 *Id.*

937 BIS, '*Corporate Responsibility: A call for views*', June 2013. Available at: https://www.gov.uk/government/uploads/system/uploads/attachment_data/file/209219/bis-13-964-corporate-responsibility-call.pdf (Accessed on March 10, 2017).

938 BIS, '*Good for Business & Society: government response to call for views on corporate responsibility*', April 2014. Available at: https://www.gov.uk/government/uploads/system/uploads/attachment_data/file/300265/ bis-14-651-good-for-business-and-society-government-response-to-call-for-views-on-corporate-responsibility.pdf (Accessed on March 10, 2017).

939 *Id.*

940 Under the theme of 'horses of courses', the majority of respondents pointed out the different roles of stakeholders in promoting the development of CSR.

941 BIS, '*Good for Business & Society: government response to call for views on corporate responsibility*', April 2014.

corporations' ability to put CSR into practice. However, the majority of respondents agreed that government could play a 'light touch' role[942] and particularly it could act as an intermediary to facilitate social dialogues between regulators, business, and other stakeholders. To live up to this expectation, the government could collaborate with a wide range of stakeholders to provide more information concerning "the government's expectation and minimum standards, case studies and, examples of best and bad practice."[943]

3.3.2.2 *Public Policies on Corporate Accountability*

In December 2012, the Department for Business, Innovation & Skill (BIS) and HM Treasury published a policy on 'Corporate Accountability (2011–2015)', with the aim of promoting responsible business.[944] To make corporations more accountable to their shareholders and also to the whole society, the UK government initiated a series of relevant policies in several specific areas: "improving corporate reporting, making company boards more representative of women, bringing in legislation that gives shareholders more power to link pay to performance, providing a national contact point for the OECD Guidelines for Multinational Enterprises, making employee ownership more accessible, and ending unacceptable bonuses in the financial sector."[945]

One priority of this policy was to improve corporate non-financial information disclosure. More particularly, the quality of corporate reporting has become a key issue on the UK policy agenda. Section 417 of the Companies Act 2006 already required companies to disclose information on general environmental, social and community issues in their annual reports.[946] As a response to the increasing pressure to improve company accountability, the UK government began to update the Companies Act 2006 to meet the changing societal expectations. For the preparation of this new law, the UK government organized a consultation on '*The Future of Narrative Reporting*' from August to October 2010,[947] to collect views on how to improve corporate transparency

942 *Id.*

943 *Id.*

944 BIS & HM Treasury, '*2010 to 2015 government policy: Corporate accountability*', May 2015. Available at: https://www.gov.uk/government/publications/2010-to-2015-government-policy-corporate-accountability/2010-to-2015-government-policy-corporate-accountability (Accessed on March 10, 2017).

945 *Id.*

946 Companies Act 2006, s.417.

947 BIS, '*The Future of Narrative Reporting*', August 2010. Available at: https://www.gov.uk/government/consultations/the-future-of-narrative-reporting-a-consultation (Accessed on March 12, 2017).

and accountability. The consultation received many replies from a wide range of stakeholders, such as companies and business, investors, trade unions, NGOs, lawyers and many other stakeholders. The summary of these replies was published in December 2010.[948] Based on the results of this consultation, the UK government published the '*The Future of Narrative Reporting: A new structure for Narrative Reporting in the UK*' in October 2012.[949] In this report, the UK government proposed a new structure of company reports, and the *Companies Act 2006* (*Strategic Report and Director's Report*) *Regulations 2013* came into force on 1st October 2013.[950]

Under the new Section 414A of the Companies Act 2006, a company is required to prepare a strategic report within the director's report. Section 414C also prescribes that in the case of a quoted company, the strategic report must include information on "environmental matters (including the impact of the company's business on the environment), the company's employees, and social, community and human rights issues."[951] Moreover, to guarantee the quality of the company strategic reports, Section 414E prescribes that "a strategic report must be approved by the board of directors and signed on behalf of the board by a director or the secretary of the company."[952] However, SMEs are exempted from the new regulations under Section 414B.

Moreover, the European Commission issued a new directive regarding disclosure of non-financial and diversity information by certain large undertakings and groups in November 2013,[953] which requires the Member States to transpose into national legislation by 6 December 2016. This requirement could be a new opportunity for the UK government to improve the quality of non-financial information disclosure.

948 BIS, '*The Future of Narrative Reporting—A Conclusion*', December 2010. Available at: https://www.gov.uk/government/uploads/system/uploads/attachment_data/file/97718/10-1318-summary-of-responses-future-narrative-reporting-consultation.pdf (Accessed on March 13, 2017).

949 *Id.*

950 BIS, '*The Future of Narrative Reporting: A new structure for Narrative Reporting in the UK*', October 2012. Available at: https://www.gov.uk/government/uploads/system/uploads/attachment_data/file/34745/12-979-future-of-narrative-reporting-new-structure.pdf (Accessed on March 13, 2017).

951 *Id.*

952 *Id.*

953 *OJ* L 330, 1 15.11.2014.

4 Sustainability Reporting Practice of European Companies

After presenting a variety of CSR/CER policies at the EU and Member States level, another focus of this chapter is to examine the actual impacts of these various public policies on corporate sustainability performance. More particularly, an important question arises here as to what extent these CSR/CER policies truly motivate companies to improve their performance towards sustainability. As already discussed in the previous chapters of this book, corporate sustainability performance varies widely across sectors, districts, and countries. As a result, the CSR/sustainability reporting practice has been selected as the main target of case studies in this book for several reasons.

First, sustainability reporting provides insight into CSR/CER performance. As one of the most popular instruments in the business community, sustainability reporting has been widely employed by companies to communicate their performance on sustainability development and CSR/CER. Today sustainability reporting has become a standard practice in the business world and it has been regarded as the 'the de facto law for business'.[954] According to a survey by KPMG, 71% of the 4100 surveyed companies across 41 countries published sustainability reports in 2013.[955] Moreover, corporate self-reporting has become the most important source for stakeholders to acquire information concerning corporate sustainable performance.

Second, sustainability reporting does address the increasing demands for corporate transparency. Corporate transparency has been a big concern for public authorities for a long time. In practice, sustainability reporting has become a priority issue on the policy agenda of CSR. The government is regarded as one of the important drivers for the rapid growth of sustainability reporting.[956] As discussed in the previous chapter[957] and also in this chapter, the EU and the many Member States have developed a broader set of initiatives and policies for promoting corporate non-financial information disclosure, which has already achieved some positive progress in this domain. For example, due to the disclosure requirements of Denmark's revised '*Financial Statements Act*', the number of large reporting companies has significantly increased from 50 to 95 percent.[958]

954 KPMG 2013.
955 *Id.*
956 KPMG *et al.* 2013.
957 See Chapter 6, Section 4.2.
958 KPMG *et al.* 2013.

Third, sustainability reporting discloses corporate impacts on environment and society. Sustainability reporting[959] refers to information disclosure about a company's impacts on the environment and the society.[960] It is generally regarded as a significant step for companies to move towards a sustainable corporate performance. In practice, sustainability reporting practices vary widely in both content and form, depending on different organizational size and industry classification.[961]

This section aims to gain more insights of sustainability reporting practices of European companies. More particularly, this section answers an important question of to what extent an increasing number of public policies on sustainability reporting has changed corporate reporting practice. Three European companies are selected from different Member States and industries. These companies are: the Dutch chemical company AkzoNobel, the French bank BNP Paribas, and the British oil and gas giant British Petroleum (BP). By analyzing the formats and contents of the sustainability reports from these selected companies, the following questions will be answered in this section:

- What is the current state of sustainability reporting practices of these companies?
- What changes have occurred with regard to their sustainability reporting practice in different periods?
- To what extent have the sustainability reporting guidelines and standards influenced the preparation of sustainability reports of these companies?

4.1 *AkzoNobel in the Netherlands*[962]

As a leading paints and coating company as well as a major producer of specialty chemicals, AkzoNobel operates in more than 80 countries around the world. As one of the sustainability leaders in the material and chemical industry, the importance of sustainability is widely acknowledged and firmly embedded into AkzoNobel's business strategy as one of the three core principles[963] and one of the five strategic focus areas.[964] In practice, AkzoNobel

959 In this book, the different countries or companies may use different terminologies, such as CSR reporting, sustainability reporting, non-financial reporting, and ESG reporting.

960 SWD (2013) 127.

961 *Id.*

962 This section gives an overview of AkzoNobel's sustainability reporting practice primarily based on the information from its 2015 report and corporate website.

963 The three core principles of AkzoNobel are safety, integrity and sustainability.

964 The five key areas include: care for the customer, reduction of product and process complexity, cash and return on investment, embedded safety and sustainability, and diverse and inclusive talent development.

has set up a range of policies to integrate sustainability into the way they run a business. Particularly in 2013, AkzoNobel adopted the new sustainability agenda called '*Planet Possible*', with the aim of delivering leading sustainability performance when building their leading market positions in paints, coatings and specialty chemicals. Based on their experience and expertise in the chemical industry, AkzoNobel strives to create more values from fewer resources through three pillars: sustainability business, resource efficiency, and capable engaged people. For each pillar, AkzoNobel also sets up specific targets for 2020. For example, in the pillar of sustainable business, AkzoNobel aims to invest 20 percent revenue for eco-premium solutions with a downstream benefit by 2020 to provide customers with a significant sustainability advantage compared with the most commonly available equivalent commercial products or industrial processes. In addition to this sustainability agenda, AkzoNobel also develops a sustainability framework to map out the detailed progress towards sustainability.

As an important part of its business strategy, AkzoNobel has a solid history in corporate reporting practices since the publication of the first annual report in 1969. However, it was not until 2004 that AkzoNobel started to publish a separate report on sustainability performance. From 2008, AkzoNobel has presented a fully integrated report consisting of detailed and consolidated financial and sustainability statements. An important reason for adopting the integrated reporting approach is to seek ways of linking sustainability performance to business results in areas, such as resource efficiency, carbon reduction, eco-premium solutions, safety, people development and engagement, and operational eco-efficiency. Particularly, since the company is committed to fully embedding the values of sustainability into their business strategy and operations, sustainability topics have been fully integrated into all sections of this report. By doing so, it could prove that a good performance in sustainability could provide positive and substantial results in financial performance as well.

AkzoNobel uses the principle of materiality to assess the important topics that should be included in its report. Among a long list of more than 200 possible material topics, AzkoNobel finally chooses 18 topics in economic, social and environmental dimensions.[965] In particular, the environmental topics involve energy, resource use, carbon emissions throughout the value chain, eco-premium solutions and value chain management, product stewardship, sustainability in the supply chain, climate change, operational eco-efficiency,

965 AkzoNobel Report 2015.

and biodiversity.[966] For every topic, there are specific requirements on what information should be disclosed in terms of qualitative and quantitative. Further, all topics are arranged in a hierarchical order based on their respective importance to business from low, medium to high degrees.

AkzoNobel also develops a set of corporate reporting tools to manage compliance and integrity at the company, such as the competition law compliance declaration, the non-financial letter for representation and share dealing statements.

As discussed above, the rapid growth of sustainability reporting practice today can be explained by various factors, such as: (1) the increasing demand and pressure from shareholders as well as stakeholders, (2) the growing acceptance of the importance and value of sustainability reporting, (3)(3) and last but not the least the amount of policies and regulations for promoting sustainability reporting. In fact, the sustainability reporting practice of AkzoNobel has been influenced by a range of policies and regulations in this domain. At the national level, the mandatory requirements on the non-financial information disclosure became one of the most important drivers for the development of sustainability reporting in the Netherlands.[967] Particularly in 2004, the Dutch Ministry of Economic Affairs established the Transparency Benchmark. In the same year, AkzoNobel started to prepare a separate sustainability report based on the pre-designed criteria of the Transparency Benchmark, including relevance, clearness, reliability, responsiveness, and coherence. As a result, AkzoNobel has received a positive evaluation from the Transparency Benchmark. In 2015 AkzoNobel ranked first on the Transparency Benchmark.[968]

AkzoNobel makes references to several important international reporting guidelines and standards, including the GRI Guidelines (the G4), the UN Global Compact, and the OECD Guidelines. In particular, AkzoNobel has built the connections between the G4 reporting indicators and its own material topics in preparing the sustainability report. As an important part of its report, AkzoNobel also provides a full overview of their reporting practices against the GRI guidelines, including an index of the G4 indicators and additional information regarding the goals and performance, policy management system, organizational responsibility, training and awareness, and monitoring/follow-up for each indicator. As a signatory to the UN Global Compact, AkzoNobel

966 *Id.*

967 See *supra* Section 2.3.

968 For more information about the Dutch Transparency Benchmark, available at: https://www.transparantiebenchmark.nl/en/about-transparantiebenchmark (Accessed on March 13, 2017).

also provides an updated summary of their progress in the implementation of the Ten Principles of the United Nations Global Compact in their reports. Further, AkzoNobel makes strong public commitments to the Caring for Climate platform. AkzoNobel is an active member of the Global Compact Netherlands Network, and it also subscribes to the UN Universal Declaration of Human Rights, the key conventions of the International Labour Organization, the OECD Guidelines for Multinational Enterprises, and the Responsible Care Global Charter, and the CEO Water Mandate.

It can be observed that the sustainability reporting policies at both national and international levels have exerted a considerable influence on the undertaking of sustainability reporting by the Dutch companies like AkzoNobel. The sustainability performance of AkzoNobel has been widely acknowledged by several influential sustainability ratings and indices. For example, in 2015, AkzoNobel has been identified as the Top Materials Industry Group of the Dow Jones Sustainability World Index (DJSI World) for the fourth consecutive year.[969] The company is consistently maintained in the Euronext Vigeo World 120 index,[970] which distinguishes companies achieving the most advanced environmental, social and governance performances and is reviewed every six months.[971]

4.2 *BNP Paribas in France*[972]

A recent survey indicated that today about two-thirds of national policies and initiatives for sustainability reporting are mandatory requirements,[973] and France is one of most cited examples of the mandatory reporting systems.[974] The sustainability reporting practices of French companies can be taken as a good example to discuss the influence of mandatory requirements on sustainability reporting practice. As one of the largest banks worldwide, the French multinational bank BNP Paribas Group (BNP Paribas) is frequently regarded as a leader in the field of sustainability and CSR/CER.

---

969 For more information, available at: https://www.akzonobel.com/for-media/media-releases-and-features/akzonobel-ranked-top-djsi-fourth-year-row (Accessed on March 13, 2017).

970 The Euronext Viego World 120 index selects the 120 most advanced companies in terms of corporate responsibility at a global level. Available at: http://www.vigeo.com/csr-rating-agency/en/actualites-a-presse/blog-9 (Accessed on March 13, 2017).

971 This index is updated in June and December of every year.

972 This section is mainly based on the information included in BNP Paribas Corporate Social Responsibility Report as well as the additional information on its official website.

973 KPMG *et al.* 2013, p. 13.

974 See *supra* Section 1.

Given its sector-specific role in the global economy, BNP Paribas makes commitments to 'act as a responsible bank' by placing its CSR commitments at the heart of its strategic priorities. Since 2002, BNP Paribas has developed a set of CSR policies. After a decade's efforts, today BNP's CSR policy consists of 4 pillars comprising 12 specific commitments.

- In the first CSR pillar about economic responsibility, BNP Paribas mainly cites three aspects: long-term financing for the economy, business ethics, and a range of responsible products.
- In the second CSR pillar about social responsibility, BNP Paribas seeks to develop a committed and fair human resources policy through recruitment, mobility and training; diversity; and responsible employment management.
- In the third CSR pillar about civic responsibility, BNP Paribas aims to combat exclusion, promoting education and culture and in order to achieve this goal, BNP Paribas makes three commitments involving: micro-finance and support for social entrepreneurship, efforts to combat exclusion and support human rights and corporate philanthropy policy, focusing on culture, solidarity and the environment.
- In the fourth CSR pillar about environmental responsibility, BNP Paribas focuses on addressing climate change via financing policy commitments in sensitive sectors, reducing the environmental footprint associated with their own operations, and supporting relevant research aimed at combating climate change.

Particularly, in order to manage the indirect environmental impacts of their financing and investment activities, BNP limits high-impact projects and supports the development of the green economy. They also actively help their clients to make an environmentally friendly investment choice by providing relevant knowledge and expertise. BNP Paribas makes significant efforts to reduce their direct environmental footprint in terms of CO_2 emissions, paper management, and waste processing. In addition to the management of the indirect and direct environmental impacts of their business activities, BNP Paribas sets up the Climate Philanthropy program to support research projects on climate change.

As mentioned above, the mandatory requirements on non-financial information disclosure play a strong role in the development of sustainability reporting practices in France.[975] In the case of BNP's sustainability reporting, the disclosure of social and environmental information in its 2002 report is in accordance with administrative order 2002-221 dated 20 February 2002 in the

975 See *supra* Section 1.

application of Article 116 of the NRE Act, and is provided in the appendices to the review of operations.[976] The NRE appendices are provided by listing every key performance indicator and the review of business operations in each aspect. For example, the environmental chapter of the NRE Act consists of 19 performance indicators.[977] For every indicator, BNP Paribas provides data or detailed information with regard to their performance and achievements over the past fiscal year. When the NRE Act was amended by the Article 225 of the Grenelle II Act in 2010,[978] some new changes occurred in BNP Paribas's CSR report as a response to the new reporting requirements. For example, BNP Paribas started to report based on the Article 225 of the Grenelle Act II and also adheres to a range of international guidelines and standards, such as the GRI guidelines, the United Nation Global Compact, ISO 26000 and UNEP.

In the case of BNP Paribas, the mandatory requirements have been regarded as one of the most important drivers for French companies to continuously improve the quality of their sustainability reports. Not surprisingly, BNP Paribas has received positive appraisals for its achievements from many prestigious rating agencies. For example, BNP Paribas ranks in second place in the banking sector for CSR on Viego's NYSE Euronext Viego World 120, Europe 120 and France 20 reference indices.[979] It also maintains its positions on FTSE4 Good Index Series, STOXX Global ESG Leaders, United Nations Global Compact 100 and DJSI World.[980] In 2015, BNP Paribas were included in the 'Global 100 most sustainable corporations in the world', which rates the top-100 companies from over 4600 global listed companies[981] in terms of sustainable development based on their assessing standards.[982]

---

976 BNP Paribas Sustainable Development Report 2002. Available at: https://invest.bnpparibas.com/ sites/default/files/documents/5576.pdf (Accessed on March 13, 2017).

977 The 19 performance indicators include: water consumption; raw material consumption; energy consumption; measures taken to improve energy efficiency; use of renewable energy sources; soil pollution; atmospheric emission of air; water and soil; noise and odor pollution; waste processing; measures taken to avoid upsetting the biological balance; measures taken to ensure compliance with legal requirements; internal department for environmental management; environmental training and information programs for employees; methods used to reduce the risks for the environment; structures to deal with pollution caused by the company to the surrounding environment; amount of compensation paid following legal decisions relating to the environment; and environmental objectives set for foreign subsidies.

978 See *supra* Section 1.

979 BNP Paribas Corporate Social Responsibility Report 2014, p. 7.

980 *Id.*

981 *Id.*

982 The rating results were analyzed by Corporate Knight from over 4600 listed companies whose market capitalization exceeds 2 billion US dollars.

4.3 *British Petroleum in the UK*[983]

As one of the world's leading oil and gas companies, BP has operations in more than 70 countries around the world and plays an important role in supporting economic development and improving the quality of life for people by providing energy. Facing the growing worldwide demand for energy as well as the climate challenge, BP recognizes the significance of sustainability for the future of their business. In order to become a world-class operator, a responsible corporate citizen and a good employer, BP believes that the best way to achieve the sustainable business is to create long-term value for both shareholders and their partners and local communities where they operate.

BP started to engage in sustainability reporting practice in the very early 1990s. Although the titles of these reports change over time,[984] the main goal of BP's sustainability reporting is to communicate the impacts of their business activities on the environment, the societies, and the economies as well as the sustainability level of their performance. In practice, BP is facing a variety of sustainability-related issues, so it is important to identify and prioritize the most relevant issues that are financially material to their long-term interests. However, the priority issues may evolve over time and vary depending on differing concerns of various stakeholders. For example, the key issues of the 2014 report included the Gulf of Mexico oil spill, the energy future, the business operation, safety, environment and society, while the top priorities for 2015 were accidents and oil spills, business ethics, climate change, human rights, local environmental impacts, managing risks and value to society. For each topic, the BP sustainability report provides detailed information regarding their activities and performance for addressing these material issues.

When BP published its first environmental report in 1991 and the first single sustainability report in 1998, there were no statutory requirements or widely accepted standards concerning the preparation, publication, and assertation of environmental and social reports. BP developed its own reporting framework, involving the detailed challenge of the contexts, selected document review, interviews with executives and managers, and site-based reviews to understand how the non-financial policies are being implemented and reported upon.[985] Today, with the rapid development of sustainability practices, there are a lot of policies, guidelines, and standards for sustainability reporting

---

983 This section is mainly based on the information included in the BP Sustainability Report as well as additional information available on its official website.

984 The differing titles of BP's non-financial performance reporting include: Environment and Social Report, Environmental and Social Overview, and Environmental and Social Review.

985 BP Sustainability Report 1998.

around the world. In this context, BP has adopted a set of international reporting guidelines and principles as its reporting standards to further improve the quality of its sustainability reports.

The first important international reporting standard for BP is the '*GRI Sustainability Reporting Guidelines*'. As early as in 2005, the BP sustainability report was prepared in accordance with the GRI guidelines for the third year. Further, as an important organizational stakeholder of GRI, BP also actively participated in the revision progress of GRI's G3 sustainability reporting guidelines which was launched in 2006.[986] Today BP continues to prepare its sustainability reports in accordance with GRI's G4 sustainability reporting guidelines to meet the core criteria. In addition to the general reporting standards, BP also reports against the '*GRI Oil and Gas Sector Supplement*' (OGSS).

The second important reporting standards are the '*Oil and Gas Industry Guidance on Voluntary Sustainability Reporting*', jointly produced by the 'Global Oil and Gas Industry Association for Environmental and Social Issues' (IPIECA), the 'International Association of Oil & Gas Producers' (IOGP) and the 'American Petroleum Institute' (API). BP for the first time reported against this sector-specific reporting standard in the BP Sustainability Report 2005. Compared to the GRI guidelines, this sector-specific sustainability reporting guidance for the oil and gas industry represents the consensus on the material sustainability issues for the oil and gas industry. Based on their expertise in this respect, BP also establishes three levels of sustainability reporting at group, country and site levels.

Since 2003, BP has entitled its non-financial performance disclosure as sustainability report. Also in this report, BP starts to participate in the UN Global Compact. As a signatory to the UN Global Compact, BP keeps updating its progress on the implementation of the Ten Principles of the UN Global Compact. BP also makes reference to the principles of the GRI guidelines[987] to report on their non-financial performance.

An overview of BP's history in the sustainability area proves that BP' sustainability reporting practice has been significantly boosted by relevant policy and regulation at international, regional and national levels. During a long period, BP has been honoured as a sustainability leader in oil and gas sector. In particular, prior to the Deepwater Horizon Spill in 2010, BP has topped many rankings on sustainability for the oil and gas sector.[988]

986 BP Sustainability Report 2006.

987 The GRI guideline was first launched in 2000 and then revised in 2002.

988 Todd Cort, 'Lessons for the CSR industry from the Deepwater Horizon spill', *GreenBiz*, July 27, 2010. Available at: https://www.greenbiz.com/blog/2010/07/27/lessons-for-csr-reporting-from-deepwater-horizon-spill (Accessed on April 24, 2017).

5 Summary and Some Concluding Remarks

The development of CSR/CER in the European context showed that in practice public authorities could play and have already played an important role in promoting CSR/CER. This conclusion is supported by a variety of CSR/CER policies and initiatives at both the EU and the Member States levels. At the EU level, we can see that the EU has been actively participating in enhancing a common understanding of CSR/CER and in stimulating CSR/CER practices across Europe. To reach this goal, the EU institutions have developed a series of CSR/CER policies and initiatives during the past decades, including the Green Paper on CSR and the 2011 EU CSR strategy. In this context, CSR/CER has emerged as a new policy field on the EU agenda.

At the Member State level, an increasing number of national governments are involved in the CSR/CER policy arena. This chapter examined the CSR/CER policies of three leading Member States: the Netherlands, France and the United Kingdom. The overview of CSR/CER policies of these three countries also reflects some major development trends in this domain. First, a combination of mandatory and voluntary policies has been observed from the CSR/CER policy framework of three countries. Second, the current CSR/CER frameworks tend to focus on large companies, listed companies, and state-owned companies, but small and medium size enterprises are usually exempt from obligations.[989] Third, the harmonization of the national framework and international framework is a common denominator, because many countries make reference to the existing and widely-accepted international guidelines, principles, and standards in their national CSR/CER frameworks.

This chapter also examined the actual effects of CSR/CER policies on corporate behaviour, particularly in the field of sustainability reporting practices. In particular, we discussed whether the sustainability practices of European companies are boosted by the relevant policies. The analysis of this chapter generally showed that positive outcomes have been observed in this domain. According to the recent survey of KPMG,[990] European companies usually outperformed other regions in terms of the number and the quality of the sustainability reports. However, it is equally argued that many problems and potential risks are associated with the current sustainability reporting practices by European companies. In 2013, the European Commission conducted an impact assessment with regard to the disclosure of non-financial and diversity information, and the results of this study showed that there is a need to further

989 KPMG *et al.* 2013, pp. 16–17.

990 KPMG 2013.

enhance the transparency of sustainability information disclosure.[991] Through this impact assessment, two major problems of the current EU reporting initiatives were identified: one is the inadequate transparency of non-financial information, and the other one is the insufficient diversity in the boards.

Despite the remaining problems associated with the current European CSR/CER framework, the European experience indeed set a good example of promoting CSR/CER. What we can learn from the European experience is that the government could play an active role in stimulating CSR/CER practices by means of various policy instruments. The case studies of the three selected European companies also showed that CSR/CER policies could encourage environmentally responsible conducts to some extent.

The AkzoNobel Reports show and substantiate the substantial progress in the CSR/CER performance of AkzoNobel over the years and also develop a long-term vision of its CSR/CER involvement, provide material information and the innovations related to that involvement. It closely follows new guidance from the GRI Guidelines and other international CSR/CER Guidance. The Reports also make reference to progress on the issues in the UN Global Compact and show progress in terms of the OECD Guidelines. AkzoNobel is a front runner in the Transparency Benchmark and has been the top performing materials industry company in the Dow Jones Sustainability Index for many years.

The BNP Paribas Reports have provided performance on various non- financial indicators for a very substantial number of years. BNP also closely follows new national requirements as well as international developments in CSR/CER guidance. BNP Paribas ranks in the top of various Banking Sector Indices.

British Petroleum has for long been a leader in sustainability reporting and performance in the UK but also in the international community. The Deepwater Horizon Oil Spill in the Gulf of Mexico showed some substantial gaps in the CSR/CER performance. This provided an unexpected end of its status as CSR/CER champion. BP also lost its top positions in all rankings on sustainability which has already stayed like that for several years.

The European experience on CSR/CER development will be quite relevant for the discussion of China's CSR/CER development in the following chapters.

991 SWD (2013) 127.

CHAPTER 8

The Chinese Approach to CSR/CER: A Theoretical Analysis

1 Introduction

Up to now the concept and practice of CSR/CER have been primarily discussed in a global context and particularly in the Western context. Despite the fact that today CSR/CER has become a global phenomenon, the interpretation and implementation of CSR/CER are to a large extent depending on the specific institutional context and the cultural background in which companies operate.[992] The emergence of CSR/CER took place at a later moment in China than in the Western countries. It was not until the beginning of the 21st century that CSR/CER became a prominent issue for both Chinese policymakers, business leaders, scholars and the public. Ever since the growth of CSR/CER has been fast in China and has become a hot topic on the policy agenda and also in academic circles. China being an important player in the international arena, the development of CSR/CER in an emerging market, like China, attracts increasing attention abroad. To better explore the Chinese approach to CSR/CER, this chapter is constructed as follows.

Section 2 starts with a brief introduction of China's institutional background in economic, societal, cultural and international dimensions. By doing so, it provides the significant difference in terms of institutional backgrounds between China and the Western countries. Section 3 focuses on the two aspects in the development of CSR/CER in China: first, it explores how the concept of CSR/CER is defined in the Chinese context from an academic and a political perspective; second, it provides the evolution of CSR/CER development in China from a historical perspective. Section 4 provides a close look at the roles of various actors in the development of CSR/CER in China, including the government, state-owned enterprises, foreign multinational enterprises, NGOs and other private actors. Section 5 addresses the key CSR/CER issues in the Chinese context. Section 6 provides a summary and some conclusive remarks.

992 Campbell 2007, pp. 946–967.

 | DOI:10.1163/9789004368132_009

2 The Institutional Background for China's CSR/CER Development

Although the current development of CSR/CER shows a tendency of convergence at the global level, the divergence of CSR/CER under the different institutional contexts should also be emphasized. Particularly it has been observed that the Western approach does not fit the Chinese reality very well, given the different institutional landscapes in China and Western countries.[993] Therefore, this section provides a brief introduction to China's institutional background, which lays the foundation for the discussion of CSR/CER development in China. In this section, China's institutional background will be analysed from a political-economic, a cultural and an international perspective.

2.1 *The Political-Economic System of China*

In a socialist society, the state[994] remains in a dominant position which is the case in China's political and economic system. In this regard, a critical step for successfully running a business in China is to understand the potential pressures that companies may encounter from the regulators. On top of that, during the past decades, the Chinese context has experienced fundamental changes as far as the relationship between the government and the business community is concerned. There are two turning points in the history of the People's Republic of China: one is the founding of the new government in 1949, and the other is the Third Plenum of the Eleventh Central Committee of the Chinese Communist Party (CPC) in 1978.

After decades of war, the People's Republic of China announced its independence on October 1st, 1949.The devastating economic and social degradation posed significant challenges to the new government as to how to reconstruct China's economy. Facing the complicated internal and external situations, the new Chinese leadership chose to embrace the doctrine of socialism. During the first Five-Year Plan (1953–1957), China achieved the transformation to socialism by adopting the Soviet model of the centrally planned economy.[995] Within this economic system, all enterprises were collectively owned and tightly controlled by the government. In other words, private enterprises were almost eliminated from China's economic structure at that time.

However, the centrally planned economy did not make the journey of China's economic recovery a smooth one but it had been hampered by

993 Wang and Juslin 2009, pp. 433–451.

994 In this chapter, the Chinese state refers to both the CPC and the Chinese governments at both central and local levels.

995 Coase and Wang 2012, p. 5.

various factors. The first important reason could be attributed to the significant lack of autonomy, which was often regarded as the fatal defect of the centrally planned system. It is widely agreed that the high-level governmental intervention in the market led to "the lack of incentives and initiatives for people at the bottom of the social pyramid, and the lack of information and accountability for those at the top."[996] Second, due to the lack of experience of the new government, the economic recovery was severely disrupted by wrong economic and social policies. More particularly, the 'Great Leap Forward' and the 'Cultural Revolution' caused tragic consequences for Chinese society.[997]

The Third Plenum of the Eleventh Central Committee of the CPC in 1978 (the Third Plenum of 1978) is widely recognized as a watershed event in China's modern history, which brought fundamental changes to China's social and economic development. On this historical meeting, the Chinese new leadership, centered on Deng Xiaoping, made the decision to move the focus of the government from the class struggle to socialist modernization.[998] In this context, the Third Plenum of 1978 is the starting point of China's transition from a centrally planned economy to a socialist market economy. To achieve this profound transformation, the Chinese government took a series of reform measures, involving agriculture reform, industry reform, the industrialization of rural areas, the promotion of the private economy, and the establishment of special economic zones.[999] As a key component of the China's market economy transition, the enterprise reform,[1000] particularly the reform of State-owned Enterprises (SOEs), has considerably influenced the development of CSR in this period.[1001]

At the beginning of the economic reform, the Chinese government first focused on one of the weakest areas of the Chinese socialist economy—SOEs, given their critical roles in China's economic and political systems. In China, SOEs were perceived by the Chinese leaders as the core of socialism,[1002] so the reform of SOEs was regarded as a focal point in the whole economic reform as well as a key step to revitalize China's economic development.[1003] In the centrally planned economy, SOEs were enterprises only in name due to the remarkable lack of managerial autonomy. Closely affiliated with the Chinese government,

996 *Id.*
997 *Id*, pp. 14–21.
998 *Id*, p. 37.
999 *Id.*
1000 For more discussion about the enterprise reform, see Section 3.2 and Section 4.2.
1001 Zhao 2014.
1002 *Id*, p. 65.
1003 *Id*, p. 43.

SOEs were under the strict supervision of governmental bureaucracy. In this period, SOEs were compelled to organize their activities in accordance with the state plan, which decided "what and how much to produce, whom to hire or lay off, how much to invest, or how to compensate managers and workers."[1004] As the adverse effects of this centrally planned economy became stronger, the Chinese government took a series of measures to improve the production and profitability of SOEs by transferring more managerial powers to SOEs. Specifically, SOEs were given more economic freedom to operate beyond the state plan, and they were also allowed to retain a certain amount of profits after fulfilling their state quotas. These reform measures achieved some progress in motivating managers and workers to improve their productivity and efficiency.

However, it is equally argued[1005] that despite a certain degree of progress, the enterprise reform of this period was unable to revitalize SOEs only through 'delegating rights and sharing profits.'[1006] In fact, these reform measures were built on a fundamental pre-requisite that SOEs should first fulfil their obligations in accordance with the state plan. Coase and Wang described this distinctive feature of the Chinese economic structure as the 'dual-track system', where the centrally planned economy co-existed with the market economy.[1007] In this situation, SOEs were still facing a variety of constraints, which to a large extent undermined their economic performance. Consequently, many SOEs still struggled to survive from insolvency during the late 1980s and the 1990s.[1008] Another impressive achievement of China's economic reform is the rapid growth of private enterprises. More particularly, the attitudes of the Chinese leadership towards non-public sectors have changed from a strong resistance to a fully supportive stance. Today, the non-public sectors have been widely recognized as an important component of China's socialist market economy.[1009]

The analysis above indicates that the changing political and economic situation has created more managerial power and independence for the business sector which has been a favourable condition for China's CSR/CER development during the past decades. However, it should be emphasized that even today SOEs are still facing a variety of constraints. A priority of China's further economic reform is to establish a modern enterprise system in which SOEs are

1004 *Id*, p. 44.
1005 *Id*, p. 69.
1006 *Id*, p. 129.
1007 *Id*, p. 45
1008 *Id*, p. 69.
1009 People's Daily, '*China reaffirms its supportive stance for the non-public sector*', March 7, 2016. Available at: http://en.people.cn/n3/2016/0307/c98649-9026173.html (Accessed on April 7, 2017).

truly free from governmental intervention and are motivated by the market disciplines. In this process, the Chinese state will position itself as the "business-friendly service provider instead of supervisors and regulators."[1010]

2.2 *The Cultural Background of China*

Another distinctive feature of China's institutional context is derived from Chinese traditional culture. Since the theory of CSR/CER is to a large extent built on Western culture and values,[1011] it is argued that the concept of CSR/CER should be understood through the lens of the Chinese traditional culture.[1012] Particularly, certain values of CSR/CER can accordingly be interpreted within the Chinese cultural context.[1013] A growing body of literature[1014] also argues that the Chinese traditional culture and philosophy shares the same values as the concept of CSR/CER.

The idea of harmony is at the heart of the Chinese traditional culture, and it has been highly worshiped by many Chinese philosophers, such as Confucius, Mencius, and Xunzi. In particular, the Confucian philosophy has a strong influence on Chinese business ethics, such as the harmonious relationships, moral codes and ethical systems.[1015] The value of harmony is frequently emphasized in the Confucian masterpiece—the Analects. In the Analects, harmony is a critical criterion for differentiating superior men (*junzi*) from inferior men (*xiaoren*). Confucius says that the superior men appreciate harmony instead of sameness, whereas the inferior men seek sameness but do not harmonize.[1016] According to Confucianism, superior men respect different opinions and more importantly they are also capable of finding out a harmonious solution to balance the conflicts among the various opinions.[1017] On the contrary, the inferior people simply look for uniformity. In the system of the Confucian philosophy, harmony does not only exist within individuals but also occurs at different levels of the family, the nation, and the world. Confucius further elaborates the harmony in five types of relationship ('*wulun*'). They are the relationship between ruler and subordinate, father and son, husband and wife, brothers, and friends. Confucius believes that if harmony can be achieved in these five

1010 Coase and Wang 2012, p. 143.
1011 Wang and Juslin 2009, p. 435.
1012 See e.g. Wang and Juslin 2009, pp. 433–451; Xu and Yang 2009, pp. 321–333.
1013 Wang and Juslin 2009, p. 433.
1014 Phoon-Lee 2006, pp. 23–26.
1015 Wang and Juslin 2009, p. 439.
1016 Analects 13. 23.
1017 *Id.*

relationships, it will lead to the '*Great Harmony*' where people could live in an absolutely harmonious way without any conflict with others.[1018]

On the way to achieve the ultimate goal of the '*Great Harmony*', Confucius believes that five virtues ('*wuchang*') should be self-cultivated by humans, and they are humanness ('*ren*'), righteousness ('*yi*'), ritual ('*li*'), wisdom ('*zhi*'), and sincerity ('*xin*'). More particularly, '*ren*' is the foremost virtue among all five virtues.[1019] It traditionally refers to the quality of being 'superior men' by fulfilling their social responsibilities.[1020] In the context of modern business, the virtue of '*ren*' requires enterprises to fulfil their responsibilities towards their shareholders, stakeholders, and the society. The second virtue worshiped by Confucian philosophy is '*yi*', the righteousness, which refers to the pursuit of ethical righteousness regardless of economic loss.[1021] The virtue of '*yi*' has been embraced as the important business ethics. This virtue generally requires that enterprises should not only focus on economic profits, but also cultivate other virtues, such as humaneness, ritual, wisdom, sincerity, and responsibility.[1022] The last virtue that is closely related to the Chinese business ethics is the sincerity—'*xin*', which simply means humans should live up to their promise. When applied to business activities, this virtue could be understood as good reputation of enterprises.[1023]

Today, the Confucian harmony also finds its values in modern society. The Chinese policymakers have translated this traditional wisdom into public policies, laws, and practices to meet their practical needs. For example, the guiding ideology of 'Building a socialist harmonious society'[1024] is in essence consistent with the Confucian idea of the '*Great Harmony*'.[1025] In this context, the Chinese traditional culture proposes a new way for both Chinese policymakers and business leaders to promote the development of CSR/CER in a Chinese context.

2.3 *The External Pressure from the Global Market*

In the age of globalization, CSR/CER is becoming a global issue beyond the concerns of one specific company or nation. Some scholars also perceived

1018 Wang and Juslin 2009, p. 441.
1019 *Id*, pp. 443–444.
1020 *Id.*
1021 *Id*, p. 444.
1022 *Id.*
1023 *Id.*
1024 For more discussion on 'building a socialist harmonious society', see Section 4.1.
1025 *Id*, p. 441.

the rapid growth of CSR/CER in China as a result of global consequences.[1026] Particularly in the wake of anti-sweatshop campaigns and the environmental movement from the 1990s, many MNEs were facing a growing demand from the customer market to improve their supply chain management.[1027] As a response, many MNEs started to incorporate CSR/CER into their supply chain management, by imposing higher or stricter environmental standards on their suppliers.[1028] The environmental or green supply chain management movement (ESCM or GSCM)[1029] has exerted great impacts on the Chinese manufacturing industry, especially those that are export-oriented.

Particularly after China's entry into the World Trade Organization (WTO) in 2001, the Chinese enterprises are facing many challenges as well as opportunities from the global market. With regard to the challenges, the green supply chain movement was first rejected by both the Chinese government and the business leaders. Viewed from their positions, the green supply chain movement was a form of protectionism, with the aim of curtailing the competitiveness of Chinese enterprises in the global market. As a result of the 'green trade barrier', the Chinese products and services were exposed to international standards, which were usually higher or stricter than the domestic standards. In this context, the Chinese manufacturing enterprises were forced to pay additional costs for implementing these standards.

In light of the opportunities, the increasing pressure from the global supply chain pushes more and more Chinese enterprises to embrace CSR/CER. This, in fact, contributed to the rapid growth of CSR/CER practices in China. Moreover, as an increasing number of foreign investments flood into China, the mature experience and the advanced technologies on corporate environmental

1026 Li, 'Lack of corporate social responsibility behind recent China accidents', *China Watch, World Institute Vision for a Sustainable World* (December 12, 2005). Available at: http://www.worldwatch.org/lack-corporate-social-responsibility-behind-recent-china-accidents (Accessed on April 7, 2017).

1027 The supply chain management encompasses all activities associated with the flow and transformation of goods from raw materials (extraction), through the end user, as well as associated information flows. Materials and information flow both up and down the supply chain. (See Handfield and Nichols 1999, p. 2).

1028 For example, some MNEs, like Wal-Mart, develop their own "Code of Conducts" to specify their specific social and environmental expectations for their suppliers. Some MNEs compel their suppliers to comply with the international standards, like the SA8000 Standard or the ISO 14000 Standard on environmental management.

1029 In current literature, there are a number of definitions of ESCM or GSCM. For example, Narasimhan and Carter (1998) described ESCM as "the purchasing function's involvement in activities that include reduction, recycling, reuse and the substitution of materials". Green *et al.* (1996) defined GSCM as "the way in which innovations in supply chain management and industrial purchasing may be considered in the context of environment."

management are also brought to the Chinese enterprises. A large body of empirical literature[1030] also indicates the positive relationship between the adoption of green supply chain management and corporate environmental performance. Some scholars, therefore, argue that the adoption of green supply chain management provides the Chinese business community with 'win-win' opportunities for improving both their financial and environmental performance. In the long run, it enhances the competitiveness of the Chinese enterprises in the global market.[1031]

3 An Overview of CSR/CER Development in China

3.1 *The CSR/CER Definition with Chinese Characteristics*

As mentioned in the previous chapters,[1032] the current CSR/CER debate has been dominated by Western academics and practitioners for a long time. When CSR/CER was first introduced to Chinese society, the conceptual understanding of CSR/CER was to a large extent built on the mainstream Western literature in this field.[1033] However, a gap has been observed between the Western countries and China on their interpretations of CSR/CER.[1034] Particularly in practice, many efforts have been made to develop the Chinese definition of CSR/CER tailored to China's unique institutional and cultural contexts.

The history of adopting the Western concept of CSR in China is only 20 years old. From a historical perspective, the concept of CSR is not new to the Chinese society. In fact, the core idea of CSR accords with the values of the Chinese traditional wisdom. As early as 2500 years ago, a group of businessmen had already engaged in the earliest form of business ethics by applying the Confucian virtues to their business,[1035] such as '*ren*', '*yi*', '*li*', '*zhi*' and '*xin*'. These merchants are appraised as 'Confucian Traders' for their decent business activities. Therefore, some scholars propose to develop the original Chinese definition of CSR by incorporating the Chinese traditional culture. Wang and Juslin described their harmony approach of CSR as follows:

> Companies should apply the concept of 'harmony' to their business, and carry on their business in a harmonious way—both interpersonal

1030 Zhu and Sarkis 2004, pp. 265–289.

1031 *Id.*

1032 See Chapter 2.

1033 Xu and Yang 2010, p. 323.

1034 Wang and Juslin 2009, p. 433.

1035 See *supra* Section 2.

> (intercompany) and man-nature harmony. The overall goal for a company in implementing CSR is to cultivate the virtues of 'humaneness', 'righteousness', 'ritual', 'wisdom', 'sincerity' and 'responsibility', and to become a 'superior enterprise, in this way to contribute to the construction of a harmonious society.[1036]

Based on this definition, the concept of CSR within the Chinese cultural context can simply be interpreted as "respecting nature and loving people".

In addition to the efforts from academia, the Chinese government also developed the definition of CSR based on its political stance. Differing from the Western approach as well as from the harmonious approach above, this definition puts more emphasis on the important role of the government in directing the development of CSR, rather than on the interests of stakeholders in this process, such as consumers, investors, employees, and civil society. Yi Xiaozhun, the then vice minister of the Ministry of Commerce,[1037] defined the Chinese CSR concept as "a concrete action taken by Chinese companies to implement the political aspiration of the new Communist Party collective leadership -putting people first to create a harmonious society."[1038] Yi further strengthened the important role of the Chinese government in promoting the development of CSR at the China-EU CSR International Forum as follows:

> Government at the central and local levels attaches increasing importance to CSR. In short, CSR does not come into being purely because of individual awakening of entrepreneurs. It also requires advocacy and promotion by the government. Over the years, governments at all levels in China have stepped up CSR publicity campaigns so that the entire society will pay attention to and become involved in this process. At the same time, the government has also reinforced supervision over CSR by making regular assessment on the law observance of companies.[1039]

In a Chinese context, the concept of CSR is closely associated with two guiding ideologies of the Chinese society—the 'Scientific outlook on development' (*kexue fazhanguan*) and the 'Building a socialist harmonious society' (*jianshe shehuizhuyi hexie shehui*). To be exact, CSR became an important part of

1036 Wang and Juslin 2009, p. 445.

1037 Yi was vice minister of Ministry of Commerce from 2005 to 2010.

1038 Newsdesk, 'A Chinese definition of CSR', *Ethical Corporation*, September 15, 2005. Available at: http://www.ethicalcorp.com/content/chinese-definition-csr (Accessed on April 7, 2017).

1039 Yi 2005.

achieving the 'Scientific outlook on development', and the 'Building a socialist harmonious society' is the ultimate goal of 'Scientific outlook on development'. Consequently, these two ideologies are regarded as the underpinning guidelines of the CSR development in China.

The 'Scientific outlook on development' was first proposed by the then Chinese leader, Hu Jintao, at the Third Plenary Session of the 16th Committee in 2003, which later served as the strategic focus of China's further social and economic reforms. The two key themes of this ideology are 'putting people first' and the other is 'a comprehensive development'. To be more precise, the CPC seeks for a comprehensive, coordinated and sustainable development featuring 'putting people first'.

Subsequently at the Sixth Plenary Session of the 16th Central Committee in 2006, the '*Decision of the CPC Central Committee on Certain Major Issues Related to Building a Socialist Harmonious Society*' was adopted. This statement set forth the 'Building a harmonious socialist society' as the long-term goal of China's social and economic development. Also in this top-level political statement, the concept of CSR is for the first time explicitly put forward. The promotion of CSR among enterprises as well as the whole society is an important measure of strengthening environmental protection and building a harmonious relationship between human and nature. At the Third Plenary Session of the 18th Central Party Committee on comprehensive reform in November 2013, the fulfilling of social responsibility has been regarded as an important part of the establishment of the modern corporate system among SOEs in the '*Decision of the CCCPC on Some Major Issues Concerning Comprehensively Deepening the Reform*'.[1040]

Moreover, the development of CSR is also included in China's Five-Year Plan on National Economic and Social Development. The 12th Five-Year Plan (2011–2015)[1041] first required Chinese enterprises to fulfil their social responsibilities, particularly when operating overseas. The development of CSR is further emphasized in the 13th Five-Year Plan, as the concept of 'Green Development' has been listed as one of the five main principles for China's economic and social development.[1042] Particularly, in Chapter 48,[1043] a series of measures has been

1040 For more information of this official document, available at: http://www.china.org.cn/chinese/2014-01/17/content_31226494_2.htm (Accessed on April 7, 2017).

1041 For more information about the 12th Five-Year Plan, available at: http://www.gov.cn/2011lh/content_1825838.htm (Accessed on April 7, 2017)

1042 The five main principles of development under the 13th Five-Year Plan are innovation, openness, green development, coordination, and inclusive development.

1043 For more information about the 13th Five-Year Plan, available at: http://news.xinhuanet.com/politics/ 2016lh/2016-03/17/c_1118366322_13.htm (Accessed on April 7, 2017).

initiated to support the development of green and environmentally friendly industries, for example, the promotion of eco-labels and green public procurement, the establishment of a green financial system, and the development of green securities and credits.

Based on the analysis above, it can be observed that both the Chinese scholars and policy makers do not develop a separate definition of CER, but take the environmental dimension as an important component of the broad framework of CSR.

3.2 *The Evolution of China's CSR/CER Development*

After exploring the conceptual understanding of CSR/CER in China, this section focuses on another important question: how CSR/CER is developed in China. Historically, the idea of CSR/CER is not new to the Chinese society, since the Chinese business ethics could find their roots in Chinese traditional culture.[1044] Some scholars perceive the Chinese business ethics embedded in Chinese culture and philosophy as the traditional form of CSR/CER engagement.[1045] However, this book takes the founding of the People's Republic of China as the starting points of discussion, and the influence of Chinese traditional culture is categorized as an important cultural background for China's CSR/CER development.[1046]

It has been observed that the attitudes of the Chinese government towards CSR/CER have experienced a dramatic shift from "a passive approach to a proactive and participatory approach."[1047] By depicting the historical evolution of China's CSR/CER development, this section aims to provide an idea of the changing attitudes of the Chinese government towards CSR/CER, as well as their changing role in promoting CSR/CER over time. There are four important periods in China's CSR/CER development.

3.2.1 The First Period (from 1949 to 1978)

In the first period, the newly founded government chose to embrace the doctrine of socialism and to the Soviet model of the centrally planning for China's economic recovery. In this period, nearly all enterprises were collectively owned and tightly controlled by the CPC and the Chinese government.[1048]

1044 See *supra* Section 2 and 1.
1045 Wang and Juslin 2009, p. 435.
1046 See *supra* Section 2.
1047 Zhao 2014, p. 67.
1048 Tang and Li 2009, p. 202.

As a result, the roles of the government and the enterprises were mixed and dislocated.[1049]

During this period, SOEs played a unique role in China's centrally planned economic system, which was far from the modern enterprises that are well known today.[1050] It is widely agreed that under the centrally planned economy, SOEs were enterprises only in name due to the significant lack of managerial autonomy. In the centrally planned economy, SOEs controlled all major industries in China, and the ownership and control of SOEs were not separated but under the administration of the Chinese government or other relevant bureaucracy. In this case, SOEs were compelled to organize their activities in accordance with the state plan, which clearly decided "what and how much to produce, who to hire or lay off, how much to invest, or how to compensate managers and workers."[1051]

SOEs could not be categorized as mere economic organizations, but more like a governmental organization with multiple responsibilities. In addition to the responsibility for the production activities, they were also responsible for providing public services, including social welfare and social security. This phenomenon is known as 'enterprises-run societies'[1052] ('*qiye ban shehui*'[1053]) or 'enterprises burdened with social responsibilities'.[1054] SOEs, as the prototypical urban work unit system (also known as '*danwei*'), were responsible for welfare, health, education and the political indoctrination of workers as well as their families.[1055] Therefore, it was a common phenomenon at that time that hospitals, schools, and many other facilities were built and operated by SOEs.

However, the undertaking of social responsibilities by SOEs of this period cannot be recognized as a form of CSR practice for several reasons.[1056] First, SOEs under the centrally planned economy system generally functioned as governmental agencies rather than pure economic organizations. In essence, they are quite different from the modern corporation as discussed in the Western economic literature. Second, the various social responsibilities of SOEs were compulsory responsibilities authorized by the Chinese government,

1049 Wang and Juslin 2009, p. 436.
1050 Kratz 2013.
1051 *Id*, p. 44.
1052 Kuo *et al.* defined the term of 'enterprises-run societies' as a society in which schools, medical facilities, and other social service institutions are run and funded by enterprises.
1053 Lin 2010, pp. 86–88.
1054 Wang and Juslin 2009, p. 436.
1055 Naughton 2006, p. 300.
1056 See e.g. Wang and Juslin 2009, pp. 433–451; Lin 2010, pp. 64–100.

which generally did not fit the common understanding of CSR of 'going beyond legal compliance'.[1057]

3.2.2 The Second Period (from 1978 to 1990)

The second period started from China's economic reform in late 1978, which has been widely recognized as a historical event in China's modern history. As the adverse effects of the centrally planned economy system gradually intensified, severe economic regression and distortions broke out in China.[1058] Especially the Great Leap Forward and the Cultural Revolution brought a series of economic and societal crises to the Chinese policy makers and the general public. As a milestone in China's modern history, the economic reform was adopted by the Chinese policy makers on the Third Plenum of the Eleventh Central Committee in late 1978. The overarching target of the Chinese economic reform was to achieve the transition from a centrally planned economy to a market economy and to build a so-called 'socialist market economy with Chinese characteristics'.[1059] As a result, the economic reform brought many fundamental changes to China's economic and social development, which laid a solid foundation for China's economic prosperity in the following decades.

The reform of SOEs is at the heart of China's transition to a market economy. Under the centrally planned economy, the immense burdens of providing social services have been criticized as the leading cause for adversely affecting the financial performance of SOEs.[1060] In this context, the monopoly of SOEs was considered as a form of market failure,[1061] and restructuring reforms of SOEs were urgently needed. The foremost goal of this economic reform was to improve the financial performance of SOEs. As a result, the Chinese government channelled many efforts to help SOEs enhance their profitability, including the privatization of SOEs, the establishment of a modern corporation system, and the massive reduction of social responsibilities.[1062] On the other hand, SOEs were required to focus on the pursuit of profit maximization in order to survive from the fierce market competition. Due to the fierce reduction of mandatory social responsibilities in this period, the introduction of CSR/CER was overlooked and even rejected by both the Chinese government and enterprises during this period.

1057 See Chapter 2.
1058 Kratz 2013.
1059 The notion of the 'socialist market economy' was first put forward at the 14th Party Congress in 1992.
1060 Lin 2010, p. 87.
1061 Kratz 2013.
1062 See e.g. Wang and Juslin 2009, pp. 433–451; Lin 2010, pp. 64–100.

3.2.3 The Third Period (the 1990s)

The CSR movement in China started from the mid-1990s[1063] when foreign multinational enterprises introduced the idea of CSR to the Chinese market through the supply chain movement.[1064] Ironically, the motivation behind this phenomenon was due to the notorious image of Chinese manufacturing industry as 'sweatshops'. As a result, the Western idea of CSR was at first rejected by not only Chinese policymakers but also by the academic scholars for many reasons.

First, from a political perspective, CSR was regarded as "intervention in China's internal affairs"[1065] by the Chinese government. CSR was even condemned as a Western hegemony and a conspiracy of developed countries to circumvent the growth of the Chinese economy.[1066]

Secondly, from the economic perspective, CSR was treated as a trade barrier[1067] set up by the developed countries for weakening the competitiveness of the Chinese enterprises in the global market.

Thirdly, from an academic perspective, the concept of CSR was also opposed by some Chinese scholars, who followed Friedman's argumentation against CSR that the only responsibility of corporations was profit maximization.[1068]

Fourthly, from a practical perspective, CSR was a luxury to Chinese enterprises at that moment. Despite the progress of enterprise reform, many SOEs still struggled to survive from insolvency,[1069] and CSR was viewed as the expense of corporate profits.[1070]

3.2.4 The Fourth Period (from 2000 to Present)

The remarkable economic growth with a single focus on profit maximization caused many social and environmental problems, such as: environmental degradation, rising inequality, and administrative corruption. As a consequence, the attitudes of the Chinese government toward CSR changed again at the early beginnings of the 2000s. More particularly, the year of 2006 is regarded as the milestone in the evolution of CSR in China, as a large group of stakeholders, including the Chinese government, business leaders, academics, and NGOs, have actively participated in China's CSR development.[1071]

1063 Yin and Zhang 2012, p. 303.
1064 Wang and Juslin 2009, p. 434; Yin and Zhang 2012, pp. 301–316.
1065 Wang and Juslin 2009, p. 436.
1066 Tang and Li 2009, p. 202.
1067 *Id.*
1068 Friedman 1970.
1069 *Id.*
1070 CSR Asia 2015, p. 17.
1071 There is no consensus regarding the year of milestone for China's CSR development and in some literature the year of 2004 or 2005 is also regarded as the turning point.

Many reasons could explain the shifts of the Chinese government towards CSR. One important reason is that the social and environmental costs of the remarkable economic growth are increasingly alarming for both the Chinese policymakers and the public.[1072] Particularly, in the wake of corporate environmental scandals, companies have been strongly criticized for their unethical and irresponsible business behaviour. From the point view of the Chinese government, the promotion of CSR is a political strategy to sustain its ruling legitimacy in Chinese society and also to enhance the reputation of China as a responsible nation in the international context. As a result, the development of CSR in China draws a broad attention from both Chinese and the international community. Several major trends of China's CSR development in this period can be observed.

First, the Chinese government becomes one of the most important drivers for CSR development, because the Chinese government has changed its attitudes toward CSR from a passive approach to a pro-active approach. CSR issues start to appear on the agenda of CPC as well as of the Chinese government. As a result, an increasing number of CSR policies and regulations have been promulgated.[1073]

Secondly, many governmental and non-governmental organizations respond quickly to the official endorsement of CSR and actively participate in supporting and promoting the development of CSR.[1074] For example, the State-owned Assets Supervision and Administration Commission of the State Council, the Ministry of Environmental Protection, the China Securities Regulatory Commission, Chinese stock exchanges, industry associations, academic institutions, and NGOs have actively participated in developing various CSR initiatives based on their respective functions.

Thirdly, the remarkable improvement of CSR practices among Chinese enterprises is widely observed. An increasing number of Chinese enterprises started to take CSR seriously. Moreover, many Chinese enterprises have gradually expanded their CSR practices from corporate philanthropy to the incorporation of CSR into their business strategies. One specific example is the rapid growth of CSR reporting practice under the requirements of the '*Guidelines to the State-owned Enterprise Directly under the central Government on Fulfilling Corporate Social Responsibilities*'.[1075] According to the Guidelines, SOEs are required to undertake CSR practices through the regular information

1072 For more discussion on the social and environmental costs of China's economic growth, see Chapter 1, Section 1.2.

1073 See Chapter 9, Section 2.

1074 *Id.*

1075 See Chapter 9, Section 2.

disclosure on their CSR performance and sustainable development. As a result, the number of CSR reports published by SOEs has increased substantially, which comprised a majority of the total number of CSR reports in China. A study of China's sustainability reporting from SynTao shows that in 2010 Central SOEs published 78% of the total number of CSR reports in China.[1076] Further, it is also reported that the number of CSR reports published by Chinese enterprises accounted for 15% of the total number of CSR reports around the world,[1077] which makes Chinese enterprises important players in the field of CSR reporting.

4 The Role of Key Actors in China's CSR/CER Development

In the case of China, a large group of stakeholders has actively encouraged environmentally responsible conduct, such as the central government, local governments, governmental departments, stock exchanges, industry associations and academic institutions. This section discusses what specific roles these different actors have played in advancing the development of CSR/CER in China.

4.1 *Government*

The government has been widely regarded as an important driver of CSR/CER development,[1078] but significant differences remain between the Western countries and China. One of those differences relates to the extent to which the government could influence the development of CSR/CER. In the Western countries, the government does play an active role in advocating CSR/CER, but it is generally agreed upon that the CSR/CER movement is primarily driven by the market demand from the private sector, particularly shareholders, employees, consumers, investors, and NGOs. This approach is well-known as a 'society-led mode' or the 'bottom-up approach'.[1079] On the contrary, the Chinese government plays a dominant role in directing the discourse of CSR/CER in China, which is often mentioned as a typical example of a 'state-led model' or a 'top-down approach'.[1080]

The prominent role played by the Chinese government attracts increasing interest from both Chinese and Western academics. Many scholars observe

1076 SynTao 2010, p. 8.

1077 KPMG 2013.

1078 Moon and Vogel 2008, pp. 303–326.

1079 Vogel 2006; Lin 2010, pp. 64–100; Ho 2013, pp. 375–442.

1080 Ho 2013, pp. 375–442.

that the Chinese government plays a more influential role in shaping the development of CSR/CER than in the context of developed countries.[1081] For example, Ho,[1082] an American scholar, conducted an in-depth research into China's state-led model of CSR/CER, by identifying the diverse approaches employed by the Chinese government for advancing CSR/CER at both national and sub-national level.

First, the Chinese government does endorse CSR/CER through direct policy statements and sustainability goals set by the Chinese central government.[1083] In particular, the promulgation of the 'Building a harmonious socialist society' is widely regarded as a strong government signal on advancing CSR/CER.

Second, the Chinese government also acts as a facilitator of CSR/CER through active promotion of research, capacity building and the adoption of voluntary CSR/CER guidelines. For example, the Ministry of Commerce has established a research centre on CSR/CER.[1084]

Thirdly, the Chinese government also recognizes the importance and necessity of building effective partnerships with NGOs and civil society in promoting the development of CSR/CER.[1085] A good example in this field is the establishment of the 'Sino-German Corporate Social Responsibility Project',[1086] with the aim to develop and implement CSR/CER policies, strategies, and guidance through public- private partnerships with industry associations and other intermediaries.

Fourthly, the Chinese government also plays a regulatory role by issuing a series of mandatory requirements on CSR/CER.

A 2008 report of the OECD[1087] suggested some possible actions that the Chinese government could take to encourage environmentally responsible conducts, such as, by strengthening the enforcement of environmental regulation; supporting the development of NGOs and civil society; promoting the disclosure of environmental information; establishing a systematic and credible mechanism for evaluating corporate environmental performance; and developing international cooperation for exchanging and sharing information and best practices of CSR/CER.

1081 *Id.*

1082 Ho 2013, pp. 375–442.

1083 *Id.*

1084 *Id.*

1085 *Id.*

1086 For More information about this project, available at: http://csr2.mofcom.gov.cn/article/ref/201410/ 20141000780102.shtml (Accessed on April 8, 2017).

1087 OECD 2008, pp. 272–274.

Based on the prior academic achievements in this field, this chapter shed lights on three specific roles of the Chinese government in encouraging environmentally responsible business conducts.

First, the government's role as a regulator of CSR/CER. The Chinese government has developed a wide range of CSR/CER-related regulations and policies with the aim of encouraging environmentally responsible business,[1088] which makes CSR/CER as an emerging approach in China's environmental policy framework.[1089] In addition to the Chinese government, a range of government agencies and departments, such as the State-Owned Assets Supervision and Administration Council, the Ministry of Environmental Protection, etc., also actively responded to the government signal by developing their CSR/CER policies and guidelines.[1090] As a result, CSR/CER is widely described as a public policy in the Chinese context, rather than as a voluntary corporate commitment. Moreover, the state endorsement of CSR/CER is regarded as the primary driver for the rapid growth of CSR/CER in China. This scenario echoes what Gond *et al.* described as —'CSR/CER as mandated by government'.[1091]

Secondly, the government's role as a promoter and facilitator of CSR/CER. The Chinese government also makes considerable efforts in raising public awareness on CSR/CER, through the promotion of relevant research and education programs, capacity building and the adoption of voluntary CSR/CER guidelines.[1092] For example, the China Academy of Social Science (CASS), in partnership with the Ministry of Commerce (MOFCOM) established the Research Centre for Corporate Social Responsibility in 2008. The importance and necessity of building effective partnerships with NGOs and civil society in promoting the development of CSR/CER are also recognized by the government. Consequently, the recent decade also witnessed the rapid growth of NGOs in China. An example is the establishment of 'Sino-German Corporate Social Responsibility Project', with the aim to "develop and implement CSR/CER policies, strategies, and guidance via public- private partnerships, industry associations, and other intermediaries."[1093] This role of the Chinese government corresponds to what Gond *et al.* described as 'CSR /CER as facilitated by government' and 'CSR/CER as a partnership with the government'.[1094]

1088 Ho 2013, pp. 375–442.
1089 For more discussion on China's CSR policies and initiatives, see Chapter 9, Section 3.
1090 *Id.*
1091 Gond *et al.* 2011, pp. 640–671; Chapter 6, Section 1.
1092 Ho 2013, pp. 375–442.
1093 Ho 2013, p. 405.
1094 Gond *et al.* 2011, pp. 640–671; Chapter 6, Section 1.

Thirdly, the government role's as a supervisor of CSR/CER. The Chinese government also focuses their efforts on improving the implementation of Chinese CSR/CER policies, considering the decoupling risk of regulation and enforcement and the possibility of greenwashing or window dressing through CSR/CER. Lin[1095] argued that due to the uncertain and unpredictable nature of Chinese CSR/CER initiatives, the effects of China's CSR/CER initiatives on corporate behaviour are quite unclear: are they legally binding or just advisory? Zhao[1096] also observed that the current enforcement of CSR/CER-related regulation in China is far from satisfactory for being unclear, unpredictable and ineffective. In this case, many scholars suggest that the Chinese government should put more emphasis on the enforcement of CSR/CER regulations. This role also fits what Gond et al. described as 'CSR/CER as mandated by government' and 'CSR/CER as facilitated by government'.[1097]

Due to the continuous efforts of the Chinese government, the past decades witnessed the rapid growth of CSR/CER initiatives in China. However, it is argued that the Chinese government has not fully played its role in promoting the development of CSR/CER. Compared to many European countries, the development of CSR/CER has not been raised as a national strategy, and there is not yet a national CSR/CER framework nor a systematic policy mechanism.[1098]

4.2 *State-Owned Enterprises (SOEs)*[1099]

Prior studies[1100] show that from the corporate perspective, the level of CSR/CER engagement is affected by various factors, such as corporate size, financial performance, ownership structure, industry sector, and geographic location. Since the economic reform, there are several different types of enterprises organized under the Chinese legal system, including the state-owned enterprises (SOEs), collective-owned enterprises, foreign-invested enterprises, partnership enterprises, and sole proprietorship enterprise.[1101]

1095 Lin 2010, pp. 64–100.

1096 Zhao 2014.

1097 Gond *et al.* 2011, pp. 640–671; Chapter 6, Section 1.

1098 For more discussion on the critics of the role of the Chinese government, see Chapter 9, Section 2.1.

1099 In this book, SOEs refer to the state-owned enterprises under the direct supervision of the State-owned Assets Supervision and Administration Commission (SASAC) of the State Council. Today, there are 106 SOEs supervised by the SASAC in 2016. In some literature, they are also referred as central SOEs.

1100 See e.g. Stanwick *et al.* 1998; Zu and Song 2009, pp. 105–117; Li and Zhang 2010, pp. 631–645.

1101 Lou and Tian 2013.

In the Chinese context, it is widely observed that the CSR/CER implementation is more prominent in SOEs, where the corporate ownership by the state is more strongly secured than in other corporate types.[1102] During the past decades, SOEs have experienced fundamental changes in various aspects, particularly after the economic reform in 1978. Notwithstanding these changes, today SOEs still play an important role in China's economy as well as in China's political and social development. They are the central force for strengthening economic growth, implementing the national strategy and maintaining social harmony and stability. As a result, the Chinese SOEs are perceived as "the division or aggression of productive assets within the loosely organized firm of China, Inc."[1103] Not surprisingly, SOEs are facing high expectations from both the government and the public to become the leading examples in the field of CSR/CER, not only in the domestic markets but also in the global market.[1104]

As discussed above,[1105] the development of CSR/CER in China is closely related to the reform of SOEs.[1106] SOEs are the major subject of many CSR/CER-related initiatives. Under the influence of various CSR initiatives, a remarkable improvement of CSR/CER practices among SOEs can be clearly observed in recent years.[1107] However, many different opinions[1108] remain with respect to the relationship between the government and SOEs when engaging CSR/CER. Lin argued[1109] that in the Chinese context, SOEs cannot be regarded as a mere economic organization, but as a unique organization embedded with both economic and non-economic objectives. The Chinese government plays a dual role in the case of SOEs: one is a shareholder and the other is the regulator. That may, however, lead to a blurring boundary regarding the respective functions of government and business. On the one hand, the Chinese government as the largest shareholder of SOEs asks SOEs and their managers to focus on profit maximization. On the other hand, the Chinese government as the regulator and the supervisor also requires SOEs to fulfil part of the public responsibilities which the government is traditionally supposed to provide. Although SOEs have been granted a certain degree of managerial autonomy after the economic reform, the Chinese government still maintains its influential

1102 Li and Zhang 2010, pp. 631–645.
1103 Zhao 2014, p. 20.
1104 Li and Zhang 2010, pp. 631–645.
1105 See *supra* Section 2.
1106 Zhao 2014
1107 See *supra* Section 4.
1108 Lin 2010, pp. 64–100; Marquis and Qian 2013, pp. 127–148.
1109 Lin 2010, pp. 64–100.

position and has 'incentives to divert wealth to obtain social stability'.[1110] Hence, the question arises how one should interpret CSR/CER if this would, in the end, only result in the government withdrawing from their primary obligation to provide public services. In this scenario, Zu and Song[1111] perceived CSR/CER as another form of government intervention in a market economy, supposing that the Chinese government could utilize CSR/CER (more particularly in the case of SOEs) to achieve its political and social goals and hence to sustain its ruling legitimacy.

4.3 *Foreign Multinational Enterprises* (*MNEs*)

Another important player in China's CSR/CER development is the foreign multinational enterprises (foreign MNEs). As China's economy becomes more integrated into the global market, the development of CSR/CER in China is also perceived as a result of global consequences,[1112] in which foreign MNEs play a major role. According to the statistics of the Ministry of Commerce,[1113] by 2014, there were around 810,011 foreign-invested enterprises registered in China, which fulfil an important role in China's economic system. Since the economic reform and 'Open-up' policy in late 1978, China's economy became closely integrated into the global market. As a lot of foreign capital flowed into China, foreign MNEs play an increasingly important role in China's economic and social development. Particularly as mentioned above, the foreign MNEs pushed more and more Chinese enterprises to embrace CSR/CER, which was an important external driver of China's CSR/CER development.[1114]

However, underperformance of foreign MNEs in implementing CSR/CER also put them at the focus of public pressure, and their environmental performance in the emerging market has become a debatable topic. In the era of globalization, an increasing number of foreign MNEs tend to establish a global supply chain around the world. By contracting with the local suppliers, foreign MNEs benefit from the rich natural resources, cheap labour, and the lax environmental standards in the host country. By doing so, foreign MNEs substantially reduce business costs and thus enhance their global competitiveness. This is the fundamental economic rationale for foreign MNEs to chase the best suppliers around the world. Also in pursuit of profit maximization, the suppliers of foreign MNEs, mostly from the developing countries, also pay

---

1110 Li and Zhang 2010, pp. 631–645.
1111 Zu and Song 2009, pp. 105–117.
1112 Li 2005.
1113 Statistics on FDI in China 2015.
1114 See *supra* Section 3.

little attention to the social and environmental impacts associated with their business activities. Moreover, to attract more foreign investments, foreign MNEs are usually given preferential treatments by the host country, such as tax preference or lower environmental standards. These factors further motivate foreign MNEs to transfer their manufacturing industry to the host country. In this process, foreign MNEs are harshly criticized for shifting their social and environmental responsibilities to their suppliers as well as the costs of pollution abatement to the host country through the global supply chain.[1115] Their irresponsible business conduct is regarded as the source of many social and environmental problems in the host country. As a result, foreign MNEs are facing an increasing pressure to manage the social and environmental implications of their suppliers and thus to contribute to the sustainable development of the host country.

In recent years, the irresponsible business conducts of foreign MNEs have frequently been disclosed by the mass media. Southern Weekend, a leading national newspaper in China, started to rank the CSR performance of Chinese companies and the World's Top 500 international companies operating in China in 2006. According to its 2006 report,[1116] large global companies underperformed in fulfilling their social and environmental responsibilities for three important reasons. First, the monopoly of these global companies threatened the economic and social security of China. Second, foreign companies exploited favourable tax policies and unfair advantages in competing with Chinese companies. Finally, many global companies lowered their environmental, labour, and ethical standards when operating in China, and by doing so they were taking advantage of the lack of regulations in the country.

Facing the increasing negative publicity, many foreign MNEs responded quickly to the increasing expectations from the Chinese government and the local markets. Particularly, in the aftermath of the Sichuan earthquake in 2008, many notable MNEs were called "iron rooster" because of their late response to disaster assistance and the insufficient amount of charity donations.[1117] This event has caused far-reaching influence on China's CSR/CER development. Before the outbreak of this scandal, many foreign MNEs claimed to pursue a global CSR/CER strategy and management system in line with international standards. Given the considerable differences in terms of institutional context and cultural background, the actual implementation of their global CSR/CER strategy met various challenges. As a result, many foreign MNEs have realized the importance of tailoring their CSR/CER strategies and practices by integrating

---

1115 Lin 2007, p. 329.
1116 Tang and Li 2009, p. 200.
1117 Yin and Zhang 2012, p. 314.

the specific context of China. Also in practice, they make considerable efforts to localize their CSR /CER strategies and practices in such a way that better fit China's realities.

4.4 *NGOs*

The non-governmental organization (NGO) plays an important role in promoting CSR/CER development in the international context and in many Western countries.[1118] On the one hand, they can address a wide arrange of social and environmental problems that public sectors are incapable of tackling. On the other hand, they have exerted considerable influence on the CSR/CER policy-making process with specific strategies. For example, some NGOs influence corporate behaviour through the well-known tactic of 'naming and shaming',[1119] while some other NGOs participate in developing their own CSR/CER guidelines.

The rise of NGOs is also an important driver of China's CSR/CER development. The Chinese NGOs, also known as 'social organizations' (*shehui tuanti*), refer to "voluntary groups founded by Chinese citizens to realize a shared objective, according to their rules and to develop non-profit making activities."[1120] In practice, there are various types of NGOs depending on their priority area of activity. According to the International Classification of Non-profit Organizations, there are 12 major types of NGOs.[1121] It is observed[1122] that the Chinese government is more tolerant of environmental NGOs than of other types of NGOs. Since the first environmental NGO emerged in 1994,[1123] the past two decades witnessed a surge in the numbers of environmental NGOs in China. According to the recent statistics from the Ministry of Civil Affairs (MOCA), by the year of 2015, there were about 7000 environmental NGOs in China.[1124]

1118 See Chapter 3, Section 5.3.

1119 *Id.*

1120 State Council of China 1998.

1121 The 12 types of NGOs include culture and recreation, education and research, health, social services, environment, development and housing, law, advocacy and politics, philanthropic intermediaries and voluntarism promotion, international, religion, business and professional associations, unions, and other.

1122 Lin 2010, p. 95.

1123 The first environmental NGO—the Academy for Green Culture—was formally registered on March 31, 1994. Now it is knowns as 'Friends of Nature'. For more information about the Friends of Nature, available at: http://china.org.cn/english/2002/Jul/36833.htm (Accessed on April 7, 2017).

1124 The data is based on the information from the Ministry of Civil Affairs. Available at: http://www.mca.gov.cn/article/sj/tjgb/201607/20160700001136.shtml (Accessed on April 7, 2017).

Schwartz[1125] categorized the existing environmental NGOs in China into three groups: traditional environmental NGOs,[1126] governmental environmental NGOs,[1127] and environmental semi-NGOs.[1128]

The capabilities of NGOs in the field of environmental protection have been gradually recognized. The Chinese government took a series of measures to enhance the public participation of environmental NGOs. A landmark event in this respect is the revision of the Environmental Protection Law of China in 2014. An important change of this revised Environmental Protection Law is to explicitly grant lawful rights to social organizations for filing public interest environmental litigation in Article 58. The introduction of Article 58 is significant progress in two aspects: on the one hand, it encourages public participation in environmental protection by providing legal channels for social organizations to bring public interest litigation against polluters; on the other hand, it motivates companies to improve their environmental performance by putting them under public supervision and monitoring.

In comparison with their international and Western counterparts, the role of Chinese NGOs in promoting CSR is facing many constraints. First, the majority of the Chinses NGOs are closely related to the government, either registered with the government or directly affiliated with the bureaucracy. In the current context of China, the close relationship with the government generally means many benefits for the operation of NGOs. However, the lack of autonomy raises on-going debates about the nature of the Chinese NGOs. Benchmarked against the widely accepted definition of NGOs, which are generally characterized as self-organized, self-supported and self-governed organizations,[1129] the Chinese NGOs cannot be categorized as truly autonomous NGOs.[1130] Second, another

1125 Schwartz 2004, pp. 36–49.

1126 Schwartz defines the traditional environmental NGOs as "organizations registered with the government ministry of Civil Affairs, that receive no state funding, and have no official ties to government beyond the necessity of a sponsoring unit". (Schwartz 2004, p. 37).

1127 Schwartz defines the governmental environmental NGOs as "organizations are both registered with the government and are directly affiliated with the state bureaucracy." (Schwartz 2004, p. 37)

1128 According to Schwartz, environmental semi-NGOs neither registered with the ministry of Civil Affairs, nor are they directly connected to the Ministry of Environmental Protection. Instead, they register within the Chinese university system. (Schwartz 2004, p. 44)

1129 Salamon and Anheier (1996) summarized five basic features of the nonprofit sector, being that they are organized (institutionalized to some extent), private (institutionally separate from the government), self-governing (equipped to control their own activities), non-profit-distributing (not returning profits generated to their owners or directors), and voluntary (involving some meaningful degree of voluntary participation).

1130 Ma 2002, p. 306.

key issue plagued with the Chinese NGOs is the lack of legitimacy. In China, the establishment of NGOs is tightly controlled and closely monitored by a specific governmental bureaucracy and strict regulation.[1131] According to the *'Regulation on the Registration and Administration of Social Organizations'*, all social organizations must register with the authorized department through a series of the screening processes.[1132] In other words, the lack of legitimacy simply indicates a variety of obstacles for NGOs, such as obtaining funding, recruitment of personnel with high expertise, and access to data.[1133] It is argued that the strict control of the government prevents the Chinese NGOs from playing a more pro-active role in influencing corporate strategy and public policies on CSR/CER.[1134]

4.5 *Other Private Actors*

Private sectors, such as academic institutions, consumers, and media, make their contributions to China's CSR/CER development in various ways.

Academic institutions. For example, the Chinese Academy of Social Science (CASS), as an important academic research institution in the area of philosophy and social science, has been actively engaged in the development of CSR/CER. In 2008, the Research Centre for Corporate Social Responsibility (the Centre) was established under the leadership of CASS Economic Division. The Centre positions itself as a researcher, facilitator, and observer of the development of CSR/CER in China. Based on their rich research experience and resources, the Centre has developed the '*Guidelines on Corporate Social Responsibility Reporting for Chinese Enterprises*', and it also published a series of research reports, including the Blue Book on Corporate Social Responsibility, and the Research Report on Corporate Social Responsibility of China.

Consumers. Consumers from both the domestic and the global market are another category of the influential private actors. As mentioned above,[1135] when CSR was first introduced to the Chinese society in the mid-1990s, the primary driver for adopting CSR/CER was to meet the growing CSR/CER demands from global buyers. Today, the increasing pressure from the global consumer market is regarded as an important force for Chinese enterprises and particularly

1131 There is a specific bureau for the registration and administration of NGOs within the Ministry of Civil Affairs.

1132 The '*Regulation on registration and administration of social organizations*' (1998). Available at: http://www.lawinfochina.com/display.aspx?lib=law&id=5613&CGid= (Accessed on April 11, 2017).

1133 See e.g. Ma 2002, pp. 305–328; Schwartz 2004, pp. 28–49; Van Rooij *et al.* 2014, pp. 3–13.

1134 See e.g. See 2009, p. 7; Tang and Li 2009, p. 2020.

1135 See *supra* Section 3.

those export-oriented enterprises to improve their environmental performance. In the domestic market, an increasing awareness of CSR/CER has also been observed among Chinese consumers. In recent years, Chinese consumers show an increasing degree of willingness to reward products or services with good environmental performance. But the consumer demand for green products is still weak in the Chinese market. Many Chinese consumers still value the physical condition and functions of products more than the information about the production process.[1136] It is also observed that Chinese consumers tend to hold higher CSR/CER expectations towards foreign brands than towards domestic brands, which is also an important cause of the less developed green market in China.[1137]

5 Key CSR/CER Issues Addressed

Many scholars have made their efforts to identify the key issues addressed by the Chinese policymakers as well as by the business leaders. These studies indicate that the focus of CSR/CER issues in China is still changing. At the early stage of CSR/CER development, the majority of the Chinese enterprises focused on two key issues: one is corporate philanthropy, such as charity donations for natural disasters, poverty alleviation, support for the education or cultural programs; the other is compliance with the CSR/CER-related regulation.

By conducting a content analysis of CSR/CER communication, Tang and Li[1138] identified three distinctive philanthropy approaches to CSR/CER as 'ad hoc philanthropy' as 'strategic philanthropy' and as 'ethical business conduct'. The findings of their study showed that in the Chinese context, it is common to observe that many companies engage in 'ad hoc-philanthropy', such as education, sports, arts and cultural activities, through donation, sponsorship, and volunteering. Yin and Zhang[1139] also observed that the Chinese understanding of CSR/CER puts more emphasis on the ethical and discretionary domains of CSR/CER, such as 'treat employees well', 'protect the natural environment', 'provide reliable products and services', 'build an ethical culture', and 'embrace humanities'.[1140]

1136 Lin 2010, p. 97.
1137 Zadek 2012, p. 16.
1138 Tang and Li 2009, p. 208.
1139 Yin and Zhang 2012.
1140 *Id*, p. 306.

In recent years the focus of CSR/CER has expanded rapidly from legal compliance and philanthropy to a more strategic approach to CSR/CER.[1141] Zadek observed an upward trend of adopting a strategic CSR/CER approach among many Chinese enterprises with the focus on "the efficiency and security of the supply chain, development of new products and services, the competition for talent, and the reputation and other gains from credible governance and accountability".[1142] Zhao echoed Zadek's findings by stating that today China's CSR/CER development follows a global trend of CSR/CER development with "the strategic concern for addressing issues such as project quality, employee management, governance and human rights, with the strong and purposeful evolution of regulatory elements for building better supply chains and attracting more international talent investment."[1143]

Some scholars place more emphasis on the unique CSR dimensions in China's specific institutional and cultural background. Xu and Yang made their efforts to identify the Chinese specific CSR dimensions by comparing the similarities and differences between CSR dimensions in Western literature and Chinese literature.[1144] Based on an inductive literature review as well as an open-ended survey among business practitioners, Xu and Yang first identified the major CSR dimensions from both Western and Chinese approaches.[1145] According to their findings, the Chinese approach shares six common dimensions with the Western approach, i.e. economic responsibilities, legal responsibilities, environmental protection, employee issues, customer focus, and charity. It can be noticed that in general there is no significant difference between these two approaches. Both approaches encompass the economic, legal, environmental, and social dimensions of CSR. But the specifications of each dimension vary depending on their respective situations. For example, the environmental dimension in the Chinese literature puts an emphasis on the conservation of resources and the improvement of the resource utilization rate.[1146] This is in line with the Chinese government's priority to improve energy efficiency.

1141 Zadek 2012, p. 3.

1142 Zadek 2012, p. 10.

1143 Zhao 2014, p. 3.

1144 Yu and Yang 2009, pp. 321–333.

1145 In detail, the Western CSR dimensions mainly consist of seven responsibilities: legal responsibilities, environmental protection, customers, employees, social donation, shareholders and equality. The Chinese CSR dimensions encompasses economic responsibility, legal responsibility, environmental protection, customer orientation, people focused, charity, employment, good faith and social stability and progress.

1146 Xu and Yang 2010, pp. 328–329.

Three unique CSR dimensions are identified in the Chinese context, and they are good faith,[1147] employment,[1148] social stability and social progress.[1149] The 'good faith' as a CSR dimension can be understood as 'compliance with business ethics', 'operating in good faith' and 'honour contractual obligations'. The dimension of employment in China focuses on 'increasing job opportunities', 're-employing lays-off', 'easing national employment pressure' and 'providing jobs for the disabled'. The last CSR dimension with strong Chinese characteristics is 'social stability and progress'. In this case, companies are expected to make their contribution in the following areas: 'ensuring social stability and harmony', 'serving and repaying society', 'supporting culture, science, and education', and 'promoting national prosperity'. This unique dimension of CSR is in essence in line with the ultimate goal of the Chinese state to achieve sustainable development and to construct a harmonious society.

6 Summary and Some Concluding Remarks

Although CSR/CER has become a global issue today, an extensive body of the literature showed that the understanding and practice of CSR/CER varies widely under different institutional contexts. This phenomenon is even more apparent in a Chinese context, given the significant difference regarding the institutional background between China and the Western countries. For a better understanding of the CSR/CER development in China, one needs to address China's political, economic, societal and cultural context. More particularly, this chapter explored the unique Chinese approach to CSR/CER, by examining the conceptual understandings of CSR and CER, the evolution of China's CSR/CER development, the key actors and drivers of the growth of CSR/CER in China and the key issues addressed in China's CSR/CER framework.

Based on the analysis above, we can see that the Chinese CSR/CER approach differentiates itself from the Western approach in several aspects. The first notable feature of the Chinese approach is the leading role of the Chinese government in directing the discourse of CSR/CER in China. As mentioned in previous chapters, public authorities have always been regarded as a key driver

1147 The dimension of good faith requires corporations to operate in good faith, honour, contractual obligations, and to provide genuine goods at fair prices. (Xu and Yang 2009, p. 330)

1148 The dimension of employment requires corporations to provide more job opportunities and to ease China's employment pressure. (Xu and Yang 2009, p. 330).

1149 The dimension of social stability and progress includes 'ensuring social stability and harmony', 'serving and repaying society', 'promoting social progress', and 'supporting culture, science and education'. (Xu and Yang 2009, p. 330).

of CSR/CER development, and in practice, many Western governments have already played an important role in promoting the development of CSR/CER. However, the influence of the Chinese government on the development of CSR/CER is much more prominent, which becomes the principal driver for the rapid growth of CSR/CER in recent years. However, the dominant role of the Chinese state also poses several constraints for the further development of CSR/CER in China. For example, a large group of private actors, including consumers, investors, and NGOs, cannot fully play their roles in promoting CSR/CER practices as has been achieved in the Western countries. Moreover, it can be observed that in the case of China the primary rationale of CSR/CER engagement is still limited to the compliance with governmental policies, and the business case for CSR/CER has not been widely recognized by the Chinese business community.

The second Chinese characteristic of CSR/CER is attributed to the strong influence of Chinese traditional culture on the understanding of CSR/CER. When the idea of CSR/CER was first introduced to Chinese society, the conceptual understanding of CSR/CER was to a large extent built on the Western CSR/CER literature. However, it is argued that the Western definition of CSR/CER was not adapted to the specific Chinese context and was therefore not widely accepted by both the Chinese state and the public. In this context, many efforts have been made to develop the indigenous CSR/CER definition by borrowing from the Chinese traditional wisdom. As a consequence, it provides a better understanding of CSR/CER in the Chinese context, which paves the way for the development of CSR/CER.

The third feature is the impressive growth of CSR/CER in China. Since the concept of CSR/CER first emerged in the Western countries in the 1920s, it took decades before CSR/CER received a prominent place in both academia and in the business world. Compared to the Western nations, the development of CSR/CER had a late start in China, but the recent decade has witnessed the surge of CSR/CER in China. Based on the analysis above, it can be observed that today China's CSR/CER development has achieved a certain degree of progress in many aspects. A large group of stakeholders pro-actively participate in China's CSR/CER development, including the government, companies, consumers, investors, NGOs and civil society. A variety of CSR/CER-related issues is also addressed by both Chinese policy makers and practitioners, beyond the roots of legal compliance and philanthropy. Moreover, China's CSR/Cer development at the policy level and in practice will be further discussed in the following chapter.

CHAPTER 9

The Landscape of CSR/CER Development in China: at Policy Level and in Practice

1 Introduction

The recent decade has witnessed a rapid growth of CSR/CER in China, as their values have been widely recognized among the Chinese policymakers, business leaders, and academic scholars. An important indicator of China's CSR/CER development is the increasing number of CSR/CER regulations and policies. As an important actor,[1150] the Chinese government has promulgated a wide range of CSR/CER policies. In addition, the private sector (such as academic circles and NGOs) has also made their contributions by developing their CSR/CER standards or guidelines. Due to the concerted efforts of the Chinese government as well as the large group of stakeholders, there is a growing trend among Chinese enterprises to integrate CSR/CER into their business strategies. However, an intensive body of literature and studies remains sceptical of the effectiveness of CSR/CER policies on improving corporate environmental performance, particularly in the emerging markets, such as China, where the enforcement of laws and regulations is relatively lax.

The goal of this chapter is to discuss China's CSR/CER development at both the policy level and in practice. More particularly, it is also important to evaluate the achievements and the constraints of the current state of China's CSR/CER development. To reach this goal, this chapter is constructed as follows. Section 2 aims to depict a broad picture of China's CSR/CER policy framework, by providing an analysis of several influential CSR/CER policies and initiatives. Section 3 turns to another important question: how is CSR/CER implemented by Chinese business practitioners in practice? It is commonly agreed that the interpretations and implementation of CSR/CER vary widely across different ownership types of corporations, due to their respective positions within China's economic structure. Therefore, a specific type of Chinese enterprises is targeted in this chapter: the state-owned enterprises (SOEs). Given the pivotal role of SOEs in China's economic and social development, Section 3 explores the undertaking of CSR/CER by SOEs by conducting the case studies of

1150 See Chapter 8, Section 1.

 | DOI:10.1163/9789004368132_010

two selected SOEs: Bank of China (BOC) and China National Petroleum Corporation (CNPC). Section 4 will have a look at the current state of China's CSR/CER development by answering two questions: first, what is the overall level of CSR/CER practices in China; second, what challenges face the further development of CSR/CER in China. Section 5 summarizes and concludes.

2 The CSR/CER Policies in China

According to a recent survey,[1151] China's CSR/CER development is boosted by various factors, including compliance with governmental policies and regulations, reputation enhancement, requirements from international buyers, trends of globalization, compliance with local government's policy, risk management, compliance with industry guidelines, compliance with international conventions, access to investment, requirements from domestic clients, talent attraction, and cost-saving. Internally, the political impetus from the Chinese government and the civil society movement contributes to the distinctive Chinese model to CSR/CER. Among all factors, CSR/CER policies have been regarded as one of the most important drivers behind the rapid growth of CSR/CER in China.

In recent years, both public and private sectors have actively engaged in developing the Chinese CSR/CER initiatives, including the central government, local governments, governmental departments, stock exchanges, industry associations and academic institutions. As a result, the forms of CSR/CER policies vary widely, including laws, administrative regulations and rules, local decrees, normative documents, industry association guidelines and non-governmental guidelines and standards. This section provides an analysis of several influential CSR/CER policies and initiatives in China.

2.1 *The Company Law of China*

The first important policy is the Company Law of China, given the natural link between the concept of CSR and corporate governance. In the case of China, the evolving attitudes of Chinese legislators towards CSR are embodied in the different revisions of Company Law over time.[1152]

1151 CSR Asia 2015, pp. 16–22.

1152 The Company Law of the People's Republic of China was adopted at the 5th Session of the Standing Committee of the 8th National People's Congress on December 29, 1993. It was revised for the first time on December 25, 1999 in accordance with the Decision of

When Chinese legislators first drafted the Company Law in the early 1990s, the concept of CSR was not widely accepted neither by Chinese policy makers nor by Chinese company law scholars.[1153] Therefore, it was not surprising that CSR was not explicitly conceptualized in the 1994 Company Law. The exclusion of the concept of CSR could be partially explained by the specific situation of that time. When the economic reform took place, the Chinese government cleared any obstacle that might endanger the profitability of SOEs by helping them extricate themselves from the function of providing social service. However, the idea of CSR was partially reflected in the 1994 Company Law. For example, the Article 14 stated that "companies must comply with the law, conform to business ethics, strengthen the construction of the socialist civilization and subject themselves to the government and public supervision in the course of business."[1154] This article to some extent echoed the core idea of CSR of going beyond the compliance with law, which has been commonly cited in defining the concept of CSR.[1155] Also, the 1994 Company Law also contained specific provisions, particularly concerning the protection of employee rights.

With the rapid growth of CSR in recent years, the 1994 Company Law was harshly criticized for not reflecting the changing business-society relationship in China. In this context, CSR became one of the debated issues in the revision process of the 2006 Company Law. As a result, for the first time, the concept of CSR was incorporated into the 2006 Company Law, which explicitly recognizes the values of CSR. To be exact, Paragraph 1, Article 5 clearly states that "a company shall, when engaging in business activities, abide by the laws and administrative regulations, observe social moralities and business ethics, act in good faith, accept the supervision of the Government and the public, and undertake

the 13th Session of the Standing Committee of the Ninth People's Congress on Amending the Company Law of the People's Republic of China. It was revised for the second time on August 28, 2004 in accordance with the Decision of the 11th Session of the Standing Committee of the 10th National People's Congress of the People's Republic of China on Amending the Company Law of the People's Republic of China. It was revised at the 18th Session of the 10th National People's Congress of the People's Republic of China on October 27, 2005. Revised for the third time on December 28, 2013 in accordance with the Decision on Amending Seven Laws Including the Marine Environment Protection Law of the People's Republic of China at the 6th Session of the Standing Committee of the 12th National People's Congress. The third revision of the Company Law of China came into effect as of March 1, 2014.

1153 Lin 2010, pp. 68–72.

1154 Company Law 1994.

1155 For more discussion on the definition of CSR, see Chapter 2.

social responsibilities."[1156] In addition, the 2006 Company Law is promulgated in accordance with the stakeholder model.[1157] According to the Company Law, the main purpose of a company is the profit maximization for the shareholders, but the interests of other stakeholders shall also be carefully protected, such as employees, creditors, consumers, government and civil society.[1158] For example, Article 17 requires companies to "protect the lawful rights and interests of its employees including employment contract, labour insurance, and in-service training and so on."[1159]

The 2006 Company Law has far-reaching influence on the development of CSR in China. Given the wide application of the 2006 Company Law to all companies irrespective of size and type, the introduction of the CSR article marks the beginning of the proliferation of CSR policy in China. Since then, a wide range of CSR initiatives has emerged. However, despite the general CSR article and the article regarding the protection of employee rights, the specific rules relevant to other key dimensions of CSR in China's Company Law are lacking, particularly regarding environmental protection.

2.2 *The Guidelines to the State-Owned Enterprise Directly under the Central Government on Fulfilling Corporate Social Responsibilities*

To comprehensively implement the spirit of the 17th CPC National Congress and the 'Scientific outlook on development', the State-owned Assets Supervision and Administration Commission of the State Council (SASAC) issued the '*Guidelines to the State-owned Enterprises Directly under the Central Government* (*SOEs*) *on Fulfilling Corporate Social Responsibilities*' (the Guidelines)[1160] in 2008. SASAC is a governmental department under the supervision of the State Council, and it is responsible for performing investors' responsibilities, supervising and managing the state-owned assets of SOEs, and enhancing the management of SOEs.[1161] In this context, the release of the Guidelines reveals the

1156 Paragraph 1, Article 5 of Company Law 2006. In the 2014 Company Law, this article is reformulated as "when engaging in business activities, a company shall abide by laws and administrative regulations, observe social morality and business ethics, act in good faith, accept supervision by the government and the public, and bear social responsibilities."

1157 Lou and Tian 2013, pp. 10–14.

1158 *Id.*

1159 Company Law 2006.

1160 SASAC 2008. The full version of the Guidelines is available at: http://www.sasac.gov.cn/n1180/n13307665/n13307681/n13307724/13333515.html (Accessed on April 7, 2017).

1161 For More information about SASAC, available at: http://www.sasac.gov.cn/n86114/n86137/index.html (Accessed on April 7, 2017).

positive attitude of the Chinese government towards CSR. More importantly, the Guidelines explicitly list the substantive requirements and measures for SOEs to undertake CSR practices.

The Guidelines consist of four parts. The first part fully explains the importance and significance of fulfilling CSR by SOEs.[1162] Particularly, the Guidelines point out four major reasons why the CSR practice of SOEs is important.[1163] First, it is a practical measure for SOEs to implement the policy of 'Scientific outlook on development'. Second, given the critical role of SOEs not only for China's economic growth but also for the welfare of the whole society, the undertaking of CSR meets the expectation of the entire society. Third, it is a necessary premise for achieving the goal of sustainable development of SOEs. Fourth, it could enhance the competitiveness of SOEs in the international market.

The second part of the Guidelines sets forth the guidelines, requirements, and principles for fulfilling CSR.[1164] By adhering to the guiding principles of the 'Deng Xiaoping Theory'[1165] and the 'Important Thought of Three Representatives',[1166] SOEs are expected to set a good example for other types of companies in promoting CSR practices.

The third part specifies the main content of CSR for SOEs, which covers eight topics: (1) complying with law and honest codes of conduct; (2) constantly improving ability of making sustainable profits; (3) improving the quality of product and service; (4) enhancing resource efficiency and environmental protection; (5) promoting independent innovation and technological advancement; (6) ensuring product safety; (7) protecting legal rights of employees; and (8) participating in social public welfare programs.

Finally, the Guidelines propose concrete measures as to how to implement CSR in practice, such as establishing awareness of CSR, completing system and mechanism for fulfilling CSR, building the CSR information reporting system, enforcing inter-enterprise communication and international cooperation, and strengthening the CPC's role in directing the CSR discourse.

1162 *Id.*

1163 *Id.*

1164 *Id.*

1165 Deng Xiaoping Theory (*Deng Xiaoping Lilun*) refers to a series of political and economic ideologies developed by the former Chinese leader Deng Xiaoping, which have served as the policy guide of the Communist Party of China.

1166 The Important Thought of Three Representatives (*Sange Daibiao zhongyao sixiang*) refers to the socio-political theory first introduced by the former Chinese leader Jiang Zemin.

2.3 *The Regulation on Environmental Information Disclosure*

The environmental information disclosure has been a priority issue on the agenda of the Chinese government, and a series of measures has been taken to propel and regulate the disclosure of environmental information. In 2007, the former State Environmental Protection Administration (SEPA)[1167] adopted the '*Measures for the Disclosure of Environmental Information* (for Trial Implementation[1168])' (the Measures), which became effective on May 1 of 2008.[1169] The Measures aim to enhance the transparency of environmental information disclosure for both environmental protection agencies and enterprises. In general, the Measures contain the general provisions and specific requirements of environmental information disclosure for both the government and the enterprises.

According to Article 4 of the Measures, the general principle of environmental information disclosure of the enterprises is the combination of voluntary disclosure with mandatory disclosure. To be exact, Article 19 explicitly encourages the voluntary disclosure of enterprise environmental information in 9 categories.[1170] On the other hand, Article 20 of the Measures prescribes the compulsory information disclosure for enterprises with 'severe pollution and whose emission of pollutants is greater than the national or local emission standard or whose total emission of pollutants is greater than the quota of total controlled emissions determined by local governments.'[1171] According

1167 The SEPA was replaced by MEP during the Reforms on the State Council organs in the 2008 National People's Congress sessions in Beijing. For more information, available at: http://www.gov.cn/test/2009-01/16/content_1207014.htm (Accessed on April 7, 2017).

1168 'Trial Implementation' means that the Measures are subject to revision.

1169 The Measures were adopted at the first executive meeting of 2007 of the State Environmental Protection Administration on February 8, 2007, hereby promulgated and came into force as of May 1, 2008.

1170 According the article 19 of the Measures, the relevant enterprise environmental information includes: (1) their environmental protection guidelines, annual environmental protection objectives and achievements; (2) their total annual resources consumption; (3) information on their environmental protection investment and environmental technology development; (4) type, volume and content of pollutants discharged by them and where the pollutants are discharged; (5) information on the construction and operation of their environmental protection facilities; (6) information on the handling and disposal of waste generated from their production, information on recycling and comprehensive use of waste products; (7) voluntary agreement entered into with environmental protection agencies for environmental improvement behavior; (8) information on their performance of social responsibility; and (9) other environmental information voluntarily disclosed by them.

1171 According to article 20 of the Measures, these enterprise should disclose to the public the following information: (1) their name, address, and legal representative; (2) names of

to Article 23 of the Measures, the environmental protection agencies provide enterprises with various incentives to encourage voluntary environmental information disclosure, such as, the public citation on major local media, the priority in the arrangement of projects with specific environmental protection funds in accordance with relevant state regulations, the priority in the recommendation of clean production exemplary projects or other exemplary projects with subsidy from the government in accordance with relevant state regulations, and other rewarding measures provided by the government.

To further improve environmental information disclosure, the 2014 Environmental Protection Law explicitly prescribes the information disclosure as one of the basic systems in China's environmental policy framework. Meanwhile, the MEP issued the '*Measures for the Disclosure of Environmental Information by Enterprises and Public Institutions*'[1172] and the '*Guiding Opinions on Further Improvement of the Corporate Environmental Credit System*'. The remarkable progress of the new policy is shown in the establishment of a corporate environmental credit system, which tracks the environmental performance of enterprise and creates corporate profiles with records of good or bad corporate behaviour. The establishment of a corporate environmental credit system has exerted far-reaching influence in various ways. First, it is an integral part of the development of the social credit system in China. Second, it aims to help companies to improve their environmental performance and to enhance their compliance with environmental regulations through the mechanism of 'incentives for good faith and punishments for bad faith'. Third, it is a creative measure for the government to achieve the functional transformation in the field of environmental protection. In particular, the information sharing regarding the environmental credit records of companies among other governmental departments and the public will improve the working efficiency of public sectors.[1173] Besides, the Guiding Opinions also specify the substantive measures for the further improvement of the corporate environmental credit system in the following five years.[1174]

---

major pollutants, method, content, and total volume of emission, information on emission that has surpassed the standards or total emission that has surpassed the prescribed limits; (3) information on construction and operation of their environmental facilities; and (4) produce plans for sudden environmental pollution accidents.

1172 This measure took effect as January 1st of 2015.

1173 For more information, available at: http://english.sepa.gov.cn/News_service/news_release/201512/ t20151221_319718.htm(Accessed on April 7, 2017).

1174 The Guiding Opinions specify five measures for the further improvement of corporate environmental credit system, including: first, to define the scope of information on the corporate environmental credit records and requires to keep and improve credit

2.4 *The Green Finance Policy*

The Chinese government also makes great efforts in greening its financial industry. Particularly, the Ministry of Environmental Protection (MEP) actively builds various partnerships with the regulatory agencies of the financial sector for promoting the green finance practices. The most notable achievements among these policies have been the 'Green Securities Policy' in the Chinese stock markets and the 'Green Credit Policy' in the banking industry.

2.4.1 Green Securities Policy

In 2008, the MEP in partnership with the China Securities Regulatory Commission (CSRC) launched the 'Green Securities Policy', which requires listed companies in 14 highly polluting industries[1175] to improve their environmental performance through environmental information disclosure and environmental performance assessment. An important element of this policy is the issuance of the 'Green IPO', which requires enterprises in highly-polluting and energy-intensive industries ('Liang Gao industries') to undergo an environmental assessment by the MEP before initiating an IPO or obtaining refinancing from banks.

Two stock exchanges in mainland China[1176] have actively implemented the Green Securities Policy by developing their CSR guidelines as well as CSR indices. They are the Shenzhen Stock Exchange (SZSE)[1177] and the Shanghai Stock Exchange (SSE).[1178] The major CSR initiatives promulgated by these two stock exchanges will be discussed in this section.

---

records; second, to make more effort to make public the industry's environmental credit information; third, to improve the information system for the industry's environmental credits, and improve the IT infrastructure; fourth, to establish a mechanism of "incentives for good faith and punishments for bad faith" for the environmental protection; fifth, to improve the environmental credits of environmental service suppliers and staff.

1175 The Green Securities Policy lists 14 highly polluting industries, involving thermal power, steel and iron, cement, aluminum, coal, metallurgy, building materials, mining, chemicals, oil, pharmaceuticals, light industry, textiles, and leather.

1176 There is another stock exchange in the Hong Kong Special Administrative Region of the People's Republic of China—the Hong Kong Stock Exchange, which will not be further discussed in this book.

1177 ShenZhen Stock Exchange, established on December 1, 1990, is a self-regulated legal entity under the supervision of the China Securities Regulatory Commission (CSRC).

1178 Shanghai Stock Exchange, founded on November 26, 1990, is also under the supervision of the CSRC.

2.4.1.1 *Shenzhen Stock Exchange Social Responsibility Instructions to Listed Companies*[1179]

As early as in 2006, the SZSE first issued the '*Shenzhen Stock Exchange Social Responsibility Instructions to Listed Companies*' (SZSE Instructions),[1180] for the purpose of implementing the Scientific Outlook on Sustainable Development, building a harmonious society and encouraging companies listed on the SZSE to actively undertake their social responsibility.[1181] The SZSE Instructions consist of eight chapters and 38 articles in total, including general provisions, protection of the interests of shareholders and creditors, protection of employee interests, protection of the interests of suppliers, customers and consumers, environmental protection and sustainable development, public relations and social welfare services, institutional building and information disclosure, and supplementary provisions. There are detailed articles under each chapter to explain how to implement the SZSE Introductions in practice. For example, regarding environmental protection and sustainable development, Article 28 specifies eight key areas that should be included in companies' environmental policies.[1182] It can be easily observed that the SZSE Instructions generally

1179 The SZSE Instructions had been replaced on by the '*Guidelines of the Shenzhen Stock Exchange for Standardized Operation of Companies Listed on the Main Board*' and the '*Guidelines of the Shenzhen Stock Exchange for Standardized Operation of Companies Listed on the Small and Medium-Sized Enterprise Board*' on September 1st, 2010, which were further revised in 2015. The main content of the SZSE Instructions has been integrated in these two Guidelines (Chapter 10 on Social Responsibility). Although the two Guidelines have simplified the SZSE instructions, they did not make substantial changes in contents. Available at: https://www.szse.cn/main/files/2015/02/11/%E3%80%8A%E6%B7%B1%E5%9C%B3%E8%AF%81%E5%88%B8%E4%BA%A4%E6%98%93%E6%89%80%E4%B8%BB%E6%9D%BF%E4%B8%8A%E5%B8%82%E5%85%AC%E5%8F%B8%E8%A7%84%E8%8C%83%E8%BF%90%E4%BD%9C%E6%8C%87%E5%BC%95%EF%BC%882015%E5%B9%B4%E4%BF%AE%E8%AE%A2%EF%BC%89%E3%80%8B.pdf https://www.szse.cn/main/files/2015/02/11/%E3%80%8A%E6%B7%B1%E5%9C%B3%E8%AF%81%E5%88%B8%E4%BA%A4%E6%98%93%E6%89%80%E4%B8%AD%E5%B0%8F%E6%9D%BF%E4%B8%8A%E5%B8%82%E5%85%AC%E5%8F%B8%E8%A7%84%E8%8C%83%E8%BF%90%E4%BD%9C%E6%8C%87%E5%BC%95%EF%BC%882015%E5%B9%B4%E4%BF%AE%E8%AE%A2%EF%BC%89%E3%80%8B.pdf (Accessed on April 7, 2017).

1180 For the full version of the SZSE Instructions, available at: http://www.szse.cn/main/en/RulesandRegulations/ SZSERules/GeneralRules/10636.shtml (Accessed on April 7, 2017).

1181 *Id.*

1182 The eight areas include: (1) to comply with the laws, regulations, and rules that govern environmental protection; (2) to reduce resource consumption, including raw materials and fuels; (3) to reduce waste generation and make every effort to recover wastes for recycling; (4) to avoid, to the greatest extent, waste generation that pollutes the environment;

adopt a multi-stakeholder approach, which encourages listed companies to not only take the interests of shareholders into account but also the interests of a large group of stakeholders, such as employees, suppliers, customers, consumers, the environment and the local community.

In addition to the protection of stakeholders' interests, another important point of the SZSE Instructions is the requirement on social and environmental information disclosure. In accordance with Article 35, listed companies are required to establish a social responsibility mechanism and publish CSR reports based on the review and evaluation of the status quo on a regular basis. In addition, the SZSE Instructions list three key points which should be included in a CSR report, and there are: (1) implementation of social responsibility relating to employee protection, impact on the environment, product quality, and community relationship; (2) assessment of the implementation of the SZSE Instructions and reasons for the implementation gap; and (3) improvement measures and schedules.

2.4.1.2 *Shanghai Stock Exchange Guidelines on Environmental Information Disclosure by Listed Companies*

Two years after the release of the SZSE Instructions, the SSE also made its contribution in developing CSR initiatives. In 2008, the SSE issued the '*Notice on Strengthening Listed Companies' Assumption of Social Responsibility*' (the Notice) and the '*Shanghai Stock Exchange Guidelines on Environmental Information Disclosure by Listed Companies*' (SSE Guidelines),[1183] aiming to encourage listed companies to disclose environmental information on a voluntary basis.

Particularly, the Notice requires all listed companies to enhance their responsibility awareness as a member of society in pursuit of not only the interests of shareholders but also the interests of other stakeholders, the environment, and society.[1184] To achieve this commitment, listed companies should establish a CSR strategy and mechanism depending on the specific features of their industries and business operations. In general, a CSR strategy should at least cover four aspects, such as protection of employee health and

---

(5) to apply environmental-friendly materials and energy-saving, waste-reducing design, technology and raw materials; (6) to minimize the adverse impact of corporate performance on the environment; (7) to provide training to employees for the purpose of enhancing environmental protection awareness; and (8) to create an environment for sustainable development.

1183 For more detailed information about the SSE Guidelines, available at: http://www.sse.com.cn/lawandrules/sserules/listing/stock/c/c_20150912_3985851.shtml (Accessed on April 7, 2017).

1184 For more detailed information about the Notice, available at: http://english.sse.com.cn/aboutsse/ news/newsrelease/c/3993550.shtml (Accessed on April 7, 2017).

safety, quality control of the company product, and promoting a sustainable environmental and ecosystem such as through pollutant reduction, conservation of water and energy, etc. Moreover, listed companies are also required to promptly disclose information about their assumption of social responsibility in their annual CSR reports.[1185]

An important innovation of the Notice is the introduction of a new concept of 'social contribution value per share' (SCVPS)[1186]—a ratio used to describe the value creation of companies on corporate social and environmental performance. In this Notice, listed companies are encouraged to disclose the social contribution value per share in their CSR reports. By doing this, the public can have a better understanding of the real value created by companies not only for their shareholders, but also for employees, customers, creditors, local communities, and the whole society. To better encourage the voluntary information disclosure by listed companies, the SSE also introduces incentives for listed companies with good performance in fulfilling CSR and preparing CSR reports, such as election priority into the 'SSE Corporate Governance Sector' and the procedure simplification in verifying their temporary announcements.[1187]

In addition to the Notice, the SSE also issued the SSE Guidelines to implement the *'Measures on Open Environmental Information (for Trial Implementation)' and the 'Guide Opinion on Strengthening Regulation of Listed Companies concerning Environmental Protection'* promulgated by the MEP. The SSE Guidelines clarify the detailed requirements of environmental information disclosure for listed companies. For example, listed companies are mandatorily required to disclose important environmental issues which are likely to have a significant influence on stock prices within two days after the issues occur. Moreover, listed companies are encouraged to disclose relevant environmental information based on their practical situations, involving: company environmental protection policy, annual environmental protection objective and effect; annual total energy consumption; environmental protection investment and environmental technology development status; emission/ pollutant type, quantity, concentration and destination; construction of environmental protection equipment and operational status; production waste treatment,

---

1185 *Id.*

1186 According to the Notice, the social contribution value per share refers to the added value created for the society on the basis of earning per share for shareholders. It is calculated by adding tax revenues created for the State, salary paid to employees, loan interest paid to creditors, donations, and other values created for stakeholders, and deducting social costs caused by environmental pollution or other factors.

1187 For more information, available at: http://english.sse.com.cn/aboutsse/news/newsrelease/c/3993550.shtml (Accessed on April 7, 2017).

disposal and recycling status; the environmental improvement agreement (signed voluntarily by the company) that the company has entered into with MEP; other information disclosed at the discretion of the company.[1188]

2.4.2 Green Credits Policy

In 2007, the former State Environmental Protection Admiration (SEPA), in partnership with the China Banking Regulatory Commission (CBRC) and the People's Bank of China (PBOC), issued the '*Opinion on Enforcement of Environmental Law and Prevention of Credit Risks*' (the Opinion). According to this Opinion, the environmental performance of loan applicants must be taken into account by banking institutions when making loan decisions. Simply, banking institutions are required to build the linkage between the credit activities and corporate environmental performance. Loan applicants with poor environmental performance records or higher environmental risks are asked to pay higher interest, and loan applicants with serious environmental violations are blacklisted and denied by banks.

In 2012, the MEP, the CBRC and the PBOC further revamped the Opinion into the '*Green Credit Guidelines*'.[1189] The main purpose of formulating the '*Green Credit Guidelines*' is to encourage banking institutions to promote the green credit business, adjust the credit structure, effectively fend off environmental and social risks and thus better serve the real economy.[1190] The Green Credit Guidelines consist of seven chapters: general provisions, organization and management, policy, system and capacity building, process management, internal controls and information disclosure, monitoring and examination, and supplementary provisions.[1191] According to the Green Credit Guidelines, all types of banking institutions, including policy banks, commercial banks, rural cooperative banks and rural credit cooperatives, are required to promote green credit activities from a strategic height, through developing client environmental and social risk assessment criteria, preparing a list of clients who are currently faced with major environmental and social risks, and establishing the working mechanism conducive to green credit innovation.

2.5 *Industry-Specific Guidelines on CSR*

Industry associations usually play an active role in promoting CSR development through developing self-regulatory standards and guidelines. In China,

---

1188 *Id.*

1189 For more information about the Green Credit guidelines, available at: http://www.cbrc.gov.cn/Engdoc View.do?docID=3CE646AB629B46B9B533B1D8D9FF8C4A (Accessed on April 7, 2017).

1190 *Id.*

1191 *Id.*

most industry associations are supported by governments or governmental departments, but the CSR guidelines they publish are usually voluntary and non-binding for member companies.[1192] However, the industry-specific CSR guidelines indeed provide important guidance for companies to interpret the concept of CSR in practice, and it also provides a valuable reference for governments to develop CSR regulations. According to a recent report, more than 40 industry associations have developed their sectoral CSR guidelines since 2006, and the textile, electronic and banking sectors are among the most active players in this regard.[1193]

In this section, the China National Textile & Apparel Council (CNTAC) is selected to exemplify the efforts of industry associations in developing self-discipline CSR standards. The '*China Social Compliance 9000 for Textile and Apparel Industry*' (CSC9000T) is considered as China's first industry-specific CSR management system issued by the industry association. In general, the CSC9000T aims to guide China's textile and apparel industry in the direction of sustainable development and thus to improve the overall quality of CSR management in the industry. The CSC9000T consists of principles and guidelines: the Principles, serving as the 'Collective Code of Conduct' for China's textile and apparel industry, involve the overall requirements for a social responsibility management system and thus help companies to set up their own goals and targets for fulfilling social responsibility; and the Guidelines specify the detailed requirements of the Principles in the management system, employment contract, child worker, forced or compulsory labour, working hours, wages and welfare, trade unions and collective bargaining, discrimination, harassment and abuse, occupational health and safety, environmental protection and fair competition.

Another remarkable progress is the publication of the '*China Sustainability Reporting Guidelines for Apparel and Textile Enterprises*' (CSR-GATES)[1194] by the Responsible Supply Chain Association of CNTAC.[1195] The CSR-GATES provides comprehensive and quantifiable indicators for textile and apparel enterprises to prepare CSR reports. It is China's first indicator system of social responsibility reporting, as well as the first CSR reporting guidelines issued by industry associations. CNTAC seeks to encourage all textile and apparel enterprises to comply with the CSR-GATES in the preparation of their social responsibility

1192 CSR Asia 2015.

1193 *Id.*

1194 For more information about the CSR-GATES, available at: http://www.ctei.cn/special/2013nzt/ 13zrnh/pdf/csr.pdf (Accessed on April 7, 2017).

1195 The RSCA is an industry-wide and professional body for the promotion of social responsibilities, which is directly under the administration of China National Textile and Apparel Council (CNTAC).

reports. In general, CSR-GATES introduces a reporting framework that consists of 201 indicators concerning business production, operation, and management activities with high relevance to stakeholders.[1196]

In addition to the sector-specific guidelines issued by one industry association, a set of cross-sector CSR standards also emerges based on the cooperation of several industry associations. In 2010, the China Federation of Industrial Economics (CFIE),[1197] a partnership with ten national industry associations,[1198] jointly released the '*Guide on Social Responsibility for Chinese Industrial Enterprises and Industry Associations 2.0*' (GSRI-CHINA 2.0).[1199] The GSRI-CHINA 2.0 aims to share a common understanding of the development of CSR for Chinese industrial enterprise and industry associations.[1200] For the purpose of continuously improving CSR performance, all industrial enterprises and industry associations are required to establish comprehensive CSR systems, promote social responsibility management, and disclose social and environmental information. In general, the GSRI-CHINA 2.0 is structured in two parts: the guide for industrial enterprise and the guide for industry associations. For each part, the GSRI-CHINA 2.0 respectively introduces the basic principles and the specific requirements in responsibility systems, the major contents of social responsibilities, and the social responsibility reports. Besides, the GSRI-CHINA 2.0 also provides a detailed reporting framework including detailed indicators, and Chinese industrial enterprise and industry associations are asked to report against these indicators.

2.6 *Other Private CSR/CER Initiatives*

The various CSR/CER guidelines mentioned above are mainly promulgated by the public sector, including government, governmental departments or organizations supported by governments. Another important player in pushing forward the development of CSR/CER in China is the private sector, such as academic institutions, NGOs, and media. In practice, private sectors have made

1196 *Id.*

1197 CFIE is a national social economic organization approved by the State Council and registered at the Ministry of Civil Affairs. Today, CFIE consists of 118 association members at both national and local levels. For more information about CFIE, available at: http://www.cfie.org.cn/2710757099819/2726451123993/1586/2873892 922653.html (Accessed on April 7, 2017).

1198 The ten national industry associations are from coal, machinery, iron and steel, petroleum and chemicals, light industry, textile and apparel, building materials, non-ferrous metals, electricity, and mining industries.

1199 The GSRI 2.0 is revised and improved based on the first version of GSRI, which was promulgated in 2008.

1200 For more information about the GSRI-CHINA 2.0, available at: http://www.cfie.org.cn/2710757099819/ 2724937977048/index.html# (Accessed on April 7, 2017).

their contribution through various ways, such as, developing CSR/CER guidelines, conducting relevant studies in the field CSR and publishing CSR reports.

The Chinese Academy of Social Science (CASS), as an important academic research institution in the area of philosophy and social science, has actively engaged in the development of CSR. In 2008, the Research Centre for Corporate Social Responsibility (the Centre) was established under the leadership of CASS Economic Division. The Centre positions itself as a researcher, facilitator, and observer in the development of CSR in China. Based on their rich research experience and resources, the Centre focuses on establishing a Chinese theoretical framework of CSR.

In 2009, the Centre released the first Blue Book on Corporate Social Responsibility, which discloses the CSR development index of China's top 100 state-owned enterprises, top 100 private- and foreign-funded entities, and 16 important industry sectors, including electricity, banking, and food. Since then, the Centre has been publishing the annual 'Research Report on Corporate Social Responsibility of China'. This annual report conducts an annual evaluation of Chinese enterprises on their performance in CSR management and the level of information disclosure by assessing four different aspects: responsibility management, economic responsibilities, social responsibilities and environmental responsibilities, and further to analyze the characteristics of the CSR development across company types and industry sectors.

In addition to the research reports on CSR, another important contribution of the Centre can be credited to the draft of the first edition of the '*Guidelines on Corporate Social Responsibility Reporting for Chinese Enterprises*' (CASS-CSR 1.0) in 2009. The publication of CASS-CSR 1.0 marks a remarkable progress in the standardization of China's sustainability reporting practices. Today, the Guidelines have been updated in their third edition—CASS-CSR 3.0.[1201] In comparison with the previous version, the CASS-CSR 3.0 set forth four major aims for promoting CSR reporting practices in China:[1202] first, it expects to help reporting companies to fully utilize the multiple values of environmental information disclosure; second, it aims to provide more practical guidelines for CSR reporting; third, it takes maximum absorption of local and international standards on CSR reporting; fourth, it integrates the international sustainability reporting standards such as the GRI reporting guidelines.

1201 In January 2014, the Centre published the third edition of its Guidelines on Corporate Social Responsibility Reporting for Chinese Enterprises (CASS-CSR 3.0).

1202 GRI and CASS, Linking CASS-CSR 3.0 and GRI'S G4 Sustainability Reporting Guidelines. Available at: https://www.globalreporting.org/resourcelibrary/Linking-CASS-CSR-3.0-and-GRI%27s-G4-Sustainability%20Reporting-Guidelines.pdf (Accessed on April 7, 2017).

TABLE 1 CSR/CER Regulation in the Chinese Legal System

CSR regulation	Regulatory body	Description	Influence
Company Law of China (2006)	The Standing Committee of National People's Congress (NPC)	"a company shall, when engaging in business activities, abide by the laws and administrative regulations, observe social moralities and business ethics, act in good faith, accept the supervision of the Government and the social public, and undertake social responsibilities" [Paragraph 1, Article 5].	It has far-reaching influence on China's CSR development.For the first time, the value of CSR is explicitly recognized in the Chinese Company Law.
The Guidelines to the State-owned Enterprise Directly under the Central Government on Fulfilling Corporate Social Responsibilities (2008)	State-Owned Assets Supervision and Administration Council (SASAC)	The Guidelines consists of four parts: i, the importance and significance of fulfilling CSR by SOEs; ii, the guidelines, requirements and principles of fulfilling CSR; iii, the main content of CSR, covering eight key topics; iv, the concrete measures for implementing CSR.	It reveals the positive signals of the Chinese government towards CSR.

Regulations on environmental information disclosure (2007)	The Ministry of Environmental Protection (MEP)	The Regulations aim to enhance the transparency of environmental information disclosure for both environmental protection agencies and enterprises.	The Regulation certainly improves the environmental information discourse in China, particularly by introducing the 'Corporate environmental credit system'.
Green securities policy (2008)	China Securities Regulatory Commission (CSRC) in partnership with MEP	It requires the listed companies in 14 highly polluting industries to improve their environmental performance through environmental information disclosure and environmental performance assessment.	To implement the Green securities policy, the two main stock exchanges in China also have developed their CSR guidelines and indices.
Shenzhen Stock Exchange Social Responsibility Instructions to Listed Companies (2006)	Shenzhen Stock Exchange(SZSE)	It consists of eight chapters and detailed articles to explain how to implement the SZSE Instructions.	the SZSE Instructions generally adopt a multi-stakeholder approach, which encourages listed companies to not only take the interests of shareholders into account but also the interest of a large group of stakeholders

TABLE 1 CSR/CER Regulation in the Chinese Legal System (*cont*)

CSR regulation	Regulatory body	Description	Influence
Shanghai Stock Exchange Guidelines on Environmental Information Disclosure by Listed Companies (2008)	Shanghai Stock Exchange (SSE)	It encourages the listed companies to voluntarily disclose environmental information.	It introduces a new concept—'social contribution per share', which is used to describe the value creation of companies on CSR.
Green Credits Guidelines (2008)	China Banking Regulatory Commission (CBRC), the People's Bank of China (PBOC) and MEP	Banking institutions are required to build the linkage between credit activities and corporate environmental performance of loan applicants.	Loan applicants with poor environmental performance will be blacklisted and denied by banks.
Industry-specific guidelines on CSR (since 2006)	Various China Industries Associations	More than 40 industry associations have developed sectoral CSR guidelines.	They indeed provide important guidance for companies from specific industries as to how to implement CSR in practice.

3 The Undertaking of CSR/CER by Chinese Enterprises

After exploring the various CSR/CER-related policies in China, this section aims to gain more insights of CSR/CER practices by Chinese enterprises, by conducting an in-depth analysis of their CSR/CER policies, the specific measures and progress to improve their CSR/CER management and performance, and their sustainability reporting mechanisms. Given the pivotal role of SOEs in China's social and economic development,[1203] this section focuses on the undertaking of CSR/CER by Chinese SOEs. Two SOEs are selected as the targets of cases studies: the Bank of China Limited and the China National Petroleum Corporation. The two case studies will be conducted by answering the following questions:

- Why are they actively engaging in sustainability reporting?
- What CSR/CER policies have they already adopted or launched?
- How can the quality of their CSR/CER practices be evaluated?

The relevant information and data for case studies are primarily from the corporate websites of the selected SOEs and also from their CSR/sustainability reports.

3.1 *Bank of China Limited*[1204]

3.1.1 Corporate Profile

As the most internationalized and diversified commercial bank in China, the Bank of China Limited (BOC) holds an important position in China's financial industry. Founded in 1912, upon the approval of Mr. Sun Yat-sen, the BOC has played different roles throughout its one-hundred-year history. In the Republic of China (from 1912 to 1949), BOC consecutively served as the central bank, international exchange bank and specialized international trade. After the national liberation in 1949, BOC was taken over by the newly founded government and was transformed to be a specialized foreign exchange bank that managed the country's foreign exchange operations.[1205] In response to the economic reform in 1978, BOC launched a series of reform measures in many aspects. In 1994, the BOC was transformed from a specialized foreign exchange bank into a wholly state-owned commercial bank. In 2004, the Bank of China Limited was established, achieving the historical transformation to a real modern

1203 See Chapter 8, Section 2.

1204 This section gives an overview of the BOC's CSR policies and practices primarily based on the information from its CSR report 2015 and corporate website.

1205 Since 1949, People's Bank of China has served as the central bank of the country.

commercial bank.[1206] In 2006, BOC successfully went public on the Stock Exchange of Hong Kong Limited and the Shanghai Stock Exchange. The BOC also plays an important role in the international financial market. Today, the BOC provides a broad range of financial services in 46 countries and regions. From 2011 to 2016, the BOC has been enrolled as one of the first Global Systemically Important Banks for five consecutive years.[1207]

The BOC is also regarded as a pioneer in China's CSR development. Throughout its long history, the BOC upholds the long-standing spirit of "promoting social welfare and contributing to a prosperous nation"[1208] and adheres to the core value of "pursuing excellence; integrity, performance, and responsibility; innovation and harmony."[1209] BOC actively carries out its development strategy of "Serving Society, Delivering Excellence" and commits to fully performing their responsibilities towards their stakeholders in China and the global community.[1210]

3.1.2 BOC's CSR/CER Policies and Sustainability Reporting Practice

As an important part of the BOC's development goal of becoming a world-class bank, the BOC has made great efforts in establishing and improving the social responsibility organization and management system in many aspects.

First, the BOC enhances a common understanding of CSR. At the BOC, the concept of CSR is interpreted as "implementing the policies of the state, serving the consumer, strengthening corporate governance, promote cultural excellence and supporting social undertakings so as to push forward the harmonious development of China's economy and society and become a world-class provider of sustainable financial services."[1211]

Secondly, from the position of the BOC in the international financial market as well in the Chinese market, the BOC identifies five priorities as follows:

- "Shouldering significant responsibility for the nation's revival;
- Possessing competitive edges in the globalization process;

1206 Since the establishment of the Bank of China Limited in 2004, the Bank of China was transferred from a wholly state-owned commercial bank to a joint stock commercial bank controlled by the State.

1207 The Global Systematically Important Banks (G-SIBs) are identified by the Financial Stability Board (FSB) in consultation with Basel Committee on Banking Supervision (BCBS) and national authorities, by using a methodology developed by BCBS.

1208 BOC, *'Corporate Social Responsibility Report of Bank of China Limited for 2015'*, p. 3.

1209 *Id.*

1210 *Id*, p. 5.

1211 *BOC, 'CSR 2009',* available at: http://pic.bankofchina.com/bocappd/report/201008/P020100804592807 644803.pdf (Accessed on April 7, 2017).

- Leading lifestyle in technological innovations;
- Earning customer loyalty in market competition; and
- Meeting the expectations of shareholders, employees, and society in the course of sustainable development."[1212]

In practice, the BOC has taken a comprehensive range of measures for fulfilling their social responsibilities in four major areas, namely, implementing China's major development strategies, enhancing global financial services, supporting charity and public interest, and performing responsibilities for stakeholders.

In the field of environmental protection, the BOC pro-actively implements the national green credit policy[1213] by "facilitating enterprise transformation and industrial innovation and supporting the development of eco-friendly industries and green technology projects."[1214] The balance of green credits has been taken as one of the key performance indicators for the BOC. The recent financial data of the BOC[1215] also shows that the balance of green credits has increased from 258,759 million RMB in 2013 to 412,315 million RMB in 2015. In 2016, the BOC has planned to issue Green Bonds in the offshore markets.[1216] In addition to green finance activities, the BOC also actively sponsors green public welfare activities, with the aim of raising CSR awareness among its employees and consumers. In order to minimize the internal environmental impact of business operations, the BOC pro-actively promotes the green office program in energy saving and emission reduction.

Thirdly, the importance of establishing effective communication channels on social responsibility has been strengthened by the BOC. Since the first CSR report was released in 2008, every year the BOC publishes a CSR report in line with a set of complete and standardized report disclosure procedures. To be exact, the BOC's CSR report is prepared in accordance with a range of CSR reporting standards at both national and international levels. At the national level, the BOC's CSR report adheres to *the 'Opinions of China Banking Regulatory Commission on Strengthening the Corporate Social Responsibility of Banking Institutions',*[1217] *'the Guidelines of China Banking Association on the Corporate Social Responsibility of Banking Institutions of China', 'the Guidelines*

1212 BOC, *'Corporate social responsibility report of Bank of China Limited for 2015'*, p. 11.

1213 See supra Section 2.

1214 BOC, *'Corporate social responsibility report of Bank of China Limited for 2015'*, pp. 75–77.

1215 *Id*, p. 9.

1216 For more information about the BOC's Green Bonds, available at: http://www.boc.cn/en/investor/ir10/ (Accessed on April 7, 2017).

1217 More information about this Opinions, available at: http://www.cbrc.gov.cn/govView_91D73B8D49484BF 4B1D87D29F9577C2D.html (Accessed on April 17, 2017).

of Shanghai Stock Exchange on Environment Information Disclosure of Listed Companies and *the Environmental*,'[1218] *'Social and Governance Reporting Guide of the Stock Exchange of Hong Kong Limited'*.[1219] At the global level, BOC adopts *the 'Guidelines of International Organization for Standardization on Social Responsibility'* (ISO 26000),[1220] *the 'Sustainability Reporting Guidelines of Global Reporting Initiative'*[1221] and *the 'AccountAbility 1000 Assurance Standard'*.[1222]

3.1.3 Analysis

After acquiring a general picture of the BOC's CSR policies, the question arises how to evaluate the BOC's practices in implementing CSR. Although it has not been a long time since the BOC pro-actively participates in the undertaking of CSR, the BOC's accomplishments in fulfilling their social and environmental responsibilities have been widely acknowledged. The BOC won the prize of *'Best Social Responsibility Bank in Asia'*.[1223] The BOC has been rewarded by China Banking Association as *'Most socially responsible financial institution'*, *'Social responsibility—best charitable contribution award'* and *'Best practice case award in social responsibilities'*. The BOC is also frequently praised as the outstanding example of socially responsible enterprises by many influential social media in China, including Xinhuanet.com, China News Service, Southern Weekend, Sina.com.cn, and China report.[1224] In terms of CSR reporting, the BOC received the *'Information Disclosure Award 2011'*[1225] for its continuously improving policy framework, well-organized daily operation and innovative practices in information disclosure management.

In the case of the BOC, the CSR-related policies are regarded as one of the most important motivations for the BOC to actively implement CSR. As a result, the implementation of the country's development strategy is a priority of

1218 See supra Section 2.

1219 More information about this Guide, available at: https://www.hkex.com.hk/eng/rulesreg/listrules/listsptop/ esg/ (Accessed on April 17, 2017).

1220 See Chapter 6, Section 5.3.

1221 See Chapter 6, Section 1.2.

1222 More information about the AA 1000 Assurance Standard, available at: https://www.accountability.org/ standards/ (Accessed on April 17, 2017).

1223 For more information about the BOC's CSR Awards, available at: http://www.boc.cn/en/aboutboc/ab2_1/2012/201306/t20130608_2306965.html (Accessed on April 7, 2017).

1224 For more information about the BOC's CSR Awards, available at: http://www.boc.cn/en/aboutboc/ab2_1/ (Accessed on April 7, 2017).

1225 'Information Disclosure Award' is the highest honour granted by domestic securities regulators in the specific area, and aims to commend those listed companies that have sound information disclosure policy system, well-managed routine works, and are dedicated to explore the innovative best practices.

the BOC's CSR policies. The BOC's CSR reports specifically reflect its achievements in implementing national development strategies, such as the 'RMB internationalization',[1226] the 'Belt and Road Initiative',[1227] the integration of the Beijing-Tianjin-Hebei region and the construction of free trade zones, bolstering the transformation and upgrading of industrial structure and the development of micro, small and medium-sized enterprises.[1228]

Furthermore, in comparison with other CSR issues, the BOC puts more emphasis on charity and the public interest through contributing to poverty alleviation and by providing support for education, science, culture, and art.[1229] However, the relationship between corporate financial performance and corporate social performance has not been clearly identified in the case of the BOC.

3.2 *China National Petroleum Corporation*[1230]

3.2.1 Corporate Profile

As one of China's largest oil and gas producers and suppliers, the CNPC is an integrated international energy corporation. Based in China, the CNPC expands its business overseas and plays a major role in the global energy market. Today the CNPC has operations in 70 countries around the world.[1231] In 2015, CNPC ranked 3rd among world's top 50 oil companies and 4th in the Fortune Global 500.[1232] As the backbone of China's economy, the CNPC makes great efforts to achieve both its sustainable development and the country's sustainable development. Under the corporate mission for "Caring for Energy, Caring for You", the CNPC aims to achieve the balance of economic, environmental and social responsibilities and strives to become an outstanding global corporate citizen.[1233]

1226 RMB internalization refers to the efforts of the Chinese government to make RMB as an international currency.

1227 The 'Belt and Road Initiative' was issued by the National Development and Reform Commission, Ministry of Foreign Affairs, and Ministry of Commerce of the People's Republic of China, with State Council authorization, on March 28, 2015. More information about this initiative is available at: http://english.gov.cn/ beltAndRoad/ (Accessed on April 17, 2017)

1228 BOC, '*Corporate social responsibility report of Bank of China Limited for 2015*', p. 11.

1229 *Id.*

1230 This section gives an overview of the CNPC's CSR policies and practices primarily based on the information from its 2015 report and corporate website.

1231 For more information, available at: http://www.cnpc.com.cn/en/aboutcnpc/aboutcnpc_index.shtml (Accessed on April 17, 2017).

1232 CNPC, '*CNPC Corporate social responsibility report 2015*', p. 4.

1233 *Id*, p. 10.

3.2.2 CNPC's CSR/CER Policies and Sustainability Reporting Practice

To build its image as an outstanding corporate citizen, the establishment and improvement of the social responsibility management mechanism have been regarded as a fundamental work for the CNPC. Due to the CNPC's consistent efforts, a relatively comprehensive social responsibility management system has been established in the CNPC, focusing on system building, organizational structure, and capacity building.

At the policy level, the CNPC first developed a set of working rules and guidelines that define the scope and the content of the economic, environmental and social responsibilities for the CNPC's business operations. Regarding the organizational structure, the CNPC established a CSR working mechanism. Within this mechanism, three CSR committees (the Social Responsibility Management Committee,[1234] the External Expert Committee,[1235] and the Social Responsibility Office for CSR Implementation[1236]) are in charge of decision making. The function departments are responsible for work organizing. And specific business sectors fulfill their respective responsibilities in practice. To enhance its capacity on social responsibility management, the CNPC also actively supports research and development (R&D) in the field of CSR, promotes CSR education and training, and raises CSR awareness among its employees.

As an oil and gas enterprise, the significant environmental impact of its business operations has been a big concern for CNPC. In this context, environmental protection has been taken as an integral part of the CNPC's CSR policy. Specifically, the CNPC focuses its efforts on priority areas: strengthening risk prevention and control, sustainable application of energy, emission control, and conservation of biodiversity and natural habitats.[1237] A remarkable accomplishment of the CNPC's efforts in this field is the adoption of eco-environmental management throughout the industry chain and in the full life cycle.[1238] Within this management system (as shown in the Figure 9), the CNPC conducts the analysis and assessment of the environmental risks throughout each stage of the industry chain, namely, the exploration and development (upstream),

1234 The Social Responsibility Management Committee is responsible for making major decisions on social responsibility policies and planning, and is composed of heads of the function departments at headquarters.

1235 The External Expert Committee is responsible for providing professional advice on social responsibility management and practices, and providing support for decision making.

1236 The Social Responsibility Office for CSR Implementation is responsible for organizing and coordinating the planning and implementation of social responsibility work.

1237 CNPC, '*CNPC Corporate social responsibility report 2015*'.

1238 *Id*, p. 31.

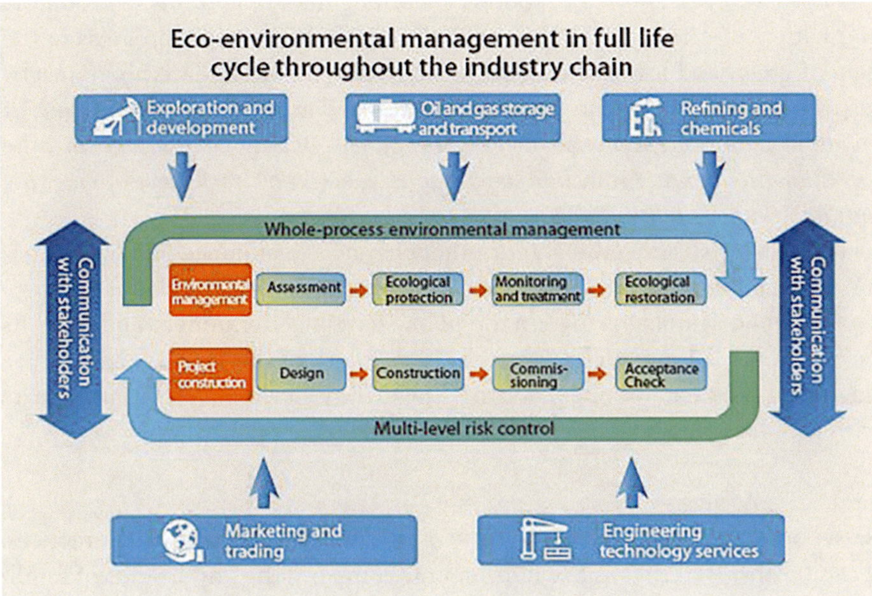

FIGURE 9 CNPC's eco-environmental management in full life cycle throughout the industry chain
RESOURCE: CNPC CORPORATE SOCIAL RESPONSIBILITY REPORT 2015

oil and gas storage and transport, refining and chemicals (midstream), marketing and trading and emerging technology services(downstream).

The CNPC also commits to combatting climate change, by reducing carbon emissions, developing low-carbon energy, improving energy efficiency, and supporting research & development of low-carbon technology.[1239]

Another priority for the CNPC's CSR work is to deepen the communication with its stakeholders, namely CSR reporting mechanism. Adhering to the principles of "honesty, interaction, and equality", CNPC made significant efforts in establishing and improving the mechanism of CSR information disclosure. The CNPC established the CSR reporting mechanism open to the public in 2006, and the first CSR report was released in 2007.[1240] Since then the CNPC has published a CSR report every year. In addition to the annual CSR report, the CNPC also discloses their accomplishments of fulfilling social and environmental responsibilities focusing on specific operation areas or issues. For example, the *'CNPC in Kazakhstan Sustainability Report'* was published in 2009 and the CNPC

1239 *Id*, p. 34.
1240 *Id*, p. 13.

also released a series of CSR reports concerning their operations in Indonesia and Latin America in 2011.[1241] In 2015, the CNPC disclosed its progress in the field of green and low carbon development and public welfare programs, by respectively publishing the *'CNPC's Natural Gas Business Development and Air Pollution Control Report'*, the *'CNPC Oil Products Quality Upgrade Report*, the *CNPC Environmental Protection Report 2014'*, the *'CNPC Green Development Report and Responsibility of an SOE*, and the *CNPC in Xinjiang'*.[1242]

The CNPC also actively expands other channels to enhance public communication and to promote transparency. For example, the CNPC launched a series of public campaigns to help the public have a better understanding of its business and CSR practices. Through the network of the new media, such as microblog, WeChat, mobile platforms, the CNPC can effectively communicate with its stakeholders.

3.2.3 Analysis

Based on a brief overview of the CNPC's CSR policies and reporting practices, it can be observed that as a leading energy company, the importance of fulfilling corporate social responsibility has been recognized in the CNPC's business strategy. In a drive to become an outstanding corporate citizen at both national and international levels, the CNPC has developed a relatively comprehensive management system on CSR. It laid a solid foundation for the company to better implement its social and environmental responsibilities. Particularly in terms of environmental protection, the CNPC indeed integrates environmental protection as an integral part of its business strategy and establishes the eco-environmental management in full life cycle throughout the industry chain. In addition to their domestic communities, the CNPC indeed pays attention to its business impacts on overseas communities. And the contributions to the social and environmental development of the CNPC have been widely recognized by the local communities. For example, the CNPC was granted the *'2015 Presidential Award for Corporate Responsibility'* in Kazakhstan, the *'Certificate of Achievement'* in Tanzania, and the title of *'Outstanding Company for fulfilling Social Responsibility'* in Oman.[1243]

In the form of CSR reporting, a CNPC report is prepared in line with a set of international CSR reporting standards, such as the GRI reporting standards, and the oil and gas industry guidance on voluntary sustainability reporting

---

1241 *Id.*

1242 *Id.*

1243 CNPC, *'CNPC Corporate social responsibility report 2015'*, p. 3.

from IPIECA/API.[1244] From the content of the report, the CNPC discloses important data on key environmental performance indicators, which reflects its accomplishments and progress in implementing social and environmental responsibilities. However, the environmental accidents caused by its business operations are not included in its CSR reports.

4 The Current State of CSR/CER Development in China

4.1 *The Overall Level of CSR/CER Development in China*

Another hot topic in both Chinese and Western academia is how to evaluate the current state of CSR/CER development in China. It is observed that a comprehensive understanding of China's CSR/CER development should be perceived from both positive and negative sides.

In recent years, the rapid growth of CSR/CER at the policy level and in practice has been widely recognized. At the policy level, CSR/CER issues become a priority on China's policy agenda. As a result, a wide range of CSR/CER-related initiatives have been developed by both the Chinese government and a large group of stakeholders.[1245] This did become the major driving force for China's CSR/CER development. Next to the concerted efforts to develop the indigenous CSR/CER framework, the Chinese government also endorsed a set of international CSR/CER standards, such as the United Nations Global Compact, the UN Guiding Principles on Business and Human Rights, ISO 26000 and Global Reporting Initiative.

In practice, a growing importance of CSR/CER has been recognized among Chinese enterprises. A report from the OECD,[1246] for example, showed that an increasing number of Chinese enterprises have actively engaged in environmentally responsible conduct through various approaches. For example, companies publish CSR/sustainability reports, implement environmental management systems, negotiate agreements with local government on environmental performance improvements, upgrade equipment and technology to be more energy efficient and environmentally friendly, install on-line monitoring staff, reduce monitoring costs and increase monitoring efficiency, launch employee education and training programs, and carry out corporate green promises by constructing gardens, lakes and green walls.[1247] More importantly, the responsible

1244 *Id*, p. 64.
1245 See supra Section 2.
1246 OECD 2008.
1247 *Id*, p. 269.

business practices of several Chinese enterprises have gained positive recognition by several well-established rating agencies at the global level. Taking China Oversea Shipping Company (COSCO) as an example, as a pioneer in the field of CSR reporting among Chinese enterprises, COSCO has published annual sustainable development reports since 2006. Their reports have been rated the highest application level of 'A+'[1248] by the GRI for eight consecutive years.[1249]

At the same time, an increasing number of cases describing poor corporate environmental performance are exposed to the public. As a result, the implementation effectiveness of CSR/CER in China is under discussion. It is commonly agreed that notwithstanding the growth of CSR in recent years, China's CSR/CER development is still at its early stage of development.[1250] For example, by conducting an inclusive study of 16 cases in China, Yin and Zhang argued that today CSR/CER is still evolving at the preliminary stage in China. Ho[1251] found out that several significant limits embedded with China's state-led approach to CSR/CER. These limitations include the dependency on government leader's awareness of CSR/CER and correspondingly the uncertainty of legal compliance; greenwashing and negotiated compliance; the borrowed legitimacy and risk shifting by contracting with third party auditors and international NGOs; the weak bottom-up demand and the constrained civic engagement; and the unclear boundaries between governmental and business responsibility in sustainable development and CSR/CER. See[1252] also equally warned that the concerted efforts of the Chinese government for advancing CSR/CER do not necessarily lead to a higher level of CSR/CER in China, particularly in the case of China's private sector. Based on his analysis of the various factors that determine the level of CSR/CER in China, See argued that the level of CSR/CER in China is affected by many variables. In addition to the government endorsement, media freedom, NGOs, social and environmental impact reporting, domestic business associations, global business associations, corporate structures, corporate governance, disclosure of social and environmental consideration by pension funds, tax treatment of philanthropy, and institutional gaps in provisions of public goods all play a role in promoting CSR/CER.

1248 There are also three Application Levels: A, B and C. When a '+' is added to the Application Level - for example, Application Level A+ - it shows that a report has been externally assured.

1249 Find more information about the COSCO's CSR reporting practices, available at: http://en.coscocs.com/col/col6917/index.html (Accessed on April 7, 2017).

1250 Yin and Zhang 2012, pp. 301–316.

1251 Ho 2013, pp. 436–438.

1252 See 2009, pp. 1–22.

4.2 *The Challenges for the Further Development of CSR/CER in China*

Despite the progress in recent years, China's CSR/CER practices are still facing many constraints in various respects, which pose significant challenges for the further development of CSR/CER in China. This section focuses on three major challenges from political, economic and legal dimensions.

4.2.1 The Political Challenge—the Level of Government Interference

The first important challenge derives from the political system in China. It is argued that the prominent role of the Chinese government has brought both positive and negative effects to the development of CSR/CER.[1253] From the positive side, the Chinese government is widely acknowledged as the primary driving force behind the growth of CSR/CER. The official endorsement of CSR/CER creates strong incentives to drive the business move towards CSR/CER because the business community needs to improve its social legitimacy by responding to government demand.[1254] The high level of governmental interference also creates a formidable challenge for the further development of CSR/CER in several aspects.

First, the motivations of the Chinese government to promote CSR/CER have been questioned. Some scholars perceive that the endorsement of CSR/CER is essentially consistent with the political interests of the Chinese ruling party.[1255] During the past decades, the rapid but unbalanced growth of China's economy has resulted in many pressing social and environmental problems. The growing conflicts between economic growth and environmental protection pose significant threats to domestic stability and the ruling legitimacy of the Party.[1256] The Chinese government gradually recognizes the institutional constraints in tackling the urgent environmental challenges, and the important role of business in this regard becomes evident.[1257] CSR/CER has been enthusiastically embraced as an instrument to complement the deficits of environmental regulation and to sustain the legitimacy of the Party. More particularly, a growing body of literature indicates that a causal relationship exists between CSR/CER and the political target of 'a socialist harmonious society' as introduced by the Chinese Communist Party.[1258] For example, Zhao observed that the new political target of 'Building a socialist harmonious society' is closely related to the concept of CSR/CER, and shares the main objectives and

1253 See e.g. Li and Zhang 2010, pp. 631–645.
1254 Li and Zhang 2010, p. 634.
1255 Lin 2010, pp. 64–100.
1256 Lin 2010, p. 93.
1257 Lin 2010, p. 66.
1258 Yin and Zhang 2012, p. 303.

values.[1259] Therefore, the pursuit of a harmonious society will contribute to the development of CSR/CER in China. However, See[1260] cast doubts as to what extent the new guiding ideology of 'building harmonious society' could contribute to the increasing CSR/CER engagement in China.

Second, other scholars argue[1261] that in the case of China, CSR/CER has also been utilized as a political strategy to improve the reputation of China's brand globally. This brand has been directly related to the violation of human rights, the abuse of labour rights, the poor product quality and the deteriorating environmental conditions. Therefore, a better performance on sustainable development and CSR/CER could substantially improve the public image of China's brand.

Third, more particularly in the specific case of SOEs, the relationship between the Chinese government and CSR/CER also attracts growing academic interest. Lin[1262] argued that in the Chinese context, SOEs could not be regarded as a mere economic organization but are in fact unique organizations with economic and non-economic objectives. The Chinese government also plays dual roles in SOEs: shareholder and regulator at the same time. That may lead to blurring boundaries regarding the respective functions of state and business. As the largest shareholders of SOEs, the Chinese government asks SOEs and their managers to focus on profit maximization. As the regulator and supervisor, the Chinese government also requires SOEs to provide public services. Although SOEs have been granted a certain degree of managerial autonomy after the economic reforms, the Chinese government still maintains its influential position and has 'incentives to divert wealth to obtain social stability'.[1263] Hence, the question arises how one should interpret CSR/CER if this would, in the end, only result in states withdrawing from their primary obligation to provide public services.

As a result, some scholars perceive[1264] CSR/CER as another form of government intervention in a market economy, supposing the Chinese government has the incentives to utilize CSR/CER (more particularly in the case of SOEs) to help achieve its political and social objectives. They, therefore, argue that the role of the Chinese government in the development of CSR/CER should be strictly limited to certain aspects of the broad landscape of CSR/CER.[1265]

1259 Zhao 2014, p. 229.
1260 See 2009, pp. 1–22.
1261 See e.g. Lin 2010, p. 65; Zadek 2012.
1262 Lin 2010, p. 66.
1263 Bai, Lu and Tao 2006, pp. 353–357.
1264 Zu and Song 2009, pp. 105–117.
1265 Ho 2013, p. 438.

4.2.2 The Economic Challenge—Is CSR/CER a Political Strategy or a Business Strategy?

At the corporate level, the implementation of CSR/CER is driven by economic and by non-economic incentives. The economic incentives refer to the market demands for CSR/CER from multiple stakeholders, such as consumers, suppliers, and investors. The non-economic pressure may generate from regulatory requirements, public campaigns from NGOs and criticism from the mass media. In general, corporate responses to CSR/CER are the results of the combination of both economic and non-economic factors.

In academic circles, there are differing opinions as to whether Chinese enterprises react to the market demands or to the policy signals on CSR/CER. Some scholars argue that the business case for CSR/CER is the primary rationale to motivate firms to move towards CSR/CER in China. For example, Zu and Song[1266] analysed the corporate responses to CSR/CER by conducting interviews with corporate managers. According to the results of their survey, three general attitudes towards CSR/CER can be identified. The first one is the true and genuine belief in CSR/CER. The second one is to improve public image and good social capital and hence to attract more economic resources or to avoid administrative penalties. The third one is to simply dismiss CSR/CER activities as they would damage the firm's economic performance.[1267] Therefore, they concluded that the true nature of their willingness behind the wide adoption of CSR/CER among Chinese business leaders could be consistent with the pursuit of economic interests.

However, many scholars remain sceptical about the nature of corporate responses for being more government-oriented than market-oriented.[1268] Yin and Zhang argued that in the context of China, CSR/CER is perceived as "a legitimacy-seeking strategy vis-à-vis key resource holders", with the aim to reduce any potential risk of regulatory interference and gain more critical resource owned by the government.[1269] Marquis and his co-authors conducted a series of studies to explore the relationship between governmental signals on CSR/CER and the corresponding corporate responses. By examining the sustainability reporting practice of approximately 1600 publicly listed enterprises in China, Marquis and Qian[1270] discussed how and why firms strategically responded to governmental pressure. Their study found out that the different

1266 Zu and Song 2008, pp. 105–117.

1267 *Id*, p. 109.

1268 Gao 2009, p. 26.

1269 Yin and Zhang 2012, pp. 312–313.

1270 Marquis and Qian 2013, pp. 127–148.

types of government-business relationships had a significant influence on the possibility as well as the level of CSR/CER engagement by enterprises. Specifically, they pointed out that some political connections, such as corporate executives serve as members of political councils,[1271] were more symbolic, resulting in symbolic CSR/CER activities. Other political ties, such as the bureaucratic embeddedness,[1272] generally related to a closer government monitoring[1273] and a more substantive CSR/CER action.[1274] Therefore, they argued that the risk of decoupling or greenwashing may commonly exist where firms could strategically make use of CSR/CER as a symbolic compliance with government policy without making any substantive changes.

Some empirical studies also prove the influence of government signals on CSR/CER engagement among Chinese enterprises. According to the results of a CSR study in China,[1275] the top 3 incentives are compliance with central government's policy, reputation enhancement and requirements from international clients. However, the business case for CSR/CER, which now becomes one of the most important rationales for global companies' CSR/CER engagement, ranks as the least important incentive for Chinese enterprises. In this context, there is a significant lack of market incentives for CSR/CER, and the strategic values of CSR/CER have not been widely recognized by Chinese enterprises and managers. In this context, it is important for both Chinese policy makers and business practitioners to broaden their understanding of CSR/CER as add-on value and the enhancement the competitiveness in the global market and more importantly the national competitiveness of China in the global economy.

Facing the increasing complexity and uncertainty when doing business in emerging markets, corporations show a higher tendency to be responsive to governmental signals on CSR/CER to sustain their license to operate. However, it also argued that the lack of strong market incentives for CSR/CER may result in corporate symbolic actions without making any substantive changes regarding their environmental performance.

1271 Ma and Parish (2006) found out that in China the firm's executives may not only be members of the Chinese Communist Party but also hold top positions in the political systems. Marquis and Qian (2013) pointed out that there are generally two types of political connections: first, corporate executives may be members of political councils such as the National People's Congress (NPC), or the Chinese People's Political Consultative Conference; second, corporate executives may themselves be governmental officials. (Marquis and Qian 2013, p. 132)

1272 *Id.*

1273 See e.g. Hiatt and Park 2013, pp. 923–944.

1274 Marquis and Qian 2013, pp. 127–148.

1275 CSA Asia 2015, pp. 16–22.

4.2.3 The Legal Challenges—the Effectiveness of the CSR/CER Regulatory Framework in China

Another worry for China's CSR/CER development is the well-known decoupling of regulation and enforcement. A gap between regulation 'on the book' and enforcement 'in practice' is widely observed in China's legal systems.[1276] Although Chinese legislators have made great efforts to develop a comprehensive and stringent legal framework on environmental protection, it is argued that the weak enforcement to a large extent impedes the effectiveness of environmental regulation. Therefore, it is still not clear to what extent China's CSR/CER regulation could stimulate enterprises to move towards CSR/CER and hence lead to an increase of social and environmental welfare in Chinese society.

A growing body of literature has examined the effectiveness of CSR/CER policies in China. Lin argued[1277] that due to the uncertain and unpredictable nature, the actual effects of China's CSR/CER initiatives on corporate behaviour are quite unclear. Zhao observed that the current enforcement of CSR/CER-related regulation in China is far from satisfactory for being unclear, unpredictable and ineffective.[1278] According to Zhao, the current situation of China's CSR/CER development is a consequence of various factors, including the deficit of governmental regulation, a poor information disclosure system, a lack of respect of human rights, and unregulated political power, and a high level of political inference in the legal system, corporate governance, and the development of CSR/CER.[1279]

Taking, as an example, sustainability reporting, which is now becoming a priority on China's CSR/CER agenda, a set of mandatory and voluntary reporting standards has been promulgated to encourage the disclosure of non-financial information. An increasing number of studies in this domain showed that the various reporting standards and guidelines created strong incentives for Chinese enterprises to participate in sustainability reporting practices. This is substantiated by an increase in the number of CSR/sustainability reports published by Chinese enterprises. According to a report on China's sustainability reporting practices from SynTao,[1280] there was only one CSR report published by the State Grid in 2006, and the number did rise to 1,722 in 2012.[1281] But the overall quality of CSR reports remains a concern. It is observed that the majority

1276 See e.g. Wang 2006.

1277 Lin 2010, p. 96.

1278 See e.g. Zhao 2014.

1279 *Id.*

1280 SynTao is a management consultancy that focuses on promoting corporate social responsibility and socially responsible investment in China.

1281 SynTao 2010.

of CSR reports in China fail to meet the criterion of materiality.[1282] Based on the content analysis of a total number of 529 CSR/sustainability reports, Kuo *et al.*[1283] found out that "41% of the sample reports fail to provide any information for the 42 CSR/CER activities[1284] which allows stakeholders to understand their CSR actions; 42% offer text descriptions of their general CSR/CER activities, but only 17% provide statistics about their achievements or other quantitative figures."[1285] Noronha *et al.*[1286] also cast their doubts on the materiality of China's environmental information disclosure practice by arguing that there is an increasing trend among Chinese enterprises to disclose a broad range of CSR/CER information without identifying the material issues in their respective business environments.

The reliability of sustainability reporting is also frequently questioned. It is unclear to what extent it conveys the correct information of a company's social and environmental performance or it is simply another form of greenwashing. Marquis and Yang argued that in the context of China, many companies could easily greenwash their reports due to the lack of monitoring mechanisms and external audit in this regard.[1287] In recent years, several greenwashing scandals have occurred in China. Companies which were lauded for good sustainability reporting practice, proved to be less environmentally responsible in practice.[1288] As a leader of sustainability in the Chinese business community, the CNPC has been praised for its outstanding performance in CSR reporting at a global level.[1289] However, in recent years the irresponsible business behaviour of CNPC has been frequently disclosed. For example, the CNPC was sued because of soil and underground water pollution in the Jilin province caused by its illegal emissions. In the overseas operations, it was fined for the violations of local environmental laws in Chad.[1290] These two examples indicate that the risk of greenwashing is widely observed among Chinese companies. Based on this evidence, Marquis and Yang suggested that the quality of sustainability reporting in China needs to be improved.

1282 *Id.*

1283 Kuo *et al.* 2011, pp. 273–287.

1284 In their study, Kuo *et al.* employed the Expert Assessment System for CSR China Honor Roll as the coding table, which consists of 42 CSR activities in 10 dimensions.

1285 Kuo *et al.* 2011, pp. 283–284.

1286 Noronha *et al.* 2011, pp. 29–42.

1287 Marquis and Yang 2014, pp. 115–116.

1288 *Id.*

1289 See supra Section 2.

1290 Petro Global News, '*Chad fines CNPC $1.2 billion for pollution*', March 31, 2014. Available at: https://petroglobalnews.com/2014/03/chad-fines-cnpc-1-2-billion-for-pollution/ (Accessed on April 7, 2017).

To summarize, it is observed that China's CSR/CER development is still at its exploratory stage and facing various constraints, and there is a big room to further improve its development.

5 Summary and Some Concluding Remarks

This chapter depicted China's CSR/CER landscape at the policy level and in practice, and it showed that the increasing importance of CSR/CER has been widely recognized by both the Chinese policy makers and the business leaders. At the policy level, a large number of CSR initiatives has been developed by a large group of stakeholders, including the government, governmental organizations, stock exchanges, industry associations, academic institutions, and NGOs. As a result, we can see that the forms of China's CSR/CER policies vary widely. There are mandatory CSR/CER standards, such as the Company Law, and the environmental information disclosure regulations, and a number of voluntary CSR/CER guidelines and standards was introduced.

In practice, the Chinese enterprises have responded quickly to the increasing expectations of the government as well as of the public. More particularly, as an important component of China's market economy, SOEs play specific roles in China's CSR/CER development. Therefore, another focus of this chapter is to have a look at the implementation of CSR/CER by Chinese enterprises. Based on the results of case studies, it can be noted that the value of CSR/CER has been widely recognized among practitioners in China. A large number of Chinese companies have made great efforts to integrate CSR/CER into their business strategies and pro-actively implement CSR in various ways and particularly through sustainability reporting mechanism. Many critical issues remain regarding the effectiveness of the CSR/CER implementation by enterprises in China. As for the Chinese SOEs, their CSR/CER practices are greatly influenced by the governmental policies and the business case of CSR/CER is hardly found among many SOEs. In this context, a question arises as to whether CSR/CER is a business strategy or a political strategy.

So far, this chapter focused on the rapid growth of CSR/CER policies and practices in China. Another key question of this chapter was how to assess the current state of China's CSR/CER development. The current state of China's CSR/CER development was primarily analyzed from two aspects: the overall level of China's CSR/CER development and the challenges for its further development. The analysis results showed that China's CSR/CER development has achieved a certain degree of progress. It is equally argued that at its early stage, the development of CSR/CER in China is facing a range of challenges and constraints, including the lower awareness of strategic CSR/CER, the limited influence of civil society, and the relatively low quality of CSR/CER practices by Chinese enterprises. In this context, many efforts should be made to improve the effectiveness of China's CSR/CER development further.

CHAPTER 10

Conclusions

1 The law and Economics Analysis of CSR/CER: a Contribution to the Current Debate

As set up in the introduction of the book, the main goal of this book was to gain new insights into the increasingly popular phenomenon of CSR/CER, its relationship with regulation, and its relevance for China from a law and economic perspective. The first important finding of this book is the new insights that the law and economic analysis could bring to the current debates of CSR/CER.

1.1 *The Traditional View of CSR/CER*

From a historical perspective, the concept of CSR is not a new topic and has experienced substantial changes over time. These changes are closely related to the evolving forms of corporations and their corresponding roles within society. As a dominant economic organization in the age of globalization, the corporation does play a critical role due to its strong economic and social powers. However, in the wake of corporate scandals, the negative consequences of business activities make corporations more vulnerable to public pressure than ever. In this context, CSR has been regarded as a possible answer for corporations to improve their social image and thus to meet increasing public expectations. As a consequence, CSR has gained enormous attention in academic circles, which can be substantiated by the historical evolution of CSR during the past decades.

The concept of CSR has been defined in different ways by numerous scholars, organizations, and governments. Irrespective of different wording, these various definitions do share some essential idea of CSR, which can be interpreted as "a company is responsible for the social, environmental and economic consequences of its business decisions and activities, beyond what the law prescribes." However, it should be noted that many unsolved disputes remain in this domain, due to some characteristics of CSR, such as the voluntary or mandatory nature, the multi-dimensional nature, and the multi-stakeholder orientation. In essence, CSR is a broader concept that covers a wide range of social, environmental and economic issues on its agenda. Within the broad framework of CSR, CER is frequently regarded as the environmental dimension of CSR. In this context, CER can be defined as "a company going beyond

 | DOI:10.1163/9789004368132_011

compliance with mandatory environmental standards by adopting higher or stricter standards on a voluntary basis."

Due to the ambiguities embedded in the definitions of CSR/CER, it is important for companies to translate this abstract concept into practice. Therefore, this book contributed to a practical understanding of CSR/CER by different industries, such as the chemical sectors, the oil and gas sector, the banking sector and the food sector. Differences were observed about how companies from different sectors integrate CSR/CER into business strategies, which could provide practical guidance for companies to implement CSR/CER depending on their own business operations.

However, the concept of CSR/CER found little appreciation for CSR/CER among a group of traditional economists, as well as law and economics scholars, mainly represented by Milton Friedman,[1291] who held that the only responsibility of business was to increase its profits. Their resentment against CSR/CER was derived from the doctrine of the 'shareholder primacy',[1292] which insisted that the primary purpose of the company was the maximization of shareholder value. In this view, the engagement of CSR/CER was perceived as a form of diverging from the profit maximization purpose of the corporation, because it came at the expense of corporate profits.

1.2 *The Strategic View of CSR/CER*

This conventional paradigm has been continually challenged by academic circles and also by the business community. More particularly, an extensive body of literature indicated that the engagement of CSR/CER did not, by all means, go against the corporate purpose of profit maximization. On the contrary, it could create added and shared values for companies under certain circumstances. This is well known as the strategic CSR/CER hypothesis. There are a variety of possibilities for companies to benefit from the engagement of CSR/CER, including:

- CSR/CER as a form of corporate philanthropy;
- CSR/CER as a marketing strategy for gaining better corporate reputation;
- CSR/CER as a strategy for reducing organizational costs and generating long-term profits;
- CSR/CER as a strategy for preventing the risk of future regulation;
- CSR/CER as a tit-for-tat strategy in regulatory compliance and enforcement.

1291 Friedman 1970.

1292 See Hansmann and Kraakman 2000–2001; Stout 2012.

More particularly, the strategic CSR/CER hypothesis has been further developed by Michael Porter, who basically argued that firms that move beyond environmental compliance will automatically not only do more investment in environmental protection but become more innovative in general.[1293] His position in this respect is well known as the Porter Hypothesis. According to Porter, the increased corporate environmental performance could become a potential source of market competitiveness.[1294]

In addition to the theoretical rationales to justify the strategic CSR/CER, a large volume of empirical literature also proved that there was a market virtue of CSR/CER, whereby companies can do well by doing good. In this domain, many scholars, such as Margolis, Elfenbein and Walsh,[1295] Eccles, Ioannou and Serafeim,[1296] have made efforts to examine the relationship between corporate sustainability performance and corporate financial performance. Their studies generally implied that a good social and environmental performance could have a positive influence on corporate financial performance to some extent. Moreover, It has been widely observed that a large group of actors, who have been directly or indirectly influenced by corporate business decisions, have actively participated in the development of CSR/CER, including shareholders, corporate managers, investors, consumers, employees, and NGOs. Although their motivations towards CSR/CER vary widely depending on their own positions and interest, they do play an important role in promoting CSR/CER practices. Moreover, we also found that despite the specific motivations of different actors, one of the most important reasons behind the increasing demand for CSR/CER is the strategic CSR/CER.

Based on the analysis of this book, it can be observed that contrary to Friedman's argument against CSR/CER, the engagement of CSR/CER could align with the profit maximization purpose of the company in various ways. More importantly, the law and economic analysis provides theoretical underpinnings to explain why CSR/CER fit the logic of profit maximization. Empirical evidence also increasingly indicated that the engagement of CSR/CER could create added value for companies and hence could become a potential source of competitiveness in the market. To summarize, the increased interest in CSR/CER could be reconciled with the traditional aversion to CSR/CER in the law and economics literature, because corporate profitability and CSR/CER should not necessarily be considered as opposites.

1293 Porter and Van der Linde 1995.
1294 Porter 1991.
1295 Margolis, Elfenbein and Walsh 2008 and 2009.
1296 Eccles, Ioannou and Serafeim 2014

1.3 *The New Insights on the Relationship between Regulation and CSR/CER*

The starting point of the law and economic analysis of CSR/CER was that an internalization of environmental externalities, which is traditionally regarded as the duty of the government, should not be voluntary and hence not take place via CSR/CER. The market failure, particularly the environmental externality, should be cured either where possible through bargaining (if transaction costs are low), or through liability rules, command and control or market-based instruments. However, the government deficit has been widely observed in regulating business activities at both national and international levels. All these problems necessitate the contribution of corporations to address environmental pollution, especially when the governmental regulation may fail for various reasons.

CSR/CER is generally defined as "going beyond the mere compliance with mandatory environmental standards on a voluntary basis." In this view, CSR/CER can be regarded as a form of self-regulation and more particularly a type of private environmental governance. The law and economic literature on self-regulation did show various advantages of this approach over other approaches, such as higher expertise of the stakeholders involved (thus leading to lower information costs), lower organizational and administrative costs, and business actors may also have a greater willingness to apply norms and standards than they would have created themselves.[1297] The application of CSR/CER in practice also supported the argument that CSR/CER could play an important role in addressing social and environmental issues as a supplement to environmental regulation.

The mere fact that CSR/CER is, in essence, a voluntary mechanism did not mean that there was no need for government intervention in any circumstances. On the contrary, many problems remained in realizing this self-regulatory approach, such as the information asymmetry in the green market (the risk of greenwashing) and the principal-agent problem as far as CSR/CER was concerned. In this context, we concluded that government regulation was still needed to accompany the success of CSR/CER. To the extent that government oversees this self-regulatory process (e.g. of sustainability reporting, eco-labelling, and certification), government regulation would merely play a supplementary role. It then fits into what is referred to as 'conditional self-regulation'.

Despite the different research focuses, a large body of literature reached a broad consensus that governments could play an important role in encouraging environmentally friendly conducts in various ways. On the basis of the

1297 See e.g. Miller 1984; Cheffins 1997.

previous studies in this domain, five roles that public authorities could play in CSR/CER were identified as: mandating, facilitating, partnering, endorsing and demonstrating. What should be noted here is that there is no strict distinction among these various roles. In some cases, governments could act as a legislator, a partner or a facilitator at the same time. At the policy level, a wide range of policy instruments has been designed and applied by governments to fulfill their commitments to promoting the development of CSR/CER. More particularly, this book also examined how these various instruments are employed in some selected areas related to CSR/CER, including the sustainability reporting system, sustainable consumption, sustainable public procurement, socially responsible investment, and awareness raising. At the international level, a set of global CSR guidelines and principles was introduced by international governmental and non-governmental organizations, such as the United Nations Global Compact, the OECD Guidelines for Multinational Enterprises, the ISO 26000 Guidance on Social Responsibility, the Global Reporting Initiative Guidelines.

2 Comparative Analysis: Convergence and Divergence of CSR/CER in EU and China

2.1 *The Convergence of CSR/CER*

Another important finding of this book is based on the comparative analysis of CSR/CER in the European context and in the Chinese context. An extensive body of studies has revealed two major trends in the domain of CSR/CER. One trend is the convergence of CSR/CER, which basically assumes that in the age of economic globalization, companies tend to adopt similar social and environmental standards.[1298] As the economic and political powers of corporations, particularly MNEs, increase substantially, the adverse consequences of irresponsible corporate behavior go beyond the concern of one specific company or nation. Not surprisingly, CSR/CER was regarded as a consequence of global business activities[1299] and has become a global phenomenon. An increasing number of intentional norms and standards on CSR/CER have appeared in this domain, such as the United Nations Global Compact, the OECD Guidelines for Multinational Enterprises, ISO 26000 on Social Responsibility, and the Global Reporting Initiative Guidelines. These global CSR/CER norms have gained wide acceptance among the business community and the national governments.

1298 Tang and Li 2009, p. 201.

1299 Zadek et al. 2001.

The trend of convergence is also observed in the development of CSR/CER in China. It fact, when CSR/CER was first introduced to Chinese society, it was the result of global supply chain movement. For a period, the conceptual understanding of CSR/CER was to a large extent built on the mainstream Western literature in this field.[1300] Today, as China' economy is more integrated into the global market, Chinese enterprises are facing the challenges as well as opportunities to implement international CSR/CER standards. In this context, the development of CSR/CER was also perceived as a result of global consequences.[1301]

2.2 *The Divergence of CSR/CER in EU and in China*

The comparative study of CSR/CER also indicated that the understanding and implementation of CSR/CER vary widely from continent to continent, from country to country and from industry to industry. Therefore, proponents of the divergence view argued that the interpretation and implementation of CSR/CER are to a large extent dependent on the specific institutional context and cultural background in which companies operate.[1302]

2.2.1 The European Approach to CSR/CER

The development of CSR/CER in the European context showed that public authorities did play an important role in promoting CSR/CER.[1303] This was proved by a variety of CSR/CER policies and initiatives at both the EU and the Member States levels. As the significance of CSR/CER has found recognition among the EU institutions, how to better promote the development of CSR/CER across Europe has become a priority on the EU policy agenda. To reach this goal, the European institutions (particularly the European Commission and the European Parliament) have taken various measures to establish the European policy framework on CSR/CER since the beginning of the 2000s. Due to the continuing efforts, the EU institutions have developed a European framework on CSR at the EU level. At the Member State level, it has been observed that an increasing number of national governments are involved in the CSR/CER policy arena as a response to the EU strategy on CSR/CER. As the key actors within this framework, Member States are expected to play a pro-active role to extend the benefits of CSR/CER across Europe. By having a look at CSR/CER policies of three Member States: the Netherlands, France and the United Kingdom, we can see that national governments have actively participated

1300 Xu and Yang 2010, p. 323.
1301 Li 2005.
1302 Campbell 2007, pp. 946-967.
1303 See Chapter 7.

in enhancing a common understanding of CSR/CER and in stimulating CSR/CSR practices across Europe.

The positive outcomes of CSR/CER policies on motivating companies to improve their performance towards sustainability were achieved among European companies, particularly concerning their sustainability reporting practices. The case studies of three selected European companies (AkzoNobel in the Netherlands, BNP Paribas in France, and British Petroleum in the United Kingdom) generally showed the European companies outperformed in terms of the number and the quality of the sustainability reports. However, it was equally argued that many problems and potential risks were associated with the current sustainability reporting practices by European companies, such as the inadequate transparency of non-financial information and the insufficient diversity in the boards.

The lessons we can learn from the European experience include: first, governments could play an active role in enhancing a common understanding of CSR/CER and stimulating CSR/CER practices by means of various policy instruments; second, at the national level, we have seen that some national governments have developed their national action plan on promoting CSR/CER, which contributed to rapid growth of CSR/CER practices; third, the various CSR/CER policies have achieved progress in encouraging sustainability reporting practices among European companies at least to some extent; fourth, in addition to the development of CSR/CER at the policy level, the measurement of corporate social and environmental performance also gained increasing importance, which could be supported by the fact that the sustainability reports of many European companies have been externally verified and evaluated by third-parties, such as a consulting agency or a sustainability rating agency.

2.2.2 The Chinese Approach to CSR/CER

Although CSR/CER has become a global issue today, the understanding and practice of CSR/CER varied widely in different institutional contexts. This phenomenon was even more obvious in a Chinese context, given the significant difference regarding the institutional backgrounds between China and the Western countries. In this case, this book contributed to a better understanding of the CSR/CER in China by taking China's political, economic, societal and cultural contexts into account.

Despite a late start in China, the recent decade has witnessed the surge of CSR/CER in China. Today China's CSR/CER development has achieved a certain degree of progress. At the policy level, a wide range of CSR/CER regulations and policies has been developed by a large group of stakeholders, including the government, governmental organizations, stock exchanges, industry associations, academic institutions, and NGOs. As a result, these various CSR/CER policies have become an important policy field in China. There are mandatory regulations, such as the Company Law and environmental information disclosure regulations. There is also a number of voluntary CSR/CER guidelines and standards. In practice, Chinese enterprises have responded quickly to the increasing expectations of the government as well as of the public. This trend was more evident in the case of state-owned enterprises. By conducting case studies of two selected Chinese SOEs (Bank of China and China and National Petroleum Corporation), we found that the value of CSR/CER has been recognized by SOEs, as they have made great efforts to integrate CSR/CER into their business strategies and to improve their CSR/CER management and performance. This can be supported by the growth of sustainability reporting practices among Chinese enterprises in recent years.

The analysis of China's CSR/CER development indicated that several Chinese characteristics were embedded in the Chinese approach to CSR/CER, which differentiates itself from the European approach.

The first difference can be attributed to the distinct models of CSR/CER development in different institutional contexts. Under the specific institutional background of China, the Chinese government plays a leading role in directing the discourse of CSR/CER in China, which is regarded as a typical example of a 'state-led model' (top-down model) of CSR/CER development.[1304] For both domestic enterprises and foreign enterprises operating in China, compliance with governmental policy ranks as the foremost incentive to implement CSR/CER in China. Although in the European context, governments also play an important role in supporting and promoting the development of CSR, the private sectors, particularly including shareholders, employees, consumers, investors, and NGOs, have exerted a strong influence on the development of CSR. Therefore, the Western approach is regarded as a 'society-led mode' (bottom-up).[1305]

The second difference lies in the different rationale for the engagement of CSR/CER between Chinese companies and European companies. According to the results of a CSR study in China, the top 3 incentives are compliance with central government's policy, reputation enhancement and requirements from international clients. However, the business case for CSR/CER, which now becomes one of the most important incentives for global companies, ranks as the least important incentive for Chinese enterprises. The results reflect that the engagement of CSR/CER is still viewed as an additional expense out

1304 Ho 2013, pp. 375–442.

1305 See e.g. Vogel 2006; Lin 2010; Ho 2013.

of corporate profits, and the strategic values of CSR/CER have not been widely recognized by Chinese enterprises.

Third, it is observed that European companies are more likely to integrate their CSR/CER policies into their business strategy, instead of some occasional philosophical donations.[1306] While for many Chinese companies, their understanding and practice of CSR/CER are still limited to philanthropic views and compliance with the public policy. For example, it is common for Chinese companies to make donations to countries suffering from natural disasters, but it is more urgent for Chinese companies to recognize and thus undertake their responsibilities towards the local communities where they operate.

Fourth, it can be observed that European companies usually outperform Chinese companies in the field of CSR/CER. This can be substantiated by the lower ranking or even the absence of Chinese companies on the influential CSR/sustainability ratings. Taking the sustainability reporting practices as an example, the average quality of CSR/sustainability reports published by Chinese companies is generally lower than their Western counterparts. In forms of CSR/CER communications, European companies are much more like to disclose the relevant information of CSR/CER on their corporate website than Chinese companies.[1307]

Although China's CSR/CER development has achieved a certain degree of progress at the policy level and in practice, at its early stage of development CSR/CER is facing a range of challenges and constraints in China. These challenges are related to various issues, such as the high-level of government intervention, the lower awareness of strategic CSR/CER, the limited influence of NGOs in promoting CSR/CER practices, and the relatively low quality of CSR/CER practice by Chinese enterprises.

3 Recommendations

The book provided some insights into China's CSR/CER development from a law and economic perspective and also from a comparative perspective. The analysis of this book showed that despite a late start, the development of CSR/CER in China has become a prominent issue at both the policy level and in practice. However, based on the experience in European countries (such as the Netherlands, France and the United Kingdom as discussed in this book),

1306 Tang and Li 2009, p. 209.
1307 *Id.*

one should notice that the development of CSR/CER is a long process[1308] and CSR/CER in China is still in its early period of development facing a variety of challenges.[1309] These challenges are related to various issues, like the lower awareness of the strategic CSR/CER, the limited influence of civil society in promoting CSR/CER, and the relatively low quality of CSR/CER practices by the Chinese enterprises. Therefore, the recommendations are formulated with a focus on how to address those challenges. Moreover, some commendations are also borrowed from the European experience in promoting CSR/CER.[1310] Notwithstanding several limitations of this book,[1311] these recommendations aim to provide some ideas about how to further improve the development of CSR/CER in China.

3.1 *The Role of Chinese Government in Promoting CSR/CER*

Based on the analysis of this book, we can see that the Chinese approach to CSR/CER is the outcome of China's unique institutional and cultural background. In this process, the Chinese government indeed plays a leading role in promoting CSR/CER, which has brought both positive and negative effects on China's CSR/CER development.[1312] From the positive side, the Chinese government is widely regarded as the primary driving force behind the growth of CSR/CER. More particularly, due to the continuous efforts of the Chinese government, the past decades have witnessed the rapid growth of CSR/CER initiatives in China, which creates strong incentives to motivate more companies to embrace CSR/CER.[1313] However, the role of the Chinese government has been subject to considerable debate.

First, the Chinese government has not fully played its role in promoting the development of CSR/CER. What we have learned from the European experience in this respect is that the development of CSR/CER has been raised as a national strategy at the EU policy agenda. Many European countries, such as the Netherlands and France, have established national policy frameworks or action plans for advancing CSR/CER. Despite the various CSR/CER public policies developed by the Chinese government, there is not yet a national CSR framework nor a systematic policy mechanism.[1314] In this context, this book

1308 Lin 2010, p. 99.
1309 See Chapter 9, Section 2.
1310 See Chapter 7; *supra* Section 1, Answers to Research Question 7.
1311 See Section 1.
1312 See e.g. Robert 1992; Li and Zhang 2010.
1313 Li and Zhang 2010.
1314 For more discussion on the critics of the role of Chinese government, see Chapter 9, Section 2.2.

suggests that the Chinese government should fully recognize the values of CSR/CER to China's sustainable development, by raising the importance of CSR/CER development on its policy agenda and by developing a national policy framework on CSR/CER.

Second, the high level of government intervention also brings formidable challenges to China's CSR/CER development. More particularly, many critical voices remain concerning the role of the Chinese government in the case of SOEs.[1315] In this book, we have observed that the development of CSR/CER is closely related to the reform of SOEs during the past decades. The Chinese government plays a dual role in the case of SOEs: the one is a shareholder and the other is the regulator. That may, however, lead to a blurred boundary regarding the respective functions of the government and the business. More particularly, as the largest shareholder of SOEs, the Chinese government, on the one hand, asks SOEs and their managers to focus on profit maximization. On the other hand, as regulator and supervisor, the Chinese government also requires SOEs to undertake part of the public responsibilities which the government is traditionally supposed to provide. Although SOEs have been granted a certain degree of managerial autonomy after the economic reform, the Chinese government still maintains its influential position and has 'incentives to divert wealth to obtain social stability'.[1316] Hence, the question arises how one should interpret CSR if this would, in the end, only result in the government withdrawing from their primary obligation to provide public services. Therefore, in a Chinese context, CSR/CER is perceived[1317] as another form of government intervention in the market economy, supposing that the Chinese government could utilize CSR/CER (more particularly in the case of SOEs) to achieve its political and social goals and hence to sustain its ruling legitimacy. In this case, this book suggests that the role of the Chinese government in promoting CSR/CER should be strictly limited to certain aspects, such as how to deter the greenwashing risk in the green market, and how to improve the transparency of corporate environmental information disclosure.[1318]

Third, in addition to the government endorsement, a large group of stakeholders indeed plays an important role in promoting CSR/CER.[1319] More particularly, NGOs have exerted considerable influence on the development of CSR/CER in the global context and in the European context. The rise of NGOs is

1315 Lin 2010; Marquis and Qian 2014.
1316 Li and Zhang 2010.
1317 Zu and Song 2009.
1318 Ho 2013, p. 438.
1319 See Chapter 3.

also an important driver of China's CSR/CER development, as the recent years witnessed the surge in the number of Chinese NGOs (more particularly the environmental NGOs).[1320] However, in comparison with their international and Western counterparts, the role of Chinese NGOs in promoting CSR is facing many constraints, such as the lack of autonomy and the lack of legitimacy. Therefore, the strict control of the government prevents the Chinese NGOs from playing a more pro-active role in influencing corporate business strategies and public policies moving towards CSR/CER.[1321] In this context, how to better promote the influence of NGOs in encouraging and supervising corporate environmental performance should be listed on the policy agenda of the Chinese government.

3.2 *The Strategic Value of CSR/CSR*

Strategic CSR/CER has been widely regarded as one of the most important rationales for corporate engagement in CSR/CER. As mentioned above,[1322] the comparative analysis of this book showed that strategic CSR/CER has found wide recognition in the European context, as an increasing number of European companies has integrated CSR/CER into their business strategies. However, the strategic values of CSR/CER have not been widely recognized by the Chinese business community. At the early stage of development, the majority of Chinese enterprises focused on two key issues: one is corporate philanthropy, such as charity donations for natural disasters, poverty alleviation, support for the education or cultural programs; the other is compliance with the CSR/CER public policies. However, the business case for CSR/CER ranks as the least important incentive for Chinese enterprises, which reflects the low awareness of business advantages of CSR/CER for Chinese enterprises and managers. Therefore, this book suggests that both Chinese policymakers and business leaders should broaden their understanding of CSR/CER beyond corporate philanthropy and legal compliance. It is important to raise awareness of the added values of CSR/CER in the business community. It is observed that as far as the market value of CSR/CER is recognized, companies do have strong incentives to improve their social and environmental performance, which could, in turn, enhance their competitiveness in the global market.

Moreover, another important lesson from the European experience in promoting CSR/CER is the wide application of assessing and comparing corporate sustainability performance by third parties, such as a consulting agency

1320 See Chapter 8, Section 4.4.

1321 See e.g. See 2009, p. 7; Tang and Li 2009, p. 2020.

1322 See *supra* Section 2.2.

or a sustainability rating agency. The increasing popularity of sustainability rating practices is largely due to the added values of corporate sustainability performance measurement for companies. Take sustainability reporting as an example, the external verification and evaluation of corporate sustainability reports could, on the one hand, guarantee the credibility of corporate information disclosure to some extent; on the other hand, it could help companies and their managers to better monitor and improve their social and environmental performance based on the scientific analysis provided by the professional agencies. In this context, a higher sustainability ranking could become a potential source of competitiveness in the global market. Not surprisingly, today many European companies have made great efforts to achieve a higher ranking on some well-established ratings and indices, such as the Dow Jones Sustainability Indices. However, it can be observed that the sustainability rating practices are largely lacking in China, which can be proved by the lower ranking or a very limited presence of Chinese enterprises on the sustainability ratings and indices. In this context, this book suggests that it is important for Chinese enterprises to recognize the values and benefits of participating in corporate sustainability performance measurement. Given what has been observed from the sustainability rating practices in the European context, the existing sustainability rating system is facing a variety of challenges, such as the lack of credibility and transparency, significant diversification, and ineffectiveness.[1323] All these problems may undermine the positive effect of sustainability ratings on improving corporate social and environmental performance. Therefore, this book also suggests that government intervention is really needed to accompany the success of the sustainability rating market for its further development.

4 Limitations and Future Research

4.1 *Limitations of This Research*

Several limitations of this book are also acknowledged in this book. First, as also mentioned in the introductory chapter,[1324] the discussion of China's environmental regulation was not included in this book. China's environmental challenges and its environmental regulation served as an important background of this research. However, the effectiveness of China's environmental

1323 See Chapter 4, Section 4.

1324 See Chapter 1, Section 3.

regulation was not the focus of this research, particularly given that a large number of studies has already been conducted to discuss various issues, related to the constraints and the effectiveness of China's environmental policy framework. Therefore, this book is based on the academic achievements of the previous studies in this domain that the limits of the current environmental policy framework in China are an important reason for private sectors, more particularly corporations, to play a role in addressing China's environmental crisis. The analysis of this book also indicated that today the role of CSR/CER in addressing social and environmental issues has been widely recognized by both Chinese policy makers and business leaders. In this context, the rapid development of CSR/CER in China has been observed at both policy level and in practice.

Another limitation of this research relates to the difficulties in evaluating the value of CSR/CER on improving corporate environmental performance and hence its contributions to China's sustainable development from an empirical perspective. In this book, we have already made some efforts to evaluate the CSR/CER practice of Chinese enterprises by conducting two case studies.[1325] The results of these case studies revealed some progress of China's CSR/CER development. For example, we observed that more and more Chinese companies have started to take CSR/CER seriously by integrating CSR/CER into their business strategies. Moreover, a wide range of CSR/CER public policies also has exerted some positive influence on encouraging and improving corporate social and environmental performance. This can be substantiated by the increasing number of sustainability reports published by Chinese enterprises under the guidance of government regulations and public policies in this respect.

However, the results of the case studies were inconclusive in reflecting the current state of China's CSR/CER practices for several practical reasons. First, the subject of the case studies in this book was limited to the specific types of Chinese enterprises, the state-owned enterprises, and other types of companies (such as SMEs) were not included. Therefore, this book could not fully reflect the current state of China's CSR/CER development. Second, another practical obstacle to evaluating China's CSR/CER practices was the significant lack of sustainability rating practices among Chinese enterprises. As a result, the lack of data provided by external parties also creates a formidable challenge for objectively assessing and evaluating CSR/CER practices of Chinese enterprises.

1325 See Chapter 9, Section 3.

4.2 *Future Research*

This book has made a contribution to a better understanding of China's CSR/CER development. The analysis of this book shows that today CSR/CER has become a dynamic and fascinating topic in China, which could potentially contribute to China's sustainability development. This research aims to trigger more discussion about China's CSR/CER development. Based on the analysis of this research, there are several interesting topics for future studies in this domain.

First, the greenwashing risk was widely observed in the European context, which implied that companies would opportunistically utilize CSR/CER as a window dressing strategy without making any substantial changes. Therefore, it is interesting to see whether this case also occurred in the Chinese context, by empirically testing whether the Chinese companies have a better environmental performance due to their engagement in CSR/CER?

Second, it is also important to have a look at whether the strategic CSR/CER hypothesis also finds empirical evidence in the case of China. Future research could make efforts to examine the relationship between corporate sustainability performance and corporate financial performance of Chinese enterprises.

Third, the undertaking of CSR/CER by Chinese SOEs also merits further research. Given the unique role of SOEs in China's political and economic systems, CSR/CER practice of SOEs also raised many disputes of being a political response to government endorsement of CSR/CER or being a business strategy for profit maximization. Fourth, it is also important to do some empirical research by interviewing Chinese business leaders or NGOs to see how they implement CSR/CER in practice, by taking China's specific political, economic, social and cultural contexts into account.

To summarize, one should also notice that at its early stage, the development of CSR/CER in China has achieved certain progress, but it is still facing a variety of challenges. This book is just the beginning rather than the end for the discussion about CSR/CER development in China. We do need further studies and refinements to see how to use CSR/CER to truly contribute to China's sustainable development.

Table of Legislations and Policy Papers

China

- 社会团体登记管理条例，国务院令第250号 [Regulation on registration and administration of social organizations] (October 25, 1998)
- 中华人民共和国公司法 [The Company Law of China] (Revised in 1994, 2006, 2014)
- 中国人民共和国环境保护法 [The Environmental Protection Law of China] (December 26, 1989, amended on April 24, 2014, as effective of January 1, 2015)
- 环境信息公开办法(试行) [Measures for the Disclosure of Environmental Information] (April 20, 2007, as effective of May 1, 2008)
- 企业事业单位环境信息公开办法 [Measures for the Disclosure of Environmental Information by Enterprises and Public Institutions] (December 19, 2014, as effective of January 1, 2015)
- 关于中央企业履行企业社会责任的意见 [The Guidelines to the State-owned Enterprise Directly under the Central Government on Fulfilling Corporate Social Responsibilities] January 4, 2008
- 关于加强企业环境信用体系建设的指导意见 [Guiding Opinions on Further Improvement of the Corporate Environmental Credit System] (December 10, 2015)
- 深圳证券交易所上市公司企业社会责任指引 [Shenzhen Stock Exchange Social Responsibility Instructions to Listed Companies] (September 25, 2006, expired on September 1, 2010)
- 深圳证券交易所主板上市公司规范运作指引 [Guidelines of the Shenzhen Stock Exchange for Standardized Operation of Companies Listed on the Main Board] (September 1, 2010, and amended on February 11, 2015)
- 深圳证券交易所中小企业板上市公司规范运作指引 [Guidelines of the Shenzhen Stock Exchange for Standardized Operation of Companies Listed on the Small and Medium-Sized Enterprise Board] (September 1, 2010, and amended on February 11, 2015)
- 上海证券交易所关于加强上市公司社会责任承担工作暨发布《上海证券交易所上市公司环境信息披露指引》的通知 [Notice on Strengthening Listed Companies' Assumption of Social Responsibility] (May 14, 2008)
- 上海证券交易所上市公司环境信息披露指引 [Shanghai Stock Exchange Guidelines on Environmental Information Disclosure by Listed Companies] (May 14, 2008)

- 中国银行业监督管理委员会绿色信贷指引 [Green Credit Guidelines] (February 24, 2012)
- 中国银监会办公厅关于加强银行业金融机构社会责任的意见 [Opinions of China Banking Regulatory Commission on Strengthening the Corporate Social Responsibility of Banking Institutions] (December 15, 2007)
- 中国纺织服装企业社会责任管理体系 [China Social Compliance 9000 for Textile and Apparel Industry] (CSC9000T)
- 中国纺织服装企业社会责任报告纲要 [China Sustainability Reporting Guidelines for Apparel and Textile Enterprises] (CSR-GATEs)
- 中国工业企业及工业协会社会责任指南第二版 [Guide on Social Responsibility for Chinese Industrial Enterprises and Industry Associations 2.0] (GSRI-CHINA 2.0)

EU

- Commission Commination on Public procurement for a better environment [COM (2008) 400 final]
- Commission Communication concerning Corporate Social Responsibility: A Business Contribution to Sustainable Development [COM (2002) 347 final]
- Commission Communication on A renewed EU strategy 2011–2014 for Corporate Social Responsibility [COM (2011) 681 final]
- Commission Communication on A resource-efficient Europe – Flagship initiative under the Europe 2020 Strategy [COM (2011) 21 final]
- Commission Communication on Implementing the partnership for growth and jobs: making Europe a pole of excellence on corporate social responsibility (CSR) [COM (2006) 136 final]
- Commission Communication on the Sustainable Consumption and Production and Sustainable Industrial Policy Action Plan [COM (2008) 397 final]
- Commission Staff Working Document Impact Assessment Accompanying the Document Proposal for a Directive of the European Parliament and of the Council amending Council Directives 78/660/EEC and 83/349/EEC as regards disclosure of non-financial and diversity information by certain large companies and groups [SWD (2013) 127]
- *Directive 2003/51/EC* of the European Parliament and of the Council of 18 June 2003 amending Directives 78/660/EEC, 83/349/EEC, 86/635/EEC and 91/674/EEC on the annual and consolidated accounts of certain types of

companies, banks and other financial institutions and insurance undertakings, *OJ* L 178/16, 17.7.2003.
- *Directive 2014/23/EU* of the European Parliament and of the Council of 26 February 2014 on the award of concession contracts Text with EEA relevance, *OJ* L 94/1, 28.3.2014.
- *Directive 2014/24/EU* of the European Parliament and of the Council of 26 February 2014 on public procurement and repealing Directive 2004/18/EC Text with EEA relevance, *OJ* L 94/65, 28.3.2014.
- *Directive 2014/25/EU* of the European Parliament and of the Council of 26 February 2014 on procurement by entities operating in the water, energy, transport and postal services sectors and repealing Directive 2004/17/EC Text with EEA relevance, OJ L 94/243, 28.3.2014.
- *Directive 2014/95/EU* of the European Parliament and of the Council of 22 October 2014 amending Directive 2013/34/EU as regards disclosure of non-financial and diversity information by certain large undertakings and groups Text with EEA relevance, *OJ* L 330/1, 15.11.2014.
- EUROPE 2020 A strategy for smart, sustainable and inclusive growth [COM (2010) 2020 final]
- European Commission (2013) 'An analysis of policy references made by large EU companies to internationally recognized CSR guidelines and principles.' Ref. Ares (2015)2100451 -20/05/2015.
- Lisbon European Council: Presidency Conclusions 29/13/2000
- Promoting a European framework for Corporate Social Responsibility [COM (2001) 366 final]
- Proposal for a Regulation on specific provisions concerning the European Regional Development Fund and the Investment for growth and jobs goal and repealing Regulation (EC) No 1080/2006 COM [(2011) 614 final]
- Regulation (EC) No 66/2010 of 25 November 2009 on the EU Ecolabel, *OJ* L 27/1, 30.1.2010.
- *Regulation (EC) No 834/2007* of 28 June 2007 on organic production and labeling of organic products and repealing Regulation (EEC) No 2092/91, *OJ* L 189/1, 20.7.2010.
- *Regulation (EC) No 889/2008* of 5 September 2008 laying down detailed rules for the implementation of Council Regulation (EC) No 834/2007 on organic production and labeling of organic products with regard to organic production, labeling and control, *OJ* L 250/1, 18.9.2008.
- *Regulation (EU) No 1301/2013* of the European Parliament and of the Council of 17 December 2013 on the European Regional Development Fund and on specific provisions concerning the Investment for growth and jobs goal and repealing Regulation (EC) No 1080/2006, *OJ* L 347/289, 20.12. 2013.

France

- Government of France, 'Preparatory document for the French national plan for the development of corporate social responsibility (CSR),' 2013.
- New Economic Regulations Act (Nouvelles Régulations Economiques, NRE Act)
- The Commercial Code of France
- The French Ministry of Ecology, Sustainable Development and Energy, 'Roadmap for Ecological Transition', 2012.
- The French Ministry of Foreign Affairs, 'The French legislation on extra-financial reporting: built on consensus', 2012.

International Level

- Global Reporting Initiative Sustainability Reporting Guidelines
- ISO 26000 on Corporate Social Responsibility
- OECD Guidelines for Multinational Enterprises
- United Nations Global Compact
- United Nations Guiding Principles on Business and Human Rights

The Netherlands

- Government of the Netherlands, 'Corporate Social Responsibility pays off', 2013.
- The Dutch Civil Code 1992
- The Environmental Management Act 2004
- The Social and Economic Council of the Netherlands (SER), 'Corporate Social Responsibility: A Dutch Approach', 2001.

The United Kingdom

- The Companies Act 2006
- The UK Department for Business Innovation and Skills & HM Treasury, '2010 to 2015 government policy: Corporate accountability', updated on May 8, 2015.
- The UK Department for Business Innovation and Skills, 'Corporate Responsibility: A call for views', June 2013.

- The UK Department for Business Innovation and Skills, 'Good for Business & Society: government response to call for views on corporate responsibility', April 2014.
- The UK Department for Business Innovation and Skills, 'The Future of Narrative Reporting', August 2010.
- The UK Department for Business Innovation and Skills, 'The Future of Narrative Reporting—A Conclusion', December 2010.
- The UK Department for Business Innovation and Skills, 'The Future of Narrative Reporting: A new structure for Narrative Reporting in the UK', October 2012.
- The UK Foreign & Commonwealth Office, *'Good Business: Implementing the UN Guiding Principles on Business and Human Rights'*, first published on September 4, 2013 and last updated on May 12, 2016.

References

Abrams, F. (1951) 'Management's responsibilities in a complex world', *Harvard Business Review* 29.3: pp. 29–34.

Adaeze, O. (2009) 'Theorising corporate social responsibility as an essentially contested concept: is a definition necessary?', *Journal of Business Ethics* 89.4: pp. 613–627.

Akerlof, G. (1970) "The market for 'lemons': quality uncertainty and the market mechanism", *Quarterly Journal of Economics* 84.3: pp. 488–500.

Albinger, H. and S. Freeman (2000) 'Corporate social performance and attractiveness as an employer to different job seeking populations', *Journal of Business Ethics* 28.3: pp. 243–253.

Ambec, S., M. Cohen, S. Elgie and P. Lanoie (2013) 'The Porter hypothesis at 20: can environmental regulation enhance innovation and competitiveness?', *Review of Environmental Economics and Policy* 7.1: pp. 2–22.

Anastas, P. and J. Warner (2000) *Green Chemistry: theory and practice*, Oxford University Press, Oxford.

Andreoni, J. (1988) 'Privately provided public goods in a large economy: the limits of altruism', *Journal of Public Economics* 35.1: pp. 57–73.

Angara, R., P. Babu, T. Eger, H. Schäfer and T. Somashekhar (2010) *'Economic analysis of law in India: Theory and application',* Oxford University Press, Oxford.

Arlen, J. and R. Kraakman (1997) 'Controlling corporate misconduct: an analysis of corporate liability regimes', *New York University Law Review* 72: pp. 687–779.

Bai, Y., M. Faure and J. Liu (2014) 'The role of China's banking sector in providing green finance', *Duke Environmental Law & Policy Forum* 24: pp. 102–150.

Bai, C., J. Lu and Z. Tao (2006) 'The multitask theory of state enterprise reform: empirical evidence from China', *The American Economic Review* 96. 2: pp. 353–357.

Bakan, J. (2005) *The Corporation: The pathological pursuit of profit and power*, Constable, London.

Baldwin, R., C. Scott and C. Hood (1998) *A reader on regulation*, Oxford University Press, Oxford.

Barnea, A. and A. Rubin (2010) 'Corporate social responsibility as a conflict between shareholders', *Journal of Business Ethics* 97.1: pp. 71–86.

Baron, R. (2008) 'The role of affect in the entrepreneurial process', *Academy of management Review* 33.2: pp. 328–340.

Barrett, S. (1994) 'Self-enforcing international environmental agreements', *Oxford Economic Papers* 46: pp. 878–894.

Baumol, W. (1988) *The theory of environmental policy*, Cambridge University Press, Cambridge.

Beaujolin, F. and M. Capron (2005) 'France—Balancing Between Constructive Harassment and Virtuous Intentions', in A. Jonker, J. Habisch, M. Wegner and R. Schmidpeter (eds.), *Social responsibility across Europe*, Springer Berlin-Heidelberg: pp. 97–108.

Beck, U. (2000) *What Is Globalization?*, Wiley, Hoboken.

Bemelmans-Videc, M., R. Rist and E. Vedung (eds.) (2011) *Carrots, sticks, and sermons: Policy instruments and their evaluation*, Vol. 1, Transaction Publishers, Piscataway. (Originally published in 1998)

Berg, M. and P. Hudson (1992) 'Rehabilitating the industrial revolution', *The Economic History Review* 45.1: pp. 24–50.

Bergstrom, T., L. Blume and H. Varian (1986) 'On the private provision of public goods', *Journal of Public Economics* 29.1: pp. 25–49.

Berle, A. (1931) 'Corporate powers as powers in trust', *Harvard Law Review* 44.7: pp. 1049–1074.

Berle, A. and G. Means (1991) *The Modern Corporation and private property*, Transaction Publisher, Piscataway. (Originally published in 1932)

Besley, T. and M. Ghatak (2007) 'Retailing public goods: The economics of corporate social responsibility', *Journal of Public Economics* 91.9: pp. 1645–1663.

Beyer, S. (2006) 'Environmental law and policy in the People's Republic of China', *Chinese Journal of International Law* 5.1: pp. 185–211.

Black, J. (2002) 'Critical reflections on regulation', *Austrian Journal of Legal Philosophy* 27: pp. 1–35.

Blonigen, B. and J. Piger (2014) 'Determinants of foreign direct investment', *Canadian Journal of Economics/Revue canadienne d'économique* 47.3: pp. 775–812.

Bowen, H. (2013) *Social Responsibility of the Businessman*, University Of Iowa Press, Iowa. (Originally published in 1954)

Bragdon, J. and J. Marlin (1972) 'Is Pollution Profitable', *Risk Management* 19.4: pp. 9–18.

Bridges, H. (1958) 'The robber baron concept in American history', *Business History Review* 32.1: pp. 1–13.

Buchanan, J. (1969) 'Demand and supply of public goods', in *The Collected Works of James M. Buchanan, Volume 5*, Liberty Fund, Indianapolis.

Buchanan, J. and W. Stubblebine (1962) '*Externality*', Economica: pp. 371–384.

Buckley, P. and P. Ghauri (2004) 'Globalisation, economic geography and the strategy of multinational enterprises', *Journal of International Business Studies* 35.2: pp. 81–98.

Calabresi, G. (1970) *The cost of accidents: A legal and economic analysis*, Yale University Press, New Haven.

Campbell, J. (2007) 'Why would corporations behave in socially responsible ways? An institutional theory of corporate social responsibility', *Academy of management Review* 32.3: pp. 946–967.

Campbell, K. and D. Vick (2009) 'Disclosure law and the market for corporate social responsibility', in D. McBarnet, A. Voiculescu and T. Campbell (eds.), *The new corporate accountability: Corporate social responsibility and the law*, Cambridge University Press, Cambridge: pp. 241–278.

Carroll, A. (1979) 'A three-dimensional conceptual model of corporate performance', *Academy of Management Review* 4.4: pp. 497–505.

Carroll, A. (1991) 'The pyramid of corporate social responsibility: Toward the moral management of organizational stakeholders', *Business Horizons* 34.4: pp. 39–48.

Carroll, A. (1998) 'The four faces of corporate citizenship', *Business and Society Review* 100.1: pp. 1–7.

Carroll, A. (1999) 'Corporate social responsibility evolution of a definitional construct', *Business & Society* 38.3: pp. 268–295.

Carroll, A. (2008) 'A history of corporate social responsibility: Concepts and practices', in A. Crane, D. Matten, A. McWilliams, J. Moon and D. Siegel (eds.), *The Oxford handbook of corporate social responsibility*, Oxford University Press, Oxford: pp. 19–46.

Carroll, A. and K. Shabana (2010) 'The business case for corporate social responsibility: a review of concepts, research and practice', *International Journal of Management Reviews* 12.1: pp. 85–105.

Cespa, G. and G. Cestone (2007) 'Corporate social responsibility and managerial entrenchment', *Journal of Economics & Management Strategy* 16.3: pp. 741–771.

Chatterji, A. and D. Levine (2006) 'Breaking down the wall of codes: evaluating non-financial performance measurement', *California Management Review* 48.2: pp. 29–51.

Chatterji, A., D. Levine and M. Toffe (2009) 'How well do social ratings actually measure corporate social responsibility?', *Journal of Economics & Management Strategy* 18.1: pp. 125–169.

Chatterji, A. and M. Toffel (2010) 'How firms respond to being rated', *Strategic Management Journal* 31.9: pp. 917–945.

Chatterji, A., R. Durand, D. Levine and S. Touboul (2015) 'Do ratings of firms converge? Implications for managers, investors and strategy researchers', *Strategic Management Journal* 37.8: pp. 1587–1614.

Cheffins, B. (1997) *Company law: Theory, structure and operation,* Clarendon Press, Oxford.

Choukroune, L. (2013) 'Corporate liability for human rights violation. The Exxon Mobil case in Indonesia', in M. Faure and A Wibisana. (eds.), *Regulating disasters, climate change and environmental harm. Lessons from the Indonesian experience,* Edward Elgar, Cheltenham: pp. 50–80.

Coase, R. (1960) 'The problem of social costs', *Journal of Law and Economics* 3: pp. 1–44.

Coase, R. and N. Wang (2012) *How China became capitalist,* Palgrave Macmillan, Basingstoke.

Cooter, R. and T. Ulen (2011) *Law and economics*, 6th edition, Prentice Hall, New Jersey.

Cramer, J. (2005) 'Refining Positions in Society', in A. Habisch, J. Jonker, M. Wegner and R. Schmidpeter (eds.), *Corporate social responsibility across Europe*, Springer Berlin-Heidelberg: pp. 87–96.

Crane, A., A. McWilliams, D. Matten, J. Moon and D. Sigel (eds.) (2008) *The Oxford handbook of corporate social responsibility*, Oxford University Press, Oxford.

CSR Asia (2015), 'A study on corporate social responsibility development and trends in China' [online] http://www.csr-asia.com/report/CSR-development-and-trends-in-China-FINAL-hires.pdf (Accessed 20 November 2016)

Dahlman, C. (1979) 'The problem of externality', *Journal of Law and Economics* 22.1: pp. 141–162.

Dahlsrud, A. (2008) 'How corporate social responsibility is defined: an analysis of 37 definitions', *Corporate Social Responsibility and Environmental Management* 15. 1: pp. 1–13.

Davis, K. (1960) 'Can business afford to ignore social responsibilities?', *California Management Review* 2.3: pp. 70–76.

Davis, K. (1973) 'The case for and against business assumption of social responsibilities', *Academy of Management Journal* 16.2: pp. 312–322.

Dean, J., M. Lovely and H. Wang (2009) 'Are foreign investors attracted to weak environmental regulations? Evaluating the evidence from China', *Journal of Development Economics* 90.1: pp. 1–13.

De Hoo, S. (2011) *In pursuit of corporate sustainability and responsibility: past cracking perceptions and creating codes*, Maastricht University Press, Maastricht.

DesJardins, J. (1998) 'Corporate environmental responsibility', *Journal of Business Ethics* 17.8: pp. 825–838.

Dewees, D, D. Duff and M. Trebilcock (1996) *Exploring the domain of accident law: taking the facts seriously*, Oxford University Press, Oxford.

Dillenburg, S., T. Greene and O. Erekson (2003) 'Approaching socially responsible investment with a comprehensive ratings scheme: Total social impact', *Journal of Business Ethics* 43.3: pp. 167–177.

Dodd, E. (1932) 'For whom are corporate managers trustees?', *Harvard Law Review* 45.7: pp. 1145–1163.

Dommerholt, E. (2012) 'Validity and comparability of the SAM and KLD screening instruments', *The Dovenschmidt Quarterly*: pp. 45–59.

Doucin, M. (2013) 'The French legislation on extra-financial reporting: built on consensus.' [online] https://www.globalreporting.org/SiteCollectionDocuments/GoF Para47PoliciesInitiatives-France.pdf

Drucker, P. (1984) 'Converting social problems into business opportunities: The new meaning of corporate social responsibility', *California Management Review* 26.2: pp. 53–63.

Dyllick, T. and K. Hockerts (2002) 'Beyond the business case for corporate sustainability', *Business Strategy and the Environment* 11.2: pp. 130–141.

Eberstadt, N. (1973) 'What history tells us about corporate responsibility', *Business & Society Review/Innovation* 7: p.22.

Eccles, R., I. Ioannou and G. Serafeim (2014) 'The impact of corporate sustainability on organizational processes and performance', *Management Science* 60.11: pp. 2835–2857.

Economy, E. (2007) 'The great leap backward?', *Foreign Affairs* 86.5: pp. 38–60.

Eijsbouts, J. (2011) *Corporate responsibility, beyond voluntarism. Regulatory options to reinforce the licence to operate*, Maastricht University Press, Maastricht.

Elhauge, E. (2005) 'Corporate managers' operational discretion to sacrifice corporate profits in the public interest', *Environmental Protection and the Social Responsibility of Firms: Perspectives from Law, Economics, and Business* 13: pp. 13–76.

Elkington, J. (1999) *Cannibals with forks: The triple bottom line of 21st century*, Capstone Publishing Ltd., Oxford.

Engel, D. (1979) 'An approach to corporate social responsibility', *Stanford Law Review* 32: pp. 1–98.

Eskeland, G. and A. Harrison (2003) 'Moving to greener pastures? Multinationals and the pollution haven hypothesis', *Journal of Development Economics* 70.1: pp. 1–23.

Esty, D. (2017) 'Red lights to green lights: from 20th century environmental regulation to 21st century sustainability', *Environmental Law Review* 47.1: pp. 1–80.

Esty, D. and M. Porter (2005) 'National environmental performance: an empirical analysis of policy results and determinants', *Environment and Development Economics* 10.4: pp. 391–434.

Falck, O. and S. Heblich (2007) 'Corporate social responsibility: Doing well by doing good', *Business Horizons* 50.3: pp. 247–254.

Fama, E. and M. Jensen (1983) 'Separation of ownership and control', *Journal of Law and Economics* 26.2: pp. 301–325.

Faure, M. (2001) *Environmental Law and Economics*, Metro, Maastricht.

Faure, M. (2011) 'Does environmental law matter?', in M. Faure and J Smits. (eds.), *Does law matter? On law and economic growth,* Intersentia, Antwerp: pp. 385–416.

Faure, M. (2012) 'Effectiveness of environmental law: what does the evidence tell us?', *William & Mary Environmental Law and Policy Review* 36.2: pp. 293–336.

Faure, M. and J. Johnston (2009) 'The Law and Economics of the Environmental Federalism: Europe and the United States Compared', *Virginia Environmental Law Review* 27.3: pp. 205–274.

Faure, M. and N. Niessen (eds.) (2006) *'Environmental Law in Development: lessons from the Indonesian experience',* Edward Elgar Publishing, Cheltenham.

Faure, M. and S. Weishaar (2012) 'The role of environmental taxation: economics and the law,' in J. Milne and M Andersen. (eds.), *Handbook of Research of Environmental Taxation,* Edward Elgar, Cheltenham: pp. 399–421.

Fox, T., H. Ward and B. Howard (2002) *Public sector roles in strengthening corporate social responsibility: A baseline study,* World Bank, Washington, DC.

Frederick, W. (2006) *Corporation, be good! the story of corporate social responsibility*, Dog Ear Publishing, Indianapolis.

Freeman, R. (2001) 'A stakeholder theory of the modern corporation', *Perspectives in Business Ethics Sie* 3: p. 144.

Freeman, R. (2010) *Strategic management: A stakeholder approach*, Cambridge University Press, Cambridge. (Originally published in 1984)

Freeman, R. and D. Reed (1983) 'Stockholders and stakeholders: A new perspective on corporate governance', *California Management Review* 25.3: pp. 88–106.

Frey, B. (1997) *Not just for the money: an economic theory of personal motivation*, Edward Elgar, Cheltenham.

Frey, B. (1999) 'Morality and rationality in environmental policy', *Journal of Consumer Policy* 22.4: pp. 395–408.

Friedman, M. (1962) *Capitalism and freedom*, University of Chicago Press, Chicago.

Friedman, M. (1970) *'The social responsibility of business is to increase its profits'*, The New York Times Magazine, New York.

Friedman, M. (2009) *Capitalism and freedom*, University of Chicago Press, Chicago. (Originally published in 1964).

Friedman, A. and S. Miles (2001) 'Socially responsible investment and corporate social and environmental reporting in the UK: an exploratory study', *The British Accounting Review* 33.4: pp. 523–548.

Gao, Y. (2009) 'Corporate social performance in China: Evidence from large companies', *Journal of Business Ethics* 89.1: pp. 23–35.

Gladwin, T. and I. Walter (1976) 'Multinational enterprise, social responsiveness, and pollution control', *Journal of International Business Studies* 7.2: pp. 57–74.

Global Footprint Network (2012) *'With no ecological bank statement, nations spend blindly'*, Annual report 2012.

Gond, J., N. Kang and J. Moon (2011) 'The government of self-regulation: On the comparative dynamics of corporate social responsibility', *Economy and Society* 40.4: pp. 640–671.

Green, K., B. Morton and S. New (1996) 'Green supply chain management practices: impact on performance', *Business Strategy and the Environment* 5: pp. 188–197.

Gunningham, N. (2009) 'Corporate Environmental Responsibility: law and the limits of voluntarism', in D. McBarnet, A. Voiculescu and T Campbell. (eds.), *The new corporate accountability: Corporate social responsibility and the law*, Cambridge University Press, Cambridge: pp. 476–500. (First published in 2007, First paperback edition in 2009).

Handfield, R. and E. Nichols (1999) *Introduction to supply chain management*, Prentice Hall, New Jersey.

Harjoto, M. and H. Jo (2011) 'Corporate governance and CSR nexus', *Journal of Business Ethics* 100.1: pp. 45–67.

Hayek, F. (1973) *Law, legislation, and liberty: A new statement of the liberal principles of justice and political economy*, Vol. 1. Rules and Order, Routledge, Abingdon.

Heald, M. (1970) *The social responsibilities of business: company and community 1900–1960*, Transaction Publishers, Piscataway.

Heyes, A. and N. Rickman (1999) 'Regulatory dealing – revisiting the Harrington paradox', *Journal of Public Economics* 72.3: pp. 361–364.

Hiatt, S. and S. Park (2013) 'Lords of the harvest: Third-party influence and regulatory approval of genetically modified organisms', *Academy of Management Journal* 56.4: pp. 923–944.

Hilton, M. (2009) *Prosperity for all: Consumer activism in an era of globalization*, Cornell University Press, Ithaca.

Ho, V. (2013) 'Beyond regulation: A comparative look at state-centric corporate social responsibility and the law in China', *Vanderbilt Journal of Transitional Law* 46: pp. 375–442.

International Monetary Fund (IMF) (2000) 'Globalization: Threat or Opportunity', April 12, 2000 [online] https://www.imf.org/external/np/exr/ib/2000/041200to.htm.

Inikori, J. (2002) *Africans and the Industrial Revolution in England: A study in international trade and economic development*, Cambridge University Press, Cambridge.

Jaffe, A., S. Peterson, P. Portney and R. Stavins (1995) 'Environmental regulation and the competitiveness of US manufacturing: what does the evidence tell us?', *Journal of Economic Literature* 33.1: pp. 132–163.

Jensen, M. (2002) 'Value maximization, stakeholder theory, and the corporate objective function', *Business Ethics Quarterly* 12.2: pp. 235–256.

Johnston, J. (2007) 'Tradable Pollution Permits and the Regulatory Game', in C. Kolstad and J. Freema (eds), *Moving to markets in environmental regulation: Lessons from twenty years of experience*, Oxford University Press, Oxford: pp. 353–385.

Jones, T. (1980) 'Corporate social responsibility revisited, redefined', *California Management Review* 22.3: pp. 59–67.

Kaplan, R. and D. Norton (1992) 'The balanced scorecard: Measures that drive performance', *Harvard Business Review* 70.1: pp. 71–79.

Keeler, T. (1984) 'Theories of regulation and the deregulation movement', *Public Choice* 44.1: pp. 103–145.

Kerr, M., J. Richard and C. Pitts (2009) *Corporate social responsibility: a legal analysis*, LexisNexis, New York.

Kitzmueller, M. and J. Shimshack (2012) 'Economic perspectives on corporate social responsibility', *Journal of Economic Literature* 50.1: pp. 51–84.

Korten, D. (2001) *When Corporations Rule the World*, second edition, Kumarian Press, Sterling.

Kotchen, M. (2006) 'Green markets and private provision of public goods', *Journal of Political Economy* 114.4: pp. 816–834.

KPMG (2013) '*The KPMG Survey of Corporate Responsibility Reporting 2013*' [online] https://www.kpmg.com/Global/en/IssuesAndInsights/ArticlesPublications/corporate-responsibility/Documents/corporate-responsibility-reporting-survey-2013-exec-summary.pdf (Accessed 20 November 2016).

KPMG Advisory, N.V., Global Reporting Initiative, and Unit for Corporate Governance in Africa (2013) *Carrots and Sticks: Sustainability reporting policies worldwide-today's best practice, tomorrow's trends*, KPMG, Amsterdam.

Kraakman, R., J. Armour, P. Davies, L. Enriques, H. Hansmann, G. Hertig, K. Hopt, H. Kanda, and E Rock. (eds.) (2009) *The anatomy of corporate law: a comparative and functional approach*, second edition, Oxford University Press, Oxford.

Kraakman, R. and H. Hansmann (2000–2001) 'The end of history for corporate law', *The Georgetown Law Review* 89: pp. 439–500.

Kratz, A. (2013) 'Reforming China's State-owned Enterprises', *China Perspectives* 1: p.94.

Kuo, L., C. Yeh and H. Yu (2012) 'Disclosure of corporate social responsibility and environmental management: Evidence from China', *Corporate Social Responsibility and Environmental Management* 19.5: pp. 273–287.

Kurucz, E., B. Colbert and D. Wheeler (2008) 'The business case for corporate social responsibility', in A. Crane, D. Matten, A. McWilliams, J. Moon and D. Siegel (eds.), *The Oxford handbook of corporate social responsibility*, Oxford University Press, Oxford: pp. 83–112.

Levy, D. and R. Kaplan (2008) 'CSR and theories of global governance: strategic contestation in global issue arenas', in A. Crane, D. Matten, A. McWilliams, J. Moon and D. Siegel (eds.), *The Oxford handbook of corporate social responsibility*, Oxford University Press, Oxford: pp. 432–451.

Li, Z. (2005) "Lack of corporate social responsibility behind recent China accidents", *China Watch, World Institute Vision for a Sustainable World* [online] December 12, 2005. http://www.worldwatch.org/lack-corporate-social-responsibility-behind-recent-china-accidents (Accessed 20 November 2016).

Li, Q. and R. Reuveny (2003) 'Economic globalization and democracy: An empirical analysis', *British Journal of Political Science* 33.1: pp. 29–54.

Li, W. and R. Zhang (2010) 'Corporate social responsibility, ownership structure, and political interference: Evidence from China', *Journal of Business Ethics* 96.4: pp. 631–645.

Lin, L. (2010) 'Corporate social responsibility in China: Window dressing or structural change', *Berkeley Journal of International Law* 28.1: pp. 64–100.

Lin, Y, C Fang., and L Zhou. (1998) 'Competition, policy burdens, and state-owned enterprise reform', *The American Economic Review* 88.2: pp. 422–427.

Lou, J. and L. Tian (2013) 'A Study on Sustainable Companies in the P. R. China', *University of Oslo Faculty of Law Research Paper No. 2013–5*[online] https://papers.ssrn.com/sol3/papers.cfm?abstract_id= 2218284 (Accessed 20 November 2016).

Lu, M. and M. Faure (2015) 'The regulation of corporate environmental responsibility', in N. Philipsen, S. Weishaar and G. Xu (eds.), *Market Integration: the EU experience and implications for regulatory reform in China*, Springer, Berlin: pp. 239–266.

Lu, M. (2017) 'The Chinese approach to CSR governance-an analysis of government-CSR relationship in China', Special Issue on the Global Governance of Corporate Social Responsibility, *International Journal of Business Governance and Ethics*, forthcoming.

Lyon, T. and J. Maxwell (2008) 'Corporate social responsibility and the environment: A theoretical perspective', *Review of Environmental Economics and Policy* 2.2: pp. 240–260.

Lyon, T. and J. Maxwell (2011) 'Greenwash: Corporate environmental disclosure under threat of audit', *Journal of Economics & Management Strategy* 20.1: pp. 3–41.

Ma, Q. (2002) 'The governance of NGOs in China since 1978: how much autonomy?', *Non-profit and Voluntary Sector Quarterly* 31.3: pp. 305–328.

Ma, X. (2016) 'China reaffirms its supportive stance for the non-public sector', *People's Daily* [online] March 7, 2016. http://en.people.cn/n3/2016/0307/c98649-9026173.html (Accessed 20 November 2016).

Ma, X. and L. Ortolano (2000) *Environmental regulation in China: Institutions, enforcement, and compliance,* Rowman & Littlefield Publishers, Lanham.

Ma, D. and W. Parish (2006) 'Tocquevillian moments: Charitable contributions by Chinese private entrepreneurs', *Social Forces*: pp. 943–964.

Maguire, M. (2011) 'The future of corporate social responsibility reporting', The Frederick S. Pardee Center for the Study of the Longer-Range Future, Boston University [online] http://blogs.bu.edu/mwm/files/2014/10/2011-Pardee-Issues-in-Brief.pdf (Accessed on April 14, 2017).

Maretno, M. and H. Jo (2011) 'Corporate governance and firm value: The impact of corporate social responsibility', *Journal of Business Ethics* 103.3: pp. 351–383.

Margolis, J., H. Elfenbein and J. Walsh (2008) 'Do well by doing good? Don't count on it', Special Issue on HBS Centennial, *Harvard Business Review* 86.1: p. 19.

Margolis, J. and H. Elfenbein and J. Walsh (March 1, 2009) 'Does it pay to be good… and does it matter? A meta-analysis of the relationship between corporate social and financial performance'. Available at SSRN: https://ssrn.com/abstract=1866371 or http://dx.doi.org/10.2139/ssrn.1866371

Marquis, C. and C. Qian (2013) 'Corporate social responsibility reporting in China: Symbol or substance?', *Organization Science* 25.1: pp. 127–148.

Marquis, C. and C. Yang (2014) 'Environmental Reporting in China still likely to be greenwash', Chinadialogue[online] https://www.chinadialogue.net/article/show/single/en/6543-Environmental-reporting-in-China-still-likely-to-be- (Accessed on April 8, 2017).

Marsden, C. (2000) 'The new corporate citizenship of big business: Part of the solution to sustainability?', *Business and Society Review* 105.1: pp. 8–25.

Marshall, T. (1964) *Class, citizenship and social development*, Greenwood Press, Connecticut.

Martinez, G. (2013) *The law and economics of eco-labels*, Erasmus University Rotterdam, Rotterdam.

Matten, D. and A. Crane (2005) 'Corporate citizenship: Toward an extended theoretical conceptualization', *Academy of Management Review* 30.1: pp. 166–179.

Matten, D. and J. Moon (2008) "'Implicit' and 'explicit' CSR: A conceptual framework for a comparative understanding of corporate social responsibility", *Academy of Management Review* 33.2: pp. 404–424.

Mazurkiewicz, P. (2004) *Corporate environmental responsibility: Is a common CSR framework possible*, World Bank, Washington D.C.

McBarnet, D. (2007) 'Corporate social responsibility beyond law, through law, for law: the new corporate accountability', in D. McBarnet, A. Voiculescu and T. Campell (eds.), *The new corporate accountability: Corporate social responsibility and the law*, Cambridge University Press, Cambridge: pp. 9–56. (First published in2007, First paperback edition in 2009).

McCrudden, C. (2007) *Buying social justice: Equality, government procurement, & legal change*, Oxford University Press on Demand.

Meadows, D., D. Meadows, J. Randers and W. Behrens III (1972) *The limits to growth: a report to the club of Rome*, Universe Books, New York.

Megginson, W. and J. Netter (2001) 'From state to market: A survey of empirical studies on privatization', *Journal of Economic Literature* 39.2: pp. 321–389.

Miller, J. (1984) 'The FTC and voluntary standards: maximizing the net benefits of self-regulation', *Cato Journal* 4.3: pp. 897–903.

Millon, D. (2015) 'Corporate Social Responsibility and Environmental Sustainability', in B. Sjåfjell and B. Richardson (eds.), *Company law and sustainability: legal barriers and opportunities*, Cambridge University Press, Cambridge: pp. 35–78.

Mokhiber, R. and R. Weissman (1999) *Corporate Predators: The hunt for mega-profits and the attack on democracy*, Common Courage Press, Monroe.

Moon, J. (2002) 'The social responsibility of business and new governance', *Government and Opposition* 37.3: pp. 385–408.

Moon, J. (2004) 'Government as a driver of corporate social responsibility: the UK in a comparative perspective', *ICCSR Research Paper Series, 20-2004*. ICCSR, University of Nottingham: pp. 1–27.

Moon, J. (2005) 'United Kingdom', in A. Habisch, J. Jonker, M. Wegner and R. Schmidpeter (eds.), *Corporate social responsibility across Europe*, Springer, Berlin Heidelberg: pp. 51–65.

Moon, J., A. Crane and D. Matten (2005a) 'Can corporations be citizens? Corporate citizenship as a metaphor for business participation in society', *Business Ethics Quarterly* 15.03: pp. 429–453.

Moon, J. and J. Richardson (1985) *Unemployment in the UK: Politics and Policies,* Gower Publishing Company, London.

Moon, J. and D. Vogel (2008) 'Corporate social responsibility, government, and civil society', in A. Crane, D. Matten, A. McWilliams, J. Moon and D. Siegel (eds.), *The Oxford handbook of corporate social responsibility*, Oxford University Press, Oxford: pp. 303–326.

Moon, J., A. Crane and D. Matten (2005b) 'Can corporations be citizens? Corporate citizenship as a metaphor for business participation in society', *Business Ethics Quarterly* 15.3: pp. 429–453.

Moratis, L. (2015) *Standardizing a Better World? Essays and critical reflections on the ISO, 26000.*

Murphy, P. (1978) 'An evolution: Corporate social responsiveness', *University of Michigan Business Review* 6.30: pp. 19–25.

Narasimhan, R. and J.R. Carter (1998) *'Environmental supply chain management'*, Center for Advanced Purchasing Studies, Tempe, Arizona.

National Bureau of Statistics of China (2014), *'China Statistical Yearbook'*, Beijing.

Naughton, B. (2006) 'Claiming profit for the state: SASAC and the capital management budget', *China Leadership Monitor* 18: pp. 1–9.

Noronha, C., S. Tou, M. Cynthia and J. Guan (2013) 'Corporate social responsibility reporting in China: An overview and comparison with major trends', *Corporate Social Responsibility and Environmental Management* 20.1: pp. 29–42.

Oates, W. and R. Schwab (1988) 'Economic competition among jurisdictions: efficiency enhancing or distortion inducing?', *Journal of Public Economics* 35.3: pp. 333–354.

Oded, S. (2013) *Corporate compliance: New approaches to regulatory enforcement,* Edward Elgar Publishing, Cheltenham.

OECD (2003) *Privatising State-Owned Enterprises: An Overview of Policies and Practices in OECD countries*, OECD Publishing, Paris.

OECD (2006) *Environmental compliance and enforcement in China: An assessment of current practices and ways forward*, OECD Publishing, Paris.

OECD (2007) *Recent trends and regulatory implications in socially responsible investment for pension funds*, OECD Publishing, Paris.

OECD (2008) *OECD Investment Policy Reviews-China 2008: Encouraging Responsible Business Conduct*, OECD Publishing, Paris.

OECD (2011) *Environmental Taxation: a guide for policy makers,* OECD Publishing, Paris.

Offe, C. (1984) *Contradictions of the welfare state*, Edited by J. Keane, London.

Ogus, A. (1994) *Regulation: Legal form and economic theory*, Clarendon Press, Oxford.

Ogus, A. (2000) 'Self-regulation', *Encyclopaedia of Law and Economics* 5: pp. 587–602.

Okoye, A. (2009) 'Theorising corporate social responsibility as an essentially contested concept: is a definition necessary?', *Journal of Business Ethics* 89.4: pp. 613–627.

Olaerts, M. and C.A. Schwarz. (eds.) (2012) *Shareholder democracy. An analysis of shareholder involvement in corporate policies,* Eleven International Publishing, The Hague.

Orlitzky, M. (2008) 'Corporate social performance and financial performance: A research synthesis', in A. Crane, D. Matten, A. McWilliams, J. Moon and D. Siegel (eds.), *The Oxford handbook of corporate social responsibility*, Oxford University Press, Oxford: pp. 113–134.

Orts, E. and K. Deketelaere (eds) (2001) *Environmental contracts: Comparative approaches to regulatory innovation in the United States and Europe*, Vol. 1, Kluwer Law International, Alphen aan den Rijn.

Pacces, A. (2011) 'How does corporate law matter? Law and Finance and beyond', in M. Faure and J. Smits (eds.), *Does Law Matter? on law and economic growth*, Intersentia NV, Antwerp.

Paine, L. and M. Moldoveanu (1999) '*Royal Dutch/Shell in Nigeria (A)*', Harvard Business School Case 9, Boston.

Patrick, M. (1978) 'An evolution: corporate social responsiveness', *University of Michigan Business Review* 6.30: pp. 19–25.

Philipsen, N. (2003) *Regulation of and by pharmacists in the Netherlands and Belgium: an economic approach,* Intersentia, Antwerpen-Groningen.

Phoon-Lee, C. (2006) "Corporate social responsibility and 'putting people first' from a Chinese cultural perspective", *The Journal of Corporate Citizenship* 22: pp. 23–26.

Pigou, A. (1951) *A study in public finance,* Macmillan, London.

Pitelis, C. and R. Sugden (2000) *The Nature of the Transnational Firm*, Psychology Press, Abington.

Porter, M. (1991) 'America's Green Strategy', *Scientific American* 264.4: pp. 168–170.

Porter, M. and M. Kramer (2002) 'The competitive advantage of corporate philanthropy', *Harvard Business Review* 80.12: pp. 56–68.

Porter, M. and M. Kramer (2006) 'The link between competitive advantage and corporate social responsibility', *Harvard Business Review* 84.12: pp. 78–92.

Porter, M. and C. Van der Linde (1995) 'Toward a new conception of the environment-competitiveness relationship', *The Journal of Economic Perspectives* 9.4: pp. 97–118.

Posner, R. (2003) *Economic analysis of law*, sixth edition, Aspen Publishers, New York.

Reinhardt, F., R. Stavins and R. Vietor (2008) 'Corporate social responsibility through an economic lens', *Review of Environmental Economics and Policy* 2.2: pp. 219–239.

Renneboog, L., J. Horst and C. Zhang (2008a) 'The price of ethics and stakeholder governance: The performance of socially responsible mutual funds', *Journal of Corporate Finance* 14.3: pp. 302–322.

Renneboog, L. and J. Horst and C. Zhang (2008b) 'Socially responsible investments: Institutional aspects, performance, and investor behavior', *Journal of Banking & Finance* 32.9: pp. 1723–1724.

Revesz, R. (1992) 'Rehabilitating interstate competition: Rethinking the race-to-the-bottom rationale for federal environmental regulation', *New York University Law Review* 67.6: pp. 1210–1254.

Richardson, B. (2015) 'Financial Markets and Socially Responsible Investing', in B. Sjåfjell and B. Richardson (eds.), *Company law and sustainability: Legal barriers and opportunities*, Cambridge University Press, Cambridge: pp. 226–274.

Rondinelli, D. and T. London (2003) 'How corporations and environmental groups cooperate: Assessing cross-sector alliances and collaborations', *The Academy of Management Executive* 17.1: pp. 61–76.

Rothbard, M. (1972) *America's great depression*, Ludwig von Mises Institute, Auburn, Alabama.

Rudra, N. (2008) *Globalization and the race to the bottom in developing countries: who really gets hurt?*, Cambridge University Press, Cambridge.

Ryan, H. and R. Wiggins (2004) 'Who is in whose pocket? Director compensation, board independence, and barriers to effective monitoring', *Journal of Financial Economics* 73.3: pp. 497–524.

Sadowski, M., K. Whitaker and F. Buckingham (May 2010a) *Rate the raters Phase One: Look back and current state*, SustainAbility, London.

Sadowski, M., K. Whitaker and F. Buckingham (October 2010b) *Rate the raters Phase Two: Taking inventory of the ratings universe*, SustainAbility, London.

Sadowski, M., K. Whitaker and A. Ayars (February 2011a) *Rate the raters Phase Three: Uncovering best practices*, SustainAbility, London.

Sadowski, M., K. Whitaker, L. Mark and A. Ayars (June 2011b) *Rate the raters Phase Four: The necessary future of ratings*, SustainAbility, London.

Sadowski, M. (October 2012a) *Rate the raters Phase Five: The company view*, SustainAbility, London.

Sadowski, M. (November 2012b) *Rate the raters Phase Five: The investor view*, SustainAbility, London.

Salamon, L. and H. Anheier. (1996) 'The international classification of non-profit organizations: ICNPO-Revision 1', *Johns Hopkins University Institute for Policy Studies* [online] http://ccss.jhu.edu/wp-content/uploads/downloads/2011/09/CNP_WP19_1996.pdf (Accessed 20 November 2016).

Salazar, J. and B. Husted (2008) 'Principals and agents: further thoughts on the Friedmanite critique of corporate social responsibility', in A. Crane, D. Matten, A. McWilliams, J. Moon and D. Siegel (eds.), *The Oxford handbook of corporate social responsibility*, Oxford University Press, Oxford: pp. 137–155.

Salzmann, O., A. Ionescu-Somers and U. Steger (2005) 'The business case for corporate sustainability: literature review and research options', *European Management Journal* 23.1: pp. 27–36.

Scalet, S. and T. Kelly (2010) 'CSR rating agencies: What is their Global Impact?', *Journal of Business Ethics* 94.1: pp. 69–88.

Scalise, E. (2005) 'The code for corporate citizenship: States should amend statutes governing corporations and enable corporations to be good citizens', *Seattle University Law Review* 29.1: pp. 275–300.

Scherer, A. and G. Palazzo (2008) 'Globalization and corporate social responsibility', in A. Crane, D. Matten, A. McWilliams, J. Moon and D. Siegel (*eds.*), *The Oxford handbook of corporate social responsibility,* Oxford University Press, Oxford: pp. 413–431.

Scherer, A., G. Palazzo and D. Matten (2009) 'Introduction to the special issue: Globalization as a challenge for business responsibilities', *Business Ethics Quarterly* 19.3: pp. 327–347.

Scherer, A. and G. Palazzo (2011) 'The new political role of business in a globalized world: A review of a new perspective on CSR and its implications for the firm, governance, and democracy', *Journal of Management Studies* 48.4: pp. 899–931.

Schwartz, J. (2004) 'Environmental NGOs in China: roles and limits', *Pacific Affairs* 77.1: pp. 28–49.

Schwartz, M. and A. Carroll (2003) 'Corporate social responsibility: a three-domain approach', *Business Ethics Quarterly* 13.4: pp. 503–530.

Schwartzman, K. (1998) 'Globalization and democracy', *Annual Review of Sociology* 24.1: pp. 159–181.

See, G. (2009) 'Harmonious society and Chinese CSR: Is there really a link?', *Journal of Business Ethics* 89.1: pp. 1–22.

Shavell, S. (1980) 'Strict liability versus negligence', *Journal of Legal Studies* 9.1: pp. 1–25.

Shavell, S. (1984) 'Liability for harm versus regulation of safety', *Journal of Legal Studies* 13: pp. 357–370.

Sheldon, O. (2003) *The Philosophy of Management*, Psychology Press, Abington (Originally published in 1924)

Shleifer, A. and R. Vishny (1997) 'A survey of corporate governance', *The Journal of Finance* 52.2: pp. 737–783.

Sjåfjell, B., A. Johnston, L. Anker-Sørensen and D. Millon (2015) 'Shareholder Primacy: The Main Barrier to Sustainable Companies', in B. Sjåfjell and B. Richardson (eds.), *Company law and sustainability: legal barriers and opportunities*, Cambridge University Press, Cambridge: pp. 79–147.

Smith, D. (1988) 'The Shareholder primacy norm', *Journal of Corporation Law* 23.2: pp. 277–324.

Smith, N. (1990) *Morality and the market: consumer pressure for corporate accountability*, Routledge, London.

Smith, N. (2003) 'Corporate social responsibility: not whether, but how.' California Management Review 45.4: pp. 52–76.

Smith, N. (2008) 'Consumers as drivers of corporate responsibility', in A. Crane, D. Matten, A. McWilliams, J. Moon and D. Siegel (eds.), *The Oxford handbook of corporate social responsibility*, Oxford University Press, Oxford: pp. 281–302.

Stanwick, P. and S. Stanwick (1998) 'The relationship between corporate social performance, and organizational size, financial performance, and environmental performance: An empirical examination', *Journal of Business Ethics* 17.2: pp. 195–204.

Steurer, R. (2010) 'The role of governments in corporate social responsibility: Characterising public policies on CSR in Europe', *Policy Sciences* 43.1: pp. 49–72.

Steurer, R., S. Margula and G. Berger (2008a) 'Public policies on CSR in EU Member States: Overview of government initiatives and selected cases on Awareness Raising for CSR, Sustainable Public Procurement and Socially Responsible Investment [J]', ESDN Quarterly Reports.

Steurer, R., G. Berger, A. Konrad and A. Martinuzzi (2007) 'Sustainable public procurement in EU member states: Overview of government initiatives and selected cases', *Final Report to the EU High-Level Group on CSR*, European Commission, Brussels.

Steurer, R., S. Margula and A. Martinuzzi (2008b) 'Socially Responsible Investment in EU Member States: Overview of government initiatives and SRI experts' expectations towards governments.' Final Report to the EU High-Level Group on CSR. Analysis of national policies on CSR, in support of a structured exchange of information on national CSR policies and initiatives. Final report to the EU High-Level Group on CSR provided by the Research Institute for Managing Sustainability. Vienna University of Economics and Business.

Stigler, G. (1971) 'The theory of economic regulation', *The Bell Journal of Economics and Management Science* 2.1: pp. 3–21.

Stout, L. (2012) *The Shareholder Value Myth*, Berrett-Koehler Publishers, Oakland.

Surroca, J. and J. Tribó (2008) 'Managerial entrenchment and corporate social performance', *Journal of Business Finance & Accounting* 35(5–6): pp. 748–789.

Swanson, D. (2008) 'Top managers as drivers for corporate social responsibility', in A. Crane, D. Matten, A. McWilliams, J. Moon and D. Siegel (eds.), *The Oxford handbook of corporate social responsibility*, Oxford University Press, Oxford: pp. 227–248.

SynTao (2010) 'A Journey to Discover Values 2010: A Study of CSR Reporting in China' [online] http://www.syntao.com/SyntaoReport_Show_EN.asp?ID=10&FID=18 (Accessed on April 8, 2017)

Tang, L. and H. Li (2009) 'Corporate social responsibility communication of Chinese and global corporations in China', *Public Relations Review* 35.3: pp. 199–212.

Temin, P. (1991) *Lessons from the great depression*, MIT Press, Cambridge, Massachusetts.

Tiebout, C. M. (1956) 'A pure theory of local expenditures', *The Journal of Political Economy* 64.5: pp. 416–424.

Turban, D. and D. Greening (1997) 'Corporate social performance and organizational attractiveness to prospective employees', *Academy of Management Journal* 40.3: pp. 658–672.

UNEP (2007), Global Environment Outlook: environment for development, GEO-4.

UNEP (2012) 'Global Environment Outlook: environment for the future we want', GEO-5.

Van Dam, C. (2011) 'Tort law and human rights: Brothers in arms on the role of tort law in the area of business and human rights', *Journal of European Tort Law* 2.3: pp. 221–254.

Van den Bergh, M. (2013) 'Private environmental governance', *Cornell Law Review* 99.1: pp. 129–199.

Van Rooij, B. (2006) 'Implementation of Chinese environmental law: regular enforcement and political campaigns', *Development and Change* 37.1: pp. 57–74.

Van Rooij, B., R. Stern and K. Fürst (2014) 'The authoritarian logic of regulatory pluralism: Understanding China's new environmental actors', *Regulation & Governance* 10.1: pp. 3–13.

Vedung, E., M. Bemelmans-Videc and R. Rist (2011) 'Policy instruments: typologies and theories', in M. Bemelmans-Videc, R. Rist and E. Vedung (eds.), *Carrots, sticks, and sermons: Policy instruments and their evaluation*, Vol. 1, Transaction Publishers, Piscataway: pp. 21–58.

Vogel, D. (2001) 'Is there a race to the bottom? The impact of globalization on national regulatory policies', *Tcqueville Review* 22.1: pp. 163–172.

Vogel, D. (2006) *The Market for Virtue: The Potential and Limits of Corporate Social Responsibility,* Brookings Institution Press, Washington D.C.

Vogel, D. (2008) 'Private global business regulation', *Annual Review of Political Science* 11: pp. 261–282.

Wang, C. (2006) 'Chinese environmental law enforcement: current deficiencies and suggested reforms', *Vermont Journal of Environmental Law Symposium* 8: pp. 159–194.

Wang, L. and H. Juslin (2009) 'The impact of Chinese culture on corporate social responsibility: The harmony approach', *Journal of Business Ethics* 88.3: pp. 433–451.

Ward, H. (2004) *Public sector roles in strengthening corporate social responsibility: taking stock*, World Bank, Washington, D.C.

Wartick, S. and P. Cochran (1985) 'The evolution of the corporate social performance model', *Academy of Management Review* 10.4: pp. 758–769.

Warr, P. (1983) 'The private provision of a public good is independent of the distribution of income', *Economics Letters* 13.2: pp. 207–211.

WBCSD (1999) *Corporate social responsibility: Meeting changing expectations*, Geneva.

WCED (1987) *Our Common Future*, Oxford University Press, Oxford.

Windolph, S. (2011) 'Assessing corporate sustainability through ratings: challenges and their causes', *Journal of Environmental Sustainability* 1.1: pp. 37–57.

Wood, D. (1991) 'Corporate social performance revisited', *Academy of Management Review* 16.4: pp. 691–718.

Wood, D. (2010) 'Measuring corporate social performance: a review', *International Journal of Management Reviews* 12.1: pp. 50–84.

Wren, D. (2005) *The history of management thought*, fifth edition, John Wiley & Sons, Inc., Hoboken.

Xu, S. and R. Yang (2010) 'Indigenous characteristics of Chinese corporate social responsibility conceptual paradigm', *Journal of Business Ethics* 93.2: pp. 321–333.

Yi, X. (2005) 'Improving corporate responsibility competitiveness to promote harmonious society', WTO Guide.

Yin, J. and Y. Zhang (2012) 'Institutional dynamics and corporate social responsibility (CSR) in an emerging country context: Evidence from China', *Journal of Business Ethics* 111.2: pp. 301–316.

Zadek, S. (2012) 'Can we believe China's corporate social responsibility rhetoric', Open Democracy [online] https://www.opendemocracy.net/openeconomy/simon-zadek/can-we-believe-chinas-corporate-social-responsibility-rhetoric.

Zhao, J. (2014) *Corporate social responsibility in contemporary China*, Edward Elgar Publishing, Cheltenham.

Zhu, Q. and J. Sarkis (2014) 'Relationships between operational practices and performance among early adopters of green supply chain management practices in Chinese manufacturing enterprises', *Journal of operations management* 22.3: pp. 265–289.

Zu, L. and L. Song (2009) 'Determinants of managerial values on corporate social responsibility: Evidence from China.' *Journal of Business Ethics* 88: pp. 105–117.

Index

Printed in the United States
By Bookmasters